CRE▲TIVE
HOMEOWNER®

ULTIMATE GUIDE TO

House
Framing

CREATIVE HOMEOWNER® ULTIMATE GUIDE TO

House
Framing
PLAN · DESIGN · BUILD

John D. Wagner

CREATIVE HOMEOWNER®, Upper Saddle River, New Jersey

VP/EDITORIAL DIRECTOR: Timothy O. Bakke
PRODUCTION MANAGER: Kimberly H. Vivas

MANAGING EDITOR: Fran J. Donegan
COPYEDITOR: Robin White Goode
EDITORIAL ASSISTANTS: Albert Huang, Evan Lambert
PHOTO RESEARCHER: Lauren Manoy
TECHNICAL REVIEWERS: Hans Bakke, Joe Wajszczuk

ART DIRECTOR: David Geer
HEAD GRAPHIC DESIGNER: Michelle D. Halko
GRAPHIC DESIGNERS: Melisa DelSordo, Jan Greco
ILLUSTRATORS: Frank Rohrback, Paul M. Schumm,
    Vincent Alessi, Cathy Dean
COVER PHOTOGRAPHY: Kim Jin Hong Photo Studio

Manufactured in the United States of America

Current Printing (last digit)
10 9 8 7 6 5 4 3 2

House Framing: Plan, Design, Build, Second Edition
First published as *House Framing*
Library of Congress Control Number: 2004113487
ISBN-10: 1-58011-235-8
ISBN-13: 978-1-58011-235-2

CREATIVE HOMEOWNER®
A Division of Federal Marketing Corp.
24 Park Way, Upper Saddle River, NJ 07458
www.creativehomeowner.com

Safety First

Although the methods in this book have been reviewed for safety, it is not possible to overstate the importance of using the safest methods you can. What follows are reminders—some do's and don'ts of work safety—to use along with your common sense.

- *Always* use caution, care, and good judgment when following the procedures described in this book.

- *Always* be sure that the electrical setup is safe, that no circuit is overloaded, and that all power tools and outlets are properly grounded. Do not use power tools in wet locations.

- *Always* read container labels on paints, solvents, and other products; provide ventilation; and observe all other warnings.

- *Always* read the manufacturer's instructions for using a tool, especially the warnings.

- Use hold-downs and push sticks whenever possible when working on a table saw. Avoid working short pieces if you can.

- *Always* remove the key from any drill chuck (portable or press) before starting the drill.

- *Always* pay deliberate attention to how a tool works so that you can avoid being injured.

- *Always* know the limitations of your tools. Do not try to force them to do what they were not designed to do.

- *Always* make sure that any adjustment is locked before proceeding. For example, always check the rip fence on a table saw or the bevel adjustment on a portable saw before starting to work.

- *Always* clamp small pieces to a bench or other work surface when using a power tool.

- *Always* wear the appropriate rubber gloves or work gloves when handling chemicals, moving or stacking lumber, working with concrete, or doing heavy construction.

- *Always* wear a disposable face mask when you create dust by sawing or sanding. Use a special filtering respirator when working with toxic substances and solvents.

- *Always* wear eye protection, especially when using power tools or striking metal on metal or concrete; a chip can fly off, for example, when chiseling concrete.

- *Never* work while wearing loose clothing, open cuffs, or jewelry; tie back long hair.

- *Always* be aware that there is seldom enough time for your body's reflexes to save you from injury from a power tool in a dangerous situation; everything happens too fast. Be alert!

- *Always* keep your hands away from the business ends of blades, cutters, and bits.

- *Always* hold a circular saw firmly, usually with both hands.

- *Always* use a drill with an auxiliary handle to control the torque when using large-size bits.

- *Always* check your local building codes when planning new construction. The codes are intended to protect public safety and should be observed to the letter.

- *Never* work with power tools when you are tired or when under the influence of alcohol or drugs.

- *Never* cut tiny pieces of wood or pipe using a power saw. When you need a small piece, saw it from a securely clamped longer piece.

- *Never* change a saw blade or a drill or router bit unless the power cord is unplugged. Do not depend on the switch being off. You might accidentally hit it.

- *Never* work in insufficient lighting.

- *Never* work with dull tools. Have them sharpened, or learn how to sharpen them yourself.

- *Never* use a power tool on a workpiece—large or small—that is not firmly supported.

- *Never* saw a workpiece that spans a large distance between horses without close support on each side of the cut; the piece can bend, closing on and jamming the blade, causing saw kickback.

- When sawing, *never* support a workpiece from underneath with your leg or other part of your body.

- *Never* carry sharp or pointed tools, such as utility knives, awls, or chisels, in your pocket. If you want to carry any of these tools, use a special-purpose tool belt that has leather pockets and holders.

Contents

Introduction 8

Section I

GETTING STARTED 10

CHAPTER 1

House Framing Materials 12
WORKING WITH WOOD 13
PLYWOOD 18
ENGINEERED LUMBER 20

CHAPTER 2

Engineering Basics 23
BUILDING LOADS 24
BEAMS, RAFTERS & COLLAR TIES 27
BUILDING PLANS 31

CHAPTER 3

Framing Tools 37
MEASURING TOOLS 38
LEVELS 39
SQUARES 40
MARKING TOOLS 41
HAND TOOLS 41
POWER TOOLS 42

CHAPTER 4

Ladders, Scaffolds & Safety Systems 45
LADDERS 46
PLATFORM JACKS 48
SCAFFOLDS 50
FALL-ARREST SYSTEMS 50

CHAPTER 5

Framing Hardware 53
NAILS 54
CONNECTORS & HURRICANE TIES 54
ANCHOR BOLTS 56
OTHER FASTENERS 59

CHAPTER 6

Essential Building Techniques 61
MEASURING ACCURATELY 62
NAILING BASICS 63
SAFE CIRCULAR-SAW USE 64
TROUBLESHOOTING LUMBER PROBLEMS 68

Section II

BUILDING THE FRAME 70

CHAPTER 7

Floor Framing 72
STRUCTURAL SUPPORT 73
GIRDERS, BEAMS & POSTS 76
FLOOR JOISTS 81
SUBFLOORS 90
UNDERLAYMENT 92

CHAPTER 8

Walls & Partitions 93
WALL FRAMING 94
ROUGH OPENINGS 100
WALL ASSEMBLY 102
SHEATHING 110
WINDOWS & DOORS 112

CHAPTER 9

Gable-Roof Framing 121

ROOF LOADS **122**
ROOF PITCH & SLOPE **122**
CALCULATING RAFTER LENGTH **123**
INSTALLING RIDGEBOARDS & RAFTERS **130**
TRUSSES **134**
SKYLIGHTS **137**
ROOF SHEATHING **138**

CHAPTER 10

Shed, Hip & Gambrel Roofs 143

FRAMING SHED ROOFS **144**
HIP ROOFS **146**
GAMBREL ROOFS **153**

CHAPTER 11

Framing Dormers 157

GABLE DORMER **158**
SHED DORMER **161**

Section III

FRAMING PROJECTS 164

CHAPTER 12

Building Stairs 166

STRAIGHT-RUN BASICS **167**
CALCULATING THE STAIRCASE SIZE **167**
STAIRCASE INSTALLATION **171**
BALUSTRADES **174**
ABOUT L-SHAPED STAIRS **179**
CALCULATING RISE & RUN **179**

FRAMING THE LANDING **181**
MAKING THE STRINGERS **183**
ASSEMBLING THE STAIRS **184**
FINISHING THE STAIRS **186**
WINDER PROS & CONS **187**
BUILDING A BASIC WINDER **187**
ADDING NOSINGS **189**

DESIGN IDEAS FOR STAIRS 190

CHAPTER 13

Basement Framing 192

ESTIMATING MATERIALS **193**
BASEMENT WALLS **193**
BASEMENT CEILINGS **197**
BASEMENT FLOORS **199**
BEAMS, DUCTS, PIPES & COLUMNS **201**

DESIGN IDEAS FOR BASEMENTS 204

CHAPTER 14

Installing a Bay Window 206

BAY WINDOWS **207**

DESIGN IDEAS FOR WINDOWS 213

PLANS TO HELP YOU BUILD YOUR
DREAM HOME **216**

HOME PLANS 218

RESOURCE GUIDE **228**
GLOSSARY **230**
INDEX **234**
CREDITS/METRIC EQUIVALENTS **239**

Introduction

Platform framing is the most popular construction method used to build today's houses. An understanding of the techniques will not only help you build a house, but the knowledge is indispensible for building additions, installing new windows and doors, reorganizing your home's floorplan, and constructing garages, sheds, and other outbuildings.

The book is designed to walk the reader through the basics of platform framing—from selecting the proper tools and materials, to laying out and erecting floors and walls, to making intricate angle cuts for rafters. The aim is to teach the basics of sound building practice and smart structural design.

To guide you through the learning experience, clear text, informative illustrations, graphic devices, and exploded diagrams help you understand the most difficult framing configurations. Labels that accompany the drawings are free of jargon and are designed to encourage even the beginner's understanding.

Section I lays out the basics of tool use and lumber selection. **Section II** builds on that knowledge as it describes how to build various aspects of a framed structure. This is the heart of the book with chapters devoted to framing floors, walls, dormers, and roofs, including gable, hip, and gambrel roofs. **Section III** covers three projects: building stairs; framing a basement using steel studs; and installing a bay window. A section of home plans from a variety of designers appears at the end of Section III.

House Framing is designed to provide information in a cumulative fashion—one chapter adds to the information that went before it. The actual framing techniques are described in step-by-step fashion where the text is supplemented by an illustration. Each task and project also begins by rating the level of difficulty of the work to be done. The level of difficulty is indicated by one, two, or three hammers:

Skill Level: Look for these estimates of job difficulty

🪶 **Easy,** even for most beginners.

🪶🪶 **Challenging,** but can be handled by do-it-yourselfers with basic tools and carpentry skills.

🪶🪶🪶 **Difficult,** but still doable by experienced do-it-yourselfers who have mastered basic construction skills and have the tools and time for the job. Consider consulting a specialist.

Section I

Getting Started

1   House Framing Materials   **12**

2   Engineering Basics   **23**

3   Framing Tools   **37**

4   Ladders, Scaffolds & Safety Systems   **45**

5   Framing Hardware   **53**

6   Essential Building Techniques   **61**

1

House Framing Materials

This book deals with platform framing, the most popular building technique used in house construction. Platform framing is popular because it requires relatively small pieces of lumber to construct a sturdy, long-lasting building. That means that young trees can provide the lumber needed for construction. In addition, the smaller components are easier to handle at the job site—an important consideration for both professional builders and do-it-yourselfers.

Before learning the building techniques of platform framing, it is important to learn about the lumber you will be using. The building and lumber industries have developed systems for rating and grading lumber components. These systems ensure that the lumber you select will meet local building codes and will help you construct a safe, durable building.

This chapter deals with the language of the lumber business. It is an important skill in its own right. Without it, you will not be able to order the materials you want and need, nor will you be able to communicate with the professionals you may hire for certain tasks. With the information contained here, you'll not only be an informed consumer, but you'll also be more familiar with these various components when you read about them later in the book and when you start to use them in framing a house or addition.

Working with Wood

Wood is one of the most important materials you'll buy for your project, so you should purchase the best-quality wood you can afford. Keep in mind that you'd be wasting your money buying expensive furniture-quality hardwoods to frame a house, just as you'd be wasting your time making furniture with framing-quality lumber. Take a close look at this section so you can learn enough about wood properties to be an educated lumber buyer.

Hardwood vs. Softwood

Wood is generally divided into two broad categories: hardwood and softwood. Common hardwoods include ash, birch, cherry, poplar, black walnut, maple, northern red oak, and white oak. Hardwoods come from slow-growing deciduous trees, or trees that lose their leaves in winter; they are therefore expensive and, in most cases, quite strong. Many hardwoods have beautiful grain patterns, and they're well suited to woodworking—joining, shaping, and routing. You won't be using hardwoods for house framing.

Softwoods come from fast-growing, cone-bearing trees called conifers, or evergreens. Usually less expensive than hardwoods and widely available at lumberyards, softwoods account for nearly all the lumber used in framing and construction. Even though hardwoods are normally stronger because they're more dense, softwoods are plenty strong enough for house framing.

Douglas fir, hemlock, eastern white pine, southern yellow pine, and spruce are all softwoods commonly used for framing houses. Douglas fir is used for most rough construction, especially along the Pacific Coast, where it is milled, whereas in the south and east you're more likely to find southern pine. There are two other softwoods you might see, redwood and western red cedar, that aren't normally used for framing because of their expense. These species are excellent for exterior siding, trim, and decks, however, because of their exceptional durability and natural resistance to decay.

Sawmills cut softwoods into standard dimensions and lengths, and that's why the lumber is sometimes called "dimension lumber." Unlike ordering hardwood (which you

order by species), ordering softwood framing lumber generally doesn't require that you ask for a specific species of wood. You simply order by dimension and grade. The lumberyard has already made a softwood choice for you by buying whatever wood is available for your region. The lumber is often simply stamped SPF for "spruce, pine, fir," and can be any one of these softwood species. To understand lumber and how to use it properly, you need to know about the properties of a tree and the milling process that turns it into lumber.

Sapwood vs. Heartwood

There are two kinds of wood in all trees: sapwood and heartwood. Sapwood, as its name implies, carries sap to the leaves. The heartwood is the dense center of the tree.

Trees that grow quickly (softwoods) tend to have disproportionately more sapwood. In fact, young trees consist of almost all sapwood. This is important to know because when you buy lumber, sapwood and heartwood behave differently in buildings. Heartwood, for instance, should be used in exposed conditions or as structural members because it is stronger and more

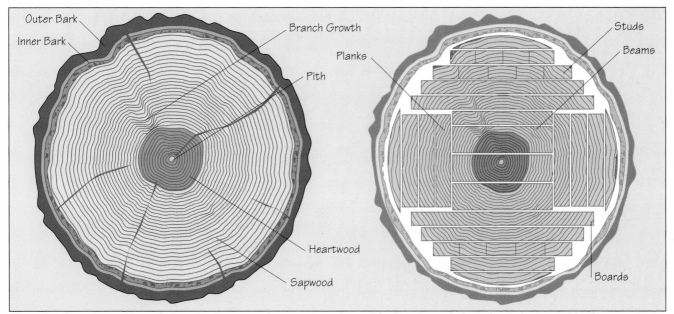

Sapwood vs. Heartwood. Because heartwood is stronger, it's used for beams, wide boards, and structural lumber pieces. Sapwood is used for planks and "light residential" lumber like studs.

durable. Sapwood is better suited for use as planks, siding, partition wall studs, and other building components subjected to little or no stress. And unless it's treated, sapwood is more susceptible to decay than heartwood.

Milling Methods

Wood can be milled in one of two ways, the quartersawn or the plainsawn method. Plainsawn, or flat-grained, lumber is the kind commonly used in framing; quartersawn wood, which can be costly, is more common in hardwoods and is used in premium furniture. The difference between these woods lies in how the wood is milled.

Quartersawn Lumber. For quartersawn lumber, the log is first quartered lengthwise. Then the boards are cut lengthwise out of each quarter-log section. This milling technique produces a stable piece of wood that's less prone to warpage because the growth rings intersect the surface at a 90-degree angle and are never fully exposed on the face of the board. Quartersawing yields narrower boards, however, and wastes a high percentage of the log. Quartersawn boards often need to be special-ordered.

Plainsawn Lumber. For plainsawn wood, the log is simply cut lengthwise, from end to end, the way you cut cheese off a slab with a knife. This milling technique yields a kind of board that is entirely different from quartersawn boards, even when they're cut from the same log. In plainsawn boards, the growth rings are at less than a 90-degree angle to the surface of the board. This exposes more face grain and makes the wood unstable and more susceptible to warpage, cupping, and twisting.

Milled Dimensions

A piece of lumber has two sizes: nominal and actual. A 2×4 may start out at 2×4 inches (its nominal size) when it comes off a log, but it soon shrinks when it is dried. Then it shrinks again when it is planed. A 2×4 soon becomes $1\frac{1}{2} \times 3\frac{1}{2}$ inches—the lumber's actual size. For wood lengths, the nominal and actual lengths are almost always the same. When you buy a 10-foot 2×4, it is usually 10 feet long (plus an inch or two).

Some lumberyards charge for lumber by the board foot, though increasingly yards are charging by the individual "stick," or piece of

lumber. If your lumberyard charges you by the board foot, here's how to figure it: Take the nominal thickness, multiply it by the nominal width and the length, and divide by 12. A 10-foot 2×6 (usually written 2×6 × 10' in the industry) would be 10 board feet.

Grading

Not all framing lumber is of the same quality. Besides sapwood and heartwood distinctions, many other wood features come into play, including moisture content, strength, number of knots, and appearance. A standardized system of lumber grading rates wood for many of these qualities. The lower the grade, the poorer the quality.

Who grades the wood? That's left up to the regional wood-inspection bureaus, which have names like the Western Wood Products Association or the Southern Pine Inspection Bureau. No matter what body inspects the wood, however, the grading system subscribes to the U.S. Department of Commerce American Softwood Lumber Standard, and the grading marks are stamped right on the lumber. The two most important grading characteristics are moisture content and strength.

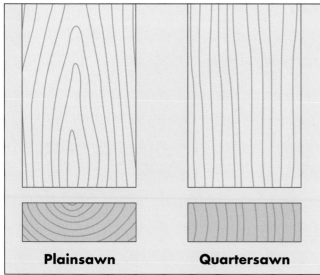

Milling Methods. Plainsawn wood (left) exposes growth rings on the face of the board and is susceptible to dimensional changes caused by weathering and moisture. Quartersawn lumber (right) is more stable because growth rings are denser and less exposed.

NOMINAL & ACTUAL LUMBER SIZES

Nominal Size (inches)	Actual Size (inches)	Nominal Size (inches)	Actual Size (inches)
1x2	$\frac{3}{4} \times 1\frac{1}{2}$	$\frac{5}{4}$x6	$1 \times 5\frac{1}{2}$
1x3	$\frac{3}{4} \times 2\frac{1}{2}$	2x2	$1\frac{1}{2} \times 1\frac{1}{2}$
1x4	$\frac{3}{4} \times 3\frac{1}{2}$	2x4	$1\frac{1}{2} \times 3\frac{1}{2}$
1x6	$\frac{3}{4} \times 5\frac{1}{2}$	2x6	$1\frac{1}{2} \times 5\frac{1}{2}$
1x8	$\frac{3}{4} \times 7\frac{1}{4}$	2x8	$1\frac{1}{2} \times 7\frac{1}{4}$
1x10	$\frac{3}{4} \times 9\frac{1}{4}$	2x10	$1\frac{1}{2} \times 9\frac{1}{4}$
1x12	$\frac{3}{4} \times 11\frac{1}{4}$	2x12	$1\frac{1}{2} \times 11\frac{1}{4}$
$\frac{5}{4}$x4	$1 \times 3\frac{1}{2}$	4x4	$3\frac{1}{2} \times 3\frac{1}{2}$

Moisture content is directly related to whether the lumber is kiln dried, air dried (with subcategories of S-dry, S-green, and MC 15), or native green. Lumber strength is divided into two categories: structural and framing.

Moisture Content. An important feature of framing lumber, moisture affects wood weight, shrinkage, and strength. Moisture content is the weight of the water in the wood, expressed as a percentage of the weight of the wood. Standing trees can have a moisture content of between 30 and 200 percent, whereas seasoned dimension lumber should have a moisture content of below 19 percent. Once the lumber's moisture level is between 15 and 19 percent, it is ready for use. In a heated building, lumber ends up with a moisture content of around 10 percent, and it shrinks while drying.

Kiln drying or air drying is how mills reach the goal of less than 19 percent moisture. As you can imagine, drying wood in a kiln is more expensive than letting it air dry in a lumberyard. If it's in your budget to buy kiln-dried lumber, it's generally a better lumber product. But air-dried lumber of nearly the same moisture content can perform just as well and costs less.

Kiln-Dried Lumber. The driest wood available, this lumber is oven-dried at the saw mill to a moisture content below 15 percent. Because kiln drying precisely controls the moisture content and shrinkage of the wood, you can count on having stable, predictable lumber dimensions. Kiln-dried 2×4s have a consistent actual size of $1\frac{1}{2} \times 3\frac{1}{2}$ inches. You'll pay more for this predictability, however. You may be just as well off with air-dried wood rated for a desirable moisture content.

Air-Dried Lumber. This kind of lumber is covered by three categories in official grading standards. "MC-15" means the lumber has a moisture content of 15 percent; "S-dry," lumber with a moisture content of 19 percent; and "S-green," lumber that has a moisture content of over 19 percent.

Native Green Lumber.
Available from local sawmills, the lumber's moisture content is usually high because it's sold unseasoned and it's not cut as precisely as standard lumberyard lumber. A 2×8 can be $2\frac{1}{4} \times 8\frac{1}{2}$, for instance, or $2 \times 7\frac{1}{4}$. It's unpredictable. Additionally, native green lumber is not as structurally stable as kiln-dried or air-dried dimension lumber. The wood is heavy and hard to work with, and it cracks and splits as it dries. Native green lumber is inexpensive, however, and you might want to use it to frame rough structures like sheds or barns. Also, you can nail it in place soaking wet when you use it for board-and-batten siding.

Structural Grade. Lumber grading for structural grade lumber is complex, with categories, grades, and subgrades. For most framing, there are four lumber categories: select structural, No. 1, No. 2, and No. 3. The higher the number, the weaker the wood; the weaker the wood, the less distance you can span. A 2×8 hemlock-fir "select structural" used as a joist and framed 16 inches on center can span 14 feet 2 inches, for instance, but a No. 3 grade can span only 11 feet. The wood gets weaker because there are more knots and less consistent grain as you move away from the select structural grade. You also pay more for stronger wood. For structural framing—joists, rafters, ridgeboards—the ideal lumber grade is No. 2.

When evaluating 2×4s, you'll find that there are three other names for the No. 1, No. 2, and No. 3 categories. "Construction" grade corresponds to No. 1; "Standard-Better," to No. 2; and "Utility," to No. 3. (A final category, "Economy," is for nonstructural use.) For wall fram-

ing, use No. 2 (Standard or Better) for load-bearing walls and No. 3 (Utility) for nonload-bearing walls. Because it's hard to sort this all out, and using utility lumber yields only marginal savings, you can safely buy No. 2 lumber for your entire project.

All lumber has a high moisture content when it is milled. So, it is either air dried or kiln dried for construction use. The acceptable maximum moisture content for wood at a lumberyard is 19 percent. Often the grade stamp for construction lumber will say "kiln-dried 19%."

Grade Stamps. All wood is stamped to let you know you have the right wood. A typical grade stamp identifies the mill, the grading service's name, the moisture content, the grade, and the species.

The mill identification number isn't really important. The same with the grading service. The species mark is mostly a curiosity, too, as the lumberyard has chosen what species you'll use, based on what's available for your region. But look closely at the biggest word in the grading stamp. You should see a word like STAND, which stands for Standard, the grade you'll use for standard household light framing. Next, look at the moisture designation. Here's where you'll see

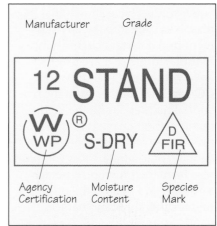

Grade Stamps. A stamp identifies the lumber's grade, moisture content, and species, along with the manufacturer and grading agency.

KD for kiln-dried, S-DRY, MC 15, or S-GRN. These are the moisture content ratings mentioned earlier.

When you go to a lumberyard with all this knowledge, you'll probably be more informed than most of the yard workers. But no matter how much you know, the lumberyard will have already made most framing lumber choices for you, at least in terms of species. You'll simply specify the grade. Check the grading stamp to make sure you've picked up the right kind of wood.

Pressure-Treated Lumber.

Pressure-treated wood (PT) is lumber that's been soaked under pressure with an insecticide and a fungicide, which ward off pests and decay, respectively. PT lumber is mostly southern yellow pine, although some other pines, firs, and hemlocks are occasionally used. These softwoods are selected because they are fast-growing, dense, and structurally sound.

Types. In the past, the most common kind of PT wood was treated with chromated copper arsenate (CCA), a compound that chemically bonds with the wood. CCA-treated lumber has a green tint from the oxidation of the copper. The retention level achieved during treatment determined its use.

CCA (and to some extent, all chemical treatments) are controversial. Some studies have shown that it dissolves back into the environment under certain circumstances. Manufacturers of these products have voluntarily withdrawn all CCA-treated lumber from the residential market. To fill the void, manufacturers have replaced CCA products with those treated with copper compounds. Most companies have their own proprietary formulas and market the products under different brand names.

Cautions. Check product data sheets for proper uses of the new treated lumber. One difference you will notice right away it that the

signature green tint of CCA-treated lumber is replaced by a brown color that eventually weathers to a gray color.

The other major difference is that there is some evidence that the chemicals used to treat lumber are more corrosive than CCA. This could be a problem with some types of fasteners. Again, check with the manufacturer about fastener selection. Some studies have shown that stainless-steel fasteners offer the best resistance to corrosion. A second choice may be nails and screws treated with a polymer coating if the fasteners are approved by the supplier.

Common Lumber Problems

Shrinkage. As with any organic thing that gains and loses water, wood swells when it is moist and shrinks as it dries. Wood also tends to shrink in the direction of the annual growth rings, or tangentially. That's why plainsawn boards rarely grow or shrink in length, but can shrink substantially across their widths. Shrinkage is a potential problem with any lumber. The combination of shrinking and swelling can lead to warping (uneven shrinking during drying), checking (cracks along growth rings), bowing (end-to-end deviation from the plane of the board's wide face), twisting (spi-

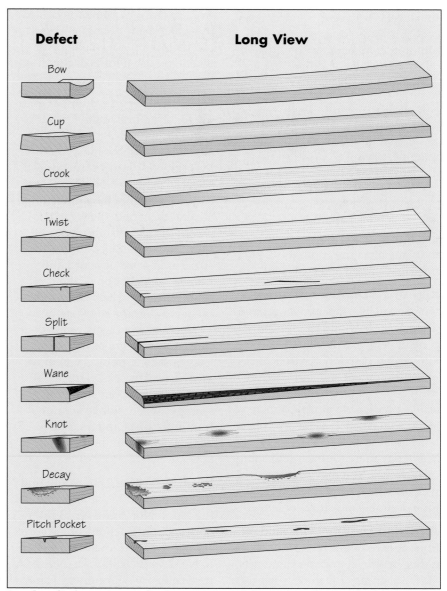

Lumber Defects. Inspect for these common defects when choosing lumber.

ral or torsional distortion), and cupping (deviation from a flat plane, edge to edge). Softwoods like pine, Douglas fir, and cedar are particularly vulnerable. With normal shrinkage, plainsawn eastern white pine can shrink across its width more than 6 percent.

Nail Popping. Shrinking wood can cause problems way down the line. When you are installing drywall, for example, and you nail through the drywall into the stud

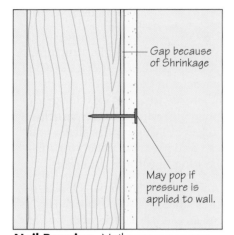

— Gap because of Shrinkage

May pop if pressure is applied to wall.

Nail Popping. Nail pops may occur when shrinking wood opens a gap between the wall and the stud or joist.

beneath it, the stud may still be in the process of drying. As the stud dries with the nail in it, it shrinks and you may get a nail pop, in which the head of the nail protrudes $\frac{1}{16}$ inch or so out from the drywall's face. Here's how you can get a nail pop: If a 2×6 stud is sold at 19-percent moisture content, it is $5\frac{1}{2}$ inches wide. As it dries down to around 10-percent moisture content, it may shrink another $\frac{3}{8}$ inch. This is especially true of juvenile wood. A gap will form between the wallboard and the face of the stud, and when someone applies pressure on the wall, perhaps just by leaning on it, the nailhead will poke through. The way to avoid a nail pop is to use seasoned wood as close to the final moisture content as possible. To do that you have to buy quality, seasoned, mature lumber (harder and harder to find these days) and properly store it on site, away from ground moisture and rain. To truly ensure against wood shrinkage, store your framing lumber in a heated place on site for as long as you possibly can before using it.

Juvenile Wood. Given the demand on the nation's forests for wood, many lumber companies have shortened their harvesting cycles or have planted fast-growing trees. When these trees are harvested, they yield juvenile wood, which can give you problems. Juvenile wood encompasses the first 5 to 20 annual growth rings of any tree, and when it's used for lumber, it doesn't have the same strength as mature wood. You may get bouncy floors, buckled walls, weakened joints, and poorly fitting windows and doors. Even kiln-dried juvenile wood can warp because of non-uniform growth-ring distribution. Inspect the lumber you're buying and look for telltale signs of juvenile wood, such as uneven grain distribution and warping, and refuse wood that is not up to par.

Weather Protection. You can't overestimate the importance of properly stacking and storing wood, both at the lumberyard (their responsibility) and after it's delivered to the worksite (your responsibility). Prepare a dry, sheltered location in

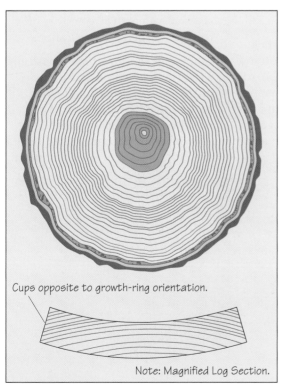

Cups opposite to growth-ring orientation.

Note: Magnified Log Section.

Juvenile Wood. Juvenile wood has an uneven distribution of growth rings and is more prone to warping.

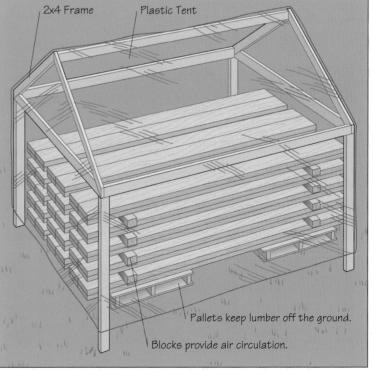

2x4 Frame   Plastic Tent

Pallets keep lumber off the ground.

Blocks provide air circulation.

Weather Protection. Storing wood off the ground and under a waterproof tent is essential for maintaining good lumber quality.

which to place your lumber when it's delivered. Allow air to pass all around the boards, especially the ends, but keep rain or snow off them. It's best to lay down pallets, use blocks to separate the rows of boards, and build a 2×4 frame to suspend a polyethylene tent above the lumber for long storage. Locate this storage spot close to the worksite.

Plywood

Once you've chosen your framing lumber, you'll need to choose plywood for decking and sheathing. Plywood comprises an odd number of thin veneer layers of wood, called plies. The veneers are cross-laminated, so that the grains of each ply run perpendicular to one another. The veneers are glued and sandwiched together and then heated to over 300 degrees F under 200 pounds per square inch (psi) of pressure. Standard plywood thicknesses are $\frac{5}{16}$, $\frac{3}{8}$, $\frac{7}{16}$, $\frac{15}{32}$, $\frac{1}{2}$, $\frac{5}{8}$, $\frac{23}{32}$, $\frac{3}{4}$, and $1\frac{1}{8}$ inches. If you order $\frac{1}{2}$- and $\frac{3}{4}$-inch plywood for your job, you'll most likely get $\frac{15}{32}$- and $\frac{23}{32}$-inch plywood, respectively. Panels are almost invariably 4 × 8 feet after factory trimming. Corner to corner, panels can be off-square by $\frac{3}{32}$ of an inch.

Every piece of plywood has a face veneer and a back veneer. These are the outside plies. The plies under the face and back veneers are called crossbands, and the center ply is

called the core. The core can be either veneer or solid lumber. Some plywoods even have fiberglass or particleboard at their cores, but you won't be using these kinds of plywood for sheathing. Veneer-core lumber is stronger than lumber-core plywood, but lumber-core plywood can hold a screw better at its edge.

Used in the right applications, plywood is strong and adds stiffness to walls and strength to floors. As wall sheathing, plywood is a vast improvement over the old style of wall sheathing, nailing 1-inch boards diagonally across the wall. A relatively thin $\frac{5}{16}$-inch plywood-sheathed wall has twice the stiffness of a wall sheathed with 1-inch diagonal boards. Besides conventional sheathing plywood, you can buy treated, fire-retardant, and waterproof plywood for special applications.

Other Panel Products

Panel products other than plywood, called nonveneer or reconstituted wood-product panels, are sometimes used for sheathing. Some of these panels are just as strong—and cheaper—than plywood. There are four types: structural particleboard, waferboard, oriented-strand board (OSB), and composite board. The products are called reconstituted because they're made from wood particles or wood strands that are bonded together with adhesive into 4 × 8-foot sheets.

The smooth-faced structural particleboard (also called flakeboard or chipboard) is simply a panel of wood particles held together by hot-pressed resin. Some exterior-rated products have a layer of resin or wax on the outside to repel water. The glue used in these products is urea formaldehyde or phenol-formaldehyde adhesive. Some building-code bodies, or organizations that determine minimum building specifications now allow you to use structural particleboard as an underlayment, a subfloor, or a roof deck.

Waferboard is just like structural particleboard, except that the wood particles in these boards are all $1\frac{1}{2}$ inches long. An exterior-grade phenolic resin glues the particles together. Where codes allow, you can also use these panels for subflooring, sheathing, and roofs.

Another panel material, OSB, also uses strands of wood, but the layers are crossed, layer for layer, just as plywood is cross-laminated to give it strength. The three to five layers of strands in OSB are bonded together with phenolic resin. These panels have a smooth face and are often rated for structural applications.

Composite board, which is basically a hybrid of plywood and particleboard, has a reconstituted wood center but a face and back of plywood veneer. Where codes allow, you can use composite-board wall sheathing and floor underlayments.

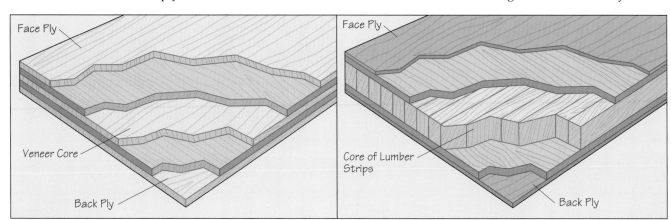

Face Ply

Veneer Core

Back Ply

Face Ply

Core of Lumber Strips

Back Ply

Plywood. Plywood is made by cross-laminating thin veneers or "plies" of wood. The core of plywood can be either a veneer ply or a lumber ply.

Rating Panel Products

When you purchase structural panels, a grading label tells you what you're buying. The leading grading association is the APA—The Engineered Wood Association and it's their stamp you're most likely to see.

Panel Grade. Panel products are also rated in a number of other categories. If you look at a typical APA grade stamp, you'll see the panel grade on the top line. This entry designates the proper application for the panel—rated sheathing, rated flooring, rated underlayment, and the like.

Span Rating. Next you'll see a large number or numbers, indicating the span rating. This rating is the recommended center-to-center spacing in inches of studs/joists/rafters over which you can place the panel. If you see numbers like 32/16, the left number gives the maximum spacing in inches of the panel when used in roofing (32 inches of allowable span along the side of the panel with three or more supports), and the right number gives the maximum spacing when the panel is used as subflooring (16 inches of allowable span along the side of the panel with three or more supports).

Thickness. In addition, the grade stamp identifies the actual thickness of the panel, often in thirty-seconds of an inch—$\frac{3}{8}$ inch, $\frac{7}{16}$ inch, $\frac{15}{32}$ inch, $\frac{23}{32}$ inch, and so on.

Exposure. The stamp also lists the exposure and durability classification for plywood: Exterior indicates exposure to weather is possible; Exposure 1 designates suitability for wall and roof sheathing; Exposure 2, for applications that will have low moisture exposure, such as subfloors.

Mill and Standards Numbers. The mill number simply identifies the manufacturer. The remaining numbers on the label—national evaluation report (NER), and performance-rated panel standard

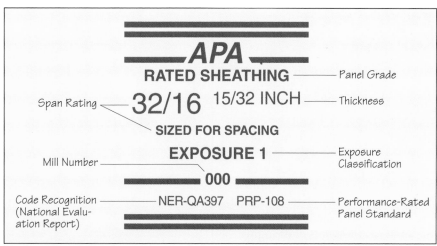

Rating Panel Products. A typical plywood grade stamp indicates the panel grade, thickness, and span rating; assures the buyer of code compliance; and identifies the grading body and the mill.

PLYWOOD VENEER GRADES (4 x 8-Foot Panels)

A	Smooth, paintable. Not more than 18 neatly made repairs, boat, sled, or router type, and parallel to grain, permitted. May be used for natural finish in less-demanding applications.
B	Solid surface. Shims, circular repair plugs and tight knots to 1 inch across grain permitted. Some minor splits permitted.
C Plugged	Improved C veneer with splits limited to $\frac{1}{8}$-inch width and knotholes and borer holes limited to $\frac{1}{4} \times \frac{1}{2}$ inch. Admits some broken grain. Synthetic repairs permitted.
C	Tight knots to $1\frac{1}{2}$ inches. Knotholes to 1 inch across grain and some to $1\frac{1}{2}$ inches if total width of knots and knotholes is within specified limits. Synthetic or wood repairs. Discoloration and sanding defects that do not impair strength permitted. Limited splits allowed. Stitching permitted.
D	Knots and knotholes to $2\frac{1}{2}$-inch width across grain and $\frac{1}{2}$ inch larger within specified limits. Limited splits are permitted. Stitching permitted. Limited to Interior and Exposure 1 panels.

Source: APA—The Engineered Wood Association

(PRP)—indicate that the panel meets all construction requirements and requisite codes.

Veneer Grades. Plywood is also rated for veneer grades, and that rating appears on the edge of the plywood, using combinations of letters. There are six categories in veneer ratings: N, A, B, C Plugged, C, and D, indicating descending order of quality. N is a smooth surface of select woods with no defects, but you won't be using N in framing. It's for use in cabinetry. For construction-grade plywood, the face-and-back-veneer grades are combinations of letters. B-C, for example, is suitable for sheathing, while you'd use A-B when both the face and back veneers will show. A-C or A-D is suitable when only the A side will show, and C-D is used for concrete forms.

Engineered Lumber

There are a number of engineered, non-wood, and steel products that you can successfully use when framing a house. Some of these products were created in response to declining wood quality and rising costs. High-quality long beams of Douglas fir are expensive and must be special-ordered. Other non-wood products were created to respond to the span requirements of changing house designs that include open floor plans, cantilevered decks and lofts, and overhanging roofs. These engineered products include glue-laminated lumber, laminated-ve-neer-lumber, and parallel-strand beams. Be aware that you must use these products in strict accordance with manufacturers' span specifica-tions. In addition, you must install them with special connectors and specified techniques.

Glue-Laminated Lumber

A glue-laminated beam is a built-up product, a beam made up of smaller pieces of wood glued to-gether lengthwise with waterproof glue. For example, six 2×4s, each measuring $1\frac{1}{2} \times 3\frac{1}{2}$ inches, will cre-ate a $9 \times 3\frac{1}{2}$-inch beam. To make a beam, high-quality lumber is fin-ger-jointed together and stacked. Finger-jointing is a technique used to join wood end to end in a single member. The ends of component wood pieces are cut to look like fin-gers and glued together.

Glue-laminated lumber can be as long as you like—25 feet or longer. Each beam is specifically engineered to support the intended building load: for heavier loads, the beam may use a more supportive compo-nent configuration, heavier com-ponent pieces, or more boards glued together.

Appearance Grades. You can use glue-laminated lumber, hidden or exposed, as ridge beams, purlins,

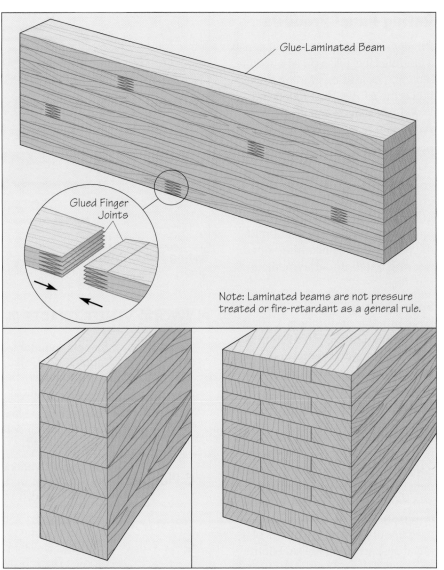

Note: Laminated beams are not pressure treated or fire-retardant as a general rule.

Glue-Laminated Lumber. Built up of finger-jointed dimensional lumber that must be engineered (sized) for your application, glue-laminated lumber can be assembled in two configurations, depending on the span and load of the application.

headers, floor girders, and garage-door headers. It comes in three appearance grades, which have nothing to do with strength: indus-trial, architectural, and premium. Industrial-grade beams are simply planed to a uniform dimension. The wood may have checks and knot-holes. Architectural-grade beams have been sanded on all four sides, and blemishes have been filled. Premium-grade beams have had all defects and blemishes fixed. All three kinds of lumber are dried, then wrapped in watertight wrapping.

Residential Grade. Residential-sized, glue-laminated lumber is a similar product made to replace

headers, the horizontal structural supports above doors and win-dows. These beams are made to standard framing widths and are designed to bear residential loads. They also have a slight bow, called a crown, which you must install upward. The top side is labeled on the wrapper.

Connectors. No matter what kind of glue-laminated lumber you in-stall, you can't just nail it in place. You may be required to use fram-ing connectors, shear plates, thread-ed rods, nail-on clips, or hangers. Be sure to double-check the manu-facturers' installation requirements and span ratings.

Cost. Glue-laminated beams are 30 to 50 percent more expensive than beams built up out of framing lumber. For shorter length applications, like headers, you'll find that a beam made of face-nailed conventional lumber is more economical. For longer spans, such as garage door headers or the structural ridge beams for large open rooms, however, glue-laminated beams offer a price advantage and dramatic labor savings. If you frame a span of 30 feet with a glue-laminated beam, you'll surely save money on labor and materials over comparable "stick-built" framing systems. You'll also gain design versatility, which you can't always put a price on. A stick-built framing system in a 30-foot-wide room would not allow for wide-open spaces, as you would have to divide the room up with partition walls to support the roof. With a glue-laminated beam, which can span 30 feet, you can keep that space open.

Laminated-Veneer Lumber

Another commonly available engineered wood material is laminated-veneer lumber (LVL). You'll use these beams where you would have used steel or an oversize glue-laminated beam. They are made, as their name implies, by laminating

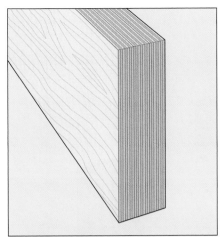

Laminated-Veneer Lumber. An LVL is a beam composed of plywood-like pieces of lumber glued together side by side.

¼-inch-thick plies together to a thickness of 4½ inches. You'll have to consult with the manufacturers' span charts to determine the size LVL to use on your job. Even when you get the span rating down, be careful, because you can't notch or drill LVLs for pipes, wires, and heating or air-conditioning ducts, and you have to use the proper framing connectors.

Parallel-Strand Lumber

Parallel-strand lumber is a kind of engineered beam that can be between 1¾ and 7 inches thick. The beams are made of matchstick-like strands of Douglas fir and/or southern yellow pine. The strands

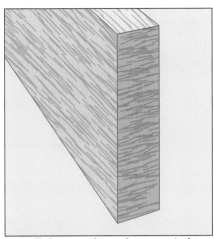

Parallel-Strand Lumber. Made from strands of softwood lumber, these engineered beams may be up to 7 in. thick.

are glued together running parallel to one another, hence the name parallel-strand lumber. These beams are more dimensionally stable than LVLs or glue-laminated lumber beams, and they serve in the same framing applications. Parallel-strand lumber tends not to cup or twist when it is stored, which is a potential problem with some glue-laminated beams and LVLs.

Wood I-Beams

Another popular engineered product, wood I-beams are dead-straight, dimensionally stable, and ideal for longer spans, say 24 feet. I-beams are light and can be in-

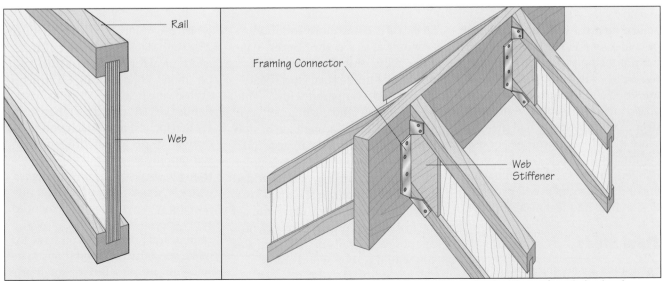

Wood I-Beams. Made with fir rails and ½-in. plywood or OSB webs, wood I-beams can take the place of costly lumber beams. Web stiffeners and framing connectors may be required.

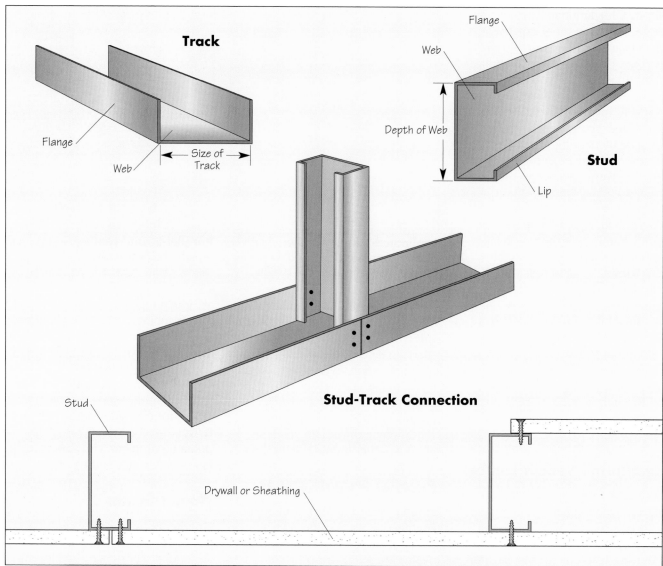

Steel Studs. An affordable alternative to conventional framing lumber, particularly in partition walls, steel studs are dimensionally stable, consistent in quality, light in weight, and perhaps most important, fireproof. U-shaped tracks act as top and bottom plates and are sized to accept the web of the studs. You can attach studs with clips, screws, or a crimping tool.

stalled by just two people. The web, or center, of a wood I-beam is typically ½-inch plywood or OSB, and the 2-inch rails at top and bottom are fir. Wood I-beams come in four sizes: 9½, 11⅞, 14, and 16 inches deep. You can simply nail them in place in many applications, or use commonly available connectors and hangers in others. The manufacturers of these products will provide design help and technical support.

Steel Studs

Steel studs are another kind of engineered product designed to replace traditional wood framing members.

Steel has become more and more economical as wood prices escalate and quality plummets. An 8-foot residential-grade steel stud costs about $1.55, compared with a similar-size wood stud costing between $1.50 and $2. The advantage of steel is that it is predictable. Every stud is precisely the same. There is no shrinkage or warping, and no added expense of building a sheltered area in which to store them. Once you get the installation process down, you can put these walls up just as fast as you would put up wood studs.

Steel studs commonly fall into two categories: NLB drywall studs,

which are nonload-bearing, made of 25-gauge steel or galvanized steel, and typical for most residential applications. Load-bearing LB structural studs are heavier. All studs have flat flanges (stud widths range from 1⅝ to 6 inches) into which you screw drywall or plywood with 8-gauge self-tapping screws made to penetrate the steel studs. For framing an entire house, you may be better off sticking with wood studs. You need some special tools for steel studs, rafters, and joists, and you have to make special accommodations to install your utilities. But for small projects like partitions and basements, steel studs are great.

Engineering Basics

Buildings need to stand up on their own and support the weight of anything that is in them, including furniture, people, the roof above, and any snow that accumulates on the roof. A lot of science goes into building a house.

Fortunately, you don't have to engineer your building from scratch. The engineering and sizing of component pieces have already been done by architects, engineers, and designers. Even better, the standardized building specifications they've come up with have been worked through using careful math and have been tested over the years in the construction of thousands of real buildings. The resulting structural engineering "common knowledge" is readily available in easy-to-read tables and charts that specify beam, rafter, and stud sizes, along with their maximum allowable loads and spans. All this information is used in drawing the blueprints for the house—the plan from which you'll build the structure. It is also used by building code officials during inspections.

Building Loads

There are five different types of forces, or "loads," that any structure must be able to withstand: dead load, live load, shear load, point load, and spread load. Some of these forces are the natural result of gravity tugging at the building, dragging it down. Some are the result of wind gusts, snow loads, or ground movement.

Defining Loads

The weight of the building itself—the framing lumber, nails, shingles, glass, doors, and the like—makes up the dead load of part of a structure. The live load is the weight of people in the building, along with anything they bring into the building, such as wood stoves, couches, dining room sets, or dance parties. The third type of load, shear load, is the force the building encounters when the wind gusts, the earth quakes, or the foundation shifts because of events like soil washout. A point load is the downward force exerted by a single heavy thing inside or on top of the structure, such as a fireplace, hot tub, or water heater. Lastly, there is the spread load, the outward force on walls caused by the downward-and-outward force of rafters, usually because of heavy snow pressing down on the roof.

If your structure isn't prepared to handle these loads, it could cave in or suffer partial collapse or failure. More likely, the framing members will bend under the loads. This bending is known as deflection.

Deflection

Deflection can cause at least four types of problems with any framed structure. If the structure itself sags, deflection can distort a window or door in its frame. If the structure's walls sag, you could end up with bulging picture windows or other large fixed windows. If windows bulge, the seals around or between the panes can break. Broken seals allow moisture and cold air to enter the building—defeating the energy savings you paid a fortune for when you bought those windows. If the ridgeboard on the roof sags under a load, then your structure will not only look bad, but you'll get cracks in the walls and perhaps some stuck doors and windows. If the deflection occurs in floors, usually because of undersized joists, you'll feel a bounce when you walk. Bouncy floors usually won't cause a building to collapse, but they can make you feel uneasy.

Dealing with the various loads that act on a house really means preventing deflection. First, use proper building-design practices, with proper spacing and alignment of framing members so that you create clean load paths. Second, use appropriate-grade, properly sized framing lumber. Third, follow building codes closely; for example, do not skimp on nailing.

Load Paths

The most common framing design errors concern load paths. A load path is the route that loads take through the house as the load exerts its force downward on the structure. Load paths must be straight vertical lines from the top of the structure to the foundation. If the load paths are not vertical or continuous, loads may bear on areas of the building that are not able to support them. The result is unwanted deflection.

Common broken-load-path scenarios include misplaced rafter struts, misaligned bearing walls, and unsupported columns not carried through to the foundation. These framing errors, described in more detail below, may seem obvious.

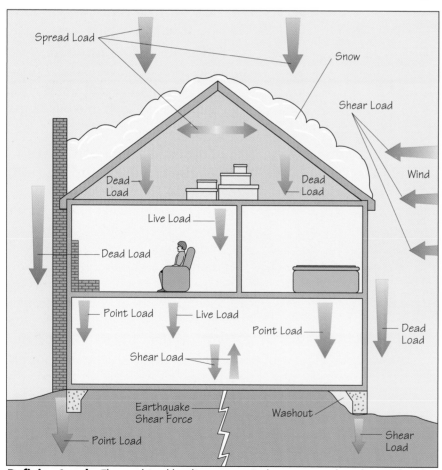

Defining Loads. The combined loading on a typical structure can be substantial and must be accounted for with proper design practices and proper beam and lumber sizing.

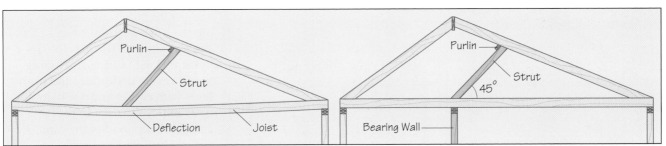

Misplaced Struts. When placing rafter struts, be sure they fall on a bearing wall, otherwise you may deflect the joist. Struts must meet the joists at no less than a 45-degree angle.

But even experienced builders make mistakes in interpreting building design and work themselves into predicaments with no good solutions. The more complicated the structure—with overhangs, cantilevered porches, or large open spaces—the more complicated the resulting design and load-path transfers will be. Building design is not for amateurs. If you're not working from designer- or architect-approved plans, have them looked over by a structural engineer. Also, never modify existing plans that an architect or engineer has already approved. Buildings are complex structures, with interrelated components. If you choose to remove a wall or even move it 12 inches from its place in the original engineered plans, you can change the entire dynamic of the structure and possibly cause a failure later down the line.

Misplaced Struts. When framing any roof—but especially irregular roofs—you may want to install a mid-rafter strut, or support, between a long rafter and the attic floor. That's perfectly acceptable practice, but only if the strut lands on a bearing wall. Bearing walls can support loads from above, as opposed to partition walls, which simply divide space.

Misaligned Bearing Walls.
Bearing walls must transfer loads through the structure to the foundation in vertical lines. If the load paths are not vertical (within an acceptable small margin of error), the joists will end up taking on the

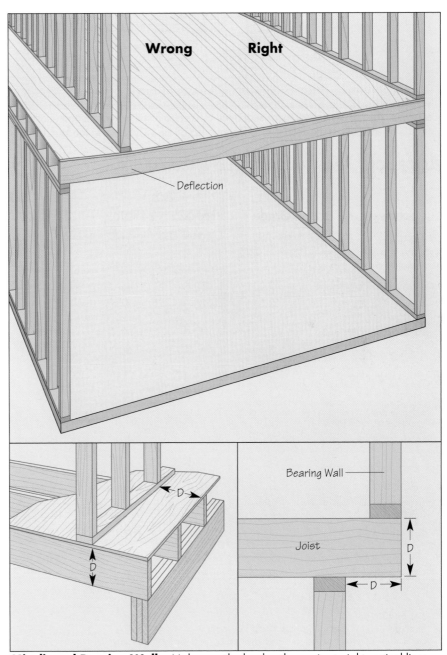

Misaligned Bearing Walls. Make sure the load paths are in straight vertical lines throughout the wall systems in any structure. A wall built on top of a floor that is not itself supported may deflect the floor joists (top). If it's impossible for bearing walls to line up, the wall should be placed no farther away from the joist end than the depth of the joist (bottom left). When a bearing wall rests on a cantilever, the distance it extends beyond the supporting wall should not be greater than the depth of the joist (bottom right).

2

ENGINEERING BASICS

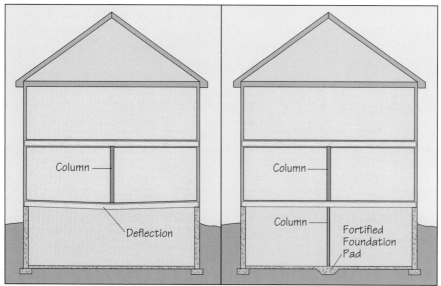

weight that the walls were designed to absorb and transfer to the foundation. The possible results are joist failures, including splits, severe deflection, and problems with cracks in drywall and gaps in floorboards. In severe cases, broken load paths can make a building collapse.

Columns. A column used to support a second-story floor must be supported from below so it can transfer the weight of the upper floors to the foundation. If a column supports a second-story floor without being supported from below, then the first-floor joists end up carrying an inordinate amount of weight.

Columns. Attic or upper-floor loads supported by a column will deflect the floor that supports the column, unless the column is itself supported all the way down to the foundation.

FLOOR JOIST SPAN RATINGS (Feet & Inches)

Species	Grade	2x8		2x10		2x12	
		16"o.c.	24"o.c.	16"o.c.	24"o.c.	16"o.c.	24"o.c.
Douglas Fir—Larch	2	13-1	11-3	16-9	14-5	20-4	17-6
	3	10-7	8-8	13-6	11-0	16-5	13-5
Douglas Fir—South	2	12-0	10-6	15-3	13-4	18-7	16-3
	3	10-3	8-4	13-1	10-8	15-11	13-0
Hemlock/Fir	2	12-3	10-0	15-8	12-10	19-1	15-7
	3	9-5	7-8	12-0	9-10	14-7	11-11
Mountain Hemlock	2	11-4	9-11	14-6	12-8	17-7	15-4
	3	9-7	7-10	12-3	10-0	14-11	12-2
Western Hemlock	2	12-3	10-6	15-8	13-4	19-1	16-3
	3	9-11	8-1	12-8	10-4	15-5	12-7
Engelmann Spruce/ Alpine Fir	2	11-2	9-1	14-3	11-7	17-3	14-2
	3	8-6	6-11	10-10	8-10	13-2	10-9
Lodgepole Pine	2	11-8	9-7	14-11	12-3	18-1	14-11
	3	9-1	7-5	11-7	9-5	14-1	11-6
Ponderosa Pine/ Sugar Pine	2	11-4	9-3	14-5	11-9	17-7	14-4
	3	8-8	7-1	11-1	9-1	13-6	11-0

Western Wood Products Association

Design Criteria:
Strength—10-psf dead load plus 40-psf live load
Deflection—Limited to span in inches divided by 360 for live load only

The "deflection of span in inches divided by 360" is another engineering standard, expressed by the equation: deflection = $l/360$, l being the length in inches of the span. The 360 figure is obviously not an arbitrary one. It is the figure that, when it divides the span length in inches, happens to result in the decimal equivalent of the required or desired deflection. If you use 180 or 240 (old codes used these numbers), you get more deflection. A 15-foot span with $l/180$ has a 1-inch deflection; a 15-foot span with $l/240$ has a ¾-inch deflection, and a 15-foot span with $l/360$ has a ½-inch deflection, which—it has been found empirically—is what people find comfortable.

Beams, Rafters & Collar Ties

Sizing Lumber

Lumber is rated for its ability to resist deflection as it spans between two bearing points, no matter where you might use it. To rate a piece of lumber, building-code bodies and lumber-grading associations have created span tables, which list the maximum allowable span for each board type, broken down by species, grade, and size. Most span tables assume a combined live and dead load of 50 pounds per square foot (psf). The 50 psf comprises 10-psf dead load and 40-psf live load. The spans listed in span tables allow a maximum deflection of $\frac{3}{8}$ inch (just perceivable) to $\frac{1}{2}$ inch (noticeable). To understand this cri-

terion better, imagine two walls a given distance apart. If you placed a board of approved size on edge between the walls and put a 50-psf load on it, the board could bend $\frac{3}{8}$ to $\frac{1}{2}$ inch under the weight. If you were to increase the load to, say, 70 psf, the board rated for 50 psf would bend more than the allowable $\frac{3}{8}$ to $\frac{1}{2}$ inch, and you would have to get a bigger board to support the greater weight.

Floor Joists. For floor joists, this rating system works well. To add a feeling of stability and solid construction, however, some designers oversize the floor joists to handle as much as 100 psf to give a firmer feeling. This doesn't necessarily mean using lumber twice as big as that used to handle 50 psf; it can mean simply spacing joists closer together. Spongy, bouncy floors

are disconcerting. By increasing joist size you may pay a little more, but you'll feel better walking on solid floors.

You can see from the span table that different lumber species have different strengths and, therefore, different allowable spans. Douglas fir (south) No. 2 grade 2×8s framed 24 inches on center have an allowable span of 10 feet 6 inches, whereas No. 3 grade of the same species can span only 8 feet 4 inches. The knots and defects in the lesser grade weaken the wood. If you follow this table or one like it, you'll have little deflection when you use the wood in properly designed buildings.

Rafters. Rating authorities size rafters similarly to joists, but there are differences. As with joists, you measure the rafter span (the distance from the ridgeboard to the outside

2

ENGINEERING BASICS

RAFTER SPAN RATINGS (Feet & Inches)

Species	Slope	2x6 16"o.c.	2x6 24"o.c.	2x8 16"o.c.	2x8 24"o.c.	2x10 16"o.c.	2x10 24"o.c.
Douglas Fir—Larch No. 2	3 in 12 or less	10-5	8-6	13-9	11-3	17-7	14-5
	Over 3 in 12	10-0	8-1	13-2	10-9	16-9	13-8
Douglas Fir—South No. 2	3 in 12 or less	10-1	8-3	13-4	10-11	17-0	13-10
	Over 3 in 12	9-7	7-10	12-8	10-4	16-2	13-3
Hemlock/Fir No. 2	3 in 12 or less	9-3	7-7	12-3	10-10	15-8	12-9
	Over 3 in 12	8-10	7-3	11-9	9-6	14-11	12-2
Mountain Hemlock No. 2	3 in 12 or less	9-6	7-9	12-7	10-3	16-0	13-1
	Over 3 in 12	9-1	7-5	12-0	9-9	15-3	12-6
Eastern Spruce No. 2	3 in 12 or less	8-5	6-11	11-2	9-1	14-3	11-7
	Over 3 in 12	8-0	6-7	10-7	8-8	13-7	11-1
Spruce/Pine/Fir No. 2	3 in 12 or less	8-8	7-1	11-6	9-4	14-8	11-11
	Over 3 in 12	8-3	6-9	10-11	8-11	13-11	11-5
Southern Pine No. 2	3 in 12 or less	10-3	8-5	13-7	11-1	17-4	14-2
	Over 3 in 12	9-10	8-0	12-11	10-7	16-6	13-6
Ponderosa Pine/ Sugar Pine No. 2	3 in 12 or less	8-6	7-0	11-4	9-2	14-5	11-9
	Over 3 in 12	8-1	6-8	10-9	8-9	13-9	11-3

Design Criteria:
Strength—10-psf dead load plus 40-psf live load
Deflection—Limited to span in inches divided by 240 for a slope of 3 in 12 or less and 180 for a slope of more than 3 in 12.

Sources: National Lumber Grades Authority, National Lumber Manufacturers Association, Southern Pine Inspection Bureau, West Coast Lumber Inspection Bureau, Western Wood Products Association.

wall plates measured horizontally), factor in the species and on-center framing, and determine what size lumber to buy by looking at a span table. Rafters sometimes have to sustain more loads than joists do, however, primarily because of wind and snow. To complicate matters further, the slope or pitch of the roof also factors into the allowable span. A steeply sloped roof, which sheds snow, will have a different load specification than a shallow or nearly flat roof, which retains it. So rafters have their own span tables, different from those for joists, which figure all this in.

You can see from the sample rafter table that 2x10 No. 2 Douglas fir (south) rafters framed 16 inches on center will have an allowable span of 17 feet with a slope of 3 in 12 or less and an allowable span of 16 feet 2 inches with a slope greater than 3 in 12. Slope is expressed as the number of inches the roof rises for every foot of its run, which is the width measured horizontally to the middle of the roof. So a 3-in-12 roof rises 3 inches for every 12 inches of run.

To determine the design rafter live load for your area in pounds per square foot (psf), check with the local building department. If the load is 40 psf or lower, you can use most standard span charts, which use 40 psf as the assumed load, when sizing rafters. (When sizing rafters make sure you have a rafter-sizing chart that accounts for slope.) If the load is greater than 40 psf (in regions of high snow, high wind, or active hurricanes), you may have to increase the size of your rafters, reduce the spans, frame the rafters closer together, or support the rafters mid-span with struts.

Collar Ties. Roofs have other components called collar ties that add to the stability of rafters. Collar ties installed in the upper two-thirds of rafters don't keep rafters from spreading under roof loads; that's the job of rafter ties, usually ceil-

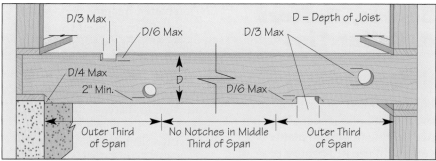

Drilling and Notching Framing Members. Notching or cutting holes in beams invariably weakens them. Don't cut holes within 2 in. of the edge of a joist or rafter, and limit them to no larger than one-third the depth of the joist. Limit notches to one-sixth the depth of the joist and no longer than one-third of the joist's depth.

ing joists or attic floor joists, to which you fasten the ends of the rafters. Collar ties stiffen the rafters and help resist wind loads. If your plans specify collar ties, you must include them. Don't leave them out, no matter how stable the rafters seem to feel.

Drilling and Notching Framing Members

When you run cables, heating ducts, or pipes, you often have to run them through joists or rafters, because running them below those members would make them poke through the ceiling below. There are ways to cut and notch joists and rafters safely, but you must stay within strict guidelines, using the board's actual—not nominal—dimensions:

■ Never cut a hole closer than 2 inches to the board's edge.

■ Never make the hole bigger than one-third the depth of the joist.

■ Never cut holes or notch the rafter or joist in the middle one-third of the board's length. That's where the wood is under the most stress from the load it bears.

■ Never cut a notch deeper than one-sixth the depth of the board, except at the ends, where the notch can be one-fourth the depth.

■ Never make your notches longer than one-third the depth of the board.

Sizing Studs, Beams, and Headers

Studs. Sizing studs is simple, because you generally have only two choices: 2×4s or 2×6s. Increasingly, structures are being framed with 2×6 studs—for a few reasons:

■ 2×6s make for a sturdier building.

■ A 2×6 wall allows more room for insulation.

■ 2×6 walls are easier to work with when running cables and pipes.

You can use 2×4s, which are about 30 percent cheaper, and have a sturdy, up-to-code wall. But you have to place 2×4s on 16-inch centers, whereas you can space 2×6s 24 inches apart, so you have to use more 2×4s and may not save that much money. It's rare to use studs that are larger than 2×6s for framing. You would do so only to add to the house's soundproofing or insulation, and in most cases other than these the benefit wouldn't be worth the added cost.

Beams. Also called girders, beams may be made from large dimensional wood, engineered lumber (LVLs or glue-laminated beams), or structural steel. Beams run horizontally—down the center of a basement, for example, to carry the floor joists above—to support the weight of some part of your structure. Most beams are built-up: made using three 2×10s or 2×12s nailed with 16d nails, 32 inches on center. Along its span, a beam may be supported

MAXIMUM SPANS FOR BEAMS (Feet & Inches)

Width of Structure (Feet)	Beam Size (Solid or Built-Up)	Bearing		Nonbearing
		One Story*	1½ or Two Stories	
Up to 26	4x6	—	—	5-6
	4x8	—	—	7-6
	6x8	7-0	6-0	9-0
	6x10	9-0	7-6	11-6
	6x12	10-6	9-0	12-0
26 to 32	4x6	—	—	—
	4x8	—	—	7-0
	6x8	6-6	5-6	8-6
	6x10	8-0	7-0	10-6
	6x12	10-0	8-0	11-6

*A dash means the beam would not be strong enough for this purpose.

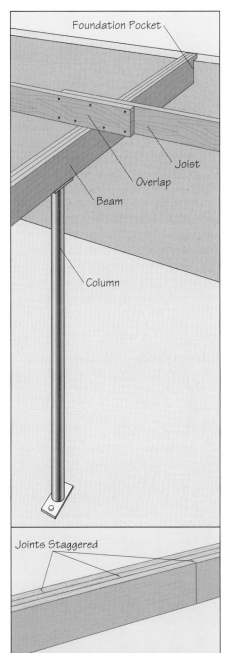

Beams. Beams are often used to support long joist spans. Beams in basement applications are set in a pocket in the foundation wall and supported by columns. When making "built-up" beams, be sure to stagger the joints of each component board.

by 4×4 wood posts or concrete-and-steel lally columns. The ends of beams typically sit in a pocket made in the foundation. (If you create a pocket for a beam, be sure to leave a ½-inch air space around the sides and beam ends for air flow.) These pockets are designed so that the top of the beam comes flush with the top of the wall's mudsill.

There are two kinds of beams: non-bearing and bearing. Nonbearing beams support the live and dead loads of the floor above it. Bearing beams support the live and dead loads of the floor above it and a wall framed directly above. A common application of a beam or girder (non-bearing or bearing) would be in a large basement. If your basement is 24 feet wide, there is no way you will span that entire distance with lumber. (A joist rated for a 24-feet span would be massive, weighty, and expensive. You'd have to go to steel.) But a wood joist can easily span a 12-foot distance. So, a commonly used design solution is to run a beam down the center of the basement, supported by columns or posts along its length. The ends of the beam would rest in pockets in the foundation wall. The floor joists (running perpendicularly) would run from the wall plates to the middle of the basement. There they would rest on the beam or sit in special joist hangers mounted on the sides of the beam.

It's easy to accidentally under-size or improperly support a beam. A typical built-up beam made of three 2×12s nailed together feels so beefy you'd think it could support any residential load. But you can see from the beam span table that a

beam made of three 2×12s (a 6×12) can span only 12 feet as a nonbearing beam in a 26-foot-wide building. If your basement will be 24 feet long and you want to run the beam the entire way, you will need a column at the halfway point to support it. Because columns are relatively inexpensive, compared with the possible damage beam deflection can cause, it's best to over-support the beam with an extra column or two. If you're building a basement that needs large open spaces without columns or one with only one column in the middle of the room, you may have to increase the size of the beam substantially or use an engineered lumber product or steel I-beam.

Headers. Headers are structural members made from two-by lumber that bridge an opening. Headers sit at right angles to joists, rafters, or studs, and support the weight from above the opening. In walls, headers assume the load that would otherwise fall on a door, window, or other wall opening. In floors and roofs, headers define the perimeters of rough openings like stairways or skylights, stiffen the joists or rafters, and assume the load of the missing joists or rafters that you cut out of the way or left out to create the opening.

You create the headers used in roofs and floors by simply doubling the lumber around the rough opening. If you're using 2×10 rafters or joists, for example, the headers will be double 2×10s properly nailed in place or in hangers at both ends of the opening, perpendicular to the rafters or joists and to the 2×10s that define the sides of the rough opening. Headers for doors and windows are different. If you're framing with 2×4s, you can't always use two 2×4s for a header if the walls will support heavy loads from above.

By checking the header table, you'll see that for load-bearing walls with an opening of 48 inches or less, a doubled 2×4 (or 4×4) is adequate if the wood species is Douglas fir (or stronger). Openings between 48 and 72 inches require a doubled 2×6 (or 4×6), and those between 72 and 96 inches call for a doubled 2×8 (or 4×8). When you make a header for a wall, you'll usually use blocking like ½-inch plywood between the two pieces of lumber. Besides the ability to carry a certain load over an opening, a doubled header (sandwiching ½-inch plywood) makes the most sense be-

cause the header will be the same thickness as a 2×4 wall, and sheet goods like drywall (inside) or plywood (outside sheathing) will come flush against the header on both sides of the wall. The ability of a single 2×8 to carry the load over a 48-inch opening does not argue for using a single 2×8 in that location. Always use doubled 2-by stock and try to make headers in walls exactly as thick as the wall in which you'll install them. If the wall is framed with 2×6s, for example, then use blocking other than plywood to make the header 5½ inches thick. Making the faces of the header flush with the outside edges of the studs

not only makes good structural sense but presents a good nailing surface for wall-finishing materials like drywall.

For nonload-bearing walls, the header does not carry loads from above. The header serves only two simple purposes: it acts as a spacer to determine the rough opening for the window or door, and it provides a nailing surface for the top of the door or window jamb. A double 2×4 is adequate in nonload-bearing wall situations for door and window openings of up to 72 inches. For larger openings in nonload-bearing walls, you'll want to increase the size of the header to a

SPAN TABLE FOR HEADERS

Lumber Size	Species	Minimum Grade	Maximum Span
4x4	Douglas fir	No. 2	48 in
4x6	Douglas fir	No. 2	72 in.
4x8	Douglas fir	No. 2	96 in.
4x10	Douglas fir	No. 2	10 ft.
4x12	Douglas fir	No. 2	12 ft.
4x14	Douglas fir	No. 1	16 ft.

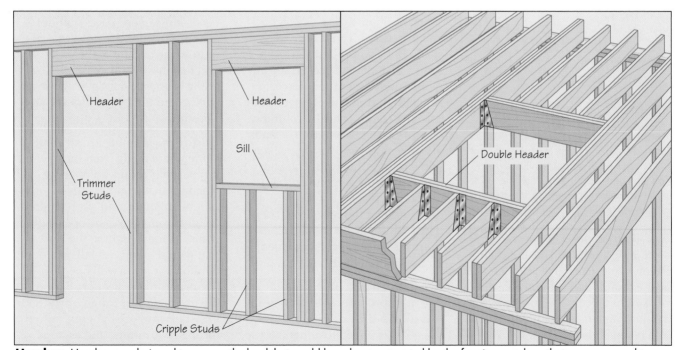

Headers. Headers are designed to assume the load that would have been supported by the framing members that were removed to create the open space. The distance between a header and the top plate may be taken up by cripple, or partial, studs (left). Headers aren't just used to carry vertical loads in walls, they are essential for stabilizing joists or rafters in rough openings in floors and roofs (right).

2×6, simply because 2×4s tend to sag or bow over longer distances. As with load-bearing walls, you should make headers in nonload-bearing walls to the thickness of the wall in which you'll install them.

Cantilevers. Because a piece of lumber has a maximum allowable span when it bridges two points of contact, you can imagine that it also has a maximum span—invariably less—when it has only one point of contact, as when it is cantilevered, or hanging out into space like a joist in an unsupported porch. Diving boards are cantilevered, and though they're specifically engineered to provide bounce, you'd be surprised how much bounce you can get out of standard dimension lumber. That's why cantilevering is subject to strict design rules.

Cantilevered beams are subject to shear and deflection, and you must account for both of these loads in your sizing. Take a deck, for example, framed with 2×8s 16 inches on center that cantilevers 8 feet. A 50-psf load will deflect the outer edge of this deck—the farthest point from the house—1 inch. A 1-inch deflection is quite noticeable. Increase the size of the joists to 2×12s, and the deflection goes down to ¼ inch—an acceptable amount. If you're going to pack the deck with friends and family

to watch sunsets or to barbecue, however, you'll have to increase the size of the joists or decrease the spacing between them to 12 inches on center, because you'll be increasing the maximum design load beyond 50 psf. Have an engineer look at your design if you plan on large loads for a cantilevered deck.

The shear point is the top edge of the joists where they meet the house. If joists are undersized, they could easily fail if you loaded the deck beyond the limit for which you sized them. Joists can fail in a number of ways, including breaking off at the shear point, though they are most likely to split. That's why you must size joists for the maximum design load, the maximum weight that you, snow, or wind will ever put on the cantilevered deck over its entire lifetime.

Here are some design rules for cantilevers:

■ Check span tables for allowable cantilever joist spans.

■ Make sure you extend the deck joists back into the structure as part of the floor system.

■ Be sure that the section of the unsupported joist is no more than one-quarter the joist's entire length. If you have a 4-foot cantilever, for example, you must have a 16-foot joist with 12 feet extending back

into the structure, nailed off as part of the flooring system.

■ Always nail a board across the joist ends to act as a header board, tying the joists together and adding stability to the deck.

Building Plans

When framing buildings of nearly any size, you need a set of plans, or blueprints, from which to work. If you walked onto any construction site, you'd likely see blueprints rolled up near the general contractor's workstation or spread out on a drafting table. Blueprints represent the guide for building the structure. The blueprints must be readily available because carpenters and subcontractors regularly refer to plans to direct them through their tasks.

Blueprints obviously can't be drawn full-size, so they're drawn to scale. Typically, a ¼-inch space or line on a blueprint represents a 1-foot space or length in the structure. Though the ¼-inch scale is popular, there are other scales in common use. You may find blueprints that use a ³⁄₃₂-inch or ½-inch scale, meaning that ³⁄₃₂- or ½-inch lines on the blueprints represent 1 foot of actual dimension.

If designers and architects were to put all the features of a building on one sheet of the blueprint, it would be difficult to read and too complicated to follow. So at the design stage, the engineer or architect breaks the building down into different plans. Each plan shows how to build different features of the house. Depending on how complicated a building is, you sometimes get as many as ten plans, covering areas of detail such as specifications, plot plans, foundation plans, exterior elevations, section views, framing plans, window and door details, finish schedule, and the like.

If you were building an architect-designed three-story house from

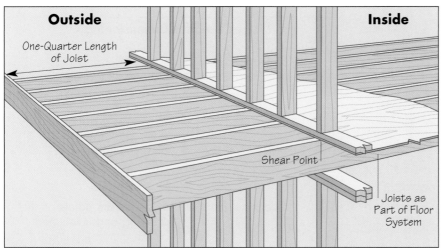

Cantilevers. Always "header-off" the ends of joists in cantilevers. A header ties the joists together and adds stability to the structure.

scratch, for example, the architect would present you with a set of plans that contains a page (or pages) for each of these different features of the building. If you were simply adding an addition or building a garage, however, you'd likely work from foundation and framing plans that include your window and door placements. Exterior elevations would reveal the way the building looks from the outside, and perhaps you would have another page that shows where to put the wires and the plumbing. All of this information would be combined onto two or three pages of a blueprint.

Reading Blueprints

Blueprints look confusing at first glance, but if you know the basics of how to read them, they become clear. First learn how to read the "lines," because it is with various types of lines that a blueprint represents a structure's component parts. Then turn your attention to the symbols and abbreviations commonly used so you can have a complete understanding of what is being represented. (See Lines Used for Drawings, below.)

Lines. A solid line on a blueprint indicates an object's visible outline. You would see a solid line along both edges of a concrete wall where it meets the floor, for instance, because those edges would be visible when the wall sits in place. A broken line indicates an object that's hidden from view.

Aspects of a building, such as a window, door, or concrete footing, often have to be located precisely along a wall or in a floor. This positioning is done with a centerline, which establishes the center point of an area or rough opening.

A section line indicates where an aspect of the building needs to be "cut," or shown in cross section, so that something inside the build-

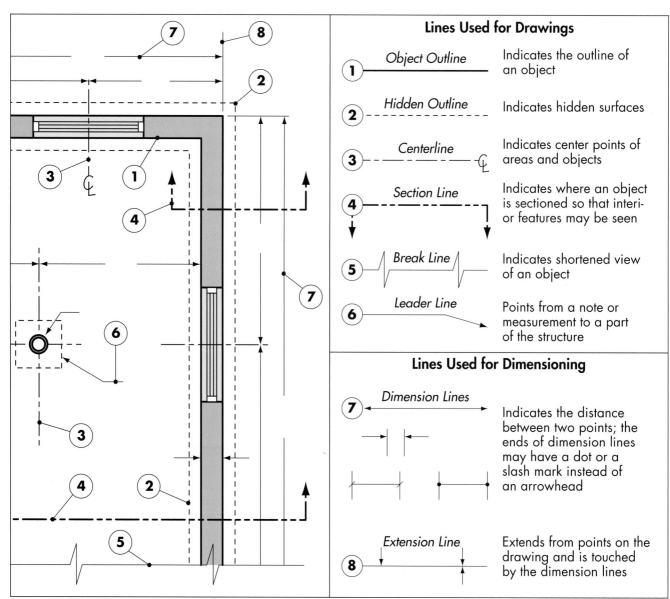

Lines Used for Drawings

1 — **Object Outline** — Indicates the outline of an object

2 — **Hidden Outline** — Indicates hidden surfaces

3 — **Centerline** — Indicates center points of areas and objects

4 — **Section Line** — Indicates where an object is sectioned so that interior features may be seen

5 — **Break Line** — Indicates shortened view of an object

6 — **Leader Line** — Points from a note or measurement to a part of the structure

Lines Used for Dimensioning

7 — **Dimension Lines** — Indicates the distance between two points; the ends of dimension lines may have a dot or a slash mark instead of an arrowhead

8 — **Extension Line** — Extends from points on the drawing and is touched by the dimension lines

Lines. In a blueprint various lines may indicate any number of things, including the outline, the center, or the dimension of an object.

ing can be seen. A break line indicates a shortened view of an aspect of the building that has a uniform predictable shape.

Blueprints also give dimensions, or distances between various points of a building, and lines play a role here, too. If the distance between walls is 10 feet, the dimension 10' 0" interrupts a solid line with arrows pointing outward on both ends. Sometimes a dimension line has dots or slanted lines instead of arrows at its ends. An extension line establishes a reference from which dimension lines are drawn.

Utility Symbols. To maintain consistency in the construction industry and to avoid confusion, blueprint floor plans use standard symbols to show the positions of various aspects of a building. Symbols represent heating and plumbing components, as well as electrical devices like outlets, switches, and power panels.

Wall Symbols. Blueprints also use symbols to indicate wall types. When a structure is drawn on a blueprint, the walls are represented as a line. But that line can be a brick wall, a wood wall, or even stucco over a wood frame, so a set of sym-

Order Plans to Build Your Own Home

To view a variety of house designs and to order blueprints to build the houses, turn to page 216.

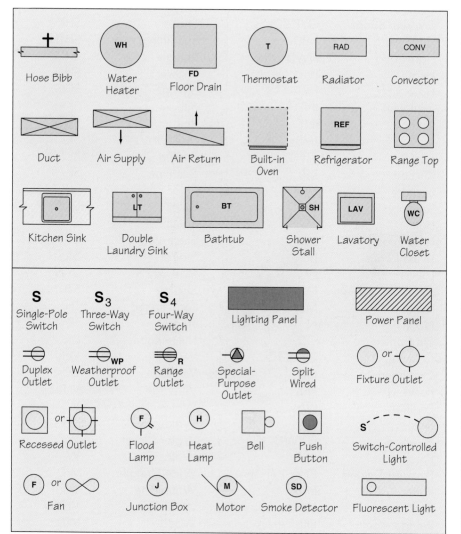

Utility Symbols. Blueprints use symbols to represent nonstructural components in a building. A few common symbols are shown here.

Wall Symbols. Symbols in floor plans represent various kinds of wall constructions.

ENGINEERING BASICS

2

bols appears on blueprints to indicate what kind of wall to build.

Abbreviations. Because the space allotted on blueprints is small, architects use abbreviations to identify various aspects of the building, such as a soffit, dormer, or door. The abbreviations are standardized. Anytime you see PT on a blueprint, for example, it means that pressure-treated wood is called for; anytime you see GL, glass is called for.

Floor Plans and Elevations

A floor plan is an overview of the floor, or story, of a building, including all the dimensions, from directly overhead. With a floor plan, you can see all the rooms in relation to one another. A floor plan is initially confusing to look at, but once you master the many lines, abbreviations, and symbols it contains, it's really quite easy to read. An elevation is a two-dimensional view of the side of a building. Every building has at least four elevations, one each for north, south, east, and west.

COMMON BLUEPRINT ABBREVIATIONS

Aluminum	ALUM	Floor	FL	Retaining Wall	RW
Anchor bolt	AB	Footing	FTG	Ridge	RDG
Bathroom	BATH	Foundation	FDN	Riser	R
Bathtub	BT	Furnace	FURN	Roof	RF
Basement	BSMT	Gauge	GA	Roofing	RFG
Beam	BM	Girder	GDR	Room	RM
Bedroom	BR	Glass	GL	Rough Opening	RO
Block	BLK	Grade	GR	Screen	SC
Brick	BRK	Ground	GRND	Sewer	SEW
Board	BD	Gypsum Board	GYP BD	Shake	SHK
Building	BLDG	Hardboard	HBD	Sheathing	SHTH
Building Line	BL	Hardwood	HWD	Shingle	SHGL
Cabinet	CAB	Heat	H	Shower	SH
Casement	CSMT	Hose Bibb	HB	Siding	SDG
Cedar	CDR	Insulation	INSUL.	Sill	SL
Ceiling	CLG	Interior	INT	Sink	SK
Center	CTR	Jamb	JMB	Skylight	SKL
Center Line	CL	Joist	JST	Sliding Door	SL DR
Chimney	CHIM	Kitchen	KIT	Soil Pipe	SP
Closet	CLOS	Laundry	LAU	Solar Panel	SLR PAN
Column	COL	Lavatory	LAV	Soffit	SOF
Concrete	CONC	Light	LT	South	S
Cornice	COR	Linen Closet	LC	Stack Vent	SV
Detail	DET	Living Room	LR	Stairs	ST
Diameter	DIAM	Louver	LV	Stairway	STWY
Dining Room	DR	Medicine Cabinet	MC	Steel	STL
Dishwasher	DW	Metal	MET	Top Hinged	TH
Door	DR	North	N	Tread	TR
Dormer	DRM	On Center	OC	Utility Room	UR
Double Hung	DH	Opening	OPNG	Ventilation	VENT
Douglas Fir	DF	Overhang	OH	Vent Stack	VS
Downspout	DS	Panel	PNL	Vinyl Tile	V TILE
Drain	DR	Partition	PTN	Water	W
Drywall	DW	Plate	PL	Waterproof	WP
East	E	Plywood	PLYWOOD	Water Closet	WC
Electric	ELEC	Porch	P	West	W
Elevation	EL	Pressure Treated	PT or P/T	Wide Flange	WF
Exterior	EXT	Rafter	RFTR	White Pine	WP
Finish	FIN	Redwood	RWD	Window	WDW
Fireplace	FPL	Refrigerator	REF	Wood	WD
Fixture	FIX	Reinforced	REIN	Yellow Pine	YP

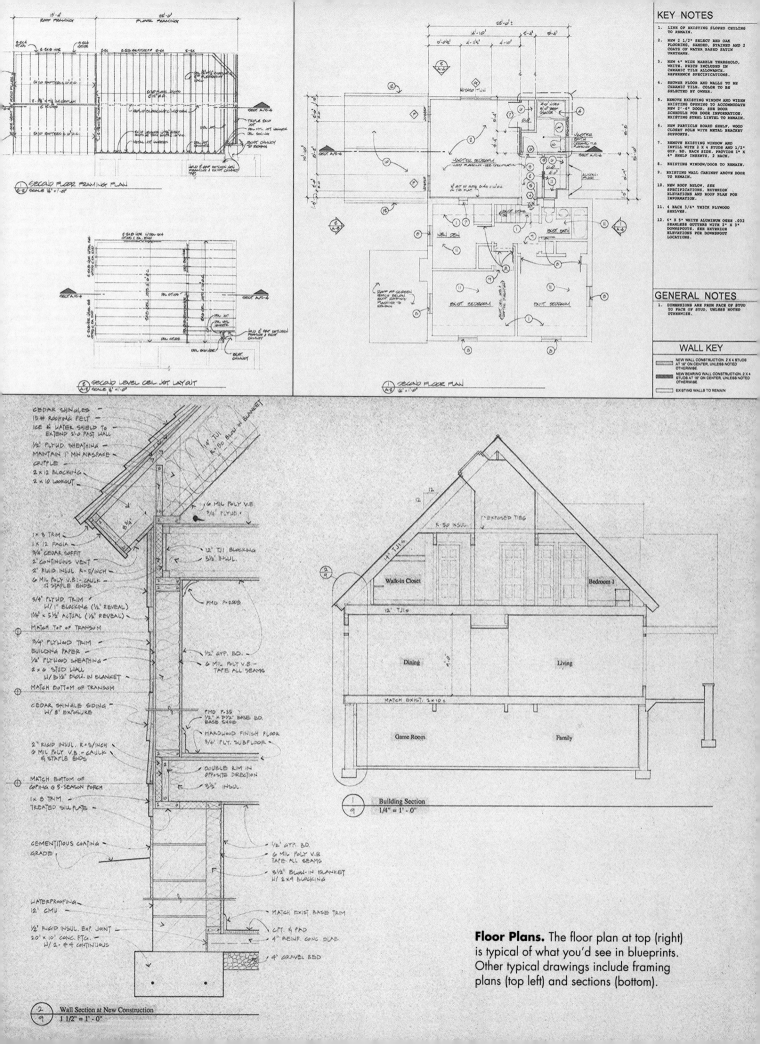

Floor Plans. The floor plan at top (right) is typical of what you'd see in blueprints. Other typical drawings include framing plans (top left) and sections (bottom).

Window and Door Sections

Most blueprints show window and door sections. The sections are detailed drawings of how to assemble window and door frames. Once you have the rough opening framed in for the window or door, you'll start to assemble the jambs, using these window and door sections as your guides. The sections show the position of such building components as the casing, the head jamb, the side jambs, and trim. They also show how wall finishes like siding or drywall butt against the window or door.

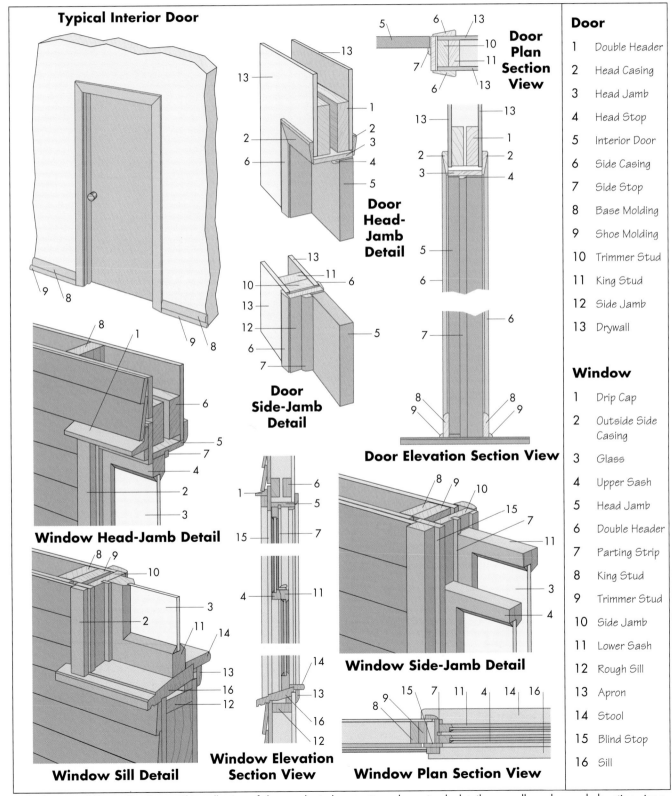

Door	
1	Double Header
2	Head Casing
3	Head Jamb
4	Head Stop
5	Interior Door
6	Side Casing
7	Side Stop
8	Base Molding
9	Shoe Molding
10	Trimmer Stud
11	King Stud
12	Side Jamb
13	Drywall

Window	
1	Drip Cap
2	Outside Side Casing
3	Glass
4	Upper Sash
5	Head Jamb
6	Double Header
7	Parting Strip
8	King Stud
9	Trimmer Stud
10	Side Jamb
11	Lower Sash
12	Rough Sill
13	Apron
14	Stool
15	Blind Stop
16	Sill

Typical Interior Door

Door Head-Jamb Detail

Door Side-Jamb Detail

Door Plan Section View

Door Elevation Section View

Window Head-Jamb Detail

Window Sill Detail

Window Elevation Section View

Window Side-Jamb Detail

Window Plan Section View

Window and Door Sections. This collection of door and window sections shows jamb details, as well as plan and elevation views.

3

Framing Tools

Most construction work requires the use of accurate laying out, marking, and cutting tools. Framing is no exception to that rule, whether you are building an entire house, a small outbuilding, or adding an addition to your home. When a ¼-inch error can lead to unsatisfactory results, it's a good idea to invest in quality tools that, used properly, will help provide accurate results. The past 15 years have seen an explosion of tools for builders, from laser-guided power miter boxes to computer-driven drills and high-tech moisture meters. Sure, some of them can make your job easier and more enjoyable, but they are expensive. However, there is a core group of standard—and inexpensive—hand and power tools that allows you to do a good job of framing if you practice diligence and pay attention to safety.

Measuring Tools

Framing houses takes precise cutting of lumber, with tolerances of at most $\frac{1}{8}$ inch. Before you can even cut boards, however, you've got to have the right tools to measure and mark them.

Measuring Tape. The most handy tool you'll use is a measuring tape. A locking 25-foot tape is well suited for framing. Heavy-duty 25-footers have ¾-inch-wide blades that stay rigid up to about 7 feet—handy when measuring something overhead or out of reach. Be sure that the tape you

buy has marks designating 16- and 24-inch on-center framing. These markings come in handy when you're laying out walls.

When you're using a measuring tape, don't rewind it too fast and let the end clip slam into the housing because this can loosen the clip's rivets and make the tape less accurate.

SAFETY EQUIPMENT

Common sense should tell you not to do construction work without first having some basic safety equipment, such as eye and ear protection.

Wear goggles or safety glasses that have aerated side guards whenever you work with power tools. Make sure your eye protection conforms to American National Standards Institute (ANSI) Z87.1 or Canadian Standards Association (CSA) requirements. Products that do will be marked with a stamp. Considering the cost of a visit to the emergency room, it doesn't hurt to buy an extra pair for the times when a neighbor volunteers to lend a hand or when you misplace the first pair.

The U.S. Occupational Safety and Health Administration (OSHA) recommends that hearing protection be worn when the noise level

exceeds 85 decibels (dB) for an 8-hour workday. When you consider that a circular saw emits 110 dB, however, even shorter exposure times can contribute to hearing impairment. Both insert and muff-type protectors are available; whichever you choose, be sure it has a noise reduction rating (NRR) of a least 20 dB.

Your construction work will create an enormous amount of sawdust. If you're sensitive to dust, it's a good idea to wear a dust mask. Two kinds of respiratory protection are available: disposable dust masks and cartridge-type respirators. A dust mask will allow you to avoid inhaling dust and fine particles. Respirators have a replaceable filter. Both are available for protection against nontoxic and toxic dusts and mists. Whichever you buy, look for a stamp indicating that the National

Institute for Occupational Safety and Health/Mine Safety and Health Administration (NIOSH/MSHA) has approved it for your specific operation. When you can taste or smell the contaminate or when the mask starts to interfere with normal breathing, it's time for a replacement.

Work gloves are also advisable to avoid injury to the hands, at least when you're moving wood or doing other jobs that don't require great tactile sense. Getting splinters is not a good way to start a workday. Similarly, heavy-duty work boots will protect your feet. Steel toes will prevent injuries to your toes from dropped boards or tools, and flexible steel soles will protect your feet from a puncture by a rogue nail. Lastly, wear a hard hat, especially when you're working in the basement or work has started on the second floor and others may be working above you.

Goggles

Safety Glasses

Foam Ear Plugs

Dust Mask

Work Gloves

Muff-Type Ear Protectors

Hard Hat

Always ease the tape into the housing: stop it with your finger near the end, and lightly push it in the last inch.

Wood Rule. Some carpenters prefer a folding wood rule, which is a stack of ruler sections, each hinged on one end. You extend the folding wood rule by unfolding each section. The best kind of folding wood rule has a thin metal ruler embedded in the first section. This little ruler slides out, and it is an excellent tool for obtaining exact short measurements. Folding wood rules are not as convenient to use for long distances as a tape measure, but for shorter distances they can come in handy. Some carpenters still prefer them.

Long Tape. These steel or fabric measuring tapes come in lengths of 50 and 100 feet and are especially handy for measuring the length of foundations to size up sill plates. The best tapes are the heavy-duty steel types used by loggers, which have ½-inch blades

and—sometimes—self-retracting features. Less-expensive steel and fabric tapes have ¼-inch blades and manual rewind.

Levels

Spirit Level. Because framing often has to be level (perfectly horizontal) and plumb (perfectly vertical), you'll need a spirit level to check your work. Bubbles in slightly bent fluid-filled vials indicate when your work is level or plumb. A 4-foot spirit level will do fine, but you may want a 6- or 8-footer for better accuracy when checking

walls for plumb. You can always place your 4-footer on a long 2×4 to extend it, but make sure the 2×4 is arrow-straight.

One way to test your level is to set it on top of a surface that reads perfectly level. Now flip the level over. The bubble should still be in the center. If it has moved, your level is off.

Digital Level. You can also buy an electronic level that beeps when it is perfectly level or plumb. The tool never goes out of whack because you can reset it electronically. Electronic levels also work as inclinometers to give you the angle of

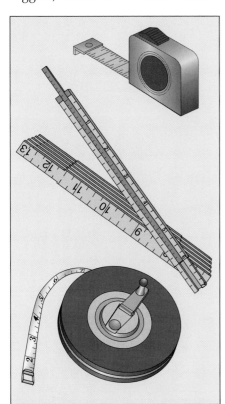

Measuring Tools. A heavy-duty measuring tape, wood rule, and long tape are handy tools on most framing jobs.

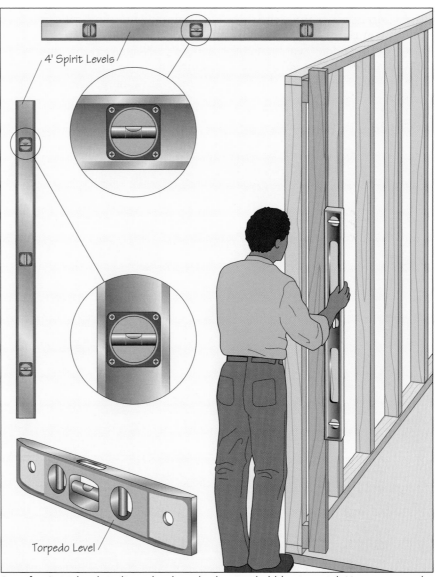

Levels. Spirit levels indicate level or plumb using bubbles in a vial. You can extend your level by holding it against a long, straight board. An 8- or 9-in. torpedo level is handy for double checking boards, floors, or pipes.

rafters and purlins. That feature can be handy when you have to match roof pitches in separate, distant locations.

Water Level. Another handy tool is a water level, which is nothing more than water in a long clear hose, with gradation marks on both ends. Because water seeks its own level, no matter what the distance or terrain, you can use the tool for all kinds of long-distance level checks. Just stretch the hose from one place to another and make sure the water line sits at the same gradation mark on both ends.

Torpedo Level. You'll never be sorry for carrying a small "torpedo level." This handy tool, about 8 inches long, is great for double checking level when you don't want to haul out your 4-footer. You can easily keep it in your nail pouch.

Squares

Framing has to be square, as well as level and plumb. You'll need at least two squares: a speed square and a framing square. Two other varieties of this tool also come in handy.

Speed Square. A speed square is a heavy-duty aluminum square in the form of a right triangle. A speed square is great for guiding your saw and marking lumber, and it's etched with common framing figures to use as a reference. You won't find a handier tool.

Framing Square. A large L-shaped square made of steel or aluminum, a framing, or rafter, square is indispensable when cutting rafters, marking long square lines, and making sure corners are square. Like the

speed square, the framing square has figures etched into it. Often, the figures are extensive rafter tables. (See "Rafter Tables on a Framing Square," page 147.)

Combination Square. You may also want to pick up a combination square, really a ruler that has a sliding bracket mounted to it at 90 degrees. The bracket has a second surface, which you can use to make 45-degree cut lines on lumber. Some squares have a pointed metal scribe to mark work for cutting. This tool is handy, but the speed square will serve most of your needs.

Sliding T-Bevel. Lastly, you may need a sliding T-bevel, also called a bevel gauge, for some complicated framing problems. You can set a sliding T-bevel at any angle and use it to transfer the same angle from one place to another.

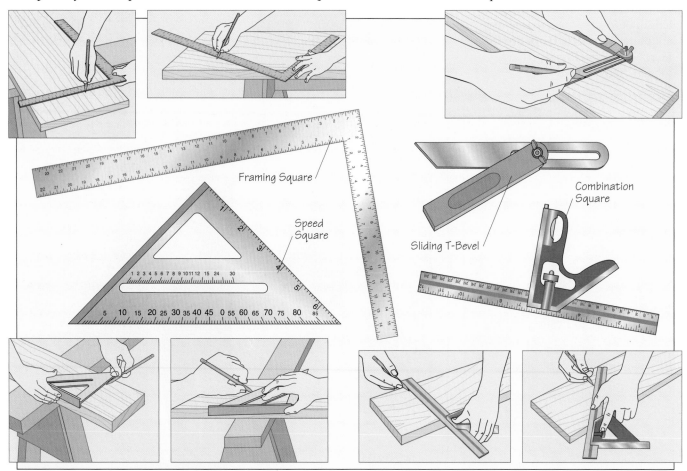

Framing Square

Speed Square

Sliding T-Bevel

Combination Square

Squares. A speed square is invaluable for marking 90- and 45-degree cut lines. It also works well as a saw guide for making cuts with a circular saw. A framing square is essential for "stepping off" rafters to determine rafter length, marking 90-degree cut lines in larger lumber, and checking whether corners are square. A combination square is good for marking 90- and 45-degree angles and for drawing consistently spaced lines from the board edge. A sliding T-bevel can be set to any angle and is ideal for transferring odd angles.

Marking Tools

Once you've measured your boards, you'll want to mark them. You'll surely need a chalk line. This is nothing more than a long piece of twine covered in chalk that you reel in and out of a chalk box. The twine has a hook or clip at one end, so it can be hooked over the ends or edges of boards or plywood. When you pull the line taut and snap it, the chalk leaves a mark. It's an indispensable tool, and can be loaded with either blue or red chalk. Other marking tools you'll need along the way include a few thick, flat carpenter's pencils (sometimes available free at lumberyard checkout counters), carpenter's crayons, and an indelible marker.

Hand Tools

Framing Hammer. At the top of anyone's list of framing hand tools should be the framing hammer. Use a 20- to 24-ounce waffle-headed, or serrated, straight-claw hammer. As for a handle, wooden (hickory) handles tend to absorb vibration better than fiberglass handles, so some people think wooden handles lessen your chances of developing repetitive motion ailments like carpal tunnel syndrome. If you get a heavy (24-ounce) hammer and your shoulder aches even after taking aspirin the first day you use it, go down in weight to the 20-ounce size.

Other Tools. You should always carry a utility knife and extra blades. Replace the blades as soon as they are dull, because working with dull blades—or any dull tools—is dangerous. With a dull tool you have to

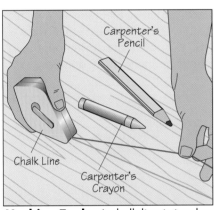

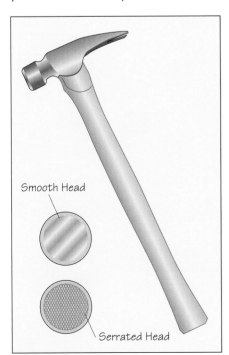

Marking Tools. A chalk line is invaluable for "snapping" cut lines on long pieces of lumber and panel material.

Framing Hammer. A hickory-handled hammer is an essential framing tool. You can buy one with a smooth or a serrated head.

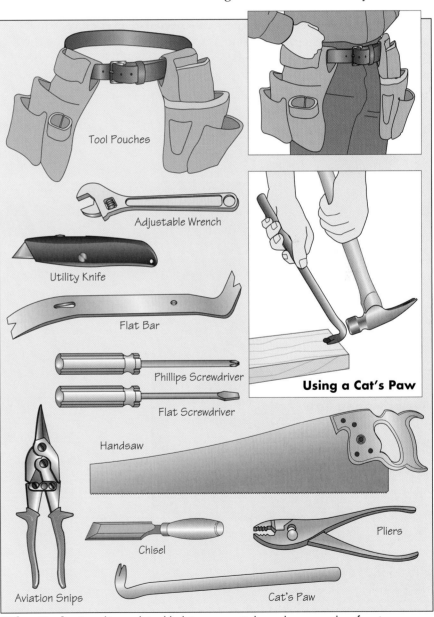

Using a Cat's Paw

Other Tools. A multi-pouch tool belt is as essential as a hammer when framing any structure. Get one that will carry your nails, tools, and measuring tape. Some framers carry an assortment of tools. You'll find that some may be more important than others.

exert more force, which can lead to uncontrolled slippage.

You'll also need a tool belt, or nail pouch, for carrying your tools. You'll find that a good-quality multipouch leather or nylon belt with an extra holster for your measuring tape is handy. Tool belts usually come with optional suspenders. Get them, because they take some of the weight off your hips. And get a padded belt if you can afford it. You won't be sorry.

Although you'll do most of your cutting with power saws, nothing will completely replace a good handsaw for certain types of cuts. A handsaw is just the thing whenever you have just a few cuts to do, spots a circular saw can't reach, or a circular saw

cut to finish off. A 15-inch saw with 10 to 12 teeth per inch (tpi) will cut well and still fit into your toolbox, even if it's small.

Other tools? It never hurts to carry along screwdrivers (flat-bladed and Phillips) for adjusting and fixing tools. Some framers won't get out of their trucks without a tool belt containing a cat's paw for removing nails, a small flat bar for muscling wood into position, a sharp chisel, pliers, aviation snips for cutting banded material, and an adjustable wrench. This stuff is weighty, however, and you may not need it all every day. You'll soon sort out what tools you should carry, and you'll leave the other tools within reach.

Power Tools

Saws

Though framing doesn't demand the precise cuts that finish carpentry does, you still need a variety of high-quality saws with sharp blades. As with all power tools, make sure the saws are double insulated or properly grounded.

Circular Saw. The tool you'll use most is a circular saw, which is capable of crosscutting, ripping, and beveling boards or sheets of plywood quickly. The most popular saws are those that take a 7¼-inch blade. This blade size will enable you to cut to a maximum depth of about 2½ inches at 90 degrees.

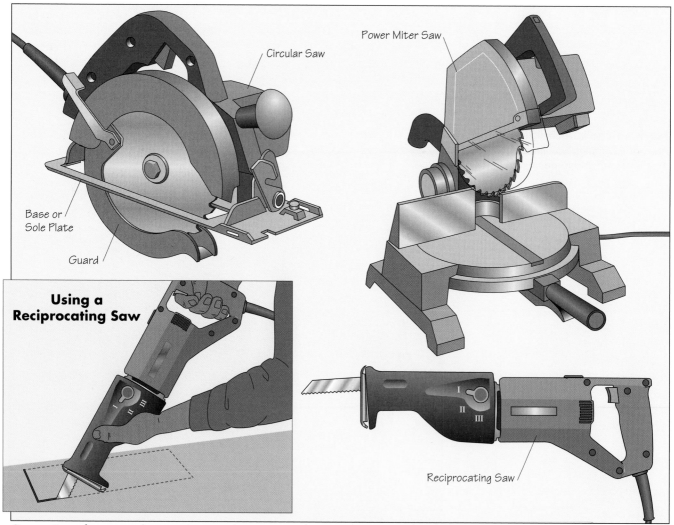

Saws. Every framer needs a circular saw. A power miter box, or chop saw, is handy for making square or angle cuts in framing lumber. A reciprocating saw is an ideal tool for cutting in those hard-to-get-at places, for cutting sheathing, and—when fitted with a metal blade—for cutting misplaced bolts or nails.

There are many options that distinguish one saw from another, the most important of which is a saw's power. Don't judge a saw's performance by its horsepower rating but by the amount of amperage that the motor draws. Low-cost saws may have only 9- or 10-amp motors with drive shafts and arbors running on rollers or sleeve bearings. A contractor-grade saw is rated at 12 or 13 amps and is made with ball bearings.

A plastic housing is no longer the mark of an inferior tool; however, a flimsy base plate made of stamped metal is. A thin stamped-steel base won't stay as flat as a thicker extruded or cast base.

For safety's sake, to minimize any chance of electric shock, be sure that your saw is double insulated. Some saws have an additional safety switch that you must press before the trigger will work. Another safety feature to look for on a saw is an arbor lock. The lock secures the arbor nut and prevents the blade from turning while you're changing blades.

There are a number of blades available, designed for cutting everything from plywood and paneling to rough lumber. For framing, use a 24-tooth carbide-tipped combination blade designed for general-purpose cutting.

Power Miter Saw. For angle cuts, you'll want to use a power miter saw, or chop saw. These tools are simply circular saws mounted on a pivot assembly, which enables you to make precise straight and angled crosscuts in boards. You can get chop saws that handle either 10- or 12-inch blades. Get the 12-inch saw, if you can afford it. These saws are expensive but well worth the cost. Use a 60-tooth combination-cut carbide blade.

Reciprocating Saw. Another handy tool to have is a reciprocating saw. It comes in handy for cutting the last ½ inch of a board that

your circular saw can't get to, for cutting rough openings in sheathing, or for cutting misplaced anchor bolts out of the way. Get plenty of wood- and metal-cutting blades, but don't confuse the two. Wood blades are more serrated than the smoother, small-toothed metal-cutting blades.

Using Saws Safely

Set up a safe sawing station by cutting an 8-foot sheet of ¾-inch plywood in half lengthwise and screwing it to sturdy sawhorses on level ground. Power should be easy to get to so cords can swing freely around the work. When you cut off a short piece of wood, it should drop freely off the end of your cutting table. When you cut large pieces, you must have someone support the wood that's hanging in midair; otherwise it will droop and bind your cut, increas-

ing the risk of kickback, one of the biggest risks when cutting. Kickback happens when a blade binds in the cut or the teeth try to take too much of a bite, and the saw kicks back at you. It happens dramatically and instantaneously, and it is quite dangerous. You can buy anti-kickback blades, which have modified tooth designs, but you can best reduce kickback by not rushing a cut and by stabilizing your work.

When you're cutting wood where you'll install it—on a second-floor deck or on a roof, for example—support the wood, preferably on sawhorses, and concentrate on each cut. Don't do anything daring or off balance. You want to go home each day with a full finger and limb count. Always keep your hands as far as possible from the cut, and clearly sight your cut line to make sure it's free of obstructions such as nails, extension cords, and the like.

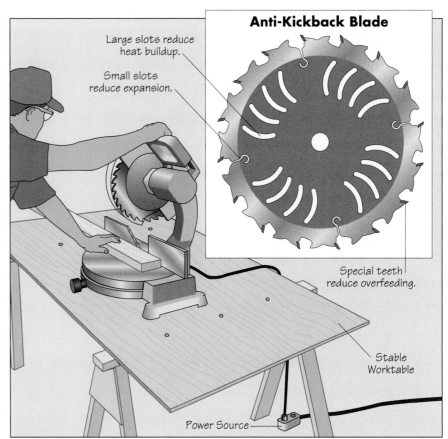

Large slots reduce heat buildup.

Small slots reduce expansion.

Anti-Kickback Blade

Special teeth reduce overfeeding.

Stable Worktable

Power Source

Using Saws Safely. A good saw station has a stable base, a wide, clean working area, and a ready, convenient source of power. Anti-kickback blades, for use with hand-held circular saws, have specially designed teeth to reduce overfeeding. By patiently letting the blade do the work when sawing, you'll reduce the risk of kickback.

Firmly place any wood you cut on a cutting surface, whether it's your sawing station table or a piece of the structure that's already firmly assembled (like a floor or wall opening). Never cut hand-held wood.

When possible, use a square to guide your cuts. A speed square is an excellent guide because it gives you a hands-free square line against which to run your saw's sole plate. You can also easily make cutting guides for panel material from a true piece of pine, some hardboard, and a couple of clamps. (See "Plywood-Cutting Guide," page 66.)

Pneumatic Nailers

Pneumatic, or air-driven, nail guns, which use magazines that can hold up to 100 or more nails, can take much of the tedium out of repetitive nailing. But you pay a price: nail guns are expensive, not only to buy but also to run. They are heavy, and you need compressors and hoses to operate them. Nail guns really don't pay for themselves—purchased or rented—unless you have a great amount of nailing to do all at one time. Stick with your hammers if you have the slightest doubt because pneumatics are not only

expensive, they can also be dangerous, especially when accidentally run at air pressures above or below that recommended for the tool (75 to 100 psi). A few years ago a building magazine ran a picture of an X-ray of a nail that was shot into a worker's skull by a pneumatic nailer. (The injured man survived.) Here's how it happened: a worker was climbing a ladder and bumped into the business end of a pneumatic nailer held by a worker who was descending the ladder. A simple mistake can have deadly consequences.

If you use pneumatics, you'll have a wide range of gun types from which to choose. Most framing guns handle 6d through 16d nails. You'll also find power staplers, which shoot heavy-duty staples for securing sheathing, shingles, and building paper, and finish nailers, which shoot finishing nails for fastening trim. You'll need a compressor, either gas-driven or electric, and 100 feet of air hose. If you have a choice, go with the quieter electric compressor. No matter what kind you use, though, be sure the proper guards protect the belt that drives the compressor. Also, make sure you set the in-line regulator to the pressure required for your tool.

Drills

You'll surely need a drill for framing. For starters, the tool is essential for drilling out holes in the sill plates so that they slip over the bolts in the top of the foundation wall or slab. You'll also need a drill to bore pass-throughs for utilities like water pipes and electrical wiring. If cost is an issue, buy a plug-in heavy-duty ½-inch drill with variable speeds. If you can afford the extra cost, you'll find a cordless drill even handier. Cordless drills come in an array of voltage ratings; the higher the voltage, the more powerful the drill. A 12-volt drill is powerful and will fill all your needs, but you can step up to more-powerful 14.4- or 18-volt drills if needed.

Cordless drills run on rechargeable batteries. Many products now have a quick-charge feature that charges batteries in less than 30 minutes. No matter how long it takes to charge the batteries, however, you'll want two of them: one to use and one to charge. So bite the bullet and buy that extra battery when you buy your drill.

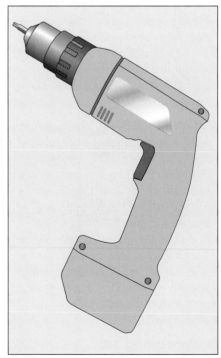

Pneumatic Nailers. A pneumatic nailer setup consists of an air compressor that drives a nailer or stapler by feeding high-pressure air through the hose, filter, regulator, and in-line lubricator. Pneumatic nailers are good for simple repetitive nailing, not intricate work.

Drills. A 12-volt cordless reversible drill with various speeds will come in handy for drilling holes and driving screws.

Ladders, Scaffolds & Safety Systems

Many of the accidents that occur on a construction site, even among professional builders, are the result of falling. This is not because construction workers are careless, it's because so much of the work of building and framing takes place 6, 10, 30, even 40 feet above the ground. You can confidently work safely, however, because there's a variety of ladders, scaffolds, and fall-arrest devices on the market today. When you use these systems properly, you can make great strides toward protecting yourself and anyone else working on your project.

Ladders

A large part of the real work of framing takes place a story or two off the ground. You've got to get up there—and eventually get down again—safely using a ladder.

There are three kinds of ladders: stepladders, fold-up (articulated) ladders, and extension ladders. A stepladder can be used for work up to 15 feet above the ground, depending on the size of your ladder. Stepladders are stable only on a level surface, however; you should never use one on a slope. The potential hazard with a stepladder is that the higher you go, the more unstable the ladder becomes. If you find you're working with your feet on or near the top three steps, you should probably move to a scaffold work platform or extension ladder.

Fold-up ladders are great for working mid-distances, between 4 and 12 feet off the ground. These ladders are handy because you can configure them in at least three ways:

■ Extend the ladder and lock it straight to act as a standard, one-section ladder.

■ Lock it in an "A" position to act as a stepladder.

■ Fold it into an "M" or into an upside-down "U" as a miniscaffold on which planks can be placed.

Extension ladders are used mostly for high outdoor work. Depending on the performance rating you use, these ladders can be quite sturdy and support the weight of a worker plus material (shingles, lumber, one end of a beam). Extension ladders are available in a wide range of sizes, typically from 20 to 50 feet.

You'll find each kind of ladder in metal (usually aluminum) or fiberglass, and many stepladders and extension ladders are made of wood. The type you'll choose depends on the work you'll be doing and how much you want to spend.

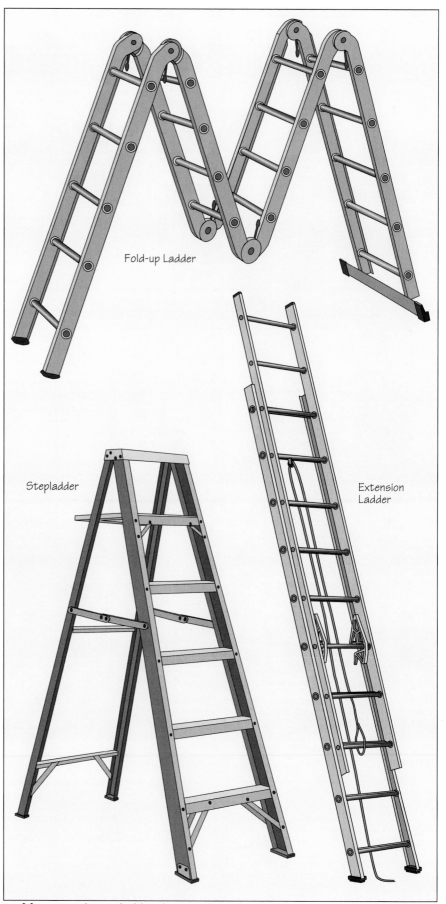

Fold-up Ladder

Stepladder

Extension Ladder

Ladders. Match your ladder choice to the task at hand.

Wooden Ladders. These ladders are not only heavy, they also wear out, crack, and splinter with use. Wooden ladders have two advantages, however: They're relatively inexpensive, and they're electrically nonconducting, so they're ideal for working around exposed electricity. A nonconducting ladder can literally be a life saver if it contacts a live power line while you're on the ladder or if your power tool is not properly grounded.

Aluminum Ladders. Inexpensive and lightweight (depending on the grade), aluminum ladders are adequate for most jobs when you place them properly. The longer the ladder, the easier it is to use if it's aluminum. Most fold-up, or articulated, ladders are aluminum. Never use an aluminum ladder in the vicinity of wiring.

Fiberglass Ladders. If you're buying for a long-term investment, get a fiberglass ladder. It may cost more, but a top-of-the-line fiberglass ladder is extremely durable, strong, noncorrosive, and nonconductive.

Homemade Ladders. You can make your own ladder, but there are strict Occupational Safety and Health Administration (OSHA) rules for safety you should adhere to. You shouldn't just nail 2×4 crosspieces on the outside face of longer 2×4s, for instance, and assume you have a safe ladder. If you make a ladder on site, the length will determine its design requirements. Homemade ladders up to 12 feet long should have an inside bottom width of 16 inches, 2×3 rails with no knots, and 1×3 crosspieces. Ladders between 12 and 20 feet long should have an inside width of 18 inches, with 2×4 knot-free rails and 1×3 crosspieces. Just as important, be sure to notch the rails so the crosspieces sit flush on the rail's face. (See the drawing above.)

Ratings. Ladders are rated for the weight they can hold. You will see a sticker on most ladders identifying

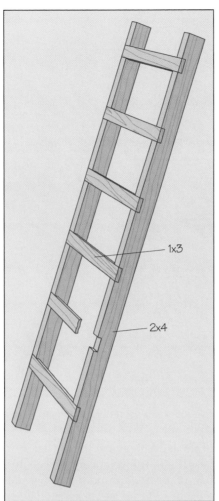

Homemade Ladders. Site-made ladders can be safe—when built correctly. Notch each crosspiece into the rails, and make the ladder the required width for its height.

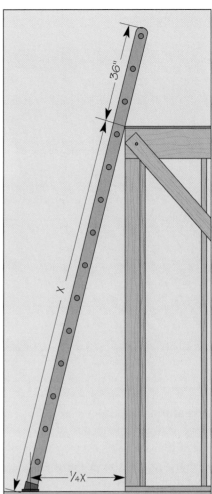

Safe Use. The distance between the ladder's base and the structure should be one-fourth the overall distance the ladder spans. Try to leave 36 in. at the top.

their "type." Type III ladders are light-duty and can carry 200 pounds per rung or step. Type II are medium-duty and can carry 225 pounds per rung or step. Type I ladders are heavy-duty industrial ladders and can hold 250 pounds per rung. Type IA ladders are extra heavy-duty and can hold 300 pounds per rung. For most residential framing jobs, a Type II ladder will serve your needs just fine.

Safe Use. When you use a straight ladder, you must set it against a vertical surface at the proper angle. As a rule of thumb, the distance between the base of the ladder and the structure should be one-quarter the distance from where the ladder contacts the ground to where the ladder rests against the structure. If your

ladder spans 16 feet, for example, it should be about 4 feet from the support surface. Anything steeper increases the risk that the ladder will topple backward when someone is on it, especially near the top, and anything shallower risks that the ladder may kick out or slide when someone is on it. If possible, allow the top of the ladder to extend about 36 inches past the point of contact. (See drawing above.)

Accessories. There are a number of ladder accessories available, some of which are essential safety features on most framing jobs. You should use a ladder stand-off when you need to work away from the structure, to trim out the exterior of windows, for example. A stand-off is a bracket you attach to the top of

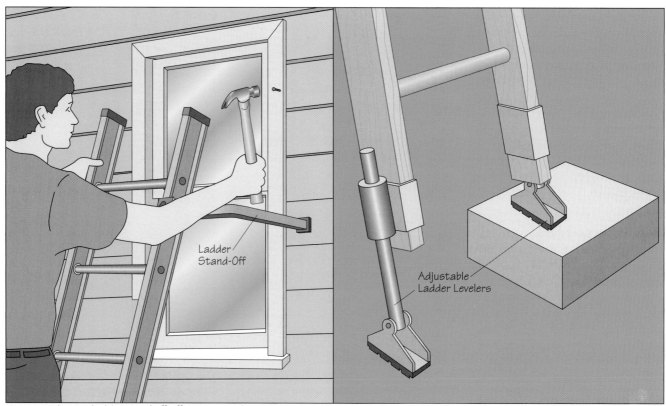

Accessories. A ladder stand-off offers you ample room to work around windows. Adjustable ladder levelers are helpful on hilly sites.

the ladder that acts as a spacer between you and the wall, providing accessibility to work.

Another handy item is a ladder leveler, which consists of two legs that you can set to different heights. Simply bolt the legs to the sides of the ladder rails at the ladder's base. Ladder levelers are especially handy for use around hilly sites and on stairs. Don't use rocks, plywood, or scrap lumber to prop up a ladder's legs. Besides being time-consuming, this slipshod practice of leveling is unsafe.

Platform Jacks

Often it's more practical to work from a platform rather than a ladder when you're framing. You can create a sturdy work platform using various kinds of brackets, called jacks, attached to a ladder, the roof, or vertical 4×4 posts.

Ladder Jacks. Essentially nothing more than heavy metal brackets that hook onto ladders, ladder jacks provide a stable, level place on which to place 2×10 wood planks or an aluminum platform. To use the jacks, you need two ladders, one for each end of the plank or working surface. There are two kinds of ladder jacks: inside-bracket and outside-bracket types.

Inside ladder jacks suspend a plank or working platform beneath the ladders as they rest against a structure. Outside ladder jacks support a plank on the front face of the ladders as they rest against a structure. Either way, the jacks hook onto the rungs of the ladder or at the junction of rungs and rails.

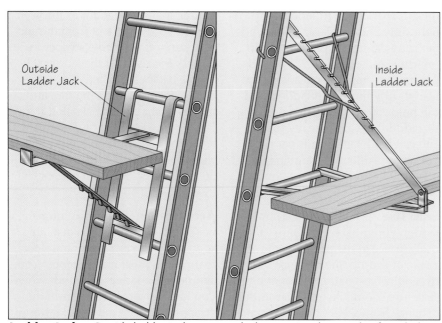

Ladder Jacks. Outside ladder jacks support planks spanning the outside of two ladders (left); inside ladder jacks support a platform suspended beneath two ladders (right).

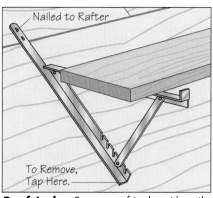

Roof Jacks. Secure roof jacks with nails driven through the roof sheathing and into a roof rafter to provide a stable surface.

Roof Jacks. Similar to ladder jacks, roof jacks support a plank. Instead of hanging them from ladders, though, you nail roof jacks directly into rafters, allowing them to sit on the roof's surface. The arms of the roof jacks that support the plank are adjustable, so you can level them properly for roofs of various pitches. The plank provides an excellent working surface for applying shingles or tar paper.

Pump Jacks. Part of a system for lifting or lowering a working plat-form made of wood or metal planks, pump jacks are metal L-shaped brackets that travel up and down 4×4 or metal posts. The vertical part of the "L" hugs an upright, and the horizontal part supports a plank or working surface. Other brackets, which you attach to structural members like rafters or studs, hold the uprights to the structure. To raise the working platform, you pump the L-shaped jacks with your foot. To lower the platform, you turn a crank. The system works on

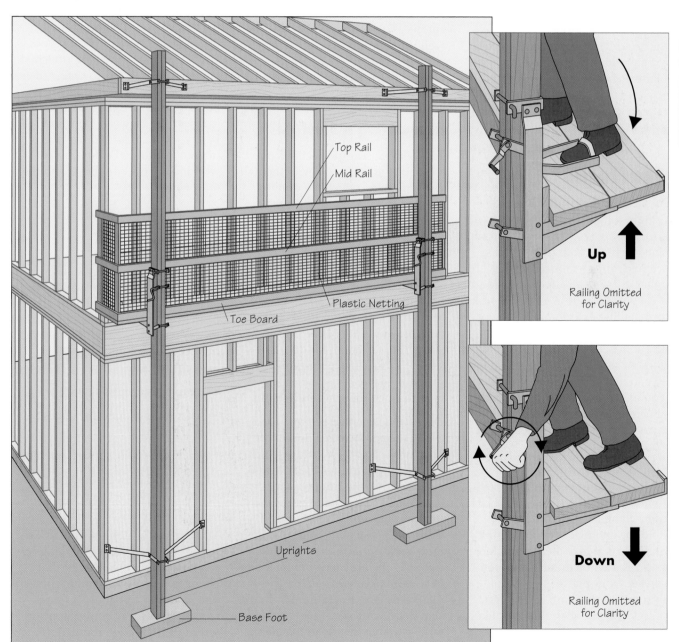

Pump Jacks. Pump jacks can offer a quick, efficient way to raise and lower a working platform. OSHA regulations require appropriate guard rails, mid rails, toe plates, and sometimes netting.

friction and depends on the weight of the platform and its cargo to hold it in place on the uprights. As you turn the crank, the bracket will chatter as it lowers. OSHA rules require that the back side of a pump-jack platform (the side against which a worker leans back when working on a structure) have a 42-inch-high top rail, a 21-inch mid rail, and a 4-inch toe board. The planks that make up the working platform can span a maximum of 10 feet. The uprights can extend a maximum of 30 feet into the air. At their bases they must bear on feet that keep them from sinking into the ground. If people are expected to be working below the pump-jack platform at any time, you must string plastic netting on the guard rails to keep things like dropped tools from falling.

Scaffolds

Prefabricated scaffolds are aluminum- or steel-tubular-framed structures that you assemble on site. You can make your own wooden scaffold, but prefabricated units are generally safer. Scaffolds provide an ideal working surface for such tasks as installing exterior sheathing or siding and working on windows and soffits. Scaffolding is certainly good to have on site, but it's expensive to rent and prohibitive to buy. You may find other ways to work at heights—such as pump jacks in particular—more cost effective for your project.

Steel pipe for heavy-duty scaffolds—the kind you're most likely to find at rental centers—is $1\frac{5}{8}$ inches in diameter. Diagonal braces hold the end pieces of the scaffold and help stabilize the frame. Once you've assembled the frame, you can set work platforms on it or, in some cases, climb it. The end pieces of some scaffolds look like wide ladders, and are available in widths of 24 to 66 inches and heights of the same dimensions.

A safe scaffold is always level; you can fine-tune a scaffold horizontally by using leveling screws at the scaffold's base. Just below the leveling screws are the scaffold's base plates, which should sit on a sturdy footing like a 2×10 plank to keep them from sinking into the ground. You may also want to consider getting a self-leveling scaffold if your site can accommodate it. A self-leveling scaffold does exactly what its name implies. The scaffold "senses" when the working platform is not level and hydraulically adjusts the legs to provide a level work surface. These systems don't work well if the ground beneath them is rough, though. They are ideal when the ground beneath them is solid and even.

Assembling a Scaffold

To assemble scaffold sections on top of one another, you join them with couplers, which are double-male-ended pins held in place by cotter pins. As the scaffold grows in height, you should tie it off to the building at least every 26 feet. It's safer to tie off scaffolding every 15 feet, especially when it's less than 48 inches wide. To tie a scaffold off to a building, run heavy rope or heavy-duty wire through a rough opening or window to a two-by cross brace that you've nailed in place. Twist the rope or wire to cinch the scaffold up tight.

Once the assembled scaffold reaches the proper working height for your project, you'll want to install a working platform, called a walkboard, within the frame of the scaffold. Walkboards made specifically for scaffolds have aluminum stiffening rails along their lengths, and they hook right on the scaffold's frame. In the absence of these kinds of walkboards, you can use 2×10 planks. Be sure to use lumber that's stamped "Scaffold Grade." Otherwise, you may overload the plank with the combined weight of you and your tools, causing it to break

and bring serious harm to anyone on the plank or below it.

The planks on scaffolds run end to end, with an overlap where the plank ends meet. OSHA rules state that this overlap be at least 6 inches and that the last planks, or the ones nearest the ends of the scaffolds, be tied off to the scaffold itself.

Before working on a scaffold, be sure all open sides and ends of any platform more than 10 feet above the ground have rails 42 inches high, with mid rails and a 4-inch toe board, just as on pump jacks. If people are working below you, you'll need plastic netting stretched between the railings to catch falling objects. Also, you must lay the planks together tightly, so no objects can slip between them and fall. Lastly, plank at least three levels of your scaffold: the one you're working on, the one above, and the one below.

Fall-Arrest Systems

A fall-protection system is any safety system that prevents workers from getting hurt because of a fall. Its use is recommended where a fall of 60 inches or more is possible. Systems include

- Guard rails around floor openings

- Guard rails around the edges of roof decks

- Guard rails across rough openings

- Full-body harnesses attached to specialty anchors nailed into the framing members of a structure

You are legally exempt from OSHA requirements if you're working on your own house; however, that changes when you employ someone, and you can get stiff fines from OSHA for noncompliance with fall-protection regulations. No matter what OSHA says, though, it's important to protect

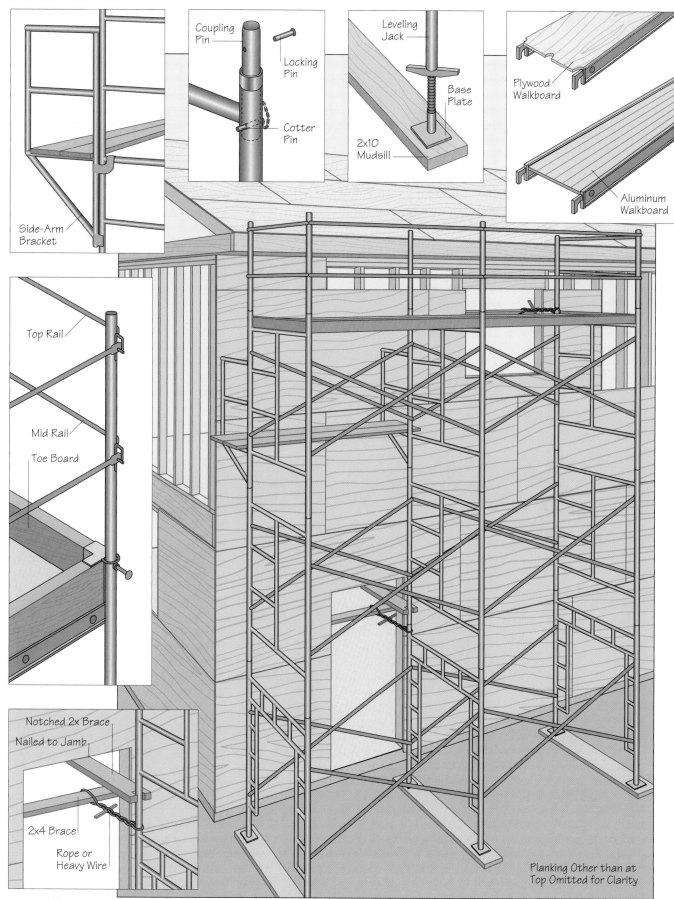

Side-Arm Bracket

Coupling Pin

Locking Pin

Cotter Pin

Leveling Jack

Base Plate

2x10 Mudsill

Plywood Walkboard

Aluminum Walkboard

Top Rail

Mid Rail

Toe Board

Notched 2x Brace Nailed to Jamb

2x4 Brace

Rope or Heavy Wire

Planking Other than at Top Omitted for Clarity

Assembling a Scaffold. An OSHA-approved scaffold system is equipped with a top rail, mid rail, toe board, and planks beneath the base plates. Tie-offs are required every 26 feet, though it's safer to install them more frequently, especially with narrow scaffolds.

yourself and your helpers—paid or unpaid—from falls.

The most efficient way to protect against falls when you're working on a roof is with a personal fall-arrest system, which consists of a full-body harness with a ring at the center of the harness's back. One end of a lanyard, or tether, clips into this ring. The other end of the lanyard clips into an ascender-type rope grab. The ascender is a one-way clamp that grabs the rope if there is any downward pull, so you can go up but not down. You can release the ascender, however, during a controlled descent.

To use an ascender, clamp it onto a rope, and clip the rope into an anchor that's securely nailed into the ridgeboard or an equally strong framing member. If you fall when wearing a personal fall-arrest system, the ascender will grab the rope, and you'll fall only as far as the slack of the lanyard and rope will allow.

These fall-arrest systems offer excellent protection and cost around $350 for a starter kit, which includes all you'll need for a residential job. Buy only OSHA-approved systems to be sure you'll be safe.

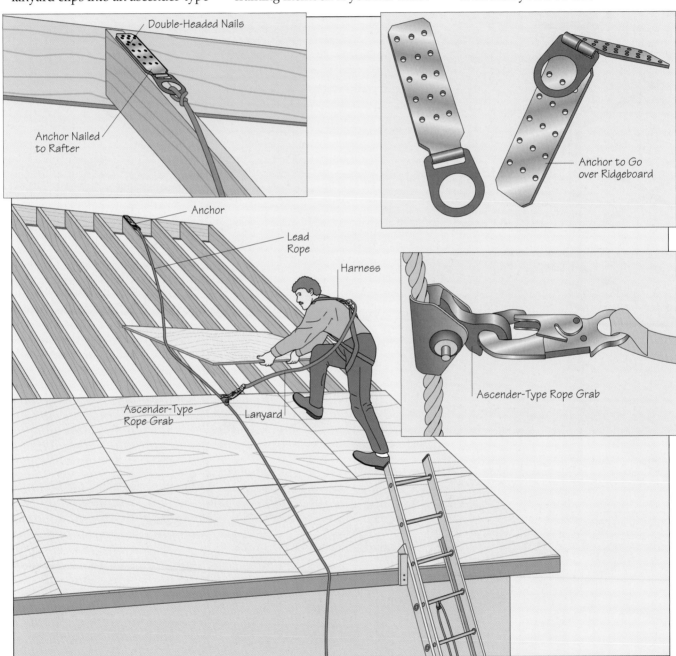

Fall-Arrest Systems. A personal fall-protection system provides excellent protection against falls and good mobility for framing work. The system consists of a harness, a lanyard, a rope-grab ascender, a lead rope, and an anchor. An ascender-type rope-grab ascends the rope by sliding. When downward pressure is exerted, as in a fall, the ascender grabs tightly. It can be released by hand for controlled descents. Plate anchors provide a place into which lead ropes can clip. The anchors must be properly nailed into ridgeboards, rafters, or other structural framing members, preferably with double-headed nails.

Framing Hardware

Modern framing techniques rely on a number of fasteners to speed the work and to add strength to the structure. Some fasteners, such as nails and screws, are familiar to most people, although even these items come in a variety of shapes and sizes. Other fasteners perform more specialized functions, and unless you've built a structure of some kind, they may be unfamiliar to you. This chapter describes framing fasteners and covers their intended uses. It starts off with nails and screws and goes on to discuss connectors, bolts, and the other specialized fasteners you may need for your project.

Nails

There are many types of nailheads and numerous kinds of nail shanks and points, each with a specific fastening task and each with different holding power. Nails come in different metals, too. Carpenters use copper, aluminum, stainless-steel, and galvanized (zinc-coated) steel nails for exposed exterior work because the nails won't rust and leave stains and streaks on wood or siding. Nails for interior work may be coated with resin or cement to increase their holding power.

Choosing the Right Nail

The trick to choosing the right nail is to match the nail to the wood-fastening task. This has largely been done for you when it comes to framing because most lumber-yards carry only a limited selection of the most popular framing nails.

Carpenters generally prefer common nails for rough framing because the nails have an extra-thick shank and a broad head. You may also see duplex, or double-headed, nails. You'd use these nails when you know you'll be removing the nail—for temporary sheathing,

safety guard rails, and the like. Duplex nails allow you to snug the bottom nailhead up tight, yet give your hammer claw a place to pull them out.

Besides common nails, the nails you'll most likely use are ring-shank underlayment nails for sub-flooring; roofing nails for applying felt paper, roofing shingles, and air-infiltration barriers (or house-wrap); and finishing nails for window- and door-jamb installation. Ring-shank nails have ridges on their shafts for extra holding power; roofing nails have large heads to hold paper securely; and finishing nails are thin, with small heads that you can drive beneath the surface of the wood with a nail set.

Sizing Nails

As commonly used, the term "penny" indicates a nail's length. The number did not originally refer to the length of the nail but to the cost of 100 nails of that size. Penny is abbreviated "d," which stands for denarius, Latin for coin, so "16-penny nails" is written "16d nails." The nails you'll use most often in framing are 6d (2 inches), 8d (2½ inches), 10d (3 inches), 12d (3¼ inches), and 16d (3½ inches).

BLUNTING NAIL POINTS

Blunt nail points before driving nails near the end of a piece of lumber. Blunting nails reduces splitting because the blunt end crushes wood fibers as it makes its way through the wood instead of splitting the fibers apart.

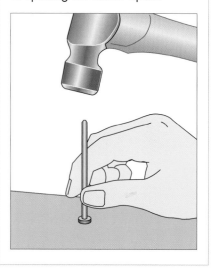

Connectors & Hurricane Ties

You can't always depend on nails to hold the connection between framing members. Sometimes you have to install a hanger, tie, anchor, or

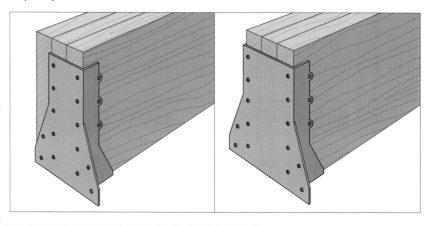

SIZING JOIST HANGERS CORRECTLY

Always use the proper joist hangers. If a joist hanger is meant for two joists, for example, don't expect it to carry the load of three. When one joist just goes along for the ride (left), its load-bearing capacity is diminished.

Choosing the Right Nail. Of all the available nail types, house framing usually requires just four or five varieties: common, double-headed, finishing, ring-shank underlayment, and roofing.

Common

Double-Headed

Finishing

Ring-Shank

Roofing

metal support to reinforce the joint. This is especially true in earthquake- or hurricane-prone areas. Some of these areas, such as Dade County, Florida, have their own strict codes for anchors.

Hangers and Ties. A number of hardware manufacturers offer a range of these anchors and ties for nearly every type of framing joint. Most of the fasteners are simply secured with nails. Of course, you wouldn't place ties or anchors at every joint in your structure, but there are a few places where they are commonly used or where you'll find that the local code requires them:

■ Where rafters meet top plates (the top horizontal board of a wall).

■ Where ceiling or floor joists butt headers or rim joists.

■ Where bottom plates (the bottom horizontal board of a framed wall) are attached to sill plates (the board attached to the foundation).

Other kinds of commonly used fasteners include post anchors, truss plates, plywood sheathing panel clips, and nail-stopping plates.

Seismic Anchors. Some anchors and ties are designed specifically for seismic areas like the San Francisco Bay area. Local codes often require extraordinary mea-

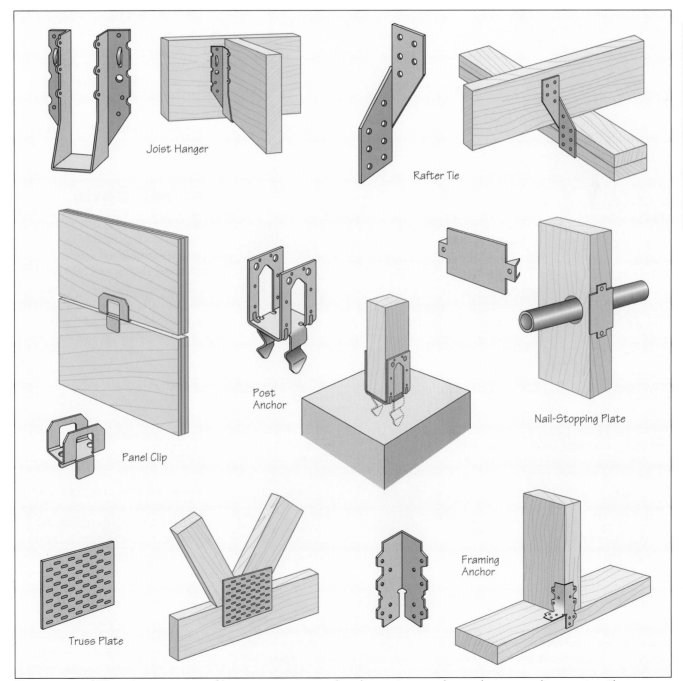

Hangers and Ties. A great variety of hangers, supports, and anchors exists to make nearly any wood connection. Those shown here are most common for framing applications.

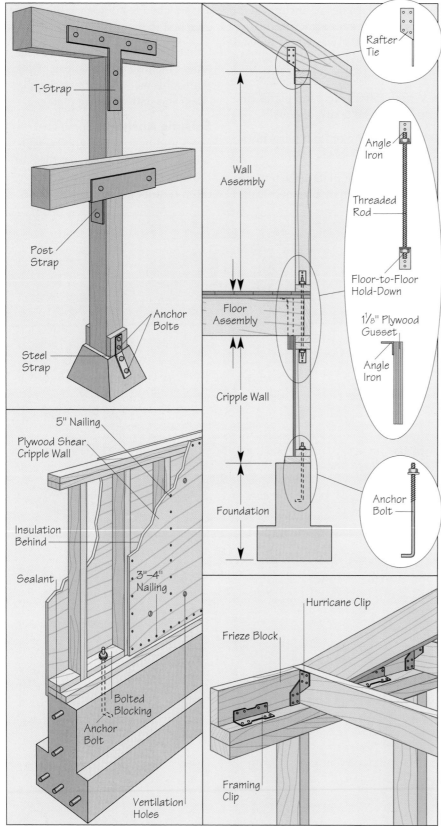

Seismic Anchors. Building codes in seismic- or hurricane-prone areas may require T-straps, post caps, and anchor bolts wherever beams and posts meet or contact the foundation (top left). They may also require plywood shear panels on cripple walls and hurricane ties, floor-to-floor angle-iron-and-all-thread hold downs, and extra-long anchor bolts at the foundation (top right and bottom left). Framing clips and hurricane ties can reinforce the connection between rafters, top plate, and rim joists or frieze blocks (bottom right).

sures for holding a house together when the ground shakes. So before undertaking any framing project, check with the local building code authority to see what regulations apply to you. Typically, seismic bracing measures require hurricane clips between joists and rim joists, framing clips between rim joists and top plates, T-straps between posts and beams, steel straps between piers and posts, and floor-to-floor hold downs at the corner of the building. The hold downs are made of angle iron and threaded steel rods. These seismic measures are not the sum of what you need to do—that depends on local building codes, which may require additional measures such as plywood shear walls on cripple, or half, walls and extra-long anchor bolts in foundations.

Anchor Bolts

Whenever you pour foundation walls, build concrete-block walls, or pour a slab, you'll attach a pressure-treated board into which you'll nail when you erect your walls. You attach this board, called a sill plate, to the top of the finished masonry using anchor bolts. There are a variety of bolts from which to choose. You must install most anchor bolts in the foundation when the concrete is still wet. It's best to position your anchor bolts before pouring concrete, tie them in place with wire, then pour your walls or slab around them.

No matter what kind of anchor you use in your foundation, the technique for fastening the sill to the foundation is essentially the same. Always use bolts of at least ½-inch diameter and, ideally, embed the end of the anchor at least 7 inches into reinforced concrete (15 inches in unreinforced concrete). Space the bolts no more than 6 feet apart and within 12 inches of the ends of the sill plates. No matter how short a sill section is, it needs at least two anchor bolts. Always use washers be-

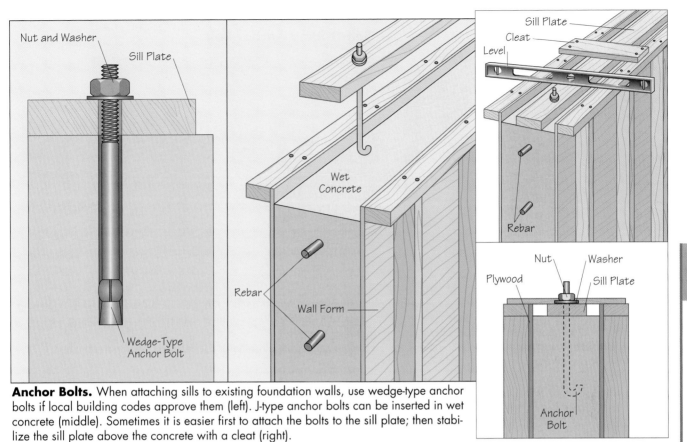

Anchor Bolts. When attaching sills to existing foundation walls, use wedge-type anchor bolts if local building codes approve them (left). J-type anchor bolts can be inserted in wet concrete (middle). Sometimes it is easier first to attach the bolts to the sill plate; then stabilize the sill plate above the concrete with a cleat (right).

neath nuts when cinching the sills down to keep the nuts from sinking into the sill plates.

You can attach sill plates when the concrete is still fresh or after it sets. If you install the plates when the concrete is fresh, you won't be able to tighten the anchor bolts until the concrete sets. In that case, you may have to install cleats across the top of the foundation to hold the sill plate in position until the concrete sets. Only then can you remove the cleats and tighten the nuts.

You can use anchor bolts for more than just holding down sill plates. Sometimes you'll use an anchor bolt to attach a ledger board onto a foundation wall or to attach a framed wall to a concrete basement wall. Anchor bolts break down into four basic categories: J-bolts, which are the most common for anchoring sills to foundations, friction-held expansion or self-drilling anchor bolts, epoxy-type anchor bolts, and expansion bolts.

J-Bolts. J-bolts are metal rods that are threaded at one end and curved into a J-shape at the other. Before pouring concrete you can hook or wire the "J" end of the anchor to a piece of reinforcement bar, or rebar, within the foundation wall or slab. You can also just insert the bolt into concrete when the concrete is newly poured. Ideally, just enough of the threaded end of the J-bolt will stick up through the sill plate so that a washer and nut can grab it and cinch down on the plate.

Friction-Held Bolts. For friction-held anchor bolts, you bore a hole with a hammer drill and slip the anchor bolt into the hole. At the base of the anchor is a wedge-shaped metal plug surrounded by a soft metal jacket. You set the anchor by applying enough force to drive that wedge back into the anchor's jacket, which then expands and grips the sides of the hole, permanently setting the anchor in place. There are a few variations on this idea, one of which is an anchor that acts as the drill bit for its own hole. When

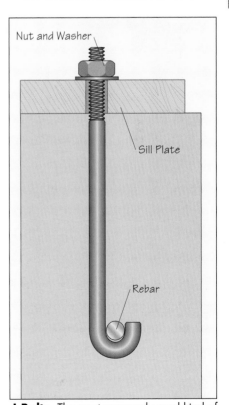

J-Bolts. The most commonly used kind of bolt for attaching sill plates to foundations, J-bolts sunk in concrete have a threaded top and a curved bottom that gets tied to the rebar. Cinch down the sill plates onto the J-bolts with a nut and washer.

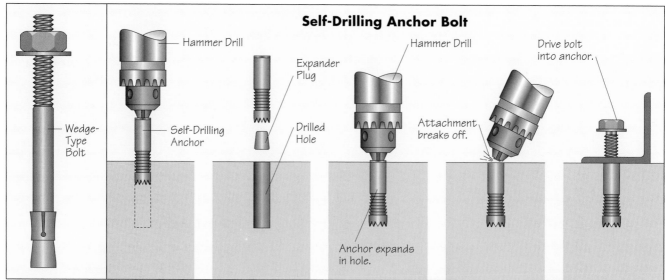

Self-Drilling Anchor Bolt

Wedge-Type Bolt

Hammer Drill — Self-Drilling Anchor

Expander Plug

Drilled Hole

Hammer Drill

Anchor expands in hole.

Attachment breaks off.

Drive bolt into anchor.

Friction-Held Bolts. Wedge-type anchors are held in place by friction. For an anchor that goes in a predrilled hole, tightening the nut drives a wedge at the anchor's base up into the metal jacket, which expands against the drill hole walls, setting the bolt permanently in place. Self-drilling anchors use the anchor jacket as the bit for drilling its own hole. When the hole is drilled, a wedge is set in place with the hammer drill, expanding the anchor's jacket against the drill hole's wall, setting the anchor.

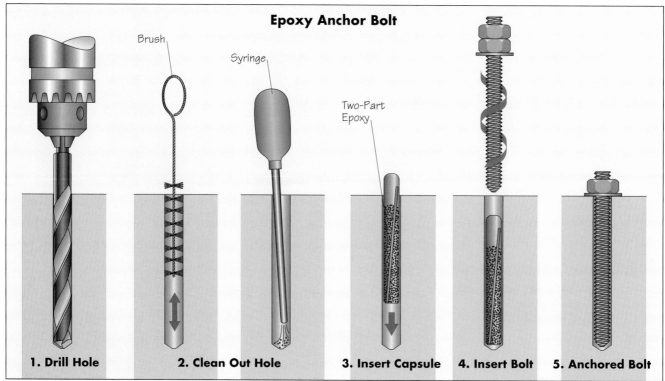

Epoxy Anchor Bolt

Brush

Syringe

Two-Part Epoxy

1. Drill Hole **2. Clean Out Hole** **3. Insert Capsule** **4. Insert Bolt** **5. Anchored Bolt**

Epoxy Bolts. For epoxy-type anchors, you insert a capsule into a drill hole. The turning action of the anchor's bolt mixes up the two-part glue, which then binds the anchor to the concrete.

you've drilled to the proper depth, you remove the anchor casing, insert a wedge in its end, reinsert it in the hole, set the wedge with the hammer drill, and snap off the top piece of the anchor, revealing a threaded shaft into which you can screw a bolt.

Epoxy Bolts. For epoxy-type anchors, you drill and clean out the bolt hole. Then you insert a two-part epoxy capsule and insert the bolt on top of the capsule. The bolt breaks the capsule, and the screwing action mixes epoxy that will hold the bolt in place.

Expansion Shields. For simple expansion anchors, you drill a hole and insert a soft-metal jacket, or shield. With the jacket in place, you insert the bolt or screw, which expands the jacket, pressing it against the shaft walls and holding it in place.

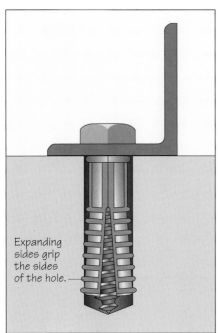

Expansion Shields. Expansion anchors use a soft metal shield that expands when a lag screw is driven into it.

Other Fasteners

Whether you're building an independent structure or adding onto a house, you'll probably need other kinds of fasteners, such as bolts, screws, and staples, at some point in the framing process.

Bolts. Bolts fall into at least three categories: carriage bolts, machine bolts, and stove bolts. Specialty bolts add many more categories. There are also about a dozen kinds of nuts and at least four kinds of washers. Each category of bolt, nut, and washer has a specific type of application and size requirement.

You probably won't find many framing applications for machine bolts, which have hex- or square-shaped heads, and stove bolts, which have rounded heads with a slot for a screwdriver. But carriage bolts, which have unslotted oval heads, can be effective when attaching boards face to face. Carriage bolts have a square shoulder just beneath the head that digs into the wood as you tighten the bolt, which prevents it from slipping and spinning in the hole, and they

are sized according to the diameter of their shanks as well as their length.

Screws. There are at least a half-dozen common screw types, but you'll probably use only three in a framing project: wood screws or bugle-head screws for decking (and maybe for sheathing) and lag screws for making heavy-duty wood-to-wood attachments, such as fastening a ledger board to a sill or rim joist. Lag screws, sometimes called lag bolts, are heavy-duty screws that you drive with a ratchet or box wrench. They have a pointed end and aggressive threads for biting into wood like a screw, but they have a hex head like a bolt. Like carriage bolts, lag screws are sized according to the diameter of their shanks: $5/16$, $3/8$, and $1/2$ inch are common sizes for lag screws.

Wood and bugle-head (also called deck) screws are also sized according to their thickness, referred to as gauge. A screw's gauge is the

diameter of its shank, or the solid shaft of the screw measured at the base of the threads near the head. Common sizes for screws are 6, 8, and 10 gauge. A 6-gauge, or No. 6, screw is $9/64$ inch in diameter, a No. 8 screw is $11/64$ inch, and a No. 10 screw is $3/16$ inch. Of course, the length for any of these screws can vary. A No. 8 screw, for example, can be nearly any length up to about $3\frac{1}{2}$ inches. The heavier the screw's gauge, the more likely you are to find it in longer lengths.

The heads on common screws can be one of four types: slotted, Phillips, square-drive (Robertson), or star-drive (Torx). The object of a screw head is to offer the maximum surface area contact between the screw drive or drive bit and screw head. A slotted screw head has about one half the surface area of a Phillips bit. The more surface area of contact, the less likely the screw is to "blow out" or strip. That's why Phillips bits are so popular around

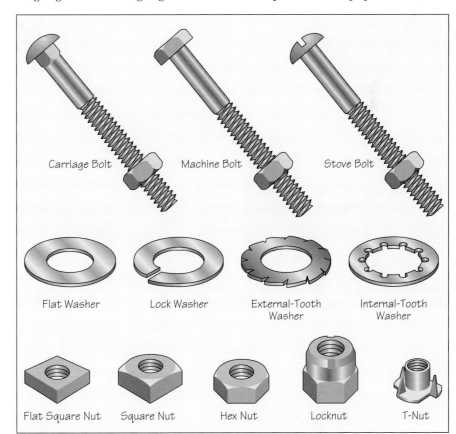

Bolts. Of the common bolt, washer, and nut types, you'll most likely use carriage bolts with flat washers and square or hex nuts in framing applications.

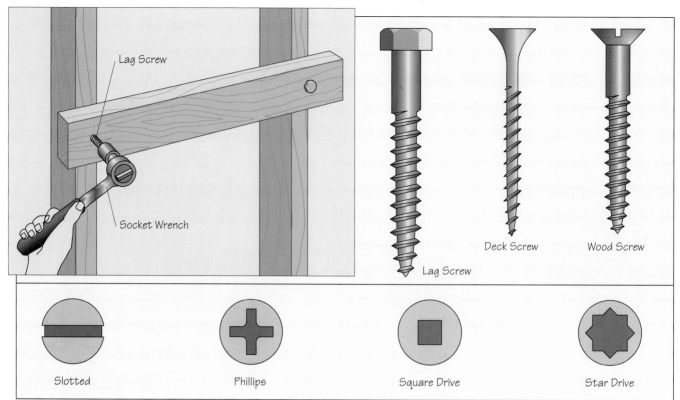

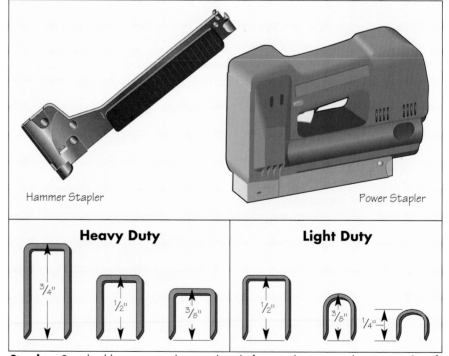

Screws. Deck screws are probably the most common screw found on construction sites. Drive heads on screws can be slotted, Phillips, square, or star-drive. The more surface area the drive head offers, the less likely that the screwdriver or drive bit will strip the screw. Lag screws are ideal for attaching ledger boards to walls and are best driven in with a socket wrench (top left).

construction sites: they provide more consistent performance when you drive them, and they don't strip as much. Some mechanics have even moved away from Phillips and use square-drive or star bits for even better performance.

Staples. Staples may be handy for securing paper in an office, but you can also use staples in construction, although they're more heavy-duty than office staples. You may use a hammer stapler to attach a vapor barrier, a wind guard, or roofing felt. If you step up to heavier gauge and longer staples, you can shoot them into place with a pneumatic gun similar to a pneumatic framing nailer and use them for trim and cabinetry work or for attaching sheathing, subflooring, and shingles.

Sheathing staples offer some advantages over nails. Staples are thinner and don't split wood as easily when driven near the end of the board. Staples also offer more holding power because they have two legs and a broad head

Staples. Standard hammer staplers are handy for attaching vapor barriers and roofing felt. Heavy-duty staples driven by a power stapler can be used to fasten plywood and subflooring. Smaller staples can be used to make cabinetry or to attach trim.

that forms a U around the material they hold in place. Before using any stapler, check the manufacturer's literature to make sure you've selected the proper staple length and gauge for your application.

Essential Building Techniques

Don't let the framing term "rough carpentry" fool you. Rough does not mean sloppy. To build a sturdy, long-lasting structure, you must measure, cut, and fasten lumber with precision. If your measurements are consistently off by so much as $\frac{1}{16}$ to $\frac{1}{8}$ inch or your saw cuts are uneven, the errors can add up quickly and cause wavy floors, out-of-square door openings, out-of-plumb corners, and loose structural connections in your building. A little attention to detail, however, can help you avoid those problems. This chapter takes a look at some tools and techniques that can help you do the job right.

Measuring Accurately

When you need to mark framing lumber for saw cutting, whether you are cutting square or angled lines, a number of tools and techniques help make the job easy and precise. Before considering marking tools, however, you need to know what a saw cut is and how to take it into account.

A small amount of wood is removed by a saw blade as it cuts. A high-quality framing job depends on exact cuts, so you must account for that wood when marking lumber. For heavy-duty saw blades, the cut can be ⅛ inch wide or more. For saber saws or reciprocating saws, the cut is much smaller. If you have a board exactly 12 feet long and you try to cut three 4-foot pieces with a heavy-duty saw blade, you'll end up with one board at 4 feet and two at 3 feet 11⅞ inches or two boards at 4 feet and one at 3 feet 11¾ inches. You must account for the cut by selecting a board slightly longer than 12 feet from which to cut. When cutting lumber, be sure you have the cut line to the outside, or waste side, of the cut line so the board you cut is the length you expect.

Using a Measuring Tape.
When using a measuring tape for *critical* dimensions, don't hook the end clip on the edge of the board or you might get an inaccurate reading. Often, the end-clip rivets come loose on measuring-tape hooks. You're better off sliding the tape so the 1-inch mark is at the end of the board, then accounting for the extra inch at the other end.

Drawing Cut Lines.
For marking angles on larger pieces of lumber, the framing square is ideal. For smaller boards, a speed square or combination square will do a fine job if the angle you want to mark is 45 or 90 degrees. For other angles use a sliding T-bevel, which you can set to copy any angle, or transfer one from a protractor.

Marking Level and Plumb Lines.
For marking level lines, use a 48-inch spirit level. A 24-inch level is handy too, though not as accurate over long dimensions.

To make sure something is perfectly vertical (plumb), you can use either a level held vertically or a plumb bob. A plumb bob is simply a pointed weight on the end of a string. Dangle the string from any point, and the weight will even-

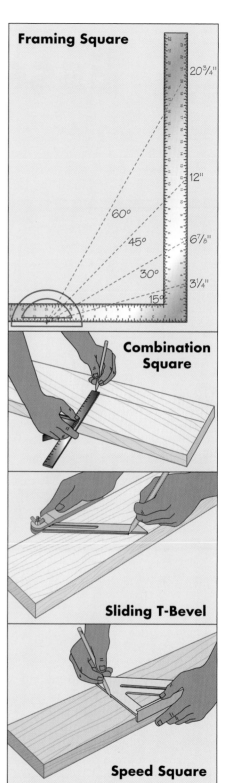

Framing Square

20¾"
60°
45°
12"
30°
6⅞"
15°
3¼"

Combination Square

Sliding T-Bevel

Speed Square

Drawing Cut Lines. A framing square can act as a large protractor when you draw a line from the 12-inch mark on the short arm to various inch marks on the long arm (top). A combination square can draw lines parallel to the board edge (upper middle). Set a sliding T-bevel to transfer any angle from one joint or board to another (lower middle). Use a speed square to mark 90- or 45-degree lines (bottom).

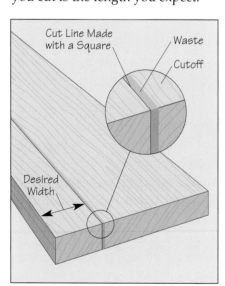

Cut Line Made with a Square
Waste
Cutoff
Desired Width

Accurate Measurements. When measuring and marking lumber to cut, account for the blade width, which will be eaten out of the wood, and place your saw so the blade is to the waste side of the cut line.

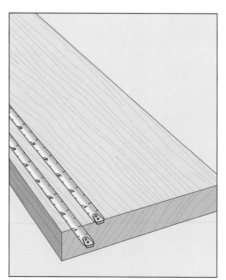

Using a Measuring Tape. The rivets on the end clip of a measuring tape can loosen, compromising accuracy. To ensure the most accuracy on critical cuts, start measuring at the 1-in. mark instead of at 0.

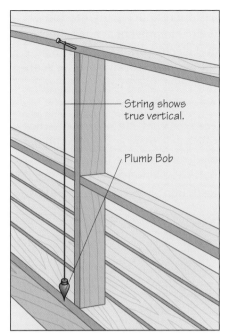

Marking Level and Plumb Lines.
Suspend a plumb bob from its end, and the string will indicate true vertical. A spirit level can be used to check both level and plumb.

tually point directly below where the string is attached. The plumb bob's string indicates true plumb, which comes in handy in a number of framing applications.

Nailing Basics

When nailing lumber, you have three choices. You can face-nail, end-nail, or toenail. Use face-nailing when two boards are flush, face to face, and you nail through the face of one board into the face of the one beneath it. End-nailing is nailing through the face of one board into the end grain of the board it abuts. Toenailing entails angling a nail in from the side and nailing down through one board into the face of a board it abuts. Toenailing requires practiced skill; it's easy to get the nail angle too steep or too shallow.

When nailing through the end of a board, stagger the nails so they don't penetrate the same grain lines; otherwise, you risk splitting the board. Also, when nailing from the face of one board into the end grain of an-

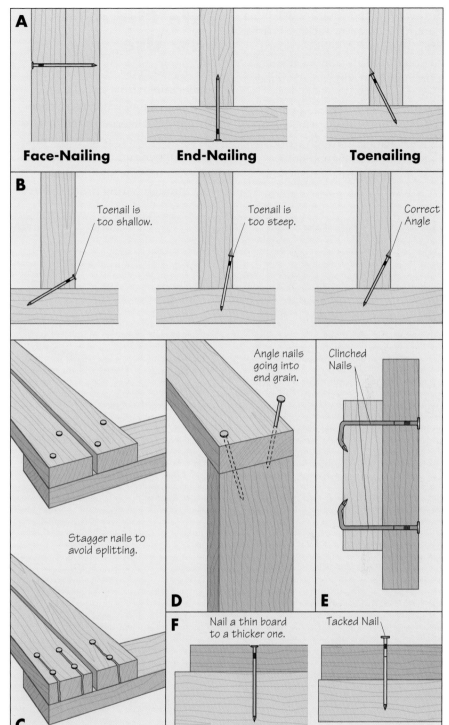

Nailing Methods. Face-nailing, end-nailing, and toenailing are common nailing techniques (A). In toenailing, it takes practice to avoid making the angle of the nail too shallow or steep (B). When nailing the ends of boards, stagger the nails so they're in different grain lines to reduce the risk of splitting the wood (C). Angle nails when driving them into end grains (D). Clinching is a nailing technique common in concrete formwork (E). When nailing together boards of different thicknesses, always nail through the thinner board into the thicker one; tack two boards together when you want to take them apart later (F).

other, angle your nails so they penetrate across the end grains. Angled nails generally hold better and are less likely to pull out. Finally, when

nailing together boards of different thicknesses, nail from the thinner piece into the thicker piece to help defeat splitting.

Tacking and clinching are two other nailing techniques. Tacking is driving a nail partially into a board so you can easily remove it later. Clinching is driving a nail all the way through two boards, then bending over the pointed end to hold the nail in place. This technique is handy in rough work where you need a good hold, as in scaffold construction and concrete formwork.

Safe Circular-Saw Use

You'll make most of your framing lumber cuts with a circular saw. An effective tool when used properly and kept sharp, a circular saw is extremely dangerous when misused or when run with faulty cords. Power to the saw should always flow through wiring protected by

a ground-fault circuit interrupter (GFCI) to prevent against shocks and electrocution. If the power source you're drawing from is unprotected, use an extension cord with a built-in GFCI.

For nonbevel cutting, be sure the saw's sole plate is square with the blade and that the blade is tight. To tighten or loosen the blade, push the teeth into a piece of wood and use

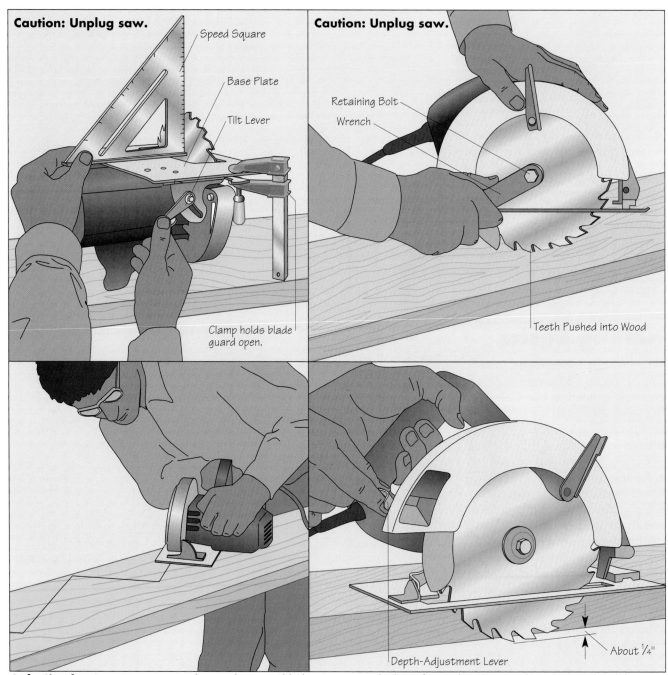

Safe Circular-Saw Use. Be sure the circular saw's blade is square to the base for nonbevel cutting by adjusting the tilt lever (top left), and that it's secure by tightening the retaining bolt (top right). Always make sure you can see the cut line so you're sure to make accurate cuts (above left), and set the saw's depth of cut to clear the lumber's thickness (above right).

a wrench on the retaining bolt. The blade should be sharp and matched to the material you're cutting. For instance, never cut framing lumber with a plywood blade because it doesn't have sufficient tooth setting. Also, make sure you can see the cut line while you're using the saw.

You'll find that your circular saw can make bevel, or angled, cuts. The base plate can tilt, offering you cuts between 90 and 45 degrees. The saw's bevel scale indicates the angle of the saw blade. When you bevel the cut by tilting your saw's base plate, however, you lessen your depth of cut. A $7\frac{1}{4}$-inch blade at 45 degrees, for example, has a depth of cut of $1\frac{7}{8}$ inches, noticeably less than the depth of cut at 90 degrees ($2\frac{3}{8}$ inches). Always be sure that the depth of cut is more than the thickness of your board—usually by at least $\frac{1}{8}$ to $\frac{1}{4}$ inch.

Choosing a Blade

The best blades for circular saws are carbide blades, the teeth of which have tungsten carbide tips for durability and long-lasting sharpness. Rip blades smoothly cut wood in the direction of the grain, generally a lengthwise cut on dimension framing lumber. Crosscut blades cut best across the grain, a widthwise cut. Combination blades are designed for both crosscutting and ripping. For the general-purpose cutting you'll be doing during the framing job, use a 24-tooth carbide-tipped combination blade.

Blade sizes are determined by what your circular saw can handle. Most saws take $7\frac{1}{4}$-inch blades. Never install a blade that's even slightly too big for your saw; it will defeat the safety offered by the saw guard.

Making Square Cuts

When making any cut, position the saw's base plate squarely on the piece of lumber and switch on the saw with the blade set back from the cut line. Allow the blade to spin up

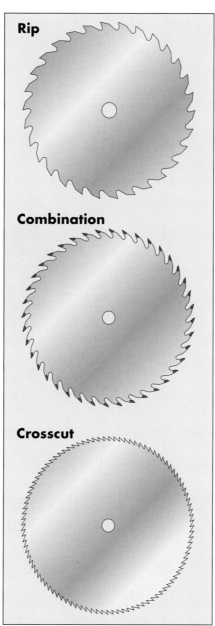

Rip

Combination

Crosscut

Choosing a Blade. There are a variety of saw blades from which to choose, including blades hardened with carbide steel and those made for crosscuts or rip cuts.

to cutting speed, free of any obstructions. Then slowly move into the cut. You'll notice that the base plate has a guide mark that indicates where the blade is cutting, but some carpenters prefer to watch the actual blade because the guide varies with blade thickness and tooth settings. As you continue with your cut, the saw guard will automatically retract, exposing the full depth of the blade. Be sure that as you finish your cut, the saw-blade guard snaps back into its original position.

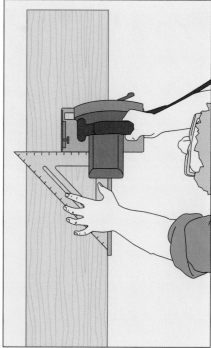

Saw Guides. A speed square makes an excellent cutting guide when cutting square cuts with a circular saw.

Saw Guides. Use a guide when you make circular-saw cuts. It takes practice to cut a straight freehand line because the circular saw wobbles easily and can wander from the intended path. Once a circular saw establishes a blade path, it tends to stay on that path. If you push the saw sideways, you risk binding the blade and burning the wood. Even when you have a good visible cut line clearly marked, use a speed square to guide the blade.

Cutting Lumber and Plywood

Crosscuts represent the vast majority of cuts you'll make in framing. Crosscutting means you cut across the grain—in most cases across the width of the board. Rip cuts go with the grain, generally lengthwise, and may run from one end of the board to the other. You won't do rip cuts as frequently because they change the width of the board rather than the length—a less common requirement.

When cutting on sawhorses, never cut between the horses. Always rest

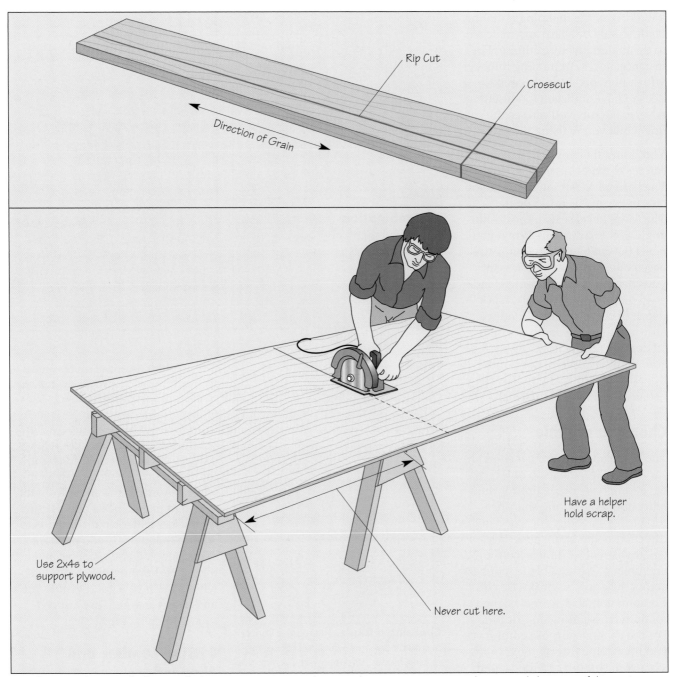

Direction of Grain

Rip Cut

Crosscut

Use 2x4s to support plywood.

Have a helper hold scrap.

Never cut here.

Cutting Lumber and Plywood. A crosscut runs across the grain lines; a rip cut runs in the general direction of the grain (top). Never make a cut between sawhorses because the boards will collapse and bind the saw, increasing the risk of kickback and injury (above). Always have a helper hold scrap wood so it doesn't droop and bind your saw.

the work on both horses, cut to the outside, and let the scrap fall away. If the piece you're cutting off is big enough to bind your cut, get a helper to support it until you finish the cut. Lastly, no matter what kind of cut you're making, always cut away from your body.

Cutting plywood takes great care. It's tempting just to zip through plywood cuts without having

someone hold the scrap piece that you're cutting away. But because plywood is so flexible, it can easily bind your saw, risking kickback. When cutting plywood, follow these simple safety precautions:

■ Always have a highly visible cut line.

■ Always have a helper supporting the weight of the piece you're cutting away.

■ Always be aware of the location of the saw cord as you work.

■ Always cut plywood on a good stable surface like a set of sawhorses.

Plywood-Cutting Guide. It's easy to allow the saw blade to wander when cutting plywood, so use a guide like a shoot board to ensure a clean, straight line. The shoot board is simply a straight-edged board that's attached to a hardboard base. For your straightedge, use any length of plywood or solid lumber that has two straight edges and is at least 2 inches wide. Fasten the straightedge to a length of ⅛-inch-thick tempered hardboard with glue and screws, allowing about 8 inches of hardboard on both sides. Screw through the hardboard into the straightedge, countersinking the screws. Trim off one side of the base by squaring the blade to the base of the saw, adjusting the depth of cut to ¼ inch, and placing the jig on a scrap of plywood. When you

make the cut, run the edge of the circular saw's base against the straightedge: this will create a straight base edge that shows the saw's exact cutting line.

To use the jig, clamp it onto the workpiece and align the edge of the base along the cutting line. Place the clamps along the extra hardboard on the untrimmed side of the jig so that the saw's motor won't run into clamps during the cut. When you get a new saw blade, retrim one side of the jig so that you know the cut line will coincide precisely with the edge of the jig.

Avoiding Kickback

Kickback occurs when a saw binds in a cut or when you are overeager and try to cut too quickly. Kickback is dangerous because you can easily lose control of the saw. The primary way to avoid kickback is to use safe sawing techniques: cut slowly, don't rush the saw, and support the scrap materials of your cut. Also, you can buy anti-kickback saw blades. (See "Using Saws Safely," page 43.) These blades have specially designed teeth that limit the amount of wood into which the saw blade can cut with each revolution. The smaller gullets, or spaces between the teeth, reduce the chance of the blade taking a deep bite into the wood and kicking back.

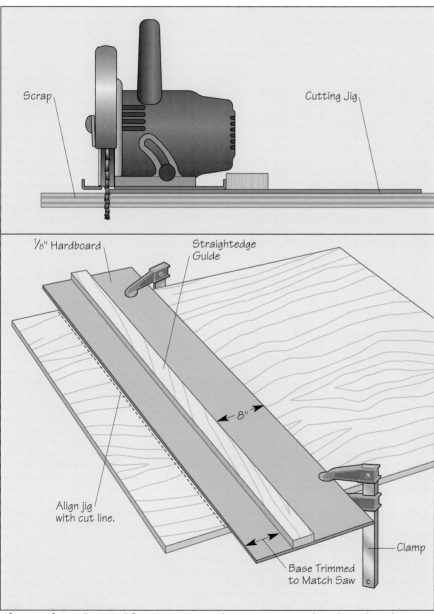

Scrap

Cutting Jig

⅛" Hardboard

Straightedge Guide

8"

Align jig with cut line.

Clamp

Base Trimmed to Match Saw

Plywood-Cutting Guide. An easy-to-make cutting jig, or shoot board, makes an excellent guide for making straight cuts on panel material.

The Pros Know

HARD-STARTING NAILS

Starting nails in out-of-reach places can be easily done using a hammer in reverse. Some claw hammer designs allow you to lodge a nail between the claws, with the point facing out. Set the nail in place, reach up, and swing the hammer once, setting the nail in place. Then jiggle the hammer loose and drive the nail home.

6

ESSENTIAL BUILDING TECHNIQUES

Troubleshooting Lumber Problems

Sometimes you can't help getting some defective lumber stock in your delivery. As the buyer, you're free to reject lumber, by piece or by lot, that isn't up to par. Some lumber will be on the verge of acceptable, however, and many framers choose to work with marginal material rather than swap it for new stock.

An established way of dealing with lumber that is substandard is to install it where it has minor impact on finished surfaces. Framed walls comprise vertical sticks of lumber called studs and horizontal sticks

HANDLING YOUR HAMMER

Grip a hammer at the end of its handle for the best leverage, and be aware of the proper pivot points to use in your arms when driving a nail. Use your elbow as a pivot point when driving medium or large nails. For really big nails—16d or more—you may have to move your shoulder into the job as well. Use your wrist as a pivot point when driving small finishing or roofing nails.

of lumber called plates. The plates need to be true and straight, so you wouldn't use marginal lumber for

plates. Also, it's crucial that the end studs be true and straight, so you'd never use marginal lumber there ei-

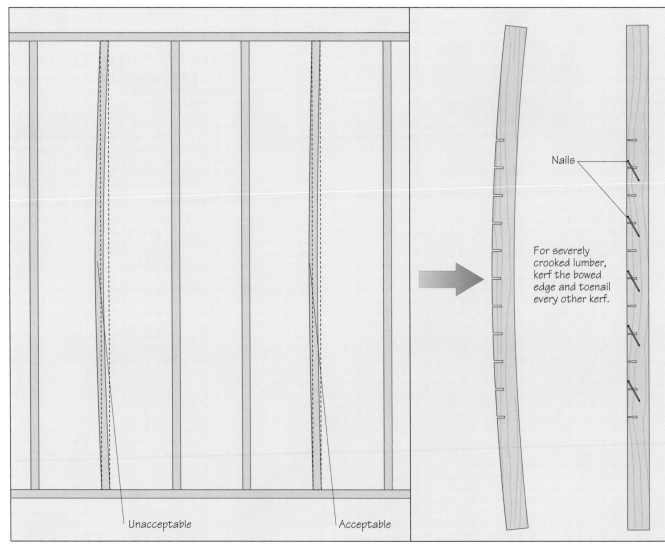

Nails

For severely crooked lumber, kerf the bowed edge and toenail every other kerf.

Unacceptable   Acceptable

Crooked Lumber and Possible Fixes. Boards that are not straight still have to fall reasonably within the on-center framing measurements so that when you cover the wall with sheathing or drywall, the studs fall where you expect them to be (left). For lumber that bows excessively side to side, you can also make a series of shallow relief saw cuts along one face, straighten the board, and toenail the cuts (right).

ther. But for the intervening studs within the wall, you might be able to get away with marginal lumber.

The important consideration here is spacing between studs. When you apply drywall or sheathing, you won't be able to see the studs beneath each sheet. You'll have to depend on their predictable location, say 16 or 24 inches on center. This means the center of the studs will occur every 16 or 24 inches, depending on your wall design. If you use wood that's so bowed or so crooked that the spacing isn't consistently within ¼ inch of the predictable on-center marking up and down the board, you could get into trouble. Wood that far out

of true is good only for safety railings, scrap, or firewood.

Crooked or warped lumber can also cause a problem if it bulges out of the plane of the wall. Correct these boards by making one or two crosscuts halfway into the stud from an edge. Hammer a tapered wood shingle into the kerf on the hollow edge or toenail the cuts on the bowed edge, or do both.

Fighting Crooked Lumber

When fighting crooked lumber stock in walls, the best thing to do is to exchange the bad piece of lumber for a good one. The amount of energy you must put into fixing a

crooked stud just isn't worth the trouble, given that they cost only about $2 apiece. If the lumber is marginal and you can't use it as a wall stud, you can bury it in the corner as a nonstructural stud or cut it down to use as blocking.

If you feel you must take extreme measures to save a piece of bowed wood, apply a trick that's usually used when building curved walls. Make a series of shallow face cuts along the outside curve of a bowed board, and you may be able to pull it back to true and toenail it. Pulling the board back to true may involve the use of a helper or at least a pry bar or flat bar when you finally install the board in a wall.

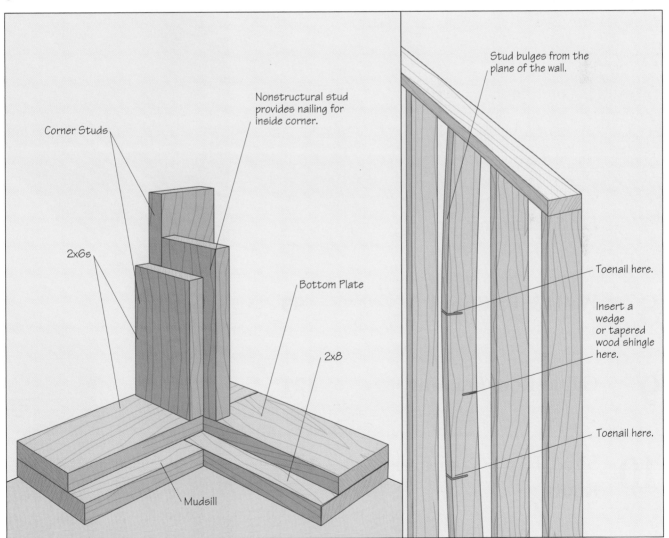

Fighting Crooked Lumber. Boards that are not straight can be buried in the corner. The corner configuration shown at left is a common one. Note that one of the studs is not a structural stud but just provides a nailing surface for drywall. You can put crooked lumber here without compromising the wall's strength. Boards that bulge substantially out of the plane of the wall are not acceptable in wall framing but may be fixed by kerfing and toenailing (right).

6

ESSENTIAL BUILDING TECHNIQUES

Section II

Building the Frame

7 Floor Framing   **72**

8 Walls & Partitions   **93**

9 Gable-Roof Framing   **121**

10 Shed, Hip & Gambrel Roofs   **143**

11 Framing Dormers   **157**

7
Floor Framing

The floor system in platform framing serves to connect the house to the foundation and to act as a base for the walls and roofing systems. Building framing for a floor is an important first step in the construction process. To make floors both firm and structurally sound, begin with proven engineering principles and designs. Then select high-quality materials that are are sized appropriately for your project. Pay particular attention to making strong connections between components, whether they be beams, girders, joists, or plywood decking. This chapter will examine time-tested design strategies and look at some of the components essential to building a good floor system.

Structural Support

In most cases, a framed structure rests on a concrete or block foundation, which can be any of a number of types, including slab, crawl space, full-wall, and concrete piers. Here's a brief look at these foundation types and how their designs affect the way you'd frame a building.

Concrete Slab

The simplest form of foundation is a slab, often called a slab on grade. A slab is a monolithic piece of concrete, meaning it is all one piece, unlike crawl-space and basement foundations, which you'd build only after you had formed and poured their footings ahead of time. Soil preparation beneath slabs is crucial, so before you have a slab poured, be sure you've prepared the soil to ensure proper drainage around and beneath the slab. Freeze-thaw cycles and frost heaving—when water contained in soil freezes and expands, heaving anything sitting on top of it—can easily crack a slab. Regional frost-line depth will determine soil preparation practices. Typically, you replace soil to 50 percent of the frost depth with ¾-inch gravel. Don't take any shortcuts. A faulty foundation is one of the hardest things to fix after framing has begun.

Crawl-Space Foundation

A crawl-space foundation is a low wall made of poured concrete or concrete block that rests on a footing. Once you've framed and decked a wood structure on top of the crawl-space wall, you'll have only enough room to crawl between the underside of the floor joists and the ground, hence the name. The minimum allowable floor-joist-to-ground space is 18 inches. If you use a girder (a wood beam made by nailing together two or three two-bys) beneath the joists, the minimum allowable space between the underside of the girder and the ground is 12 inches. The

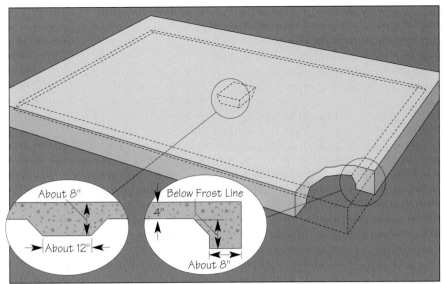

Concrete Slab. Slabs are monolithic pieces of concrete. Thicker edges support the building's live and dead loads, and thick interior sections support load-bearing posts or walls. Soil beneath slabs must be carefully prepared to ensure drainage.

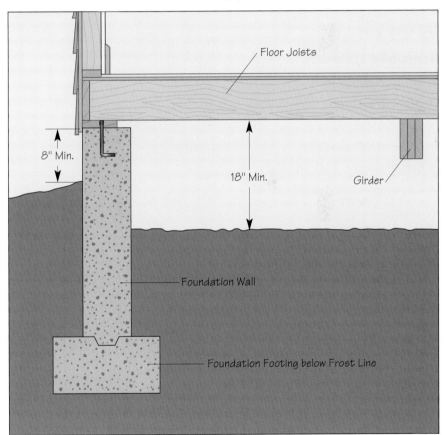

Crawl-Space Foundation. Crawl-space foundations are short walls set on footings. Sills are attached to the walls using J-bolts.

minimum distance between the outside bottom of the wood structure and the ground is 8 inches.

The footings beneath crawl spaces serve the same purpose wider sections of slabs serve: they spread the building's live and dead loads over a wide footprint, distributing the building's weight over a larger area. Prepare the soil beneath the footing to ensure proper drainage, just as you would with a slab.

Basement-Wall Foundation

Poured-concrete or concrete-block basement-wall foundations are common in many areas. Typical modern basement walls are 8 feet high, but you must account for the basement floor-slab depth when calculating the height of your forms for footings for poured-concrete walls or the number of courses you'll have laid for concrete-block walls. If you form or build a basement wall at 8 feet, your walls will have an inside ceiling height of 7 feet 8 inches, because the slab takes up 4 inches.

Attaching Sill Plates to a Foundation

Difficulty level:

Tools and Materials

- Basic carpentry tools
- Framing square
- Circular saw
- Drill and ⅝" spade bit
- Socket set or adjustable wrench
- Two-by pressure-treated lumber
- Sealant
- Nuts and washers for anchor bolts

1 Measure sills to find bolt position. For slabs, use two-by pressure-treated lumber of the same dimension you'll make the walls—usually 2×4s or 2×6s. For crawl-space or basement foundations, you need to use pressure-treated 2×8s as the sill plates. Using a framing square, measure in from the edges and ends of the slab or foundation to determine where on the sill plate the anchor bolts will poke through. Double-check that your sill lumber is pressure-treated, then mark and drill the ½-inch diameter holes for the bolts.

2 Undercut the rough openings. You'll eventually need to remove the sill plate where rough openings for doors will occur.

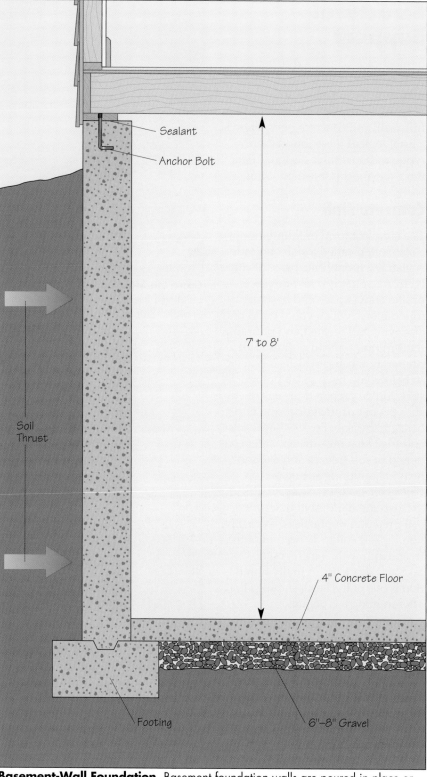

Sealant

Anchor Bolt

7' to 8'

Soil
Thrust

4" Concrete Floor

Footing

6"–8" Gravel

Basement-Wall Foundation. Basement foundation walls are poured in place or built with concrete block on top of a footing. After the walls are in place, a basement floor is poured right up against the foundation walls.

Cutting through the installed sill is difficult. To make that job easier, cut a saw kerf halfway through the lumber on the underside of the sills to mark the inside edges of rough openings before putting the sill plates in place. Later, you'll be able to cut the sill plates out of the way using a reciprocating saw or circular saw set to the proper depth.

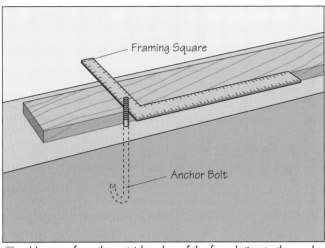

1 Measure from the outside edge of the foundation to the anchor bolt. Then on the sill, mark that distance in from the sill edge.

2 Cut a ¾-in.-deep kerf in the sill plate beneath rough openings for doors to make removing this section of sill easier later.

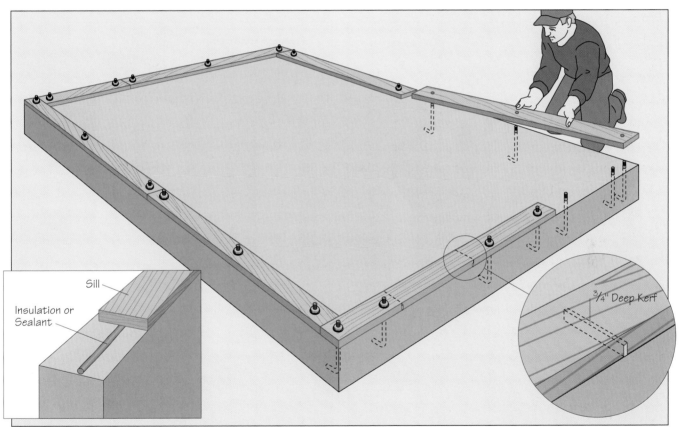

3 Fasten the sills to the slab using J-bolts. Seal between the sills and foundation, and use shims where necessary to keep the sills level.

3 **Set the sill plates.** Place the sill plates on top of the slab or foundation walls. The connection between the sill and the foundation is apt to leak cold air, so it's a good idea to seal this area. You can accomplish this task easily by using foam insulation between the sill and the foundation. Most building supply stores carry ropes of pinkie-finger-thick foam insulation or ⅛-inch-thick sheets of foam the same width as the sill. By laying this insulation down on top of the foundation and putting your sill in place, you sandwich the foam between the sill and the foundation, blocking air infiltration.

When you set the sills, the anchor bolts should poke through the holes you drilled. The outside edge of the sill plates should align with the outside edge of the slab or foundation. With washers and nuts in place, use a socket wrench or adjustable wrench to tighten the sill plate against the slab or foundation. Make sure the sill is level, and shim it where necessary to make it perfectly straight.

Pier Foundations

Pier foundations are not foundations in the traditional sense, but rather concrete pillars on which wood posts, joists, beams, or plates directly sit. Though some structures, such as sheds, are constructed on top of piers, you're more likely to find piers supporting decks or porches. The reason is that piers are susceptible to shifting out of plumb in areas where there are freeze-thaw cycles or loose soils. If you use piers, prepare the soil where they sit with the proper gravel and drainage to reduce frost problems.

Wood Foundations

Lastly, there are wood-framed foundations, which tend to be rare but are inexpensive and easier to construct than concrete foundations. Wood foundations are much like standard sheathed walls, except that instead of being sided they're backfilled with soil and gravel. You erect a 2×4 or 2×6 stud wall with top and bottom plates, then sheathe it with plywood. If you have a wood foundation built, use pressure-treated lumber for all the wall parts: studs, plates, and sheathing. Untreated wood foundations can be easily damaged by decay and termites.

Girders, Beams & Posts

A structure's outside walls transfer a great deal of the load in any building directly to the foundation walls, but an enormous load also bears down through the center of the structure. How that central load is carried determines, in part, the design of your basement. If you want your basement to be a wide open area, with no columns in place, then the load that bears down on the center of the floor must be transferred to the foundation walls through a steel I-beam. The I-beam ends sit in

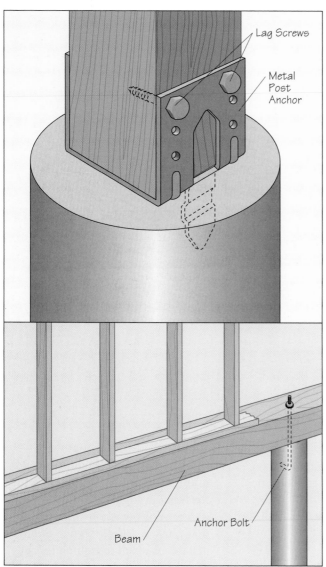

Pier Foundations. Metal brackets make a structurally sound connection between concrete piers and wood posts (top). Piers may attach directly to joists, girders, and beams using anchor bolts (bottom) or brackets.

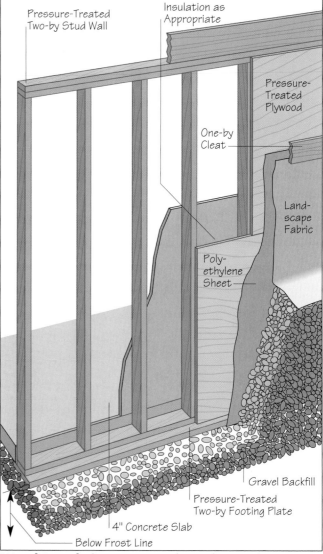

Wood Foundations. Increasingly rare but popular in certain parts of the United States and Canada, wood foundations use treated wood and are built much like standard walls, with studs, plates, and plywood sheathing.

pockets in the foundation walls at each end of the room and—if it's sized properly—will adequately support the load from above.

If you don't mind having a column or two in the basement or if a costly steel I-beam is out of your budget, then you can use simple wood girders, which carry the house loads between columns. The columns, in turn, transfer part of the load to the basement floor.

Usually when you install a girder or I-beam, you'll have to shim it to the correct elevation. Foundation wall pockets are left ½ inch or so lower to leave space for adjustment. Broken pieces of slate are usually used for shimming rather than wood, which compresses too easily.

Joists that don't overlap beams or girders will likely rest partially on blocking (for I-beams) or ledger boards (for girders). The blocking and ledgers determine the elevation at the top edge of the joists, which must be level and consistent, especially where they meet at the girder or beam. If the joists butt a girder, joist hangers can also hold them in place. If the joists lap face-to-face as they rest on a girder or I-beam, you need to install blocking between them to keep them from tilting or flopping over.

Wood Girders

In most wood-framed structures, a girder is the main supporting beam. Made of wood, the girder runs the length of a building, bearing large loads from above and partially transferring them to support columns or posts.

Girders that are a solid piece of dimension lumber, or a timber, are expensive and hard to obtain, so most girders are made by face-nailing together smaller pieces of dimension lumber, like four 2×10s or three 2×12s, to create a structural girder. The size of the girder depends on what loads it will carry.

Larger girders can carry heavier loads longer distances between supporting columns.

Wood girders should sit in a foundation pocket and bear at least 4 inches on the bottom of the pocket. The depth of the pocket depends on the size of the girder. Because the girder is wood, leave ½ inch on either side of the pocket for ventilation. The elevation of the pocket must be precise, so the top of the girder sits at the same elevation as the top of the sill plate.

Girder Support. Girders are supported by walls and posts or columns, generally spaced 8 to 10 feet apart. Posts and columns should stand plumb and are attached to the underside of girders with metal brackets that are lag-screwed into place. Posts are made of wood; columns, called lally columns, are heavy-gauge steel pipes usually filled with concrete. The base of a wood post or lally column should always be supported by a footing that helps distribute the load it carries.

Steel I-Beams

Let's say you have a basement that's 30 feet long and 30 feet wide. It would be easy to divide this space by running load-bearing columns or a wall across the room to support a girder, making the longest span 15 feet, a distance easily handled by properly sized framing lumber. But if you wanted that space open—for a play room, utility room, workshop, or game room, for instance—you wouldn't want to divide it down the center of the room.

For wider spans, therefore, it may be necessary to install an I-beam supported by one column—or even none—spanning where a column-

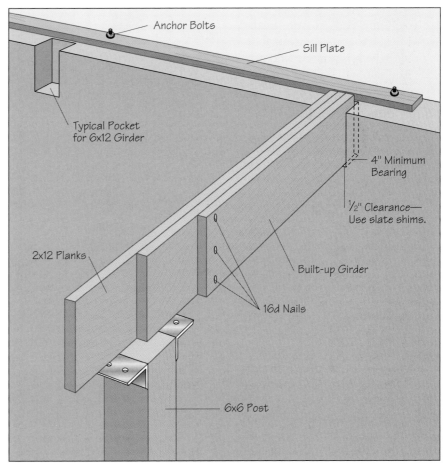

Girder Support. Pockets in the foundation provide a seat in which girders sit, but the girder must bear at least 4 in. on the foundation and have ½ in. of clearance on each side for air circulation. The top of the girder should come flush with the top of the sill plate.

supported girder would otherwise be to transfer the loads from the building to the outside walls. I-beams are typically made of steel and are shaped like the capital letter I (in cross section), with horizontal webs at the top and bottom. Steel beams are far more costly than wood, but they have the capacity to span long distances without deflection and can carry great loads. (Don't guess at what size beam to get; have an engineer specify it for you.) The ends of steel I-beams usually rest in a pocket in the foundation wall and must bear on that pocket at least 4 inches. The elevation of the foundation wall pocket must be precisely positioned, because the top web of the steel I-beam should be flush with the top of the sill plate.

Installing Columns and Posts

Lally columns and pressure-treated wood posts rest on a concrete footing over which is poured a floor slab. The slab will seal the column or post and footing in place.

Lally-Column Installation.
You fasten lally columns to footings with four short anchor bolts or J-bolts. Before pouring a slab, form and pour a 12 × 12-inch lally-column footing 8 inches deep using two-by lumber. During the pour, have a wood template ready with holes positioned to match the bolt holes in the lally-column plate.

Insert J-bolts into the holes of the template, and hand-tighten the nuts to hold the J-bolts in place. When you pour the footing, lay the template in place so you can properly insert the J-bolts into the fresh concrete. Once the footing concrete has cured, remove the template, plumb the lally column in place, and cinch down on the J-bolts' nuts and washers to attach the lally column to the footing. With lally columns positioned, you can then pour the basement floor slab.

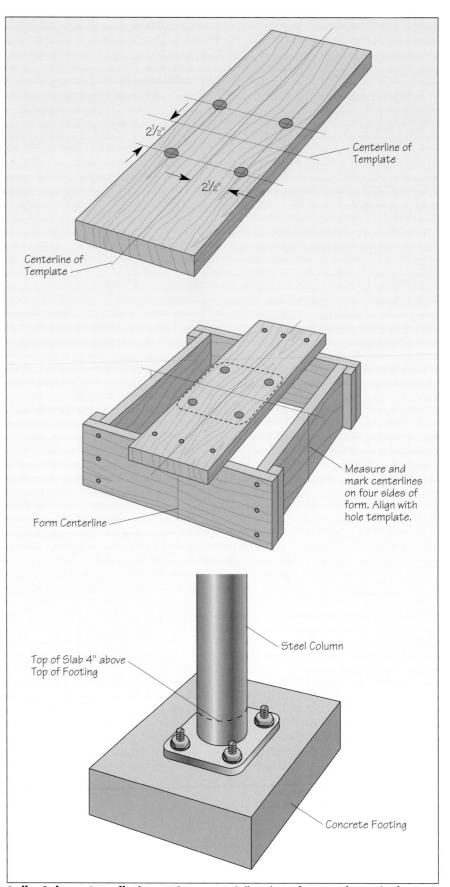

Lally-Column Installation. When setting lally-column footings, frame the footing with wood, and hold the lally column's anchor bolts in place with a wood template that matches the holes in the bottom of the column.

Wood-Post Installation. For the base of wood posts, as with columns, you'll create a concrete pier footing (ideally with a connector or a steel rod protruding from its center) that you seal in concrete when you pour your floor. Before pouring the slab, use two-by lumber to create 12 × 12-inch concrete piers 8 inches deep. During the footing pour, insert either a steel rod or a post anchor in the wet concrete. If you're using a steel rod, drill a hole in the base of the post to receive the steel rod.

Once the pier concrete has cured, plumb the pressure-treated post in place. Lag-screw the post to the anchor if you've used anchors. Pour the slab around the concrete pier. If you're installing posts in a crawl-space foundation, the posts should be seated on properly set concrete piers in well-drained soil. Be sure to position the concrete piers directly beneath the girder or beam the posts will support.

The Pros Know

CUTTING POSTS SQUARE

When cutting posts with a handsaw, install temporary cutting guides at the cut line. You can use any straight, thin material.

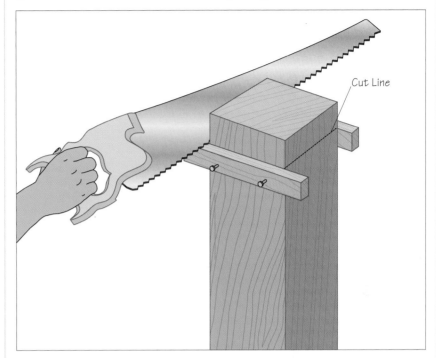

Cut Line

FLOOR FRAMING

7

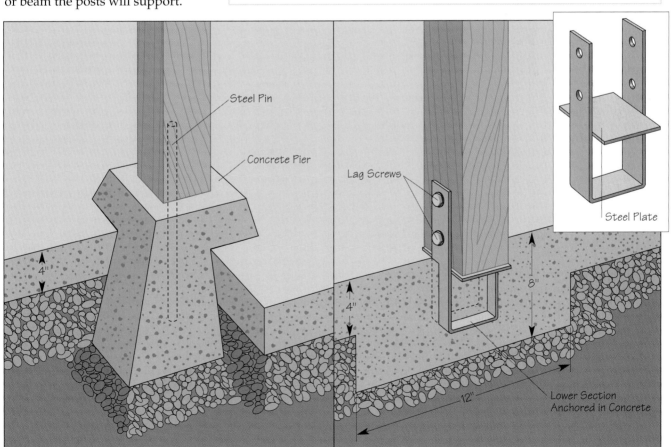

Steel Pin

Concrete Pier

Lag Screws

Steel Plate

4"

4"

8"

12"

Lower Section
Anchored in Concrete

Wood-Post Installation. When setting wood posts on piers, install a steel rod in the pier that will protrude into a predrilled hole in the post, or use brackets set in concrete to support the post with a plate and straps.

Column and Post Attachment.

Columns and posts attach to the underside of girders or I-beams. Columns have flat flanges at their tops that accommodate four bolts. The bolts fasten the flange to the bottom of I-beams. For girders, the column's flange should sit flush on the underside of the girder. Insert lag screws through the column's flange, and tighten them with a socket wrench. Wooden posts attach to girders and I-beams with angle-iron brackets or metal post caps.

Preparing Girders and I-Beams for Floor Joists

Normally when you install floor joists, you lap them over the top of the girder or I-beam. If you want the joists to be flush with the top of the girder or beam, you may have to install ledger boards or blocking along the bottom of the member's outside faces. A ledger board is essentially a shelf on which the joists rest. When the joists are in place you can join the tops of the joists across the girder or I-beam with scab boards, or if you've set them high enough, you can notch the joists to join each other over the center of the girder or beam. If you use scab boards, make sure they extend at least 12 inches onto each

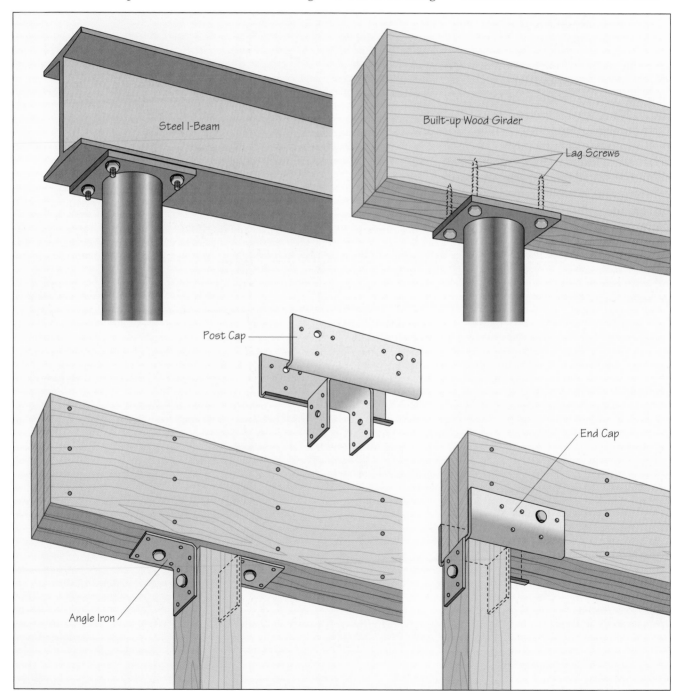

Column and Post Attachment. Bolt lally columns to steel I-beams through a flange at the column's top; fasten them to wood girders with lag screws. A variety of brackets are available to secure wood posts to wood girders.

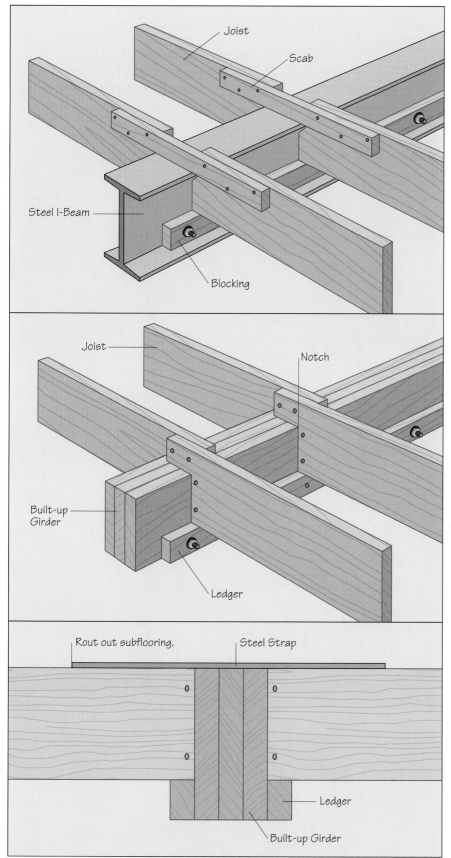

Preparing Girders and I-Beams for Floor Joists. Use ledgers and scabs to attach floor joists to an I-beam (top) or girder if you don't set the joists on top. You can also notch boards (middle), but that takes more work. If the top edges of joists sit flush with the girder's or I-beam's top, you can tie them in place with a steel strap (bottom).

joist. If the joists come flush with the top of the girder or I-beam, join them with flat steel straps. If the floor joists are the same depth as the wood girder and you want them flush at the top and bottom, use proper joist hangers.

To attach the ledgers or blocking, drill holes for $\frac{1}{2}$-inch carriage bolts through the girder or I-beam every 48 inches, $1\frac{1}{2}$ inches up from the bottom. Drill the ledger boards with holes to match those you just drilled, and then position the ledger boards on both sides of the girder or I-beam. Insert bolts, washers, and nuts, and then use a socket wrench to tighten the bolts.

Floor Joists

The next step is to install the floor joists. But where exactly do you put them? Before placing the floor joists on the sill, you must mark the sill plate (and any girder or beam the joists will cross) with an X where joists will be. Floor joists are usually placed 16 inches on center, which means that the center-to-center measurement from one joist to the next is 16 inches. Note that your measuring tape has 16-inch demarcations in color (usually red) that you can use for laying out floor joists along your sill plates. Also note that 16-inch on-center framing allows the edge of 4 × 8-foot plywood or waferboard panels to fall on the center of every fourth floor joist. Because the first joist will have the panel flush to its outside, the distance from the first joist to the second one should be $15\frac{1}{4}$ inches on center.

When determining joist lengths, consult a span table like that on page 26, and then account for the thickness of a header joist—a board that's nailed into the end grain of floor joists. Header joists stabilize floor joists, provide a clean edge to which you can attach floor decking, and provide a continuous nailing surface for any sheathing that extends down over the foundation. Remember to account for the thickness of the header joists when you cut floor joists for length: subtract twice the thickness of the header from the end-to-end length of joists.

Installing Floor Joists

Difficulty Level:

Tools and Materials

- Basic carpentry tools
- Lumber
- Level
- Circular saw
- 8d and 16d nails

1 **Locate the joists.** Mark an X at the end of the sill plate to locate the first joists. Measure 15¼ inches and make a pencil

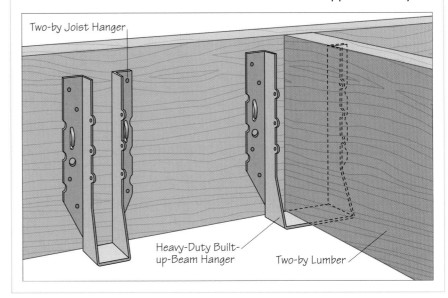

The Pros Know

CHOOSING THE RIGHT CONNECTOR

Never use a hanger for anything other than the framing member it was intended for. A built-up-beam hanger, for example, would be oversized and ineffective if it were used to support a two-by.

Two-by Joist Hanger

Heavy-Duty Built-up-Beam Hanger

Two-by Lumber

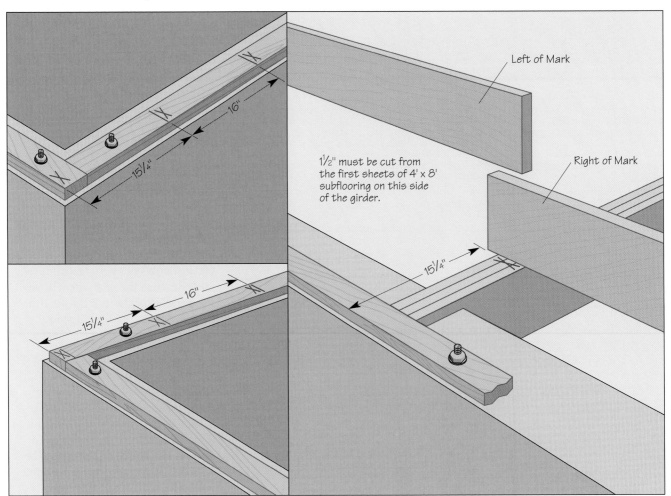

Left of Mark

Right of Mark

1½" must be cut from the first sheets of 4' x 8' subflooring on this side of the girder.

15¼"

16"

15¼"

16"

15¼"

15¼"

1 Mark the sill plates at 15¼ in. in from the edge and at 16-in. intervals thereafter. Place the joists to the left or right of the marks, depending on the wall on which they rest, and lap them over the girder.

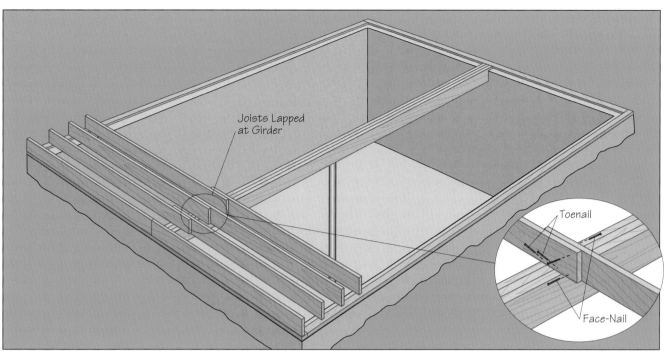

Joists Lapped at Girder

Toenail

Face-Nail

2 Where joists overlap and rest on girders, toenail them in place. Then face-nail the joists to each other with three 8d nails, two from one side and one from the other.

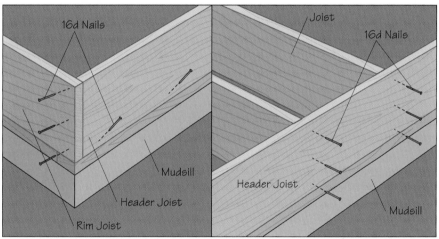

16d Nails

Mudsill

Header Joist

Rim Joist

Joist

16d Nails

Header Joist

Mudsill

3 Nail rim joists with three 16d nails at corners; toenail them to the sills along their lengths (left). End-nail floor joists to header joists using three 16d nails (right).

The Pros Know

TAPERING JOISTS

It's tempting to taper joists so they fit below low-pitched roofs. But tapering a joist too much weakens it. Never taper a joist more than one-half its depth. Also, the angle of the taper should extend a maximum of three times the joist depth.

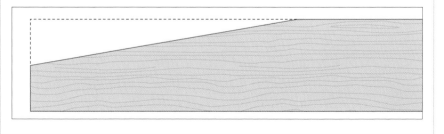

mark for the second joist. Using 16-inch distances, mark all the remaining joists. Go back to the marks and, using a combination square, draw a straight line at each mark. Then mark an X to the right of each line you've drawn to indicate where the joist will sit. If you'll lap the joists over the girder or I-beam, set the joists on one wall to the right of each mark and set the joists on the opposite wall to the left.

2 Install the joists. Rest the joists on edge above each X that you marked. Toenail each joist to the girder and sill using 16d nails. Where joists overlap a girder or beam, lap them at least 4 inches and face-nail them with three 8d nails, two from one side and one from the other.

3 Install the header joists. Mark the headers for joist positions as you did the sill plate. Place the header joists, and tack them at each end to the first and last joists. One by one, plumb each joist and end-nail the header joists to the floor joists using three 16d nails. Remove the tack nails, and plumb and nail home the first and last joists.

Blocking and Bridging

Because the joists are on edge, they are not as stable as if they were lying flat. It's essential to stabilize them by either bridging or blocking them. Bridging is a technique that uses $\frac{5}{4} \times 3$s (angled on both ends at 45 degrees) that form an X between joists. (You can also install prefabricated metal bridging.) You install bridging every 6 feet along the joist's length. Blocking employs the same stabilizing principle, except that you install blocks square between joists. Blocking is often used in small spaces where bridging isn't practical and over girders or beams.

Installing Bridging

Difficulty Level:

Tools and Materials

- Basic carpentry tools
- $\frac{5}{4} \times 3$ bridging lumber
- 8d nails

1 **Lay out the bridging.** Precut all the bridge pieces. To determine length, measure diagonally from the bottom edge of one joist to the top edge of the next one. Most joist spacing is consistent, so this dimension should work for almost all the bridging pieces. Cut parallel 45-degree angles at the ends of the bridging. Snap a chalk line across the joists as a guideline.

2 **Install the first bridging leg.** Working in one direction, install one leg of the bridging X all the way down the row of joists, alternating on either side of the chalk line. Drive nails only into the top of the bridging, leaving the bottom unnailed.

3 **Install the second bridging leg.** With one leg of the bridging installed, work back in the other direction, installing the second leg of the X. Nail the top end of the bridging to hold the pieces in place. Nail the bottom end of the bridging only after you've installed

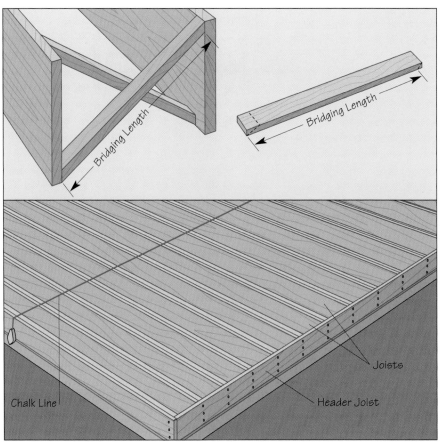

1 Snap a chalk line across joists as a guide to align bridging.

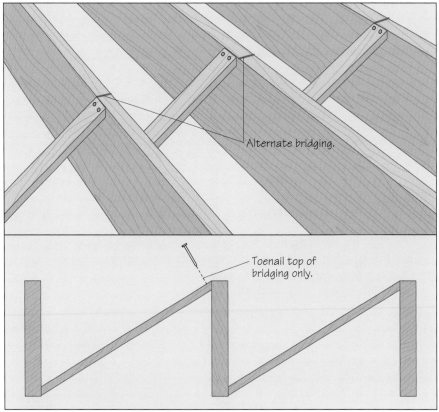

2 Install bridging by moving first in one direction across the floor's width. Nail only the top of the bridging until after decking is in place.

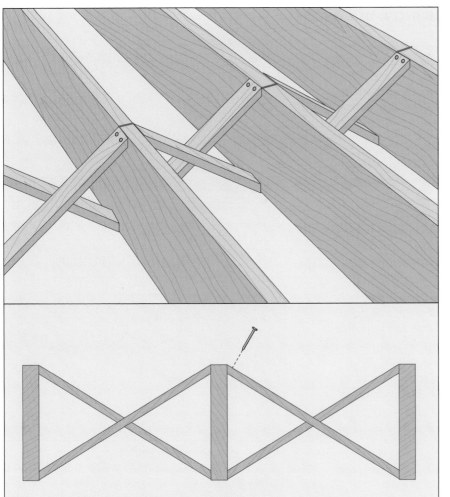

the subfloor on the joists. The sub-floor will hold the joists in place at a consistent elevation. If you nail the bridging into place, top and bottom, before the decking is on, you risk misaligning the joists, making for an uneven floor.

Installing Blocking

Difficulty Level: 🐾

Tools and Materials

- Basic carpentry tools
- Two-by blocking lumber (same dimensions as joists)
- 8d nails

1 Cut the blocking. Cut blocks out of the same type of lumber used for joists. (Use 2×10 blocks if the joists are 2×10, 2×12 blocks for 2×12 joists, and so on.) Measure between the joists exactly where you'll put the blocking, and cut the blocks so they fit snugly.

2 Install the blocks. Insert the blocks between joists. Stagger them 1½ inches over girders to make it easier to nail through the joists into the blocks' end grain.

3 Install bridging in the other direction. After decking is installed, drive home nails on the bottom of both sections of bridging.

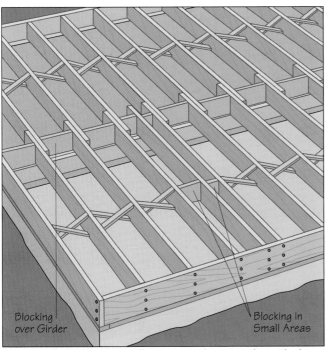

1 Install blocking in small spaces and over girders. Blocking should fit snugly.

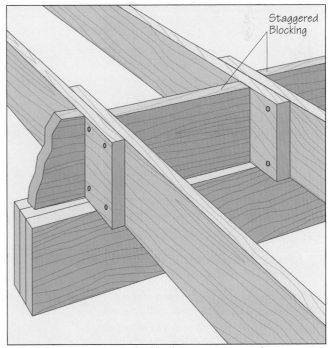

2 Alternately stagger the blocking 1½ in. to make it easier to nail into the end grain of the blocks.

ACCOMMODATING WIRING, PLUMBING & DUCTWORK

A piece of lumber's strength depends on its entire dimension, without any notches or holes made in it. The more holes and notches you put in the lumber, the weaker it becomes. During house construction, it's often necessary to drill or notch lumber to make room for running wires, heating ducts, and pipes through the walls. It's easy to do this the wrong way, by hacking at the wood wherever it's convenient. By following a few simple rules, however, you can safely notch and drill wood. When calculating the sizes of notches and holes, use actual, not nominal, dimensions.

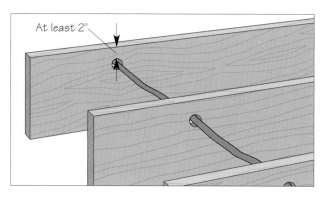

At least 2"

■ Try not to cut a hole in a joist closer than 2 inches to the edge. Doing so weakens the joist considerably and increases the risk of nicking wires, pipes, or ducts with fasteners screwed or nailed through the decking.

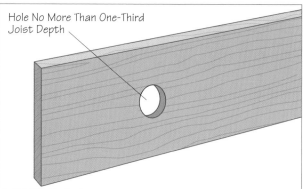

Hole No More Than One-Third Joist Depth

■ Never cut a hole bigger than one-third the depth of the joist. This weakens the joist too much because you're removing one-third of its strength at that particular point. If you're using 2x10 joists, make the maximum hole size 3 inches; for 2x12s, make it 3¾ inches.

■ Never make a notch in the middle third of a joist's length. This is where the loads really test the joist, at its mid-span, so avoid anything that would compromise its strength in this crucial section.

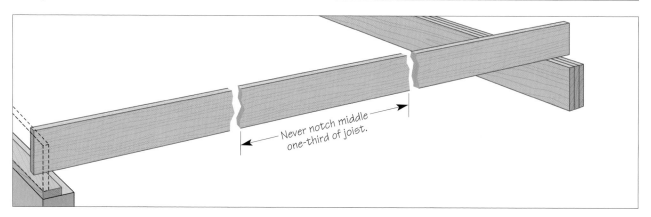

Never notch middle one-third of joist.

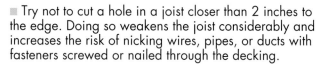

■ Notches in joists should be no deeper than one-sixth the joist's depth (one-quarter the depth near the end of the joist) and no longer than one-third the joist's depth. Cover notches with steel plates.

The rules listed above apply mostly to running wires or pipes. If you get into running ducts, zero-clearance chimney pipes, or items larger than one-third the depth of the joists, you'll likely either build a special chase or passageway for running these services or suspend them using metal straps.

Additionally, be aware that electricians and plumbers commonly over-drill and over-notch joists for running their wires and pipes. It may be your job to see that they are aware of the structural principles listed above.

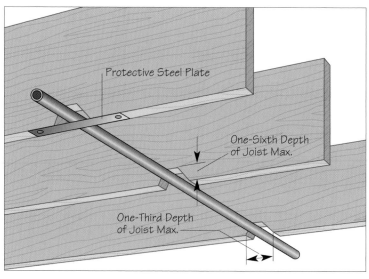

Protective Steel Plate

One-Sixth Depth of Joist Max.

One-Third Depth of Joist Max.

Rough Openings in Floor Joists

Most joist-framed floors have rough openings in them for such things as stairways or chimneys. Framing rough openings in floors follows a simple logic: the joists that define the rough opening—called trimmers if they run lengthwise and headers if they run perpendicular to floor joists—are usually doubled because they have to carry the load that would have been carried by the joists that were removed to create the rough opening. Doubling the trimmers and headers reinforces these extra-load-carrying joists.

Framing a Rough Opening

Difficulty Level:

Tools and Materials

- Basic carpentry tools
- Circular saw
- Level
- Two-by joist lumber
- 16d nails

1 Install the trimmer joists.
Measure the rough-opening dimensions on the plan, and cut the necessary lumber accordingly. Double up joists on both sides of the rough opening, but don't just scab the extra trimmer joists on. All trimmer joists should have bearing points on both ends. Face-nail the trimmers every 48 inches with three 16d nails.

2 Install the header joists.
Mark the header positions on inside trimmer joists at both ends of the rough opening. Install the headers by running a double thickness of joist lumber perpendicular to the floor joists. As you install the headers, check for square and to make sure you maintain the rough opening's required end-to-end inside-to-inside joist dimensions. Use joist hangers.

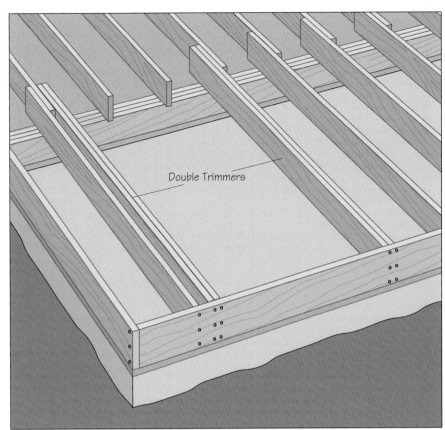

1 Rough openings in floors demand that trimmer joists be doubled and have two bearing points to carry extra loads.

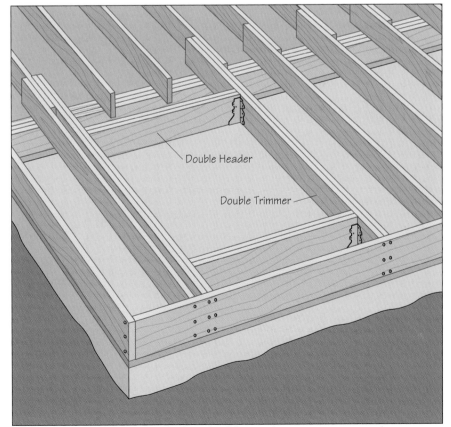

2 Install double headers at both ends of the rough opening using joist hangers.

3 **Install the tail joists.** Often you'll run shorter joists, called tail joists, from the headers to the rim joists and girder or beam. Space the tail joists according to the 16-inch-on-center spacing of the regular floor joists. Tail joists won't carry much of a load, but they're essential for spacing and for maintaining a consistent nailing surface for when decking goes down.

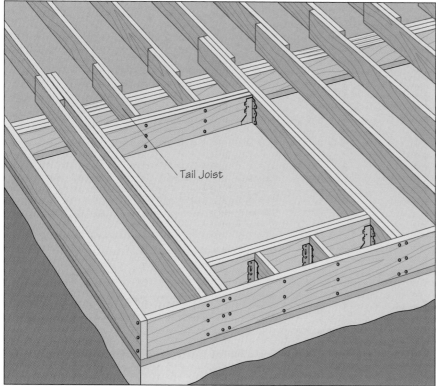

Tail Joist

3 Install short joists, called tail joists, between the double header and the rim joists or girder. Use joist hangers.

The Pros Know

TEMPORARILY HOLDING A BEAM IN PLACE

When nailing a cross piece of lumber without using a joist hanger, temporarily suspend it from bent nails at one end while you nail the other end.

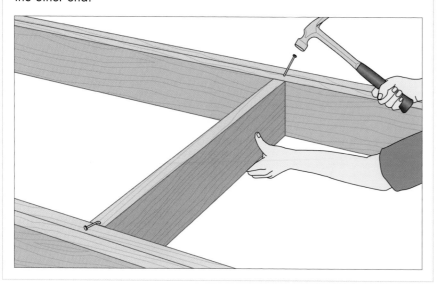

Cantilevered Joists

Cantilevered, or overhanging, joists can add an attractive design feature to any structure. There are two kinds of cantilevers: one that supports a load-bearing wall and one that creates a postless porch or deck that doesn't support a bearing wall. (See "Cantilevers," page 29.) These porches are often ideal for second-floor balconies, though many people use cantilevered full decks on first floors.

The time to build cantilevered decks or porches is during the installation of the building's main floor joists. If you try to create a postless porch hanging out in mid-air after you've framed and floored the house, it would not be structurally sound. You can't expect structural support from a ledger board that you've scabbed onto the side of a sheathed house.

Cantilever designs follow strict rules, because overhanging a cantilever too far can cause severe joist deflection or outright joist failure. The unsupported overhanging length of a joist should be about one-third the length of the overall joist, and the remaining length should extend back into and be tied to the main building's structure. If you cantilever out 3 feet, for example, the joists for the cantilever should be at least 9 feet long, extending 6 feet (minimum) back into the building. If you're expecting to support extraordinary loads, like a hot tub or frequent large groups of people for barbecues, use the more conservative "one-quarter rule" mentioned on page 31: extend the joists no more than one-quarter their overall length, with three-quarters extending into the building.

There are two common cantilever designs: one in which the cantilevered joists run perpendicular to the floor joists and another in which the cantilevered joists are an extension of the floor joists. The same principle of overhang distance applies to both cases.

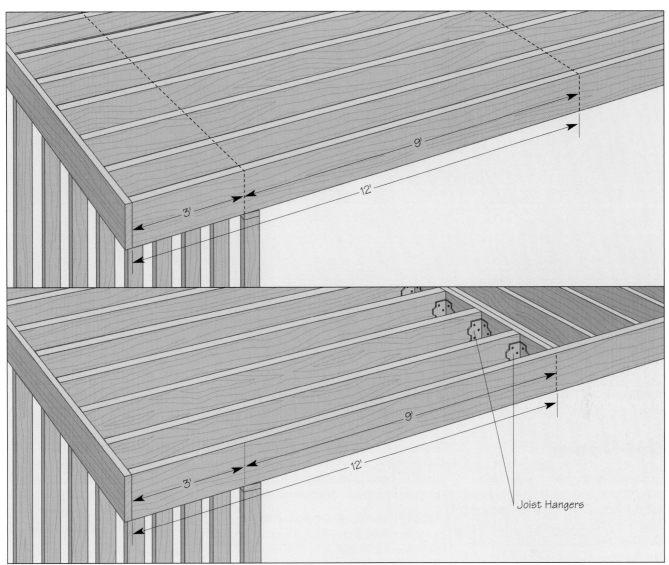

Cantilevered Joists. Cantilevers may be extensions of floor joists (top) or perpendicular to them (above). For every 12 in. a heavily loaded cantilever overhangs, 36 in. should extend back into the building.

Load-Bearing Cantilevers.

Load-bearing cantilevers are entirely different from porch cantilevers. An example of a load-bearing cantilever would be a bearing wall that rests on a joist jutting out from a building. The laws of structural design severely restrict the length of a cantilever that supports a load-bearing wall: the cantilever can extend no more than the depth of the joist it rests on. If you're framing with 2×12 joists, for example, then the cantilever supporting a load-bearing wall can be no longer than 11¼ inches to the outside edge of the joist. If you cantilever any more than that, you risk shearing off, crushing, or bending the joists.

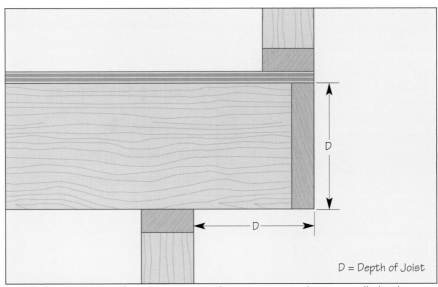

Load-Bearing Cantilevers. For a cantilever to support a bearing wall, the distance it extends beyond its supporting wall must not exceed the depth of the joists.

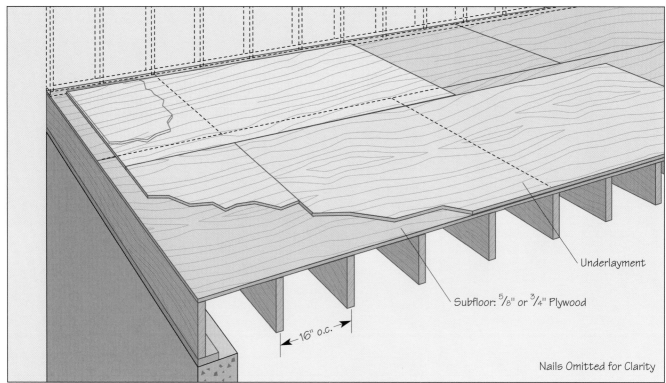

Underlayment

Subfloor: $\frac{5}{8}$" or $\frac{3}{4}$" Plywood

16" o.c.

Nails Omitted for Clarity

Subfloors. Subfloors, which sit on joists, are made of plywood or other panel products. Subflooring offers structural support to underlayment and/or finished flooring like vinyl, ceramic tile, and wood flooring.

Subfloors

With the floor joists in place, it's time to put down floor decking, or subflooring. The subflooring forms a base for floor coverings like carpet or wood boards or planks. For finish flooring like tile or vinyl, you'll need to add another layer of panel material (called underlayment) on top of the subfloor. Of course, you could leave the subflooring as the finished floor if you're going to use the room as a workshop.

Use $\frac{5}{8}$- or $\frac{3}{4}$-inch tongue-and-groove plywood for subfloors. Install the thinner plywood if you're going to use an underlayment for finished flooring; install the thicker material if you're planning to lay carpet or install wood floors. Use $\frac{3}{4}$- to 1-inch plywood if you're leaving the subflooring as the finished floor. Choose lumber-core plywood for floor decking, since much of the nailing is along the edges.

Other panel materials you can use as subflooring include waferboard and oriented-strand board (OSB).

Note, however, that building codes allow these materials only when they've been manufactured using an exterior-grade phenolic resin.

Panel products are labeled with a stamp from the APA—The Engineered Wood Association. (See "Rating Panel Products," page 19.) Check the stamp to see whether the APA approves the plywood or other material for subflooring, and check the allowable span (also on the stamp) to make sure you can install the panels over your joist spacing.

Installing Subflooring

Difficulty Level: 🔨

Tools and Materials

- Basic carpentry tools
- Circular saw
- Plywood suitable for your subfloor
- Tubes of construction adhesive
- Caulking gun
- 8d or 6d ring-shank nails or 2-in. deck screws and drill

1 Apply adhesive. Use a caulking gun to apply a bead of construction adhesive to the tops of all joists. Adhesive creates a good bond between joists and plywood and cuts down on squeaky floors.

2 Lay the plywood. Because plywood expands and contracts, leave a $\frac{1}{16}$-inch gap between end joints and a $\frac{1}{8}$-inch space between edge joints. If you use nails, choose 6d ring-shank nails for material up to $\frac{7}{8}$ inch thick and 8d nails for heavier panels. If you'd rather screw down the plywood, use 2-inch deck screws. Always stagger panel edges so seams don't line up across the width or length of the floor. Start the first row of plywood with a full panel, and then start the second row with a half panel.

3 Fasten the plywood. Nail or screw the subflooring every 12 inches along the edges and in the field of the plywood. If you choose not to use adhesive, nail or screw every 6 inches along the outside edges and 10 inches along the panel's interior.

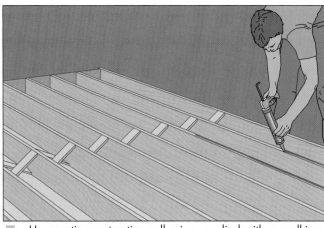

1 Use mastic construction adhesive, applied with a caulking gun, to bond subfloors to joists.

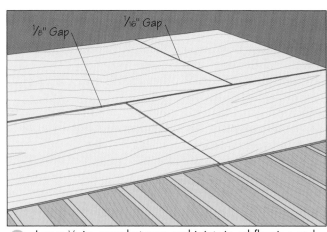

2 Leave ¹⁄₁₆-in. gaps between end joints in subflooring and ¹⁄₈-in. gaps between edge joints, staggering the seams.

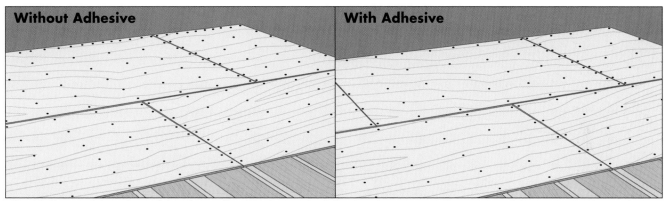

Without Adhesive   **With Adhesive**

3 Nail around the edges of the plywood and in the interior following the proper nailing pattern: 6 in. on center along edges and 10 in. in the interior for panels without adhesive; 12 in. everywhere with adhesive.

Avoiding Springy Floors

Springy floors are almost always the result of undersized joists. If you find that the floor seems to flex when you walk across it, chances are you misread the joist span table and either used joists that aren't deep enough (say, 2×10s instead of 2×12s) or spanned too great a distance with the joists. This problem is difficult to correct after the fact, so be sure to size joists properly.

Avoiding Spongy Floors

Spongy floors are generally the result of inadequate attachment of the plywood subfloor to the joists. Small gaps between the joists and the underside of the subfloor will give you a spongy feeling when you walk across the decking. To avoid this problem, carefully follow fastening schedules and use adhesive. If the floor feels spongy anyway, it may be because of slightly warped plywood or joists. Go back and install more nails or screws until the decking feels secure.

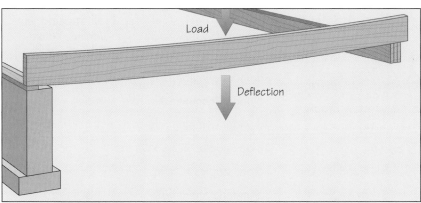

Avoiding Springy Floors. Floors that are springy may be framed with joists that are undersized and are deflecting under the load. Bridging helps in avoiding deflection by distributing loads to adjoining joists.

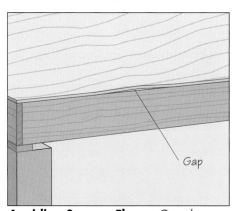

Avoiding Spongy Floors. Gaps between joists and the underside of subflooring can make a floor feel spongy.

Underlayment

Though some builders use the words "subflooring" and "underlayment" interchangeably, they are not the same. Subflooring is the structural panel material you lay down on floor joists. Underlayment is a thin panel material you install on top of subflooring to provide a smooth, durable surface on which to put a finished floor like sheet vinyl.

Underlayment must be stable, water resistant, and free of defects. Vinyl flooring, for example, will show up even small underlayment defects like raised grain, splits, or knotholes. And if the underlayment is not water resistant, it may absorb spilled water or other liquids and swell. Tile adhesive and ceramic-tile grout will quickly fail with water-swollen underlayment, and vinyl or ceramic tiles will come loose.

Types of Underlayment

There is a variety of underlayment materials available, including hardboard, particleboard, OSB, and plywood. Of these various underlayments, every type except plywood has exhibited failure in one or more applications. Hardboard and particleboard, for example, expand when moist, and the APA has not approved all OSB as underlayment.

You can use APA-approved plywood underlayment beneath carpet, ceramic tile, vinyl, and wood flooring. Be sure the APA stamp says "underlayment" or "plugged cross bands," and be sure the exposure rating on the stamp is either "Exposure 1" or "Exterior." Those ratings indicate that the plywood is glued with a water-resistant phenolic resin and can withstand exposure to moisture. Be sure the underlayment has a "fully sanded" face (not "plugged and touch-sanded"), and install the better face up.

Installing Underlayment

Difficulty Level:

Tools and Materials

- Basic carpentry tools
- Circular saw
- 3d or 4d nails
- Plywood underlayment

Lay the plywood underlayment panels with the long edges perpendicular to the floor joists, and stagger the underlayment seams at least 2 inches with the subflooring seams. Also, because you staple or nail underlayment to the subfloor, it's not necessary—or even desirable—for underlayment end joints to land directly on joists. Establish a gap between panel edges of just $\frac{1}{32}$ inch. Nailing schedules vary, depending on the underlayment thickness and subfloor type, so match up your conditions with those in "Recommended Underlayment Nailing Schedule."

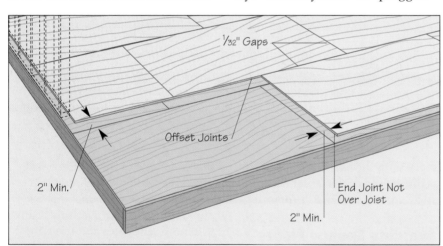

Installing Underlayment. Install APA-approved plywood underlayment over subflooring. Leave $\frac{1}{32}$-inch gaps at the edges, and don't align seams with subfloor seams or with joists.

RECOMMENDED UNDERLAYMENT NAILING SCHEDULE

Underlayment	Subfloor	Underlayment Thickness (in.)	Fastener (positioned $\frac{1}{2}$ in. from panel edges)	Nail Spacing (in.) Along Edges	Within Field
Plywood	Plywood ($\frac{1}{2}$ in. or thicker)	$\frac{1}{4}$	3d underlayment nails	3	6
Plywood	Plywood ($\frac{1}{2}$ in. or thicker)	$\frac{1}{8}$ to $\frac{1}{2}$	3d underlayment nails	6	8
Plywood	Plywood ($\frac{1}{2}$ in. or thicker)	$\frac{5}{8}$ to $\frac{3}{4}$	4d underlayment nails	6	8
Plywood	Plywood ($\frac{1}{2}$ in. or thicker)	$\frac{1}{4}$	18-ga. staples x $\frac{3}{16}$ x $\frac{7}{8}$ in.	3	6
Plywood	Plywood ($\frac{1}{2}$ in. or thicker)	$\frac{3}{8}$ and thicker	16-ga. staples x $\frac{3}{8}$ in.	3	6
Plywood	Boards up to 4 in. wide	$\frac{1}{4}$	3d underlayment nails	3	6
Plywood	Boards 4 in. wide and wider	$\frac{3}{8}$	3d underlayment nails	6	8

Walls & Partitions

O nce you begin framing the walls you will begin to feel as though you are making real progress on your project. It is probably the most gratifying and enjoyable part of building a house or addition because you see the building and individual rooms begin to take shape. Wall framing is relatively easy to do with simple, straightforward carpentry tasks. Perhaps the most important thing to keep in mind when erecting walls is that errors left uncorrected at this stage of building will turn into hard-to-fix problems later on. If a wall is not plumb or if the room you frame is not square, for example, not only do the building's load paths change slightly but the dimensions change, too. Sheet goods that you apply to the wall inside or outside—drywall or sheathing—may need time-consuming trimming and may have unsightly, hard-to-hide joints and corners.

In this chapter you will find explanations of the components you'll need to build various types of walls, as well as proven strategies for laying out walls, erecting them, and checking them to make sure they're square and plumb—limiting possible problems down the line.

Wall Framing

Modern "stick" framing takes one of two forms: balloon framing or platform framing. Balloon framing, a predecessor to platform framing, was widely used in the nineteenth century after the development of mass-produced lumber. The method was innovative for its time. It enabled people to build structures out of "sticks" (2×4s and 2×6s) rather than heavy posts and beams. The exterior-wall studs in balloon framing run in one piece from the mudsills to the rafter plate.

These days, the vast majority of houses are platform framed be-cause balloon framing requires extra-long 2×4s or 2×6s. Though these longer pieces of lumber are available, they are often a special order, and the quality is inconsistent. Platform framing is also easier when building multistory structures because, as the name implies, you work from framed platforms for each story. Platform framing breaks the framing job into discrete components, which are easier to work on than a whole building at once. Though we will cover balloon framing only briefly, many of the wall-building and wall-raising techniques used in platform framing apply to balloon-framed houses.

2x4s vs. 2x6s

Most load-bearing interior and exterior walls are framed with 2×4s or 2×6s, depending on structural and insulation demands. Because 2×6s are larger than 2×4s, they are stronger, so a 2×6 wall is structurally stronger than a 2×4 wall. These days, builders are increasingly using 2×6s, which may be framed 24 inches on center, as opposed to 2×4s, which must be framed 16 inches on center.

Besides the structural advantage 2×6-framed walls offer, the wider studs provide more space for insulation. An insulated 2×4 wall can have an insulating value of between

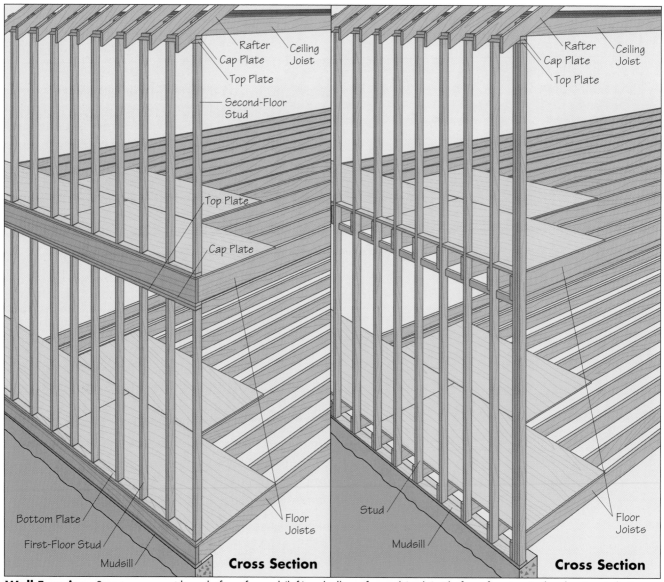

Wall Framing. Structures are either platform framed (left) or balloon framed (right). Platform framing is the dominant design strategy used today.

R-13 and R-15. The "R" stands for resistance to heat flow; walls with a higher R-value are more energy efficient. An insulated 2×6 wall can have an insulating value of between R-19 and R-21.

Clearly 2×6 walls offer advantages over 2×4 walls in spaces that need to be well insulated and structurally sound, like the walls of your house, addition, or dormer. The 2×6s cost only marginally more, and for the performance you get, the extra expense is worth it. If you're building a shed or a garage, however, 2×4 walls framed 16 inches on center will do fine. Of course, you'll have to follow your blueprints. If you want to upgrade to 2×6 construction on any project, make sure your architect or designer knows before you get the final approved set.

Wall Studs. Before you can lay out a wall for framing, you must know how walls are constructed. All walls have a bottom, or sole, plate, a top plate (doubled in bearing walls), and vertical members called studs. There are three kinds of studs: king studs, trimmer studs, and cripple studs. Trimmer and cripple studs are sometimes called jack studs. King studs run from the bottom plate all the way to the top plate. Trimmer studs run from the bottom plate to the underside of a header. Cripple studs run from the bottom plate to the underside of a rough opening's sill or from the top of a header to the top plate, filling in between the top and bottom of any rough frame.

Laying Out Plates

Difficulty Level:

Tools and Materials

- Basic carpentry tools
- Circular saw
- Level
- Framing square
- Two-by framing lumber
- 16d nails

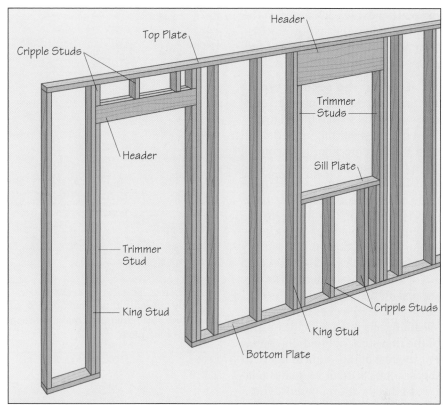

Wall Studs. King studs run between the top and bottom plate. Headers support the wall load above windows and doors. Trimmer studs support headers, and cripple studs run from the underside of sills to the bottom plate or from the top of the header to the top plate.

1 Mark the plate ends. You'll lay out and assemble the first stud wall on the floor, and then raise it into position. Start by choosing two lengths of two-by lumber to form the top and bottom plates. Lay

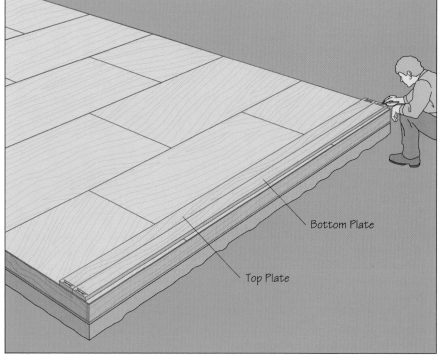

1 Lay the top and bottom plates on the subfloor, and mark the positions of the end studs.

the plates next to each other on the subfloor. Begin the layout process by marking an X at the ends of the plates for the first king studs.

2 Lay out the second wall stud.

You must position exterior wall studs so that the edge of the 4x8-foot sheathing material falls on a stud's centerline. To accomplish this, place the second wall stud 15¼ inches from the end of the plate for 16-inch-on-center framing (2×4s or 2×6s) or 23¼ inches from the end of the plate for 24-inch-on-center framing (2×6s). This is the stud from which you'll make your 16- or 24-inch-on-center marks for the rest of the wall. You set the stud at 15¼ (or 23¼) inches because the sheathing sits flush with the outside of the first stud, not with its center. For the rest of the studs to fall with their centers at 16 or 24 inches relative to the sheathing panels, you must subtract one-half the width of a stud, or ¾ inch, from this first layout dimension. Sometimes this stud spacing works out for sheet goods (drywall, paneling) applied to the inside of the framed wall; more often you'll have to trim the edge of your first piece so that it breaks across the center of the stud. Bury the trimmed edge in the corner, and put the factory edge on the outside stud.

3 Lay out the remaining studs.

Make a small vertical mark, with an X to the right of it, along the remaining lengths of both plates where king studs will occur, every 16 or 24 inches on center from the second stud marked in Step 2. Mark a T on just the bottom plate where trimmer studs will fall. Mark a C where cripple studs will occur. Set cripple studs to maintain the 16- or 24-inch-on-center spacing wherever king studs are missing. Mark an H on the top plate where you'll put the headers. After you've marked all the stud positions, go back and square up your tick marks using a combination square, and then draw a full line across the width of the plates.

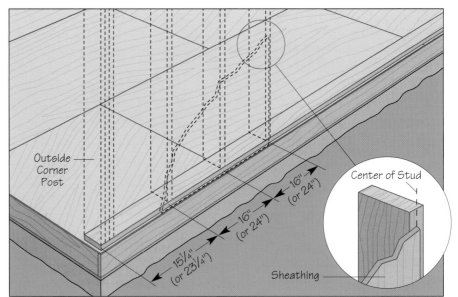

2 Lay out studs to accommodate 4 x 8-ft. sheet goods so that they break at mid stud. This requires locating the second stud at either 15¼ or 23¼ inches in from the end of the plate.

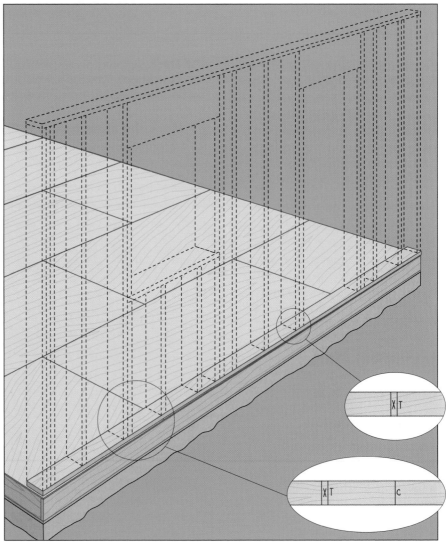

3 Mark an X where king studs sit, a T where trimmer studs sit, and a C where cripples sit.

QUICK-SET FRAMING

The Pros Know

For laying out long walls without a lot of openings—or even setting trusses—make this jig to do the job without having to measure every time. Lay out $1\frac{1}{2} \times 1\frac{5}{8}$-inch notches on two long 2x4s at 16 or 24 inches on center. Set the jigs 5 or 6 feet apart, and insert framing members into the notches, all ready to be nailed up.

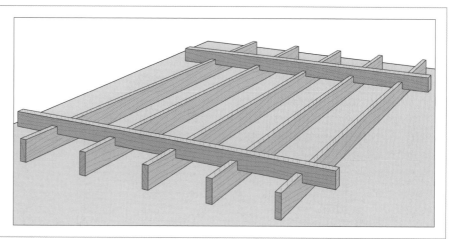

Stud Configuration for Corners

There are two types of corners you will frame: inside corners and outside corners. Inside corners occur where interior walls, or partitions, butt into another stud wall. Outside corners are the corners of walls. Both corner configurations use nonload-bearing studs or blocking, spaced blocks that simply provide backing.

Marking Plates for Inside Corners

Inside wall corners use triple studs or blocking and two studs. The blocking takes the place of the center stud. The two outer studs provide extra support and a nailing surface for sheet materials.

Whether you're using 2×4s or 2×6s to frame the exterior walls, use a 2×4 as the middle stud or the blocking for the interior partition's first stud when you make an inside corner. In most cases interior partitions are framed using 2×4s, except walls that will contain plumbing drainpipes, which may be framed using 2×6s.

1 Locate the interior wall. Determine where the interior partition wall will butt into the exterior stud wall, and mark the plates where the center of the partition wall will occur.

2 Mark the blocking. The mark you made for the center of the partition wall will be the

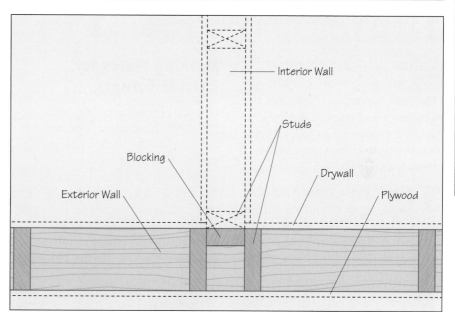

Marking Plates for Inside Corners. Plan view of a typical partition wall corner shows that sheet goods on all walls have a nailing surface.

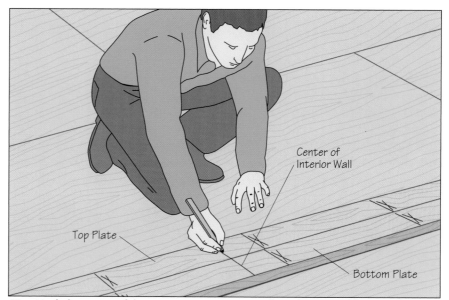

1 Mark the center of the intersecting partition wall on the top and bottom plates.

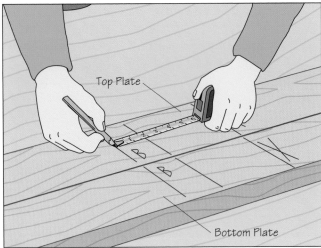

2 Measure the plates for the blocking.

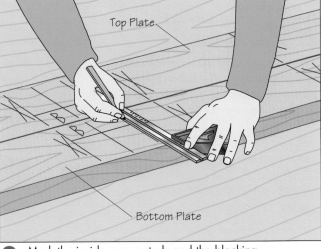

3 Mark the inside-corner studs and the blocking.

center of an inside-wall corner block. Measure from each side of this mark 1¾ inches (2¾ inches if, for some reason, you'll use 2×6s on the interior wall as well). Then make two short lines, and label the space B for block.

3 **Mark the studs.** Mark the locations of the inside-corner studs. Measure 1½ inches along the lines defining the B space, and connect the lines.

Marking Plates for Outside Corners

Outside corners are a combination of two stud configurations, one for each wall of the corner. On one wall you'll simply end the frame with a single stud. On the connecting wall (for 2×4 walls) you may use three studs, stacked face to face to face. The interior stud may comprise three blocks instead of a full stud. For 2×6 walls you can use blocking

as shown in the drawing below, left. There are two alternative configurations you may want to use. One uses three studs in the pattern shown in the drawing below, middle. The other uses one stud in each wall and metal drywall stops on the stud nearest the corner (drawing below, right). This configuration allows you to run insulation almost to the end of each exterior wall. The latter two designs are not as strong as the conventional corner, however.

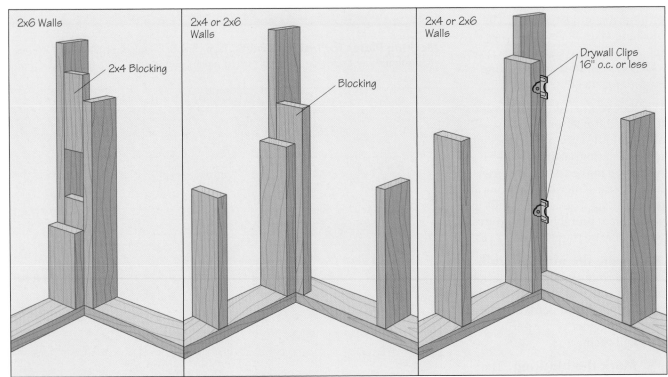

Marking Plates for Outside Corners. Outside corners may be made of four studs (or three studs and blocking, at left), three studs (middle), or two studs and drywall clips (right).

MARKING FOR STUDS

When you need to mark the position of a stud, you can use a framing square. The tongue of the square is $1\frac{1}{2}$ inches wide, the same width as a 2x6 or 2x4 stud.

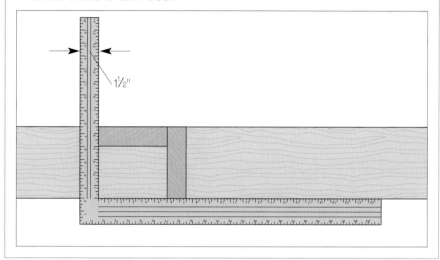

$1\frac{1}{2}''$

NAILING CORNERS

When you nail corners together, use five 16d nails. Start about 6 inches up from the bottom and down from the top, and then drive the remaining three nails evenly spaced between the first two.

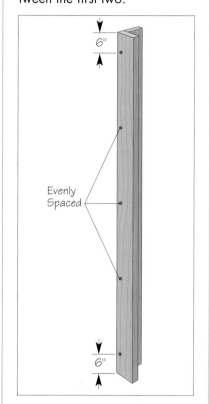

6"

Evenly Spaced

6"

1 **Lay out the first wall.**
Draw a line for the first stud at the end of the plates, measuring in from the end $1\frac{1}{2}$ inches. Then mark for a stud perpendicular to that stud on the interior of the wall. This is usually the first exterior wall you lay out, with the first full wall stud being $15\frac{1}{4}$ (or $23\frac{1}{4}$) inches from the end. (See "Laying Out Plates," Step 2, page 96.)

2 **Lay out the second wall.**
On the single-stud wall, draw a line $1\frac{1}{2}$ inches in from the end of the plates, and mark an X for a single end stud. Mark the second wall stud $11\frac{1}{4}$ inches from the end for a 2×4 wall and $9\frac{1}{4}$ (or $17\frac{1}{4}$) inches from the end for a 2×6 wall to account for the width of the adjoining wall studs plus the sheathing thickness of $\frac{1}{2}$ inch.

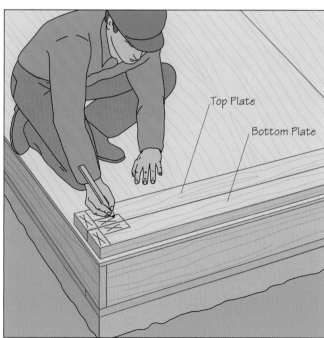

Top Plate

Bottom Plate

1 Lay out one wall with perpendicular studs. You can also use four studs or two studs and panel clips for the corner.

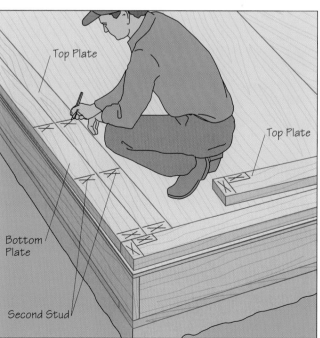

Top Plate

Top Plate

Bottom Plate

Second Stud

2 Lay out the other wall for one end stud. Set the second stud to accommodate the width of a stud and the sheathing thickness.

Rough Openings

Stud placement is crucial for rough openings, which are the spaces in walls where you insert doors and windows. You should take care to keep rough openings only about ½ inch to ¾ inch wider than the unit width to allow for plumb and level adjustments. Excessive shimming is not only troublesome and time consuming, but it may weaken the connection between the studs and the window or door frame. When you nail through the window or door jambs, for instance, the nail should penetrate a trimmer stud. If the nail only picks up shimming materials, the window or door may not be properly attached. You'll most likely be installing windows and doors with jambs already attached. The paperwork accompanying the units will indicate the rough-opening size. Be sure you match these sizes carefully.

Marking Plates for Window Rough Openings

1 Lay out the trimmer studs. Determine the centerline of the rough opening, and mark it on the bottom plate. Measure one-half the rough-opening width to each side of the centerline to define the outside edges of the rough opening, and mark the bottom plate with a T for trimmer studs. Double-check your measurements. The inside-to-inside distance of the trimmer studs should equal the width of the rough opening. If there are no king studs already positioned next to the trimmer studs, mark them to the outside of the trimmers.

2 Lay out the cripple studs. Cripple studs run from the bottom plate to the underside of the rough sill. Using 16- or 24-inch-on-

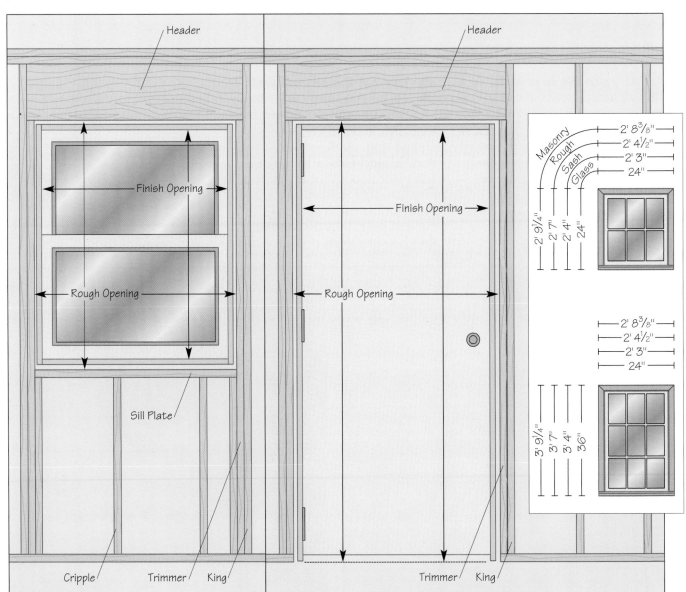

Rough Openings. The rough openings for a window and a door are similar, except for the bottom sill and cripple studs. Make the opening as accurate as possible. Manufacturer specs give you appropriate dimensions. (Specs courtesy of Rolscreen Co.)

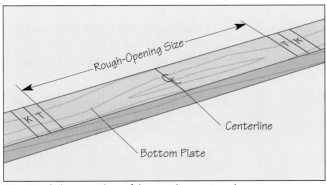

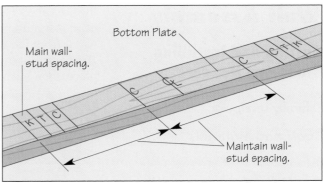

1 Mark the centerline of the rough opening; then measure one-half the opening size to each side to locate the trimmer studs.

2 Mark the center cripple stud on the bottom plate; then measure from the king studs for any remaining cripple studs.

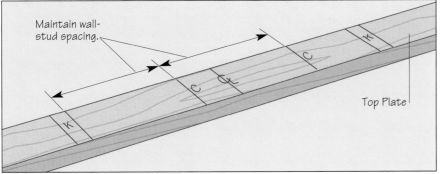

3 Mark the top plate for cripple studs that correspond with the bottom cripples or with an H for the header location.

center spacing (depending on the stud size and wall design), mark Cs for any cripple studs that will sit beneath the rough sill, measuring from the wall's main king studs to maintain consistent on-center spacing for the studs. Be sure there's at least one cripple stud in addition to the support on each side of the rough sill (provided by trimmer or cripple studs).

3 **Mark the top plate.** The top plate above a window will have marks only for king studs and the header or any cripples that run from the top of the header to the underside of the top plate. It will not necessarily have marks for trimmer studs. Mark the king studs that correspond to the king-stud marks on the bottom plate. If the header runs from the top of the rough opening to the underside of the top plate, just mark an H for it.

If the header is narrow and needs cripple studs for support, mark the studs that correspond to the cripples on the bottom plate.

Marking Plates for Door Rough Openings

1 **Mark the bottom plate.** Determine the center of the rough opening for the door you

plan to install, and mark it on the bottom plate. Measure one-half the opening to each side of the centerline, and make marks. Mark for two 1½-inch spaces on each side to the outside of this rough-opening dimension: one for the trimmer stud and one for the king stud.

2 **Mark the top plate.** Mark top plates above door rough openings for king studs and a header. A header above a door often fills up all the space between the top of the door jamb and the top plate, so you won't always be installing cripples here. If cripples are necessary, however, mark them now. Measure 16 or 24 inches on center from the nearest main wall studs.

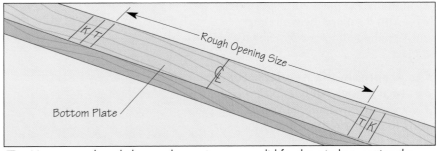

1 Measure and mark the rough opening as you did for the window, setting the trimmer- and king-stud locations.

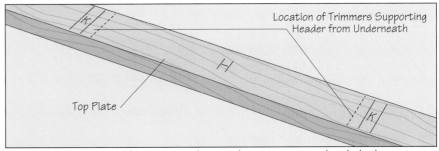

2 Mark the king-stud locations on the top plate to correspond with the bottom plate, and mark the header or cripple-stud locations.

8

WALLS & PARTITIONS

Wall Assembly

Cutting and Installing Studs and Headers

Difficulty Level:

Tools and Materials

- Basic carpentry tools
- 2x4s or 2x6s
- Two-by lumber for header stock
- ½-in. plywood
- 8d nails

1 Cut and attach the main wall studs. With the top and bottom plates marked for all the wall studs and rough openings, it's time to cut the studs. A power miter box makes this job go quickly. King studs will be full length—91½ inches plus an inch or so for 8-foot ceilings. Trimmer studs will be king-stud length minus the combined height of the header and cripples above. You can cut the cripples and sills to length after you put the trimmers and headers in place.

Separate the plates, and insert the king studs at the ends of the plates and along the wall as marked. Nail through the top plate with two 16d nails. You'll square the walls after you've nailed all the wall members in place.

2 Assemble the headers. For each header, cut two 2×12s or whatever two-by material you're using to fill in the space above the window or door. (See "Headers," page 29.) Use this two-by material as a guide to mark a piece of ½-inch plywood to size. Cut the plywood; sandwich it between the two pieces of two-by material (for a 2×4 wall); and nail the assembly with six to 12 12d nails spaced 12 to 16 inches apart. For a 2×6 wall, assemble the header with 2½-inch blocking to be the same width as the wall.

3 Complete the rough openings. For each door or window rough opening, insert the header in the area above the opening. The header should be snug and square; nail it from the top and sides with 16d nails. Put the trimmer studs in place; then measure and cut any cripple studs and sills. Mark the position of the sills on the trimmer studs and the position of the cripple studs on the underside of the sills. Remove the trimmers, and lay

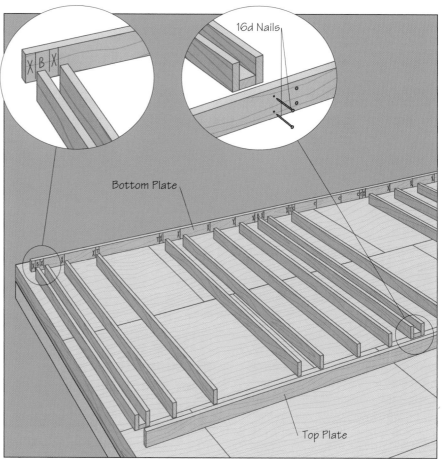

1 Cut the king studs to length; place them in position between the plates; and nail them with two 16d nails at the top and two at the bottom.

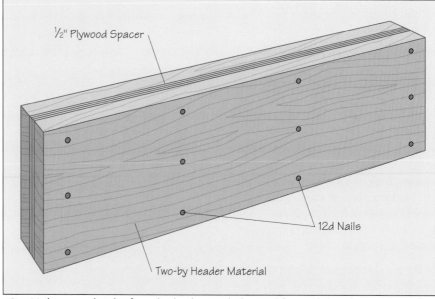

2 Make a sandwich of two-by lumber and plywood for each header, and nail the pieces together with 12d nails.

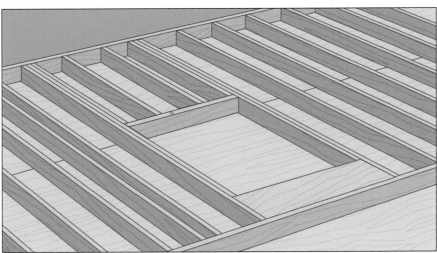

3 Assemble each window and door rough opening with 16d nails.

them on the floor. Drive 16d nails through the trimmers into the sills and through the sills into the cripples; then insert the completed assembly into the rough opening. Attach the bottom plate to the cripples and trimmers with 16d nails, and then nail the trimmers to the king studs with 8d nails.

FIRE BLOCKING

Most building codes require fire blocking—two-by stud material that runs horizontally from stud to stud—every 10 feet measured vertically in stud bays, the spaces between the studs. Fire blocking interrupts the upward flow of flames and heat. If there were no blocking and a fire started in the basement walls, it could easily and quickly reach the roof and consume the house in flames by following the unobstructed chimney-like path of the stud bays.

If you're framing typical 8-foot walls, the first-floor top plate will serve as fire blocking for the first 10 feet and the second-floor top plate for the next 10 feet. If you're building walls that extend 10 feet or more vertically without blocking of some sort, however, you must install fire blocking.

Squaring and Bracing Walls

You need to check all walls to make sure they're square before you stand them in place. If you're using structural sheathing, install 1×4 diagonal braces across the face of the wall to stiffen it and keep it square.

Tools and Materials

- Basic carpentry tools
- 50-ft. measuring tape
- Circular saw
- Sharp chisel
- 1x4 lumber

1 Measure diagonals. With the stud wall lying flat on the subfloor, measure the wall diagonally from the one end's top corner to the other end's bottom corner. Write down the measurement. Measure the same wall from the first end's bottom corner to the other end's top corner. Write down this measurement, as well. Compare the two measurements. If they don't match exactly, the wall is not square.

2 Square up the wall. To square the wall, tack two cleats to an end wall stud and tack one to the floor so you can push on the

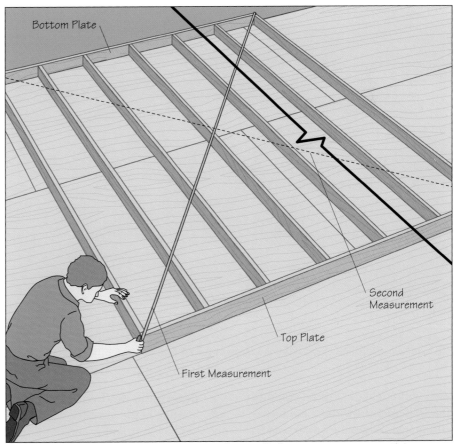

Bottom Plate

Second Measurement

Top Plate

First Measurement

1 Check walls for square by measuring diagonally from corner to corner. If the measurements match, the wall is square.

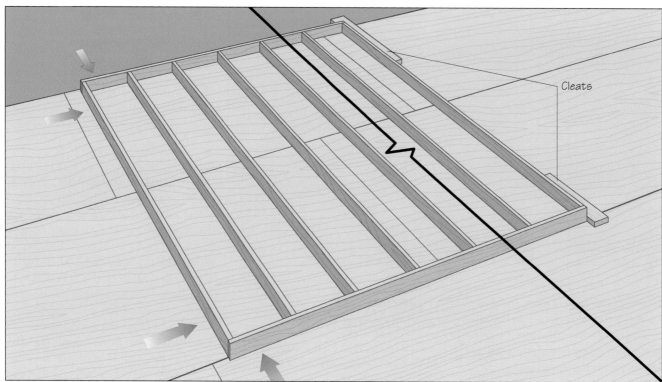

Cleats

2 Tack the framed wall to cleats, and then nail the cleats to the subfloor after you've squared up the wall.

1x4 Brace

3 Snap a chalk line to position one edge of a 1x4 brace. Lay the brace in place along the line, and mark the other side with a pencil.

wall without sliding it. As you push the wall, retake the diagonal measurements. When they match, tack the other cleat to the floor to hold the wall square.

3 Determine the brace length. Starting at the top or bottom one stud bay in from the end of the wall, measure diagonally along a line that is no longer than the wall is tall.

If the wall is 96 inches tall, for example, the brace need be no more than 96 inches long. Make pencil marks at both ends of the line, and then snap a chalk line between these two and cut along the chalk and pencil lines. Make multiple passes between the two saw cuts; then chisel out the remainder to make a path for the 1×4. Lay the 1×4 in place, and nail it with two 8d nails at each stud.

Erecting Walls

Difficulty Level: 🦇🦇 manpower intensive

Tools and Materials

- Basic carpentry tools
- 16d nails
- Completed, squared wall
- Long 2x4s for bracing
- Cleats to nail into the subfloor and headers
- 48-inch level

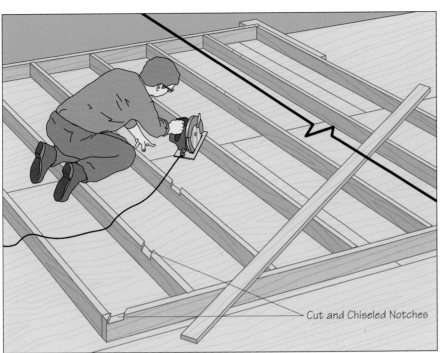

Cut and Chiseled Notches

4 Cut along the lines with a circular saw, and chisel out enough wood so the brace's face sits flush with the face of the wall.

points. Use the chalk line to position a 1×4. With one edge of the 1×4 lined up with the line, draw a pencil mark along the other edge. Also,

cut the angle the top and bottom plates make on the 1×4.

4 **Install the brace.** Set your circular saw depth to ¾ inch,

1 **Position the wall.** Before erecting any wall, snap a chalk line along the subfloor to establish a reference guide for positioning the inside edge of the wall's bottom plate, and nail cleats to the rim joist.

 8

WALLS & PARTITIONS

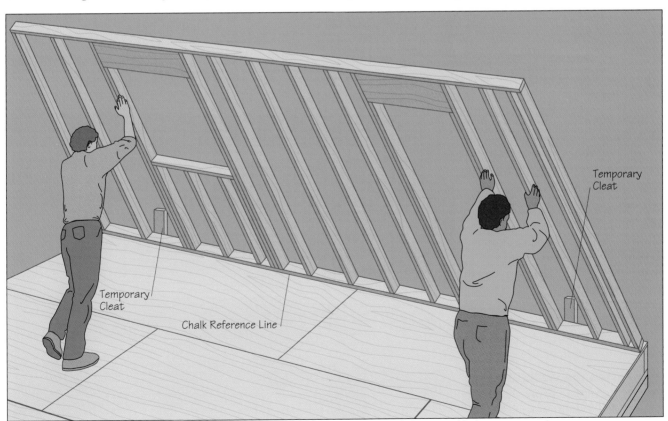

Temporary Cleat

Temporary Cleat

Temporary Cleat

Chalk Reference Line

1 Snap a chalk line as a reference for the inside face of the wall, and stand the assembled structure in place.

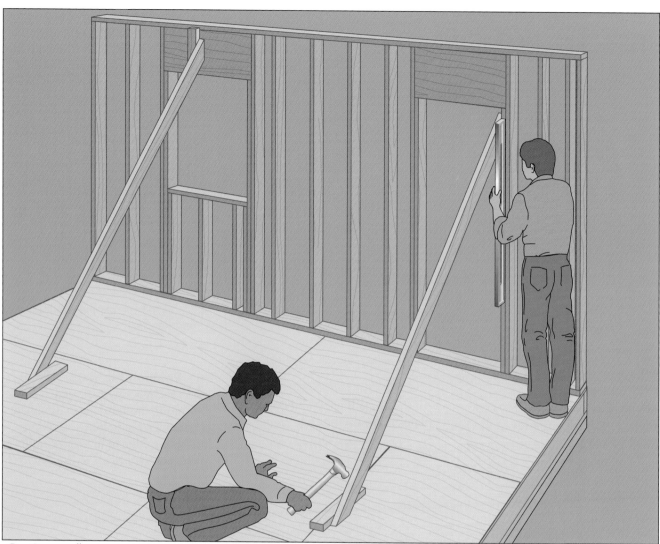

2 Once walls are erect, temporarily brace them using two-by lumber secured by cleats that are nailed to the subfloor.

With as many people as you need, slide the wall into position so that when you raise it, it will stand close to the guideline. Erect the wall, and align it with the line.

2 Brace the wall. Using a 48-inch level, get the wall as close to plumb as possible. You'll fine-tune it for plumb when you install the adjacent wall. Run braces from studs or from cleats on headers to cleats that will be tacked to the subfloor. When you have the wall plumb, have a helper nail the cleats to the subfloor.

3 Fasten the wall. With the bottom plate properly positioned, nail it to the rim joists and to the floor joists with 16d nails, one nail per stud bay.

3 Nail the bottom plate to the rim joists and to the floor joists using 16d nails. Stagger the nails from stud bay to stud bay.

Final Plumbing and Alignment of Walls

Plumb walls are essential; a stud wall that is not plumb will haunt you through the entire building process, right up to the ridgeboard. Plumb the walls as you complete them; once all the outside walls are up, fine-tune them for plumb and align them.

Difficulty Level:

Tools and Materials

- Basic carpentry tools
- Extended level
- Scissor-type two-by lever
- Nails
- String
- Three identical ¾-in.-thick blocks
- Two-by lumber the same dimension as the top plates
- 16d and 10d nails

1 Check for plumb. To check whether a wall is plumb you can use an extended level. Hold a 48-inch level against a straight 2×4. To make it easier to hold the extended level in place, cut two identical one-by blocks and screw them at each end to act as stand-off blocks. Hold the extended level in place on both the side and face of the stud wall. If the studs are not plumb when you read the side of the wall, the wall isn't square. Using a scissor-type lever wedged between the subfloor and the top plate, apply force to the wall until the studs read plumb. To make a scissor-type lever you need two boards, each one a little shorter than the wall. Cut the end of one at a 75-degree angle. This will be the vertical member of the scissor device. Then at one end of the other board, the horizontal member of the scissor, cut two 45-degree angles to make a point on the board. Two-

thirds or more up the vertical member, attach the second piece at about its halfway point with a carriage bolt so the horizontal member can swing freely. Place the vertical member so that it sits on the decking against a cleat, and lodge the pointed end of the horizontal member into a corner where a stud meets the underside of the top plate. As a helper presses down on the horizontal board, the vertical board will brace against the cleat and push the wall to one side. When the wall reads plumb, tack the vertical board to a stud to hold the wall in place until you can sheathe it with plywood.

2 Check for lean in/out. Hold the extended level on the face edge of the studs at about every fifth stud bay. If the studs are not plumb, the wall is leaning in or out. Release any line braces you attached in Step 2, "Brace the Wall," and adjust the wall until it's plumb. (See "Erecting Walls," page 105.) Apply force to the

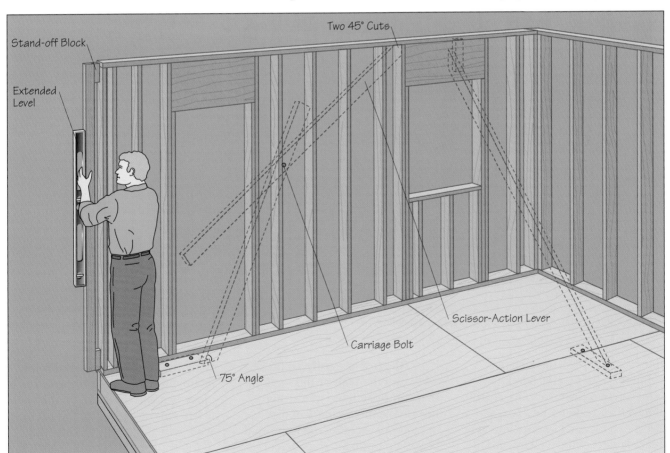

Stand-off Block

Extended Level

Two 45° Cuts

Scissor-Action Lever

Carriage Bolt

75° Angle

1 Check the walls for plumb using a level. Use a scissor-action braced lever to correct out-of-plumb studs.

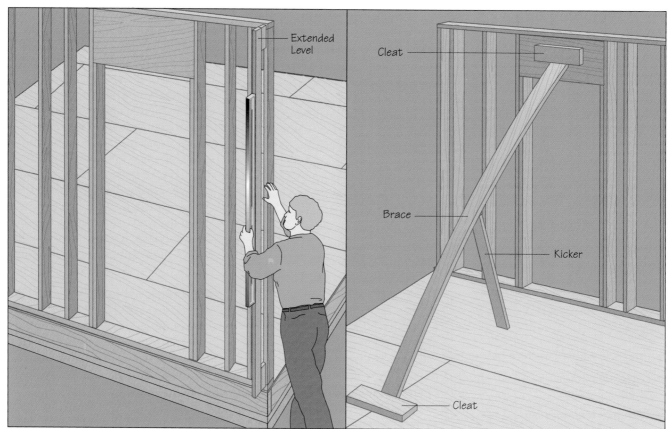

2 Check the walls for lean-in/out. To pull walls inward, nail a flat brace to cleats on the subfloor and on the wall, and then apply force by wedging a two-by kicker between the floor and the brace.

3 Use stand-off blocks and string to indicate whether a wall is straight. The wall is true if the string barely touches the hand-held block.

line braces to push the wall out. To bring the wall in, attach a flat brace between two cleats (one attached to the wall and one to the floor) and use a two-by as a kicker to bow the brace and force the wall inward. Re-tack the line braces to hold the wall in its proper position.

3 **Align the wall.** To make sure the wall or the sections that comprise it are in a straight line, make three identical blocks of wood, ¾-inch thick. Mount two blocks on opposite outside corners of the same wall, and stretch a string tightly between them,

tying the string to nails so it is taut against the blocks. Run the third block beneath the string. If the wall is true, the string will stand off the wall ¾ inch along the full length of the wall and just barely touch the block. If the wall is out of alignment and the string either stands off the

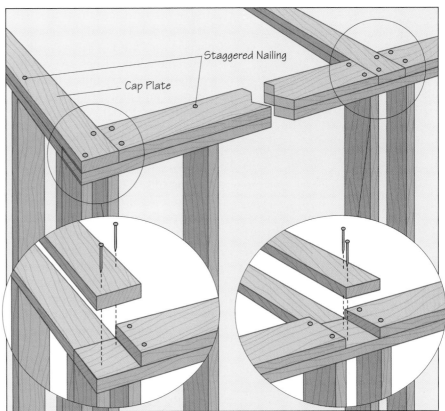

block or lies on it too tightly, apply force using one of the devices described earlier to set the wall right.

4 **Install the cap plate.** Walls should have two top plates, a cap plate and the wall's top plate below it. You've already nailed the top plate on top of the studs. Now that you've plumbed and braced the walls, a cap plate is essential for tying the walls and various partitions together where they meet in corners or Ts. The basic principle is as follows: a wall's cap plate should always lap the butt joint made by the top plates of the adjoining walls. Drive two 10d nails at each end of the cap plate and one 16d nail over each stud in the wall in a staggered pattern. Also, when a cap plate or a top plate forms a butt joint, the joint should always fall over a stud. Joints in the cap plate should always be at least 48 inches away from those in the top plate.

4 Lap the cap plate over the top-plate joint at corners and Ts, and nail it with two 10d nails. Drive 16d nails at each stud, staggering them along the plate's length.

Framing Connectors

After you've plumbed and aligned the walls and nailed all the cap plates in place, you may want to install metal fasteners to reinforce the stud joints. Seismic or hurricane codes in your area may even require these fasteners. Stud-to-stud nail-on plates are especially helpful in reinforcing the top-plate connections where walls meet at corners.

Seismic Bracing. Earthquakes and wind are two forces that can easily destroy a building. The damage from wind comes mostly when windows break, admitting wind-

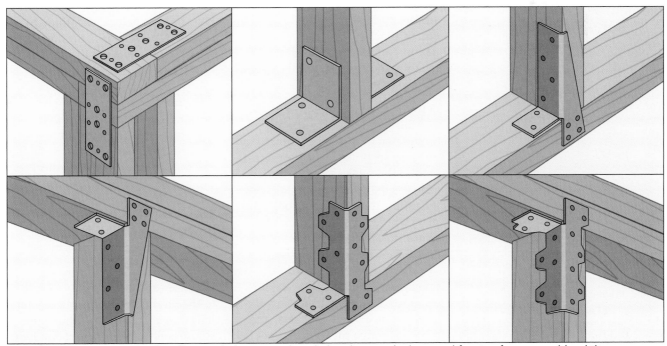

Framing Connectors. Nail-on flat metal plates, metal angle brackets, and other metal framing fasteners add stability to any wall and may be required by code in your area.

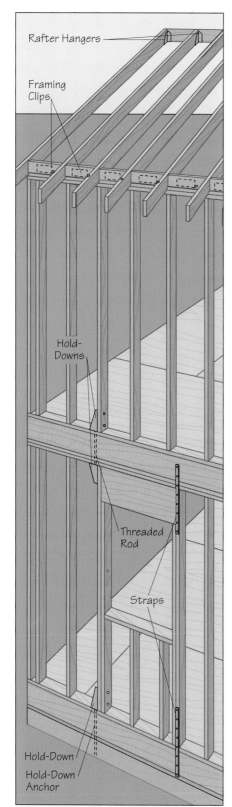

Rafter Hangers

Framing Clips

Hold-Downs

Threaded Rod

Straps

Hold-Down

Hold-Down Anchor

Seismic Bracing. Seismic connectors include hangers between the ridge and rafters, framing clips between rafter blocking and top plates, hurricane hold-downs and straps between floors, straps that hold walls to rim joists, and foundation hold downs between the first floor and the foundation.

driven projectiles or gusts that can lift off a roof. The walls of a house also create a kind of sail against which the wind pushes, so even if your windows stay intact, the wind can push and pull on a house with enough force to damage it severely.

Earthquakes, on the other hand, tend to exert sheer forces. They can also vibrate a house and shake it off its sills. Whether you are using structural reinforcement to protect against wind or earthquake, the object is to keep the various framing components somehow tied together, including connections between the sill and foundation, between the first- and second-floor floors, between the second floor's top plate and the rafters, and between the rafters and the ridgeboard.

There are a variety of specialized hurricane and earthquake connectors available for framing. (See "Seismic Anchors," page 55.) Extended anchor bolts between the foundation and the sill are essential in areas subject to seismic forces. Between the first floor and the foundation, a hold-down anchor in the form of a metal strap is a good idea. This strap will wrap around the bottom plate, span across and attach to the sill plate, and anchor it into the foundation. If you're attaching posts to your foundation, foundation hold-downs in the form of heavy-duty L-brackets may be required.

Between the first floor's top plate and the second floor, a strap-type hold-down may also be required to tie these sections of the house together. Roof connectors or hurricane ties may be required for tying the rafters to the second floor's top plate where the frieze blocks, top plates, and rafters meet. Strap-type connectors are sometimes used to tie rafters to the ridgeboard. Between floors, some codes call for a floor-to-floor hold-down consisting of a steel rod and angle brackets, and even a 1⅛-inch plywood gusset between floor joists. As a matter of course, codes require the use of

plywood sheathing to strengthen walls. Some carpenters install plywood on both the inside and outside of first floor walls, especially if they're cripple walls, which are particularly susceptible to collapse during earthquakes.

Sheathing

With the exterior walls plumb, square, and braced, it's time to sheathe them. You can apply sheathing vertically or horizontally. Horizontal sheathing is generally a better choice, although some codes require that you put blocking behind horizontal sheathing between studs. Vertical sheathing may be a good choice on 8-foot-high walls where you have a nailing surface along all four edges of the plywood. On most walls, however, where the inside height is 8 feet and you need to fill in strips to make up for joist framing and the like, vertical application compromises the superb racking resistance of plywood and OSB. Installing fill strips between full horizontal sheathing panel maintains racking resistance.

All kinds of sheathing materials are available—from gypsum and fiberboard nonstructural sheathing to oriented-strand board to conventional plywood—and in a variety of thicknesses. Your plans will probably specify the kind of sheathing with which the building was designed. One-half-inch CDX plywood is the most common for sheathing. Also, most wall designs call for the bottom edge of sheathing to overlap the sill plate and extend down to cover some of the foundation or slab. This overlap provides the wall with the best shear resistance and helps to seal out drafts and insects.

When sheathing walls, it's easiest to sheath right over the rough openings that you created within your stud framing. When you're finished sheathing you can mark the openings and cut them out.

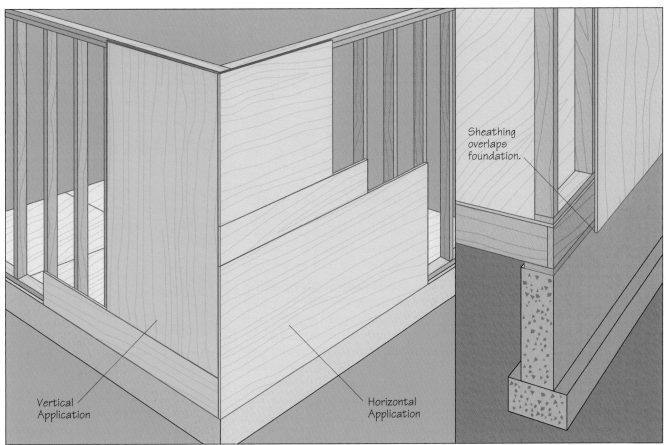

Vertical
Application

Horizontal
Application

Sheathing
overlaps
foundation.

Sheathing. You can install sheathing horizontally or vertically; in most cases it's best to overlap the foundation.

Installing Sheathing

Difficulty Level: 🦇🦇

Tools and Materials

- Basic carpentry tools
- Sheathing material
- 6d or 8d common nails
- Chalk line
- Circular saw
- Handsaw or reciprocating saw

1 **Attach the sheathing.** When laying out panels, leave a ⅛-inch gap between the long edges of the panel and a ¹⁄₁₆-inch gap where panel ends meet to allow room for the panel's natural expansion. Using 6d nails for panel thickness of ½ inch or less and 8d nails for panel thickness of more than ½ inch, nail through the panel into the studs, all the way around the panel. Space the nails 6 inches on center around the outside edge,

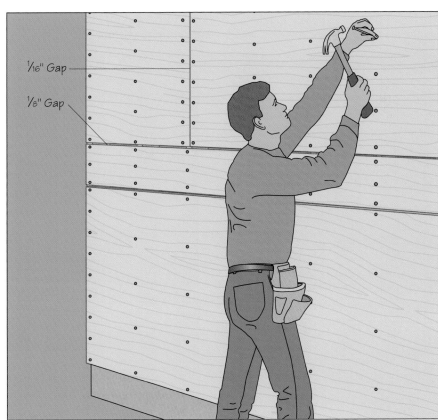

¹⁄₁₆" Gap

⅛" Gap

1 Install ½-in. sheathing using 6d nails, with a ⅛-in. gap at the long edge and a ¹⁄₁₆-in. gap at the ends.

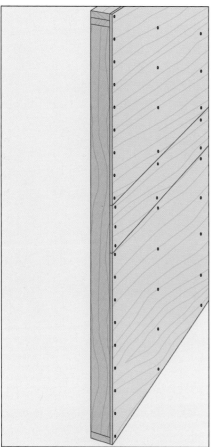

2 Always place narrow panels of sheathing between two larger panels. Never stack large panels and run a strip at the top or bottom.

and 12 inches on center along the plywood's interior. Always work from one end of the sheathing to the other. Never nail all four corners before nailing the interior, because this can lead to bulges.

2 Fill any gaps. In horizontal applications, if the sheathing doesn't quite reach the top of the wall, you'll need a strip of filler plywood. Don't install this strip across the top of the wall, where the top-plate-to-plywood nailing is essential for stabilizing the structure. Instead, install this strip in the middle of the wall.

3 Mark the rough-opening corners. For each rough opening, drive a nail or drill small holes from inside through the sheathing at the four corners. Use these nails or holes to locate a chalk line on the outside of the sheathing. Snap a line connecting the corners to create a box, and use this as your cut line.

4 Cut out the openings. Start the cutting with your circular saw. Plunge-cut into the sheathing, and continue cutting into the cor-

ners of the box. If you cut any farther than the corners, you risk nipping at the header or sills. Finish the cuts with a handsaw or reciprocating saw, and then remove the piece of sheathing you've cut out.

Windows & Doors

To finish the side walls properly, you should install all exterior doors and windows. Carpenters often install windows and wood doors only after they've installed the roof and weatherproofed it with at least roofing felt to protect the expensive units from water and weather damage.

Windows

Among the many window varieties, there are five most common types:

■ Fixed, or stationary, windows are the simplest kind of window because they don't open. A fixed window is simply glass installed in a frame that's attached to the house.

■ Double-hung windows are perhaps the most common. They consist

3 From inside, drive nails or drill holes to mark the corners of openings. Snap chalk lines connecting the corners outside.

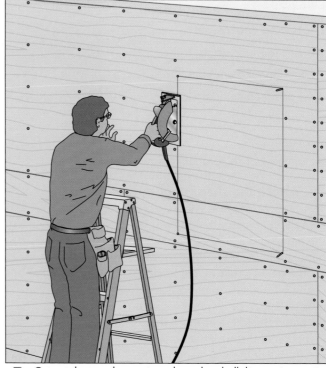

4 Cut out the rough opening along the chalk lines using a circular saw with the depth of cut set to sheathing thickness.

ACCOMMODATING WIRING & PLUMBING

- Drywall screws can easily puncture or penetrate copper pipe or wire, so you must set plumbing and wiring back from the side of the stud that will be receiving screws. Mark for holes so that when the tubing or wire is in place it will be no closer than 1½ inches from the stud edge.

- Maintain a consistent elevation from one stud bay to the next, especially for pipes, which are inflexible.

- Drill for wires with a ⅝-inch spade bit and for tubing with a ⅝- to 1-inch spade bit, depending on the size of the tubing. Drill for larger plumbing members like drains only in nonstructural partition walls.

- Where it is impossible to set the wire or tubing back from the wall at least 1½ inches, install a metal shield (1/16 inch in thickness) on the edge of the stud's inside face to prevent screws from entering. You'll find the protective metal plates in plumbing- and electrical-supply stores as well as home centers.

of two framed glass panels, called sash, that slide vertically, guided by a metal or wood track. One variation, called a single-hung window, consists of a fixed upper sash and a sliding lower sash. The sash of some double-hung windows allows you to tilt them inward to make it easier to clean the outside. The tilt feature is particularly handy for upper floors because windows are accessible from the outside only by ladder.

- Casement windows have hinges on one side and swing outward from the window opening when you turn a small crank. You can open casements 90 degrees for maximum ventilation. What's more important, you may use these windows as egress because most of the sash area is unobstructed when you open the window.

- Awning windows are similar to casements in that they swing outward, but they have hinges at the top. A useful feature of this window is that you can let it remain open slightly for ventilation, even during a light rain. One variation, called a hopper window, has hinges at the bottom. You can open a hopper outward or inward.

- Sliding windows are similar to a double-hung window turned sideways: The glass panels slide horizontally. You might use a slider where you need a window that's wider than it is tall.

8

WALLS & PARTITIONS

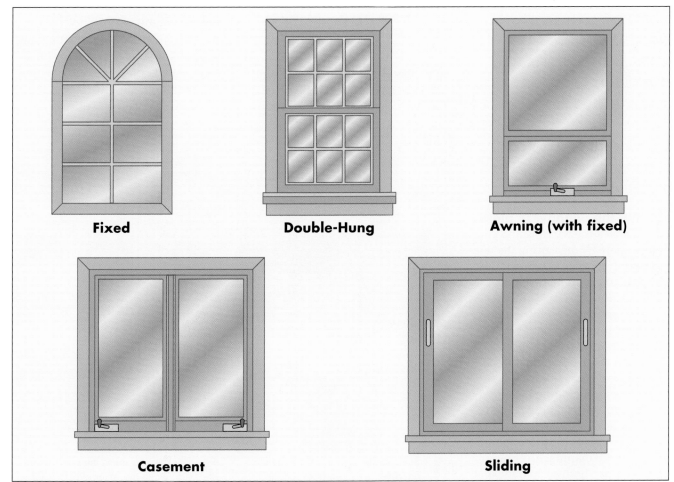

Fixed **Double-Hung** **Awning (with fixed)** **Casement** **Sliding**

Windows. Although windows may be divided into five general categories, there is great variety within each type.

Carpenters generally install windows in one of two ways, depending on the construction of the window. You can install some windows by driving nails through the exterior casing, sometimes called brickmold, and into the sides of the rough opening. You secure other windows—usually metal, vinyl, aluminum-clad wood, vinyl-clad wood, and some all-wood windows—by nailing into the sheathing and framing through a perforated flange that surrounds the window. The following steps detail basic installation. Always refer to the instructions included with your window, however, because details vary according to the manufacturer.

Installing Windows with Brickmold

Difficulty Level:

Tools and Materials

- Basic carpentry tools
- Building paper
- 1-in. roofing nails or staples
- Windows
- 48-in. level
- Shims
- Caulking gun and caulk
- 10d casing nails
- Flashing

1 **Put the window in place.** Unpack the window and check it for square by measuring the window jambs corner to corner. The diagonal measurements must match. If there are any braces or reinforcing blocks on the window, leave them in place until you've nailed the window securely to the house. Some manufacturers recommend that the sash be removed before window installation to prevent glass breakage, while others recommend leaving the sash in place to stiffen the jambs. If the manufacturer permits, remove both sash to make the window easier to carry up

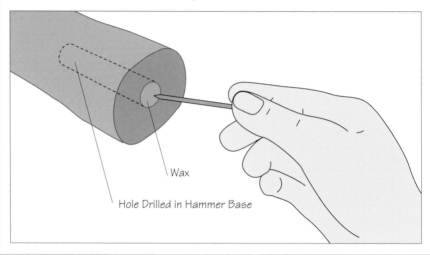

The Pros Know

DRILLING FOR NAIL WAX

Dabbing paraffin wax on a finish nail can help make it go easily into trim lumber, often with less splitting. Store paraffin wax in a drilled-out section at the base of your hammer.

Wax

Hole Drilled in Hammer Base

the ladder. Staple or nail 15-pound building paper over the sheathing, wrapping it around the top, bottom, and sides of the rough opening. Lift the window into the opening and hold it as an assistant helps from the inside.

2 **Level the window.** Shim the sill for level beneath each jamb leg as needed. If the window

is wider than 30 inches, shim the sill midway between legs as well. Check the sill frequently throughout the installation to ensure that it has not shifted out of position. Tip the window away from the opening just enough for your assistant to run a bead of exterior-grade caulk behind the brickmold, and then press the window against the wall.

Felt Paper

1 Remove the sash from a double-hung window before installation to make it easier to lift.

2 One person shims the window inside while the other checks it for level and plumb outside.

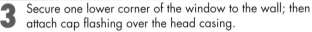
3 Secure one lower corner of the window to the wall; then attach cap flashing over the head casing.

4 Plumb and shim the jamb from inside as needed. Check the window for square, especially if you've removed the sash.

3 **Set the window.** Drive a 10d galvanized casing nail through the casing, securing one lower corner of the window to the wall. Casing nails are similar to finishing nails, but their shanks are heavier. Attach cap flashing over the head casing. If flashing did not come with the window, buy it at a building-supply store.

4 **Plumb the window.** Check the window for square; this is particularly important if you removed the sash earlier. Check the window for plumb. If necessary, adjust the frame by slipping shims between the jamb and the framing. When the window is plumb, use another nail to tack it in place on the outside.

5 **Nail the window.** Install both sash, and open and close them a few times. If they work properly, complete the nailing. If the sash bind, however, you may have to reposition the window. Use a high-quality exterior-grade caulk to fill any gaps beneath the sill or around the window opening. Inside, use fiberglass or a foam sealant to seal

5 Install the sash. If they slide smoothly, finish nailing the window into place.

the gap between the window jambs and the rough opening. Foam expands as it cures, so spray it gradually to prevent it from pushing the jambs out of position.

The Pros Know

USING NAILS AS PILOT BITS

For finishing nails that need predrilled holes, use the nail itself (with its head cut off) to serve as the pilot bit in a pinch.

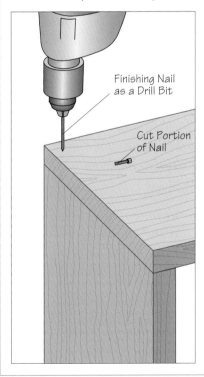

Finishing Nail as a Drill Bit

Cut Portion of Nail

1 Wrap the rough opening with felt paper; run a bead of caulk; and place the window in position.

2 Level and shim the window from inside, and then begin nailing it at one corner through the nailing flange.

3 Finish nailing the window, checking for plumb before driving the nails home. Nail just above the top flange.

Installing Flanged Windows

Difficulty Level:

Tools and Materials

- Basic carpentry tools
- Building paper
- 1-in. roofing nails or staples
- Windows
- 48-in. level
- Shims
- Caulking gun and caulk
- 1¾-in. roofing nails
- Flashing

1 Set the window in the rough opening. Staple or nail 15-pound building paper over the sheathing, wrapping it around the top, bottom, and sides of the rough opening. Caulk the perimeter of the opening, and then place the window in the rough opening.

2 Level the sill. Check the sill for level, and shim beneath the window from inside the house as necessary. Begin nailing the window in place on one side, using 1¾-inch roofing nails through existing slots in the flange.

3 Nail the window. Nail through the flange on the other side of the window, checking for plumb. The best technique is to drive the first few nails partway, fully driving them home only after you're sure the window is plumb and level. After several nails are in place, check the operation of the window by opening and closing it several times. Don't nail through the top nailing flange. Rather, start the nail just above the flange to allow the head to catch the top edge of the flange, or use 8d nails and bend them over the flange. Secure the window in this way in case the header ever sags: if you placed nails through the top flange and into the header, pressure from a sagging header would transfer to the window frame, causing the window to bind or the glass to crack.

EASY-CUTTING WEDGES

Wedges can sometimes be hard to cut after they've been set in place. Make it easier to chop off the excess by cutting wedges across the grain. Be extra careful when handling these wedges, though, because wedges cut this way are more fragile.

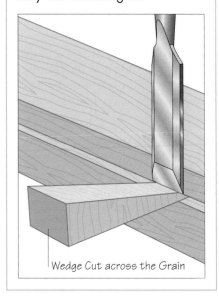

Wedge Cut across the Grain

Installing Prehung Doors

Most exterior doors are made of wood or metal. Exterior metal doors often have a core of wood or rigid foam insulation surrounded by a metal skin. The metal may be embossed or stamped to give it the look of a wood door. Most wood doors are built in one of two ways: as individual panels set in a frame (called a panel door) or as a single plywood sheet (facing) secured to each side of a wood framework (called a flush door).

Prehung exterior doors come with top and side jamb pieces, stops, and thresholds. The doors are typically attached to the jamb assembly and held in place with shipping braces. The doors are generally 80 inches tall and 36 inches wide. Some doors come with sidelights and/or double doors in one unit. Most prehung doors come with complete installation instructions, including the rough-opening size.

Difficulty Level:

Tools and Materials

- Basic carpentry tools
- Wood shims or shingles
- 8d casing nails

1 Set the door in place. If the door comes with shipping braces, keep them intact. Before setting the prehung unit in place, run a couple ¼-inch beads of non-hardening caulk between the floor and threshold for a good seal. Place the unit in the opening so that it'll swing in the desired direction. Residential exterior doors usually swing inward. Remove the braces; then check the clearance between the top of the door and the head jamb. It should be a uniform $\frac{1}{16}$ to $\frac{3}{32}$ inch, or about the thickness of a dime.

2 Attach the jambs. Use a level to plumb the hinge jamb on the face and edge, inserting shims behind the jamb at the points to be nailed. Adjust the shims. If the jamb is twisted, insert two nails side by side through the jamb to correct the problem. Nail the jamb in three places from top to bottom.

Before attaching the lock and head jambs, recheck the tolerances. Remember, the space should be a uniform $\frac{1}{16}$ inch between the jamb and door. If the lock side is too tight, adjust the shim under the lock jamb to correct the situation. Plumb, shim, and nail the lock jamb framing; then shim and nail the head jamb at the center to prevent sagging.

3 Trim the shims. Once you've attached the jambs, cut off the protruding parts of the shims around the door with a handsaw.

Locksets

The term "lockset" refers collectively to the complete door-latch system: latch-bolt assembly; trim; and handles, knobs, or levers. A latch bolt is a spring-loaded mechanism that holds a door closed and may or may not have a lock incorporated in it. A deadbolt, on the other hand, isn't spring loaded; you can operate it only with a key or a thumb-turn mechanism. A deadbolt will always have at least one keyhole. Sometimes deadbolts require keys for both interior and exterior operation to provide added security.

8

WALLS & PARTITIONS

1 Run caulk beneath the threshold. Then set the door in place.

2 Plumb and shim the hinge jamb, and then nail it in three places.

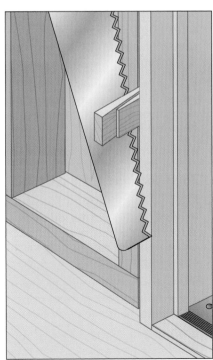

3 Cut off all the shims flush with the door jambs using a handsaw.

The Pros Know

REMOVING FINISHING NAILS

To remove finishing nails, don't pull them out with a claw hammer. Instead, pull them through the board using end nippers or pliers and a block of scrap wood.

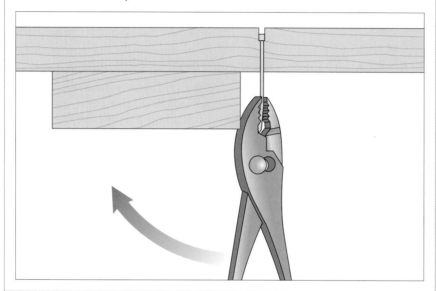

Every door needs a latch or lockset, which are available in many styles, from sleek and contemporary to detailed traditional designs, and in various materials, from burnished aluminum to solid brass. When you buy such door hardware, look for heavy-gauge metal, fine machining without sharp or rough edges, and a plated finish to withstand heavy use.

Match the hardware to the door. A solid, heavy entry door, for instance, should have a substantial handle-and-latch lockset rather than a small knob. Think about security when selecting hardware like locksets and deadbolt assemblies for exterior doors. The following steps explain the basic procedure for installing a lockset, although you should always refer to the manufacturer's instructions, which come with most sets.

FRAMING DETAILS

All residential doors hang in a wood (or sometimes steel) frame made of these elements.

■ The head jamb is at the top, flanked by side jambs, one on the lock side and one on the hinge side.

■ The sill, or threshold, which is often eliminated on interior doors, lies underfoot.

■ Stops, narrow strips of wood nailed to the head and side jambs, prevent the door from swinging too far when it closes.

■ The strike plate, or the metal strip mortised into the side jamb on the lock side of the door, accepts the latch.

■ Wood casings at the top and sides cover the framework and any gaps, and add the finishing touch to the installation.

■ Weather stripping, ideally incorporating interlocking metal strips, should be included all around the frame of an exterior door.

■ The door frame sits within a "rough opening" in the wall formed by wall studs and a header. The framing of interior walls does not always require a header. The

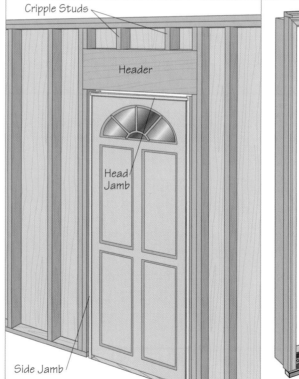

Cripple Studs

Header

Head Jamb

Side Jamb

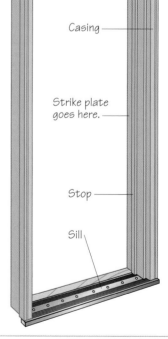

Casing

Strike plate goes here.

Stop

Sill

rough opening is always large enough so that you can set the door frame into place and adjust it vertically or horizontally. You might slip pairs of wood shims between the door frame and the studs to adjust the frame. You'll cut the shims flush with the door frame later.

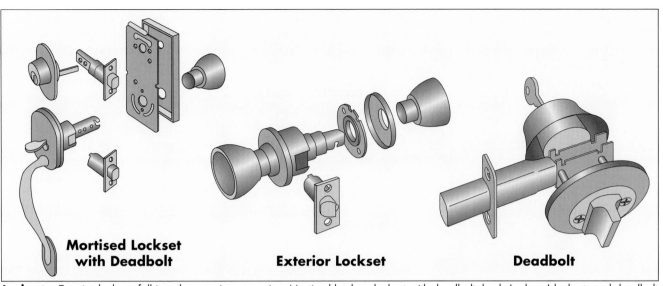

Mortised Lockset with Deadbolt

Exterior Lockset

Deadbolt

Locksets. Exterior locksets fall into three main categories: Mortised latch or lockset with deadbolt, knob (or lever) lockset, and deadbolt.

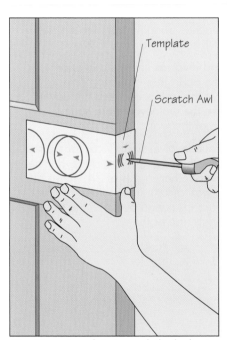

1 Use a template to mark the lockset and latch holes.

Installing a Lockset

Difficulty Level: 🦇🦇

Tools and Materials

- Basic carpentry tools
- Lockset
- Awl
- Drill with assorted bits and holesaws
- ¾-in. wood chisel

1 Locate the holes. Prehung wood and metal entry doors usually have holes predrilled for locksets. If yours doesn't, you'll have to cut them in. Using an awl and the template included with the instructions, mark positions for the lockset assembly holes.

The knob or handle should be 36 to 38 inches from the floor. Its hole should be 2⅜ inches or 2¾ inches from the edge of the door, depending on the lock.

2 Drill the holes. Bore a hole for the lock tube into the face of the door. Drill from one side until you barely break through the other side. Then drill from that other side to avoid splintering the wood. Next, drill a hole into the edge of the door for the latch.

3 Install the lockset. Insert the cylinder assembly and latch into the door. Mortise the latch plate into the edge of the door using a ¾-inch wood chisel. Note that on residential metal doors, the edge is still wood; it's only the thin faces of the door that are metal.

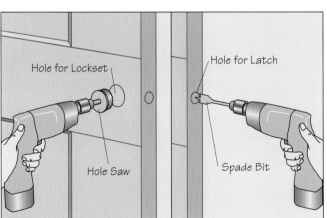

2 Bore holes in the door using a power drill with a hole saw and a spade bit.

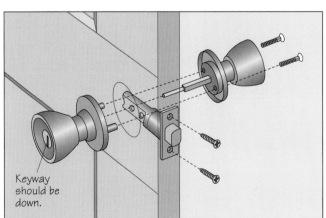

3 When installing a keyed lockset, align the keyway as shown, with the slot facing down.

8

WALLS & PARTITIONS

4 **Mark the door edge.** Place the strike plate over the latch, and mark the plate's position on the edge of the door as reference marks for when you cut the strike plate into the door jamb with the chisel.

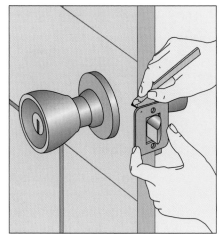

4 Mark the plate's position on the door to help align the plate on the jamb.

5 Remove the plate and close the door. Locate the strike and plate.

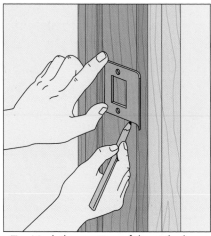

6 Mark the position of the strike by tracing the strike plate on the jamb.

5 **Center the latch.** Using a sharp pencil, pinpoint the spot where the center of the latch hits the door jamb.

6 **Mark the strike location.** Hold the strike plate on the door jamb, centering the hole over the pencil mark made for the latch. Also, make sure the plate is flush with the top and bottom marks you made on the edge of the door. Trace the location of the strike plate and the latch on the door jamb. With a sharp chisel, cut a mortise into the jamb equal to the depth of the strike plate. If you make the cut too deep, use cardboard to raise the plate so it's flush. To make room for the latch, use a drill or chisel to bore a hole into the center area of the strike plate. Fasten the strike plate to the jamb using screws, checking the alignment again.

SOUNDPROOFING

You can attempt soundproofing 2x4 partition walls, the nonload-bearing walls that divide the interior of a structure. Although you can't expect to make any walls in the house truly soundproof, you can effectively attenuate, or cut down, the transmission of sound through some walls. Walls separating bedroom and bathroom are prime candidates for soundproofing. There are a number of approaches, ranging from the simple to the complex, depending on how much sound you want to block.

A simple approach to controlling sound involves filling the interior partition wall with batts of R-11 unfaced fiberglass insulation or rigid foam rated at around R-11. The mass of the insulation helps cut down sound transmission. If you want to make the wall even more soundproof, double the drywall on each side of the wall.

Probably the best soundproofing technique involves using 2x6s for the top and bottom plates and framing the wall with staggered 2x4 studs. Set the studs at 12 inches on center, so that every other stud is at 24 inches on center on the same plane. Though this wall arrangement alone is effective, it's best to weave unfaced fiberglass insulation between the studs and use double layers of drywall on each side of the wall.

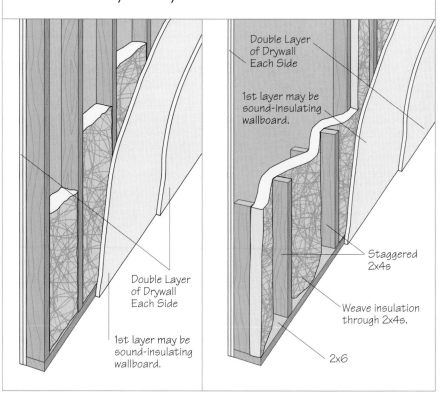

Double Layer of Drywall Each Side

1st layer may be sound-insulating wallboard.

Double Layer of Drywall Each Side

1st layer may be sound-insulating wallboard.

Staggered 2x4s

Weave insulation through 2x4s.

2x6

Gable-Roof Framing

Roof framing can be intimidating, mainly because you must calculate the length of the rafters and the necessary angles at the ridge and the rafter tails in order for the roof to come out right. The process involves some basic arithmetic and geometry that you may not have used since high school, so you may be a little rusty when it comes to laying out the roof. But don't worry. This chapter shows how to break down the process into small, manageable segments. The chapter even provides the necessary math you will need to do the job right. Once you see the principles at work in this chapter, you'll be marking and cutting rafters with confidence.

Roof Loads

Like floor joists, rafters must be selected to span distances. A beefier piece of lumber can span greater distances, so a 2×8 rafter will have a longer allowable span than a 2×6 rafter of the same grade. A 2×12 will have a greater allowable span than a 2×10 of the same grade, and so on. Unlike floor joists, however, rafters are set in position at an angle. A low angle (one closer to level) puts more strain on a rafter than a high angle (one closer to vertical), so a rafter's allowable span is affected by the roof's angle, called pitch or slope. A steep roof has a high angle, while a less inclined roof has a lower angle.

On-center framing distances also affect allowable rafter span. Because rafters placed 16 inches on center are closer together than those set at 24 inches on center, they take on less load and can be a smaller dimension. You may find that you need 2×10s for a roof with 24-inch-on-center framing but that you can use 2×8s if you frame them at 16 inches on center.

Finally, the grade of the lumber affects allowable rafter span. No. 1 Douglas fir will have a greater span than No. 2 Douglas fir, and so on. So be sure that you calculate your rafter spans using the wood species and grade available to you. If you change species or grade, recheck the span table for the recommended size for the lumber you're buying. (See "Rafter Span Ratings," page 27.)

When referring to a span table, make sure it's a rafter table and not a joist table. They are different. On a rafter table you'll notice that there are two categories of span. You know that slope affects the rafter's capacity to bear loads, but rather than list span tables for each different roof angle, the tables typically break the slopes down into two categories: steep-sloped roofs and low-sloped roofs. Low-sloped roofs on a rafter span table have slopes of less than 4 in 12; for steep roofs, the slopes are 4 in 12 or greater.

Roof Pitch & Slope

Pitch. Roof pitch is the angle of a roof as a ratio of total rise to span. The total rise is the vertical height of the roof at its ridge measured from the top plate of the structure's end walls at the wall's midpoint; the span of a gable roof is the distance from wall to wall. A 24-foot-wide structure, for example, with a gable roof that rises 10 feet in the middle has a pitch of $^{10}/_{24}$, or $^{5}/_{12}$. A pitch of $^{1}/_{4}$ or $^{1}/_{3}$ is common for gable roofs. A Cape Cod-style house might have a $^{1}/_{2}$ pitch.

Slope. The more commonly used slope is expressed as the rafter's vertical rise in inches, or unit rise, per 12 inches of horizontal run, or unit run. If a slope has a unit rise of 4 and a unit run of 12, it means the roof surface rises 4 inches for every 12 inches along the run line. This dimension is expressed as 4 : 12 or 4 in 12. On most design drawings of roofs, you'll notice a right triangle off to the side that identifies a roof—in this case 4 in 12—with a 12 at the top of the triangle on one leg of the right angle and a 4 on the other leg. The hypotenuse of the triangle shows you the angle of slope. The higher the number of inches in unit rise, the steeper the roof. An 8-in-12 roof rises 8 inches in elevation for every foot of run; a 12-in-12 roof, common in Cape Cod-style houses, rises a foot in elevation for every foot of run (a 45-degree angle).

Figuring Total Rise. If you know the slope of a roof but don't know the total rise, you can determine that dimension using the total run. Divide the span in half to get the total run. Let's say your structure has a span of 20 feet. The total run is 10 feet. Now multiply the unit rise by the number of feet in the total run. An 8-in-12 roof with a total run of 10 feet means the total rise is 80 inches (8 × 10), or 6 feet 8 inches. If you increase the run, the slope doesn't change, but the total rise increases. For example, if you have a 12-foot run with an 8-in-12 roof, the total rise is 96 inches (8 × 12), or 8 feet.

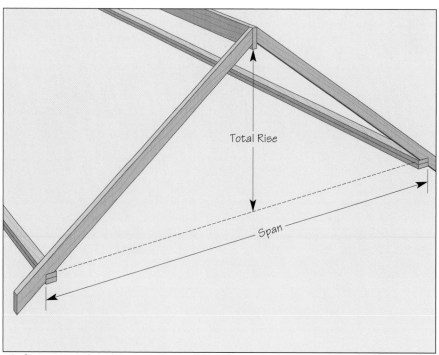

Pitch. Expressed as the ratio of a roof's total rise to its span, pitch is usually written as a fraction: $^{1}/_{3}$ pitch, for example.

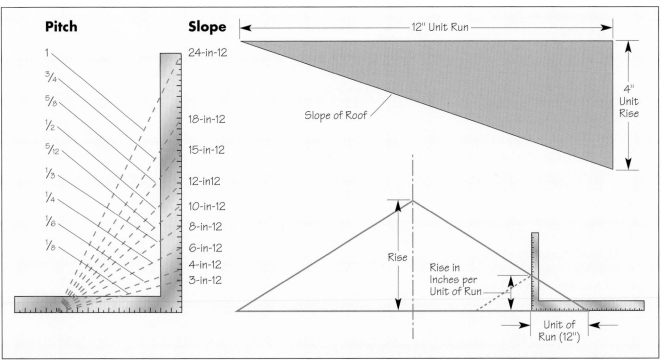

Slope. Another way of describing a roof's angle is its slope: the number of inches the roof rises for each unit of run, usually 12 in.

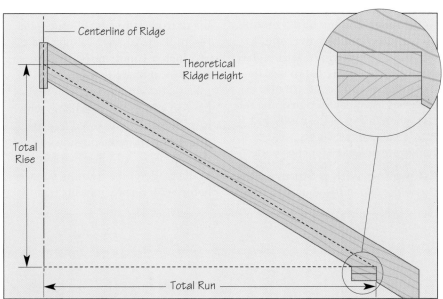

Figuring the Total Rise. Total rise is the vertical measurement from the cap plate to the theoretical ridge height. To find the rise in feet, multiply the run by the unit rise and divide by 12.

When you frame a roof, it's important to know precisely what the rise defines. When you determine rise, you use a measurement along a line (the measuring line) from the cap plate's top outside edge to the ridge's centerline. The point at which the rafter measuring line and the ridgeboard centerline intersect is known as the theoretical ridgeboard height. The rise is the distance from the cap plate to the theoretical ridgeboard height.

To determine the inside height of the ridgeboard, or the height at the bottom of the ridgeboard above the top plate, you must remember that rafters must have a notch to sit securely on the double top plate, usually with a 3¾-inch plumb cut on a 2×10 that sits on a 2×6 top plate. Therefore, the bottom of the ridge will be lower by 3¾ inches (or whatever the length of the plumb cut line is) plus an inch or so to account for the flat edge of the ridgeboard.

Calculating rise and run correctly is essential for three principal reasons. First, rise and run determine where to position your ridgeboard; second, a precise calculation will help you size rafter stock; third, rise and run are required for determining rafter lengths.

Calculating Rafter Length

You'll use a framing square, pencil, and calculator to figure and mark common gable rafters. Because all the common rafters in a simple gable roof are identical, the easiest thing to do is to mark one, cut it, and put it in place. If that first rafter fits perfectly against the ridgeboard and cap plate, use it as the master rafter, or template, for marking all the others. To calculate the total number of rafters you need, do the following:

9

GABLE-ROOF FRAMING

- For 16-inch-on-center framing, multiply the length of the building by three-quarters, and add 1 (L × 0.75 + 1 = X rafters).

- For 24-inch-on-center framing, multiply the building length by one-half and add 1 (L × 0.5 + 1 = Y rafters).

Before you order rafter lumber, you must know what size boards to get. You can approximate the sizes using a framing square and measuring tape. To determine the exact rafter lengths, you can use any of three methods: work with rafter tables; use the Pythagorean theorem; or step off the rafters with a square. First, however, you need to determine the roof slope and identify the cuts you'll need to make.

Determining the Roof Slope.
To mark rafters, you need to find the roof slope indicated on the building's plans. The rafter length will be determined by the roof slope and the width of your building, which you'll also find on the plans. The rafter-length measurement will determine where you'll make the cuts on the rafters.

Three Crucial Cuts.
There are three cuts in most rafters: the ridge cut, where the rafter rests against the ridgeboard; the tail cut, which

The Pros Know

DRAWING 45-DEGREE ANGLES

Position a framing square at the 12-inch mark along the outside edge of its blade and tongue, and you can establish 45-degree lines accurately enough for framing work.

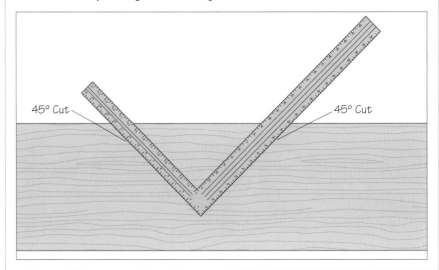

45° Cut   45° Cut

determines the shape of the tail end of the rafter; and the bird's-mouth cut, where you notch the rafter to sit on the cap plate. The tail cut may be plumb or square (drawing) or a combination. The tail cut also establishes the outside edge of the rafter, where it forms the eaves and may create an overhang. Most overhangs are at least 12 inches wide.

Estimating with a Square.
Let the wide arm of the square, or the blade, represent the total run and the narrow arm—the tongue—represent the total rise. Using a scale of 1 inch = 1 foot, measure the distance from blade to tongue to find the length of the rafter. You'll also have to add in any overhang, which is traditionally measured as a level dimension from the outside edge of the cap plate. Add that extra length to the blade of the framing square before you do any measuring.

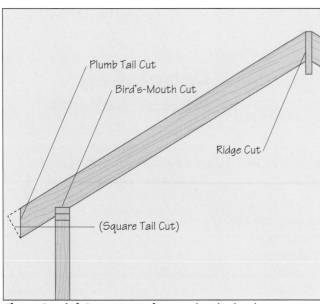

Plumb Tail Cut

Bird's-Mouth Cut

Ridge Cut

(Square Tail Cut)

Three Crucial Cuts. Most rafters need a plumb ridge cut, a bird's-mouth cut at the plate, and a plumb and/or square tail cut.

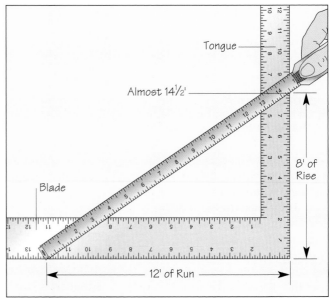

Tongue

Almost 14½'

Blade

8' of Rise

12' of Run

Estimating with a Square. Use a framing square and measuring tape to estimate the length of a rafter.

Using a Rafter Table

The rafter table found on a framing square contains work-saving data and is useful for many essential framing calculations. You need look only at the first line of the table, which gives unit rafter length, for common gable rafters. Unit length is the common rafter length required, in inches and decimals, at any given slope to gain a foot of run, or a foot of horizontal distance. A rafter at a steep 10-in-12 slope, for instance, has to be longer to cover a foot of run than a rafter at a less-inclined 4-in-12 slope.

To find the unit length you need, look on the blade (which also contains the table) below the inch designation that corresponds to your slope. If, for example, you're framing a 6-in-12 roof, look at the number below the 6-inch mark on the framing square's blade. You'll find it reads 13.42.

If your total run is 14, multiply 13.42 by 14 to get 187.88 inches. Divide 187.88 by 12 to get 15.656 feet, or 15 feet 7⅞ inches. (See "Decimals of a Foot," on page 126.)

Create An Overhang. The rafter length is the distance from the ridge to the edge of the building. To create an overhang, you need to add extra rafter length beyond the building line. The overhang is a level dimension from the edge of the building, but the actual rafter length is longer because of its slope. If you want an 18-inch, or 1.5 foot, overhang on the 6-in-12 roof, for example, you must multiply 1.5 × 13.42. The result is 20.13. Divide 20.13 by 12 to get 1.68 feet, or 1 foot 8³⁄₁₆ inches. This is the distance to add along the top edge of the rafter beyond the building line to yield a 1-foot 6-inch overhang.

Calculating the Length

The calculations used here to determine rafter length are an example and are not meant for all rafters, but

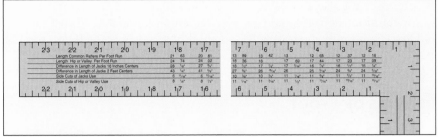

Using a Rafter Table. Better framing squares have a rafter table that contains valuable information for making rafter calculations.

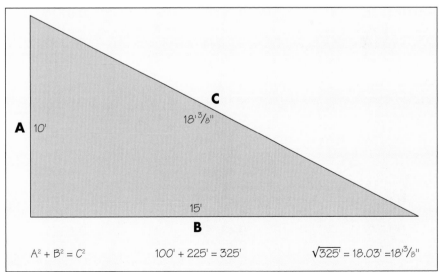

Create an Overhang. An overhang is a level dimension from the edge of a building, but you need more rafter length than the overhang width because of the slope.

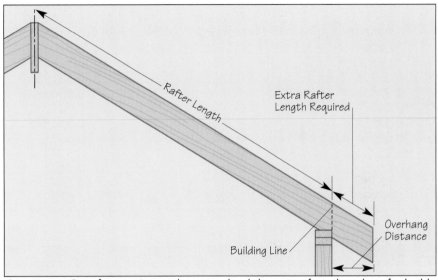

Calculating the Length. The total run and total rise represent the base and altitude of a right triangle; the hypotenuse is the common rafter length.

you can use the principles for any common gable rafter.

■ Determine the roof slope. Here, assume a slope of 8 in 12. Remember, that means the roof rises 8 inches for every 12 inches it runs horizontally.

■ Determine the building width. For this example, assume the building is 30 feet wide.

■ Determine the run. The run is usually one-half the building's width. In this case, the run is 15 feet.

9

GABLE-ROOF FRAMING

■ Determine the rise. Once you know the slope (8 in 12) and run (15 feet), you know the roof will rise 10 feet from the top plate to the ridge (8 × 15 = 120 inches, or 10 feet).

You're now ready to figure the rafter length for an 8-in-12 roof on a building 30 feet wide. If you think of half the roof as a right triangle, you already know the base (15) and

altitude (10). You need to figure the hypotenuse of this right triangle, which represents the rafter length. Using the Pythagorean theorem, $A^2 + B^2 = C^2$:

DECIMALS OF A FOOT

Decimal	Inch	Decimal	Inch	Decimal	Inch	Decimal	Inch
0.0000	0	0.2500	3	0.5000	6	0.7500	9
0.0052	$1/16$	0.2552	$3^1/16$	0.5052	$6^1/16$	0.7552	$9^1/16$
0.0104	$1/8$	0.2604	$3^1/8$	0.5104	$6^1/8$	0.7604	$9^1/8$
0.015625	$3/16$	0.265625	$3^3/16$	0.515625	$6^3/16$	0.765625	$9^3/16$
0.0208	$1/4$	0.2708	$3^1/4$	0.5208	$6^1/4$	0.7708	$9^1/4$
0.0260	$5/16$	0.2760	$3^5/16$	0.5260	$6^5/16$	0.7760	$9^5/16$
0.03125	$3/8$	0.28125	$3^3/8$	0.53125	$6^3/8$	0.78125	$9^3/8$
0.0365	$7/16$	0.2865	$3^7/16$	0.5365	$6^7/16$	0.7865	$9^7/16$
0.0417	$1/2$	0.2917	$3^1/2$	0.5417	$6^1/2$	0.7917	$9^1/2$
0.046875	$9/16$	0.296875	$3^9/16$	0.546875	$6^9/16$	0.796875	$9^9/16$
0.0521	$5/8$	0.3021	$3^5/8$	0.5521	$6^5/8$	0.8021	$9^5/8$
0.0573	$11/16$	0.3073	$3^{11}/16$	0.5573	$6^{11}/16$	0.8073	$9^{11}/16$
0.0625	$3/4$	0.3125	$3^3/4$	0.5625	$6^3/4$	0.8125	$9^3/4$
0.0677	$13/16$	0.3177	$3^{13}/16$	0.5677	$6^{13}/16$	0.8177	$9^{13}/16$
0.0729	$7/8$	0.3229	$3^7/8$	0.5729	$6^7/8$	0.8229	$9^7/8$
0.078125	$15/16$	0.328125	$3^{15}/16$	0.578125	$6^{15}/16$	0.828125	$9^{15}/16$
0.0833	1	0.3333	4	0.5833	7	0.8333	10
0.0885	$1^1/16$	0.3385	$4^1/16$	0.5885	$7^1/16$	0.8385	$10^1/16$
0.09375	$1^1/8$	0.34375	$4^1/8$	0.59375	$7^1/8$	0.84375	$10^1/8$
0.0990	$1^3/16$	0.3490	$4^3/16$	0.5990	$7^3/16$	0.8490	$10^3/16$
0.1042	$1^1/4$	0.3542	$4^1/4$	0.6042	$7^1/4$	0.8542	$10^1/4$
0.109375	$1^5/16$	0.359375	$4^5/16$	0.6093	$7^5/16$	0.859375	$10^5/16$
0.1146	$1^3/8$	0.3646	$4^3/8$	0.6146	$7^3/8$	0.8646	$10^3/8$
0.1198	$1^7/16$	0.3698	$4^7/16$	0.6198	$7^7/16$	0.8698	$10^7/16$
0.1250	$1^1/2$	0.3750	$4^1/2$	0.6250	$7^1/2$	0.8750	$10^1/2$
0.1302	$1^9/16$	0.3802	$4^9/16$	0.6302	$7^9/16$	0.8802	$10^9/16$
0.1354	$1^5/8$	0.3854	$4^5/8$	0.6354	$7^5/8$	0.8854	$10^5/8$
0.140625	$1^{11}/16$	0.390625	$4^{11}/16$	0.640625	$7^{11}/16$	0.890625	$10^{11}/16$
0.1458	$1^3/4$	0.3958	$4^3/4$	0.6458	$7^3/4$	0.8958	$10^3/4$
0.1510	$1^{13}/16$	0.4010	$4^{13}/16$	0.6510	$7^{13}/16$	0.9010	$10^{13}/16$
0.15625	$1^7/8$	0.40625	$4^7/8$	0.65625	$7^7/8$	0.90625	$10^7/8$
0.1615	$1^{15}/16$	0.4115	$4^{15}/16$	0.6615	$7^{15}/16$	0.9115	$10^{15}/16$
0.166667	2	0.416667	5	0.666667	8	0.916667	11
0.171875	$2^1/16$	0.421875	$5^1/16$	0.671875	$8^1/16$	0.921875	$11^1/16$
0.1771	$2^1/8$	0.4271	$5^1/8$	0.6771	$8^1/8$	0.9271	$11^1/8$
0.1823	$2^3/16$	0.4323	$5^3/16$	0.6823	$8^3/16$	0.9323	$11^3/16$
0.1875	$2^1/4$	0.4375	$5^1/4$	0.6875	$8^1/4$	0.9375	$11^1/4$
0.1927	$2^5/16$	0.4427	$5^5/16$	0.6927	$8^5/16$	0.9427	$11^5/16$
0.1979	$2^3/8$	0.4479	$5^3/8$	0.6979	$8^3/8$	0.9479	$11^3/8$
0.203125	$2^7/16$	0.453125	$5^7/16$	0.703125	$8^7/16$	0.953125	$11^7/16$
0.2083	$2^1/2$	0.4583	$5^1/2$	0.7083	$8^1/2$	0.9583	$11^1/2$
0.2135	$2^9/16$	0.4635	$5^9/16$	0.7135	$8^9/16$	0.9635	$11^9/16$
0.21875	$2^5/8$	0.46875	$5^5/8$	0.71875	$8^5/8$	0.96875	$11^5/8$
0.2240	$2^{11}/16$	0.4740	$5^{11}/16$	0.7240	$8^{11}/16$	0.9740	$11^{11}/16$
0.2292	$2^3/4$	0.4792	$5^3/4$	0.7292	$8^3/4$	0.9792	$11^3/4$
0.234375	$2^{13}/16$	0.484375	$5^{13}/16$	0.734375	$8^{13}/16$	0.984375	$11^{13}/16$
0.2396	$2^7/8$	0.4896	$5^7/8$	0.7396	$8^7/8$	0.9896	$11^7/8$
0.2448	$2^{15}/16$	0.4948	$5^{15}/16$	0.7448	$8^{15}/16$	0.9948	$11^{15}/16$

$10^2 + 15^2 = C^2$
100 feet + 225 feet = 325 feet

The square root of 325 feet is 18.03 feet, which equals 18 feet $\frac{3}{8}$ inch. If your rise and/or run are not in whole feet but in feet and inches, then convert to inches, do the math, and convert back to feet. Use the table "Decimals of a Foot" (left) when you divide the resulting number of inches by 12 on a calculator to arrive at feet.

Calculate the Overhang. You can also use the Pythagorean theorem to figure out the dimension you'll have to add to the rafter length for the overhang. If you want an 18-inch overhang on the same 8-in-12 roof, envision the overhang area as a miniature roof. The run is 18 inches (the horizontal dimension of the overhang) and the rise is 12 inches ($8 \times 1.5 = 12$). Therefore,

$12^2 + 18^2 = C^2$
144 inches + 324 inches = 468 inches

The square root of 468 inches is 21.63 inches, which is 1.80 feet, or 1 foot $9\frac{5}{8}$ inches.

Stepping Off the Length

Rather than do any calculations, you can accurately measure a rafter by "stepping off" with a framing square in 12-inch units of run.

Lay a straight piece of rafter stock across two sawhorses. Sight down the edge of the rafter, and position yourself so that you're on the crowned side, which will be the top of the rafter. It's easier to hold and work with the framing square from that position.

Difficulty Level: 🦇🦇

Tools and Materials

- Framing square with stops
- Pencil
- Rafter (to serve as a template)

1 **Adjust the square.** Let's say you want to lay out a roof with an 8-in-12 slope. Lay the square on the left end of the stock. Hold the square's tongue in your left hand and its blade in your right. Pivot the square until the edge of the stock near you aligns with the unit rise mark (8 inches in this example) on the outside of the tongue and the 12-inch mark on the outside of the blade. Mark along the outside edge of the tongue for the ridge plumb line. You'll use this mark as the reference line for stepping off full 12-inch units. To make accurate marking easier, attach adjustable stops called stair nuts or stair buttons to the square to set the rise and run positions. (See drawing.)

If the span is an odd number of feet, say 25, with a run of $12\frac{1}{2}$ feet, you'll have to include a half-step to accommodate the extra length. Mark off the partial step first, then go on to step off full 12-inch units.

Holding the square in the position in which you had it to mark the ridge cut, measure and mark the length of the odd unit along the blade. Shift the square to your right along the edge of the stock until the tongue is even with the mark you just made. Mark off a plumb line along the

tongue of the square. When you begin stepping off full units, remember to start from the new plumb line and not from the ridge cut line.

2 **Step off the rafter.** Working with the same 8-in-12 slope and a run of $12\frac{1}{2}$ feet, start to step off the rafter from the partial step mark. Continue stepping off to your right by marking where the stock intersects the blade and shifting the square until the outside of the

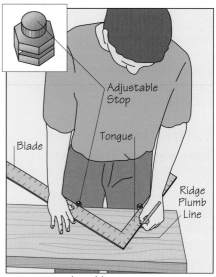

1 Using adjustable stops, set your square's tongue to the roof unit rise and the blade to the unit run. Mark the ridge line.

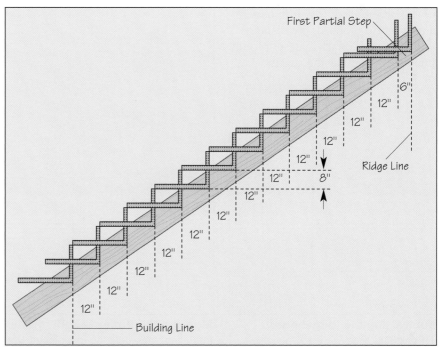

2 Step the framing square off to the right, once for each foot on run in the roof. Work from the ridge line or the first partial step.

tongue aligns with that mark. Perform this step a total of 12 times.

On the last step, mark a plumb line along the outside of the tongue. This plumb line, also called the building line, marks the outside of the cap plate.

3 **Step off the overhang.** To measure the overhang, step off the additional distance in the usual way, starting from the building line. For an 18-inch overhang, for example, make an additional 1½ steps. If the rafter board is running short and there's not enough room on which you can rest the square while you're doing the marking, turn the square over and measure straight off the building line.

Subtracting the Ridgeboard Thickness

You have calculated the length of the rafter to the center of the ridgeboard. You must therefore shorten the rafter to accommodate the width of the board. If you haven't marked the plumb ridge line on a rafter, do so as discussed in "Stepping Off the Length." Measure back from the center of the ridge line a distance of one-half the thickness of the ridgeboard. If you're using a two-by ridgeboard, the distance will be ¾ inch. Mark another plumb line at this point as the cut line.

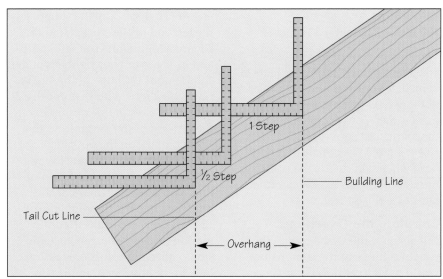

3 Starting from the building line, step off a distance equivalent to the overhang width.

Marking the Rafter Length

If you haven't stepped off the rafter, you must still mark it for length. Measure from the original ridge line, not the cut line you just marked, the total rafter length. Do not include the overhang. Measure along the top, or crowned, edge of the rafter.

Set the framing square at the proper slope; position it at the length mark; and draw a plumb line like

the line drawn at the ridge. This is the building line. Add the overhang length you calculated, and make a mark.

Marking the Rafter Tails

At their tail ends (the ends that overhang the walls), you can cut rafters either plumb, ending in a vertical line parallel with your structure's walls, or square, ending in a line that is square with the rafter. Plumb-cut

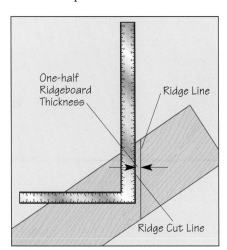

Subtracting the Ridgeboard Thickness. Measure back from the ridge line a distance of one-half the ridgeboard thickness.

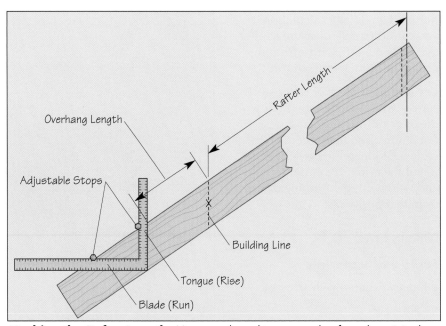

Marking the Rafter Length. Measure along the crown edge from the original ridge line, and mark the rafter length you determined earlier, not including the overhang. Then add the overhang length, and mark the end of the rafter with a plumb or a square line.

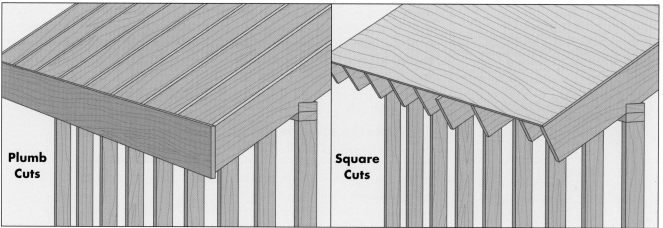

Marking the Rafter Tails. Cut the ends of the rafters plumb or square. Square cuts must be exactly the same length because the edge of the roof emphasizes any irregularities.

rafters may also have their pointed tails nipped off with a line parallel with the structure's floor. Plumb-cut rafters are best for accommodating fascia boards and for creating screened or sealed-in cornices: simply make a plumb cut line at the overhang mark.

If you choose to leave the rafters square, with the ends at an angle to the building's walls instead of parallel, make a square cut line across the rafter at the overhang mark. Measure off the overhang dimension, and mark the cut line starting at the bottom edge of the rafter. Be sure the rafters are all exactly the same length: the roof sheathing will create a sight line that will make obvious any rafters that are too short or too long, even by a small amount.

Making the Bird's-Mouth, Ridge, and Tail Cuts

Once you have the ridge and tail cut lines marked, it's time to mark the bird's mouth and make all the cuts. The building line you drew on the rafter already marks the plumb cut of the bird's mouth. Use that line as a reference to draw the horizontal, or seat, cut line for the bird's mouth.

Difficulty Level:

Tools and Materials

- Framing square
- Pencil
- Circular saw
- Handsaw
- Rafter (to serve as the template)

1 **Mark the plumb cut.** The amount you notch out along the plumb cut must not exceed one-third the depth of the rafter; otherwise the rafter will lose some of its span rating. Note, however, that the rafter will actually "gain" thickness by being positioned at an angle. Although the actual width of a 2×10 is 9¼ inches, its working width in position may be more like 11 inches. One third of that width is about 3¾ inches. Mark the allowable depth on the building line, measuring from the bottom edge of the rafter.

2 **Mark the seat cut.** The seat cut is the horizontal line that will rest on the cap plate. It should be as wide as the cap plate. So if you are framing your walls with 2×6s, the seat cut should be 5½ inches. Align

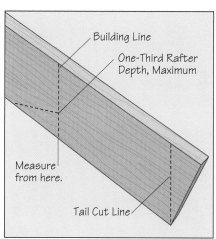

Building Line
One-Third Rafter Depth, Maximum
Measure from here.
Tail Cut Line

1 Measure up from the bottom one-third the rafter width, and make a mark.

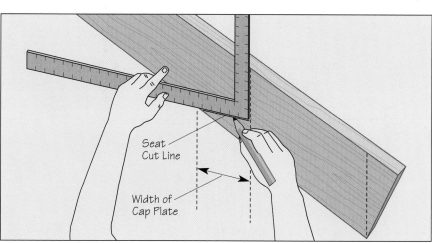

Seat Cut Line
Width of Cap Plate

2 Align the framing square with the building line, and make the seat cut line as shown.

3 Make the ridge and tail cuts; then make the bird's-mouth cuts, finishing with a handsaw.

PROPERLY BEARING RAFTERS

Roof sag can be one result of a rafter that improperly bears on a top plate. If the toe of the rafter (with no overhang) rests on the top plate, for example, the rafter may split, causing the sag. But if the heel rests on the top plate, the rafter is far more stable.

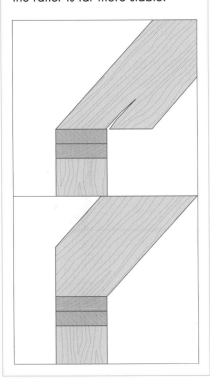

the framing square with the building line, and move it up or down until the dimension from the building line to the rafter edge equals the wall-stud width. Draw a line, which should be at or below the mark you made in Step 1.

3 **Make the saw cuts.** Using a circular saw, make the rafter's ridge and tail cuts. Make the initial bird's-mouth cuts with a circular saw, but finish them with a handsaw, as a circular saw will overcut and eat too far into the body of the rafter. The rafter is now ready for you to put it in place against the ridgeboard when it's erected. If the cuts all line up, use this rafter as a guide to cut the remaining rafters.

Installing Ridgeboards & Rafters

Once you've measured, marked, and cut the sample rafter, you're ready to start framing the roof. The most likely scenario is that you'll install a ridgeboard and rafters over a one- or two-story structure with a ceiling just below the roof. The ceiling joists act as rafter ties; you must install them before you

erect the roof frame. If you're not installing a floor in the attic space below the roof, you'll have to install a temporary floor while you work.

Erecting the Roof

Difficulty Level:

Tools and Materials

- Basic carpentry tools
- Ridgeboard
- Rafters
- Two-by lumber for supports and braces
- 10d nails
- 16d nails

1 **Set the ceiling joists.** In stick construction you place the ceiling joists and rafters parallel at the plate and face-nail them together with three or more 10d nails. Attach the ceiling joists prior to installing the rafters, and cut the ends of the joists to fit the slope of the rafters at the plate. To cut the joists properly, measure the height of a rafter as it would sit on the top plate at the end of the bird's mouth and along the plumb line. Transfer this measurement to the end of the ceiling joist. Align the framing square with the

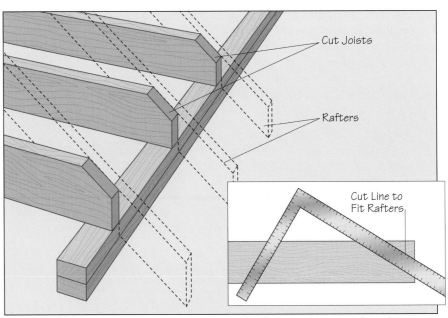

1 Align the square on the joists according to the slope as shown, and cut the joists.

top edge of the ceiling joist, with the tongue showing the unit rise and the blade showing the unit run. Slide the square until the blade intersects the rafter-height mark; then pencil a mark along the blade. Cut the joist along the mark, and then toenail the joist to the cap plate with three 16d nails.

To provide a place to work and a temporary support for ridgeboard bracing, tack three rows of sheathing panels perpendicular to and down the middle of the ceiling joists.

2 Splice the ridgeboard. The ridgeboard may be a straight one-by or two-by. Sight the board and make sure the crown, if any, faces up. Use a width that will allow full contact with the plumb cut of the rafter. Fit the ridgeboard to the length of the building plus the gable overhang at each end. You may have to join two boards. Use a scarf joint, which you make using a 45-degree angle cut into each piece. Carefully position this joint so that a rafter lands right on it, giving it extra strength. Add a temporary scab board onto the joint to support it during the ridge-raising operation.

3 Mark the ridgeboard. Lay the ridgeboard perpendicular to and across the ceiling joists, centered in the structure. Allow for the gable-end overhang. Mark an R for rafter placement using the joists as guides. Position the rafters so that they're flush with the ceiling joists and can be face-nailed.

4 Determine the ridgeboard height. The height of the ridgeboard is crucial because you've precisely cut the master rafter to sit a certain distance above the top plates. Calculate the dimension as follows:

(Total rise) + (Height of plumb line from the bird's-mouth seat cut to the top of the rafter) - (Depth of ceiling joist) - (Thickness of temporary sheathing panels) - (Depth of ridgeboard)

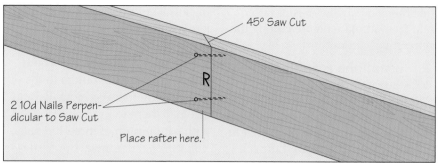

2 Use a scarf joint to join two or more pieces of lumber when making a long ridgeboard. The ridgeboard splice should break on a rafter.

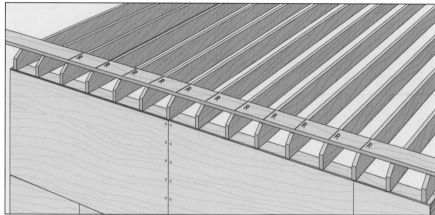

3 Mark the rafter locations on the ridgeboard. For 16-in.-on-center spacing, set each rafter so it's adjacent to a ceiling joist.

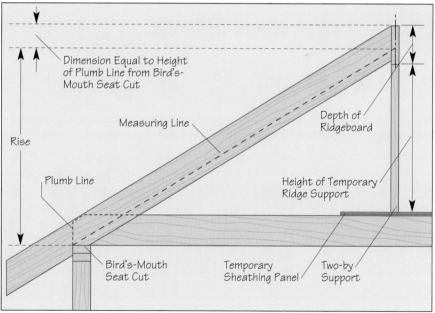

4 To get the ridgeboard height, add the rise and the rafter plumb-line height; then subtract the sheathing thickness and the joist and ridgeboard depth.

5 Raise the ridgeboard. Set the ridgeboard in place using vertical two-by braces nailed onto its side. Attach diagonal braces to the vertical two-by braces, and nail them to cleats on the temporary decking.

With the ridgeboard positioned, set the master rafter in place to see whether all the cuts you made fit snugly. If they do, mark and cut the rest of the rafters, using the master as your guide. If the cuts are off, ad-

9

GABLE-ROOF FRAMING

just them; cut a new master rafter; and try it in place before cutting the remaining rafters.

6 Install the rafters. Position the rafters in place in pairs. Face-nail the first rafter with three 16d nails at the ridgeboard, and then face-nail the matching rafter at an angle. (See drawing.) If the ceil-ing joists lap a bearing wall, the raf-ters will be offset by 1½ inches, and you'll be able to face-nail straight through the ridgeboard into both rafters. Toenail the rafters to the wall plate with three 16d nails, and face-nail them to the ceiling joists with a minimum of three 10d nails. You can also use metal hurricane ties to secure the rafters. If the plans call for collar ties, install them after you've installed the rafters.

7 Install sway braces. Once you've installed all the rafters, remove the temporary supports and sheathing if you're not putting down a subfloor. Nail a 6- to 8-foot 2×6 down the middle of the ceiling

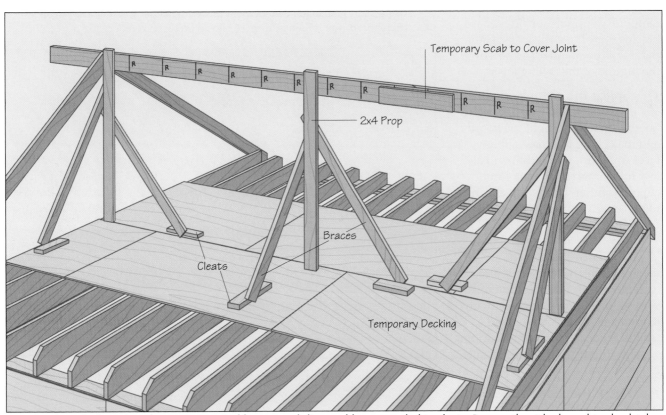

5 Set the ridgeboard in place using vertical braces and diagonal braces nailed to cleats. Be sure the ridgeboard is absolutely straight, and position the crown side (if any) up.

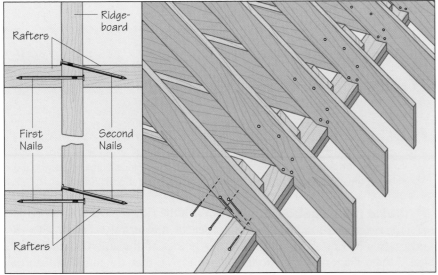

6 Nail the rafters to the ridgeboard using 16d nails as shown, and then attach the rafters at the wall plates.

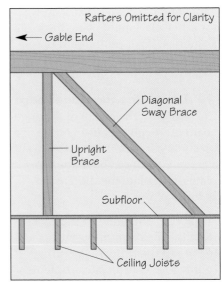

7 Brace the ridgeboard with vertical and diagonal sway braces.

joists at each gable end. Brace the ridgeboard near each end, 12 inches from the building's edge, with a 2×4 upright and a 2×4 diagonal cut at 45-degree angles to prevent roof sway.

Framing the Gable-End Overhang

The gable end of a roof needs an overhang that matches the eaves overhang. An overhang not only looks good but also keeps water away from the structure. Framing an overhang is relatively simple, but you must plan in advance.

Difficulty Level:

Tools and Materials

- Basic carpentry tools
- Four extra common rafters (two for each end of the roof)
- 2×6s for the outriggers
- 16d nails

1 **Frame the gable end.** After you've framed the roof with common rafters, use a plumb bob to find the center of the gable-end cap plate directly under the ridgeboard. If you'll be installing a gable-end vent, measure one-half its width to

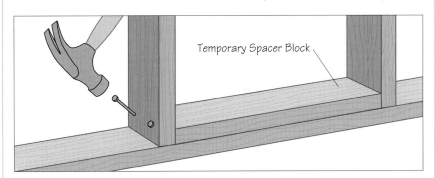

EASY TOENAILING

Sometimes you have to toenail, and when you do, a stud may shift off the layout lines as you drive the nails. Hold the studs in place with a temporary spacer block cut to fit your stud spacing. Make sure the nails don't hit the block, and remove it when you've finished nailing.

Temporary Spacer Block

each side of the center mark and mark for the first full studs. Continue to mark along the cap plate at your established stud spacing. Set a stud at a full stud position, plumb it, and mark where it intersects the end rafter. Set the stud at the next stud position and mark it again. The difference in height is the common difference between studs. Cut notches (corresponding to rafter height) 5 to 6 inches long and 1½ inches deep into the tops of several studs, using a sliding T-bevel to transfer the proper rafter angle for the bottom of the notches. Cut the

studs to fit between the top plate and the end rafters, using the common difference you determined earlier. Toenail the studs to the cap plate; then toenail and face-nail through the rafters into the notches using 16d nails.

2 **Notch the end rafters.** On each end rafter, notch out for a minimum of three outriggers. Outriggers are 2×6s that you face-nail into the crown edge of the end rafter and end-nail into the last common rafter. Set your circular saw to cut 1½ inches deep; make two marks 5½ inches apart where you'll place

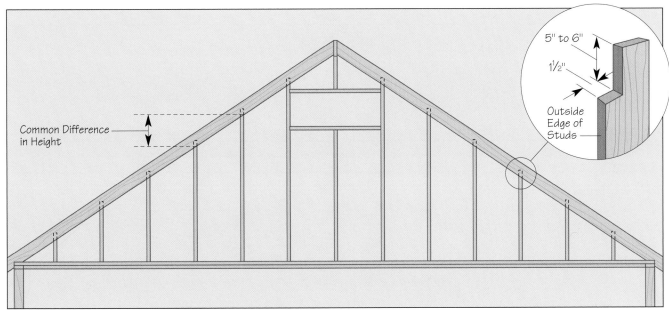

5" to 6"

1½"

Outside Edge of Studs

1 Notch wall studs to size and set them in the gable end, toenailing and face-nailing to secure them.

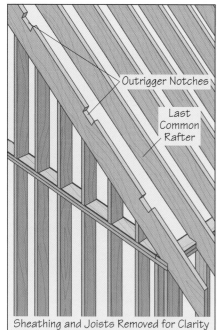

Outrigger Notches

Last Common Rafter

Sheathing and Joists Removed for Clarity

2 Cut notches in the end rafters 1½ x 5½ in. for 2x6 outriggers.

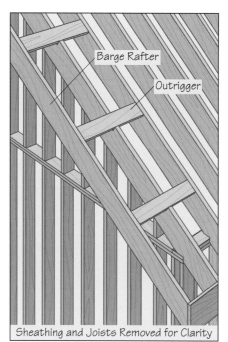

Barge Rafter

Outrigger

Sheathing and Joists Removed for Clarity

3 Cut each outrigger; nail it in place; and attach barge rafters.

each outrigger; and cut several kerfs between the marks. Plow out the cut areas with a chisel to complete the notches.

3 Cut and install the outriggers and barge rafters.
Measure and cut each outrigger to fit the width of the overhang plus the distance from the building line to the last common rafter. Install each outrigger by fitting it into one of the notches you cut in the end

rafters and butting one end against the last common rafter. Fasten the outriggers by face-nailing two 16d nails at the notches and end-nailing two 16d nails at the last common rafter. The barge rafters are really common rafters without bird's mouths. Face-nail the barge rafters to the outriggers using 16d nails; fasten them to the ridgeboard, also with 16d nails; and secure them at their tail ends with fascia boards and 10d finishing nails.

Trusses

If you're nervous about cutting rafters from scratch and you don't mind losing the open attic space, roof trusses are a roof-framing option. Roof trusses are difficult to install, but you can order them in custom sizes and configurations. Trusses are nothing more than 2×4 webs and 2×4 or 2×6 chords held together by gussets, which are flat metal or plywood plates. The two top chords and one long bottom chord form the shape of a gable roof. Webs tie the chords together. Cutting any one of the members compromises the structural integrity of the entire truss. Residential roof trusses commonly come in two forms, the W-type and Howe truss. End trusses often don't have the same web configuration as the trusses for the interior of the roof. Instead, the "webs" are vertical two-by studs installed at 16 or 24 inches on center.

You erect trusses right on the top plates, with one truss per stud bay. If you've framed the walls at 24 inches on center, the trusses will occur every 24 inches as well. Order trusses from a truss manufacturer by specifying the desired length of the bottom chord, which should be as long as the structure's span. You

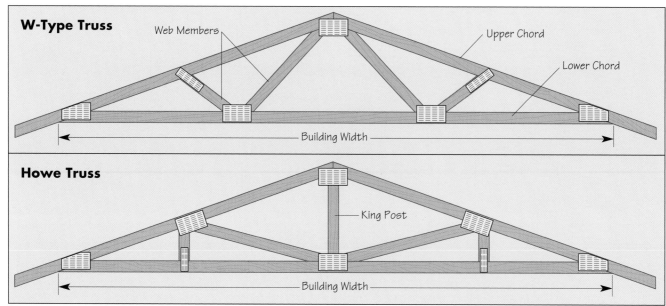

W-Type Truss

Web Members

Upper Chord

Lower Chord

Building Width

Howe Truss

King Post

Building Width

Trusses. In a standard truss, chords define a triangle; webs brace the chords; and scabs, gussets, and splices hold the truss together.

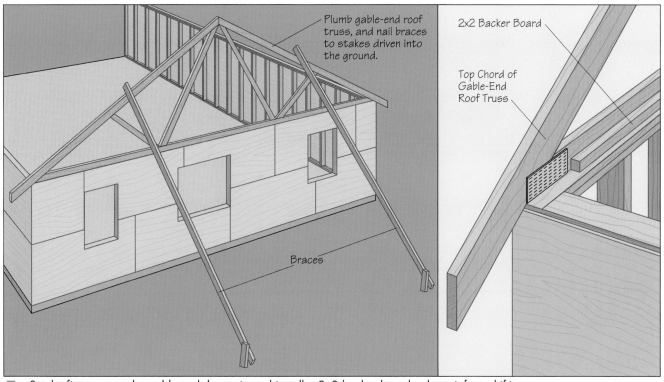

Set the first truss on the gable end; brace it; and install a 2x2 backer board to keep it from shifting.

may not have much control over ridge height.

The drawback to trusses is that they cut off attic storage space and deny you the opportunity to build second-story dormers or finish off an attic room. You'll find trusses most commonly used for storage buildings and garages.

The easiest way to erect trusses is with a crane, a potentially hazardous job as the trusses hang from a single sling attached to the apex of the truss triangle.

Erecting Trusses

Difficulty Level: 🐾🐾🐾

Tools and Materials

- Basic carpentry tools
- Crane and hoisting sling
- Two-by braces 6 to 10 ft. long
- 2x2 backers
- 12d and 16d common nails

1 **Position the first truss.**
Have the first truss lifted by

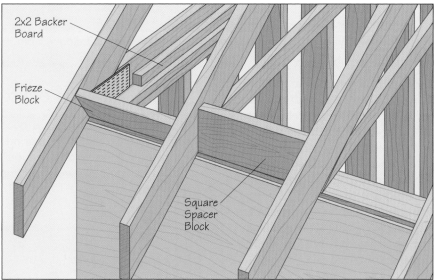

Set the remaining trusses in place, and install spacer blocks between them at the plates.

crane, and position it at the gable end of the roof on the cap plate. Fasten the truss using toenailed 16d nails or metal anchor brackets. Using 2×4s attached to stakes as diagonal braces, plumb the truss with a level, and nail it off to the braces. Leave the 2×4 braces in place until you've installed and braced all the trusses and nailed down the roof sheathing. Install a 2×2 backer board

to keep the base chord of the truss from moving out of position, and nail the truss to the 2×2 backer.

2 **Set the remaining trusses.**
Position the remaining trusses, installing spacer blocks between the trusses at the plates as you proceed. For 24-inch-on-center spacing, use 2×4 or 2×6 blocks 22½ inches long. Install same-length blocks between

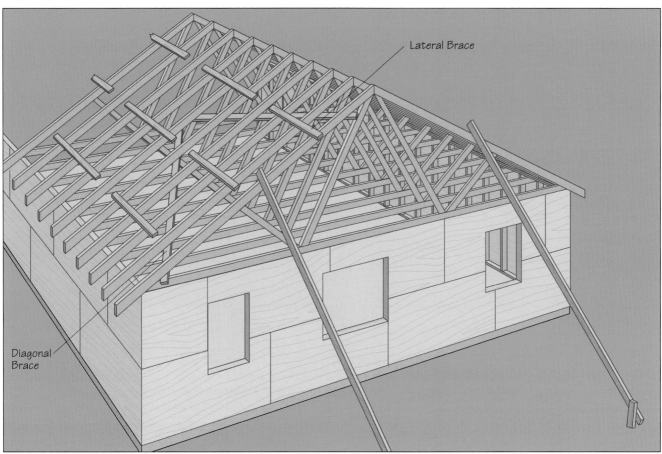

Lateral Brace

Diagonal Brace

3 Attach two-by lateral braces, each connecting three trusses, and diagonal braces underneath.

the trusses at the peak to form the ridgeboard and ensure proper spacing at the top. You can set the spacer blocks at the plate vertically, flush with the outside edge of the plate, or as a frieze block, set square with the truss and extending out from the top plate. Spacer blocks with vents are available from truss manufacturers. Install blocks with two 12d nails at each truss, face-nailing through the truss.

3 **Install the braces.** With three trusses installed, tack a 2×4 brace across the top on each side. Tack braces on additional trusses as you set them in position, midway and then near the bottom of the span. Also, for lengths of 20 feet or more, run a 1×4 diagonal brace at about a 45-degree angle from the cap plate to the peak on each side. Nail the diagonal to the underside of the truss top chord. You can leave the diagonal braces in place for greater stability of the roof.

The Pros Know

MISSING CONNECTORS

Connectors are a good idea when attaching joists to rim joists, or in any other load-bearing area of the framing. Without connectors, the only thing holding the joists in place is the end nails, and under stress, joists can pull away from rim joists, compromising their ability to carry loads.

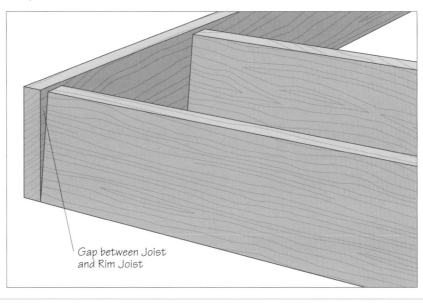

Gap between Joist and Rim Joist

Skylights

Installing a skylight in a roof is a good way to bring light to a windowless bathroom or to a large open space like a master bedroom suite. There's no secret to framing for a skylight. The trick is to prevent leaks when you do the finish work by flashing the skylight and applying shingles properly. Here's how to frame the skylight rough opening within the rafter bays. If you install a skylight in a roof above an attic, it may be necessary to create a skylight shaft to bring light into the living area.

Framing for a Skylight

Difficulty Level: 🦅🦅

Tools and Materials

- Basic carpentry tools
- Two-by rafter lumber that matches the dimensions of the rafters
- Two-by joist lumber

1 Frame the ceiling opening. First determine the correct rough opening by referring to the skylight manufacturer's literature, and then decide where in the room the skylight should go. Create an opening by doubling up the nearest ceiling joists on each side of the skylight. Install a double header on each end, perpendicular to the ceiling joists. Use framing connectors or 16d nails for all the connections. If the opening between the joists is too wide, use trimmers to narrow it.

2 Frame the roof opening. Use a plumb bob or level to define the rough roof opening above the ceiling opening. Double the entire rafter, from plate to ridge, on each side of the skylight's rough opening. Make a double header above and below to define the opening within the rafter bays, and install trimmers to adjust the space between rafters. Use framing connectors or 16d nails for all the connections.

3 Build the shaft. Use partition-wall-framing principles to create a skylight shaft. Build a stud wall between the floor joists and the underside of the rafters using 2×4s. Measure the angles with a sliding T-bevel, and cut the angles accurately. Install the studs as shown in the drawing, perpendicular to the headers and parallel with the joists and rafters. Toenail the studs with 10d or 12d nails. When you do the finish work, you'll insulate the shaft walls and apply drywall to them. A more careful approach is first to sheathe the walls with plywood to create a more stable shaft and minimize cracking of the drywall joints. Once you sheathe the roof, but before you attach the roofing shingles, install the skylight according to the manufacturer's instructions.

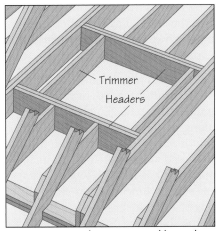

1 Determine the correct width, and install double headers and trimmers.

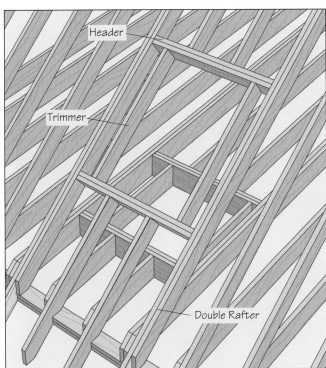

2 Header off the roof opening in a manner similar to that used for the ceiling opening.

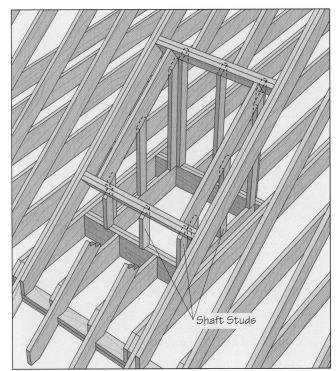

3 Connect the roof and ceiling openings with studs to form a shaft. Use a sliding T-bevel to mark the shaft studs.

9

GABLE-ROOF FRAMING

Roof Sheathing

Roof sheathing comes after all the rafters are in place. Sheathing stabilizes the roof and provides a nailing surface for the roofing material. Roof sheathing can be $\frac{3}{8}$ inch (only for 16-inch on-center rafters) or $\frac{1}{2}$ inch thick (for 16- or 24-inch-on-center rafters). There's not much cost difference. Plywood is the choice sheathing material, but your building code may allow less expensive nonveneer sheathing materials like oriented-strand board (OSB). Whether you use plywood or OSB, be sure the panels are APA-rated Exposure 1 where you'll enclose the soffit. For open soffits, use panels marked Exterior or Exposure 1 of the appropriate grade to permit painting or staining. Be sure to stagger the sheathing-panel joints so the seams don't line up.

Sheathing the Roof

Prolonged exposure to the weather can damage the framing, so waterproof the structure as soon as possible. Use caution: the greater the roof slope, the more hazardous the job. On steep roofs, nail down 2×4 cleats for footing support as you work up the roof.

Difficulty Level:

Tools and Materials

- Basic carpentry tools
- Plywood sheathing
- 8d nails or powered stapler
- Panel clips (for 24-in.-on-center framing)
- Drip edge
- 15 lb. asphalt-impregnated roofing felt
- $\frac{7}{8}$-in roofing nails

1 Make the sheathing layout. Draw a scaled sheathing layout for the entire roof on paper, showing panel sizes, placement, and number of panels; graph paper is easiest to use. Plan any panel cutting on one side so you can use the cut-off portions on the opposite side. You can start at the eaves with a full 4-foot-wide panel, provided you don't end up at the top having to use a strip less than 16 inches wide. A narrow strip may be too weak to support a person or provide a solid backing for the roofing. Trim the panels of the first row to adjust the width of the last row. Stagger the panels in succeeding

rows so the ends fall on different framing members. The sketch will reveal the number of panels required over open soffits; use the appropriate grade panels previously mentioned over these areas.

2 Install the panels. Begin panel installation at a bottom corner of the roof, placing the long side perpendicular to the rafters and positioning the end joint over the center of a rafter. Use H panel clips on panels installed on 24-inch-on-center rafters. Locate clips midpoint between the rafters. Make the panel edges flush with rafter ends and the edge of fascia rafters. Leave a $\frac{1}{8}$-inch space between panels for expansion.

Fasten each panel using 8d common, spiral-threaded, or ring-shank nails. Space nails 6 inches apart along panel ends and 12 inches at intermediate supports. If you use a powered staple gun, use 1½-inch staples for ½-inch plywood. Drive the staples 4 inches apart along the edges and 8 inches in the interior of the sheathing. Start the second course with a half (4 × 4-foot) panel. Stagger the panels by at least one rafter as you go up the roof.

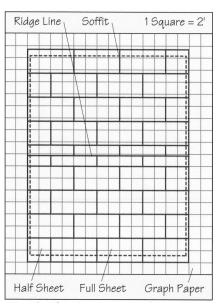

1 Plan for sheathing installation by drawing a scaled layout of panel placement.

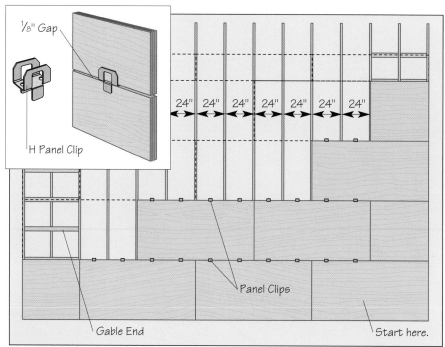

2 Start from a bottom corner of the roof, and use panel clips where rafters are placed 24 in. on center.

INSTALLING FLASHING

Install flashing where the roof of an attached structure joins the house, around chimneys, around skylights, and in valleys. All metal flashing must be at least 26-gauge (0.019-inch, or 0.48mm) corrosion-resistant coil stock (preferably aluminum or copper). For chimneys, skylights, and garages where a gable roof butts a vertical side wall, you'll weave metal step flashing with the roof shingles.

For chimneys, you start with an apron flashing. Cut the flashing as shown in the drawing, install it over the shingles; then continue with the step flashing. Install a section of flashing, then a shingle, and so on. You finish with another apron on the up-roof side, which goes under the shingles. Step flashing pieces are rectangular, usually 10 inches long and 2 inches wider than the exposed face of the roofing shingles. Roofing shingles with a 5-inch exposure, for example, require 10x7-inch step flashing. Fold the 10-inch length in half so that it can extend 5 inches onto the roof deck and 5 inches up the chim-

ney, skylight, or wall. For chimneys, a second metal flashing, called cap flashing, is set about 1½ inches into the mortar joints of the chimney and bent over to cover the step flashing. Then you install a roof-like cricket on the up-roof side (drawing), and cover it with roll roofing, overlapping the shingles by 4 to 5 inches.

When you use step flashing on an attached gable roof, begin installation at the base of the roof by placing a section over the end of the roofing starter strip. Position the flashing so that you'll cover it with the tab of the end shingle in the first course of shingles. Secure the vertical arm of the flashing using one nail.

Apply the first course of roofing shingles. Then place the second piece of flashing over the end shingle in the first course of roofing shingles. Position the flashing shingle 5 inches up from the butt so that you'll completely cover it with the tab of the end shingle in the second course. Apply the second course of roofing shingles, flash the end, and so on.

For a shed roof against a vertical wall, you'll lay shingles up the roof until you have to trim a course to fit the base of the vertical wall. The last, trimmed, course must be at least 8 inches wide, so it may be necessary to adjust the exposure of preceding courses to achieve this dimension. Check your spacing well before you come to these last courses so that you can make adjustments.

Install a continuous piece of 26-gauge metal flashing over the last shingle course. Fold the flashing strip so that it will extend a minimum 5 inches up the wall and 4 inches onto the last course of shingles. Embed the flashing strip in asphalt plastic roof cement, and nail it to the wall. There's no need to nail the flashing to the roof. Apply a row of shingle tabs over the metal flashing strip, trimmed to the width of the strip and embedded in roof cement.

Bring the siding down over the flashing at the wall as cap flashing. Leave space between the siding and the roof to allow for painting.

9

GABLE-ROOF FRAMING

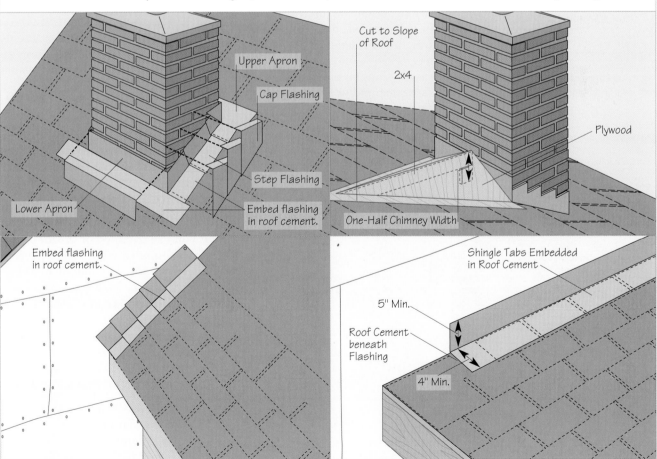

Upper Apron

Cap Flashing

Step Flashing

Lower Apron

Embed flashing in roof cement.

Cut to Slope of Roof

2x4

Plywood

One-Half Chimney Width

Embed flashing in roof cement.

Shingle Tabs Embedded in Roof Cement

5" Min.

Roof Cement beneath Flashing

4" Min.

3 **Install the drip edge.** The drip edge, or drip cap, is a molded metal strip that fits the edges of the entire roof, both eaves and rakes, to divert water runoff. The edge comes in 10-foot lengths. Install the drip edge with 7/8-inch roofing nails along the eaves before applying roofing felt. Later, apply the felt so that it overlaps the edge. At the rake ends, install the drip edge over the felt.

4 **Lay the roofing felt.** Use asphalt-impregnated roofing felt as an underlayment under asphalt shingles. Attach the felt with corrosion-resistant roofing nails long enough to penetrate sheathing or with 1/2-inch staples using a

hammer tacker or powered staple. In general, roof slope dictates the method of felt installation: in temperate climates, apply one layer of 15-pound felt on roofs having a 4-in-12 slope or greater. Lap the felt 2 inches horizontally and 6 inches vertically to shed water. Overlap the ridge by at least 6 inches.

On roofs having less than a 4-in-12 slope, start with a 19-inch-wide sheet at the eaves. Lay a 36-inch-wide sheet over the first, and then lap each subsequent sheet 19 inches horizontally and at least 12 inches vertically. This layout, in effect, provides a double layer of felt.

Installing Shingles

You can buy shingles in conventional three-tab strip styles and in architectural styles, which mimic the look of slate or wood shakes. Three-tab strip shingles are available in a self-sealing asphalt and fiberglass base. The shingle size most commonly used is 36 inches wide and 12 inches long, installed with 5 inches exposed to the weather. Approximate weight per square, or 100 square feet, is 215 pounds, with—in most cases—shingles packaged in three separate bundles to the square.

Asphalt shingles have an asphalt-saturated organic base. Fiberglass shingles are essentially the same except that glass fiber replaces the organic base. You can buy shingles rated to last anywhere from 20 to 50 years.

While roofers often have their own methods of applying strip shingles, this discussion will cover the 6-inch, 5-inch, and 4-inch trim methods with a 5-inch exposure. If you're installing architectural-type shingles, the same general principles apply, but follow the manufacturer's instructions carefully to achieve the proper look.

Difficulty Level:

Tools and Materials

- Basic carpentry tools
- Shingles
- Flashing
- 1 1/4-in. roofing nails (2 1/4 lbs. per square) or staples

1 **Apply the starter strip.** The starter strip can be a row of shingles trimmed to the manufacturer's specifications, a strip of mineral-surface roll roofing at least 7 inches wide, or a course of shingles turned so that the tabs face up the roof. The starter strip protects the roof by covering the spaces under the cutouts and the joints of the first course of shingles. Extend the strip beyond the drip edge at the rake ends and the eaves by 1/4 to 3/8 inch.

If you use trimmed or upside-down shingles, cut 6 inches from the end of the first shingle in the starter strip to ensure that the cutouts of the first course won't fall over the starter strip joints. Nail along a line parallel to the eaves and about 4 inches above it. Place nails so they don't show under the cutouts of the first course.

You might use 36-inch-wide roll roofing as a starter strip to protect against ice damming in a cold climate. If so, nail the roll roofing along

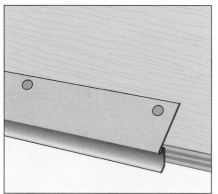

3 Attach metal drip edge along the eave and rake ends using roofing nails.

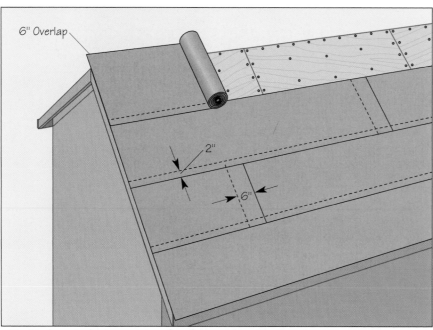

4 Nail or staple down the roofing felt, overlapping the edges.

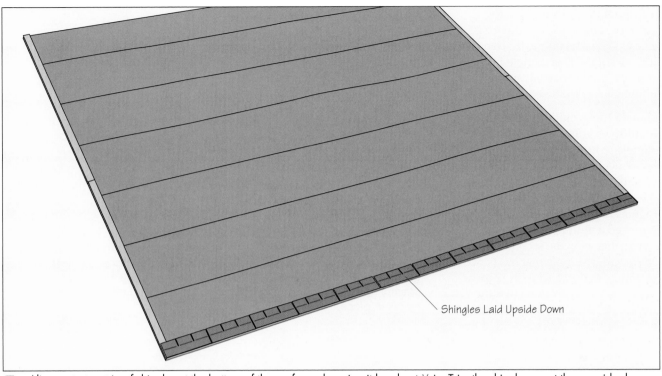

Shingles Laid Upside Down

1 Align a starter strip of shingles at the bottom of the roof, overhanging it by about ¼ in. Trim the shingles or set them upside down.

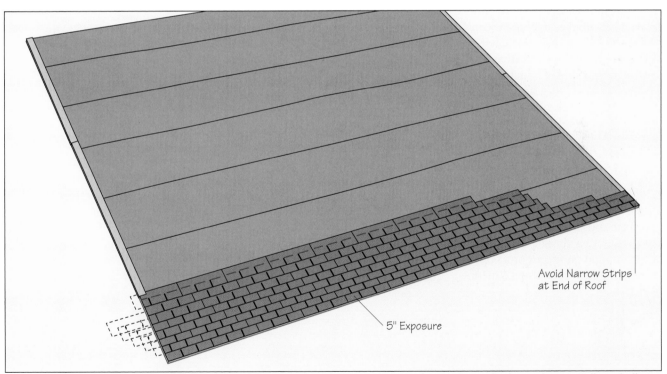

Avoid Narrow Strips at End of Roof

5" Exposure

2 Start the first course with a full shingle, and then trim the other courses according to the method you choose. Follow chalk lines snapped parallel to the eaves every few courses.

a line 4 inches above the eaves, with nails spaced 12 inches apart.

2 Lay the courses. Keep the cutouts in a straight line as you work up the roof. Measuring from the edge of the roof and snapping chalk lines to guide every few courses will help you keep the shingles aligned. Begin the first course with a full-length shingle. On most of the remaining courses you'll trim a little off the first shingle to conform to the method of installation selected.

Depending on the length of your roof and how the shingles fit it, you'll use the 6-inch, 5-inch, or

4-inch method, named for the amount removed from the first shingle in each course. By removing part of the first shingle in each row, the cutouts in that course will not line up with the course below.

Choose the installation method that leaves you with the widest shingle strip at the finish end. With the 6-inch method, also called the centered alignment method, begin the second through sixth courses with a shingle from which you've removed a multiple of 6 inches. It works this way: the second course starts with a shingle that has 6 inches removed; the third with 12 inches removed, the fourth with 18 inches, the fifth with 24 inches, and the sixth with 30 inches. The adjacent shingle in each course is full-width. Begin the seventh course with a full-width shingle, and repeat the pattern.

The 5-inch method works the same way, except that each of the second through sixth courses starts with a shingle from which you've removed a multiple of 5 inches. The seventh course would normally start with a 1-inch-wide piece, which is too small, so start with a full shingle. The 4-inch method follows the same procedure, except that the trim-off is a multiple of 4 inches.

Some roofers use a method different from those described above, starting with a shingle cut in half, a full shingle on the second course, a half shingle on the third course,

NAILING TIPS

■ Use the recommended size and grade of fasteners, such as corrosion-resistant 12-gauge nails with a $\frac{3}{8}$-inch head or approved staples.

■ Use four fasteners—one 1 inch from each end and one centered over each of the two cutouts.

■ Align shingles so you cover all nails or staples with the course above. When you lay shingles with a 5-inch exposure, place the nails on a line $\frac{5}{8}$ inch above the top of the cutouts.

■ Drive the nails straight, not at an angle. Do not break the shingle surface with the fastener head.

■ Don't drive fasteners into cracks in the roof sheathing.

■ Don't nail into or above the sealing adhesive. Align each shingle correctly and keep nails at least 2 inches from the cutouts and the end joints of the underlying course. Start nailing from the end nearest the last shingle laid, and continue across the shingle. This prevents buckling. Do not attempt to realign the shingle by shifting the free end after more than one nail is in place.

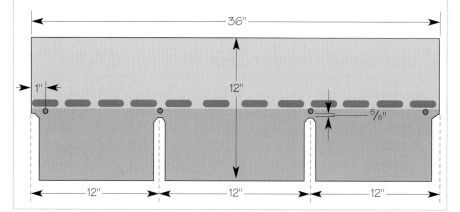

and so on up the roof. To ensure a professional job, follow the manufacturer's instructions.

3 **Cap the ridge.** Begin by cutting full shingles or pieces of scrap shingles as shown. Make sure the tapered ends are narrower than the exposed portions to end

up with a neater job. Apply shingles with a 5-inch exposure. Start at the ridge end that's opposite the prevailing wind direction. Drive one nail on each side at a point about 5½ inches from the exposed end of the shingle and 1 inch up from the edge. You may need longer nails for the cap shingles.

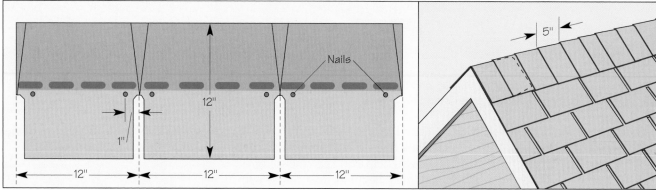

3 Make tapered cuts in the shingles for the ridge cap, and install them with a 5-in. exposure, nailed as shown.

Shed, Hip & Gambrel Roofs

While gable roofs may be the most popular type of roofing design used on residential buildings, there are other types of roofs that are specified often, including shed, hip, and gambrel roofs. The kind of roof you use will depend on your architectural taste, the climate in which you live, and the building's function. Shed roofs, also called lean-to roofs, are often used on animal barns and wood sheds. These roofs are easy to build and require minimal carpentry skills, but in heated, insulated structures they may be hard to vent. Hip roofs offer an appealing design, but they are difficult to frame. Gambrel roofs are also attractive, their distinctive shape being reminiscent of English country houses, and they are practical because their rafter configuration provides extra second-floor space. Because of their practicality, gambrel roofs are often used on barns. Each roof type requires a different style of cutting and assembling rafters. This chapter will cover the framing requirements for each type.

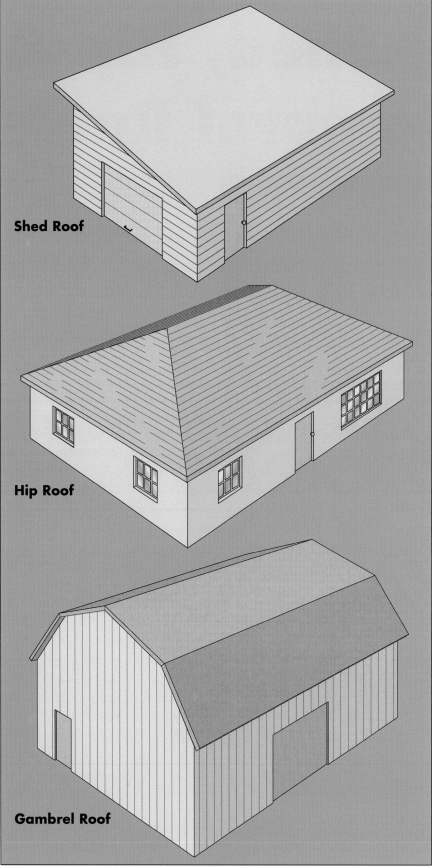

Shed, Hip & Gambrel Roofs. Three alternative roof types include shed, hip, and gambrel. Cutting rafters for each type of roof applies the same principles of span and slope but different principles of rafter design.

Framing Shed Roofs

Shed roofs, popular on porches, dormers, vacation homes, and smaller utility buildings, tend to have shallow slopes. A shed roof is essentially one-half a gable roof. Both ends of the roof rest on top plates, except on porches and dormers, so marking and cutting shed-roof rafters is simple. Your blueprints will give you the correct wall heights to which you should build for a shed-roof structure.

Marking Shed Rafters

1 **Determine the rafter length.** Your blueprints will likely specify the dimension rafter lumber to use. If not, use a span table to choose the lumber. (See "Rafter Span Ratings," page 27.) Next, you'll need to determine the rafter length. First obtain the roof slope and the run from your plans; then determine the rise. Note that, unlike a gable roof, the run is the total span of the building minus one wall thickness. Estimate the length stock you'll need, and then use the rise and run of your building and the Pythagorean theorem to determine rafter length, or use a framing square. (See "Rafter Length Measurement," page 123.)

2 **Lay out the rafters.** Sight each rafter, and make sure the crown edge is up. Starting at the higher end of the rafter, use the framing square to mark the building line. For a 3-in-12 roof, make the mark by setting the framing square at 3 inches along the tongue and 12 inches along the blade. When the rafter is in position, this line will be plumb and will determine the outside edge of the top plate. Subtract from this the width of the wall plate, and draw another plumb line. The second line will indicate the inside edge of the front wall. Measure the rafter length from the first building line you drew, and make a mark along the crown edge to establish the inside edge of

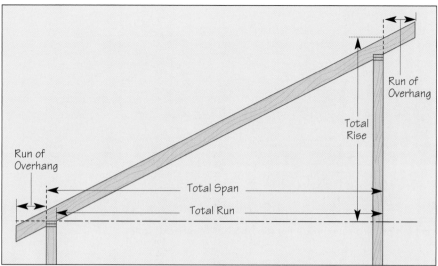

1 Obtain the slope and run from your plans, figure out the rise, and then determine the rafter length you'll need.

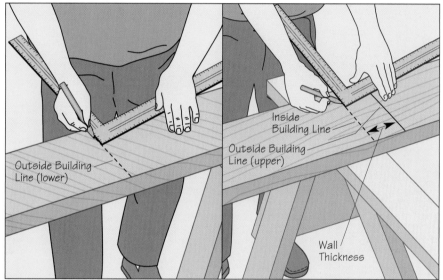

2 Align the framing square for a 3-in-12 slope, and draw the building reference lines, top and bottom.

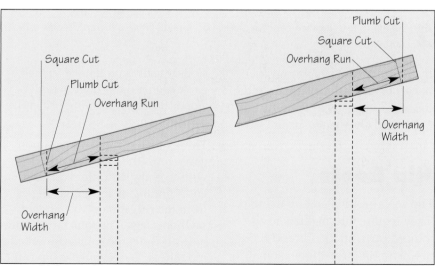

3 Add the overhangs to the outside building lines, and cut the rafters plumb or square, according to your design.

the back wall. Add the width of the wall plate; position the framing square at 3 and 12 at this mark; and draw another building line here. With the rafter in position, this line will be plumb and will mark the outside edge of the back wall.

3 Calculate the overhangs.
Now it's time to add overhangs to each of your building lines. The unit length on a rafter table of a 3-in-12 roof is 12.3. (See "Using a Rafter Table," page 125.) So if you want an 18-inch (1½-foot) overhang on each end, multiply 12.3 by 1.5, and you get 18.45 inches, or 18½ inches. At each end of the rafter, measure along the lower edge 18½ inches. Make a mark and, with your framing square set at 3 and 12, use the mark to draw either a plumb line (if you're installing a fascia) or a square line (if you want the rafter to end square). This will give you an overhang of 18 inches. Note that on a low-sloped roof the desired overhang width is near equal to the overhang run (a difference of ½ inch in this case).

Installing Shed-Roof Rafters

Difficulty level: 🦇🦇

Tools and Materials

■ Basic carpentry tools

■ Framing square

■ Rafter stock

Shed rafters, like common gable rafters, need a bird's mouth notched into them wherever the rafters will sit on the cap plates. Shed roofs are a little tricky, however, because both ends of the rafters sit on cap plates. Remember that the upper building line (the first line you drew) marks the outside of the building, but you'll need to cut the bird's mouth on a plumb line that marks the inside of this wall. So be sure to draw the upper bird's mouth using the line you drew after you measured back the width of the wall plate.

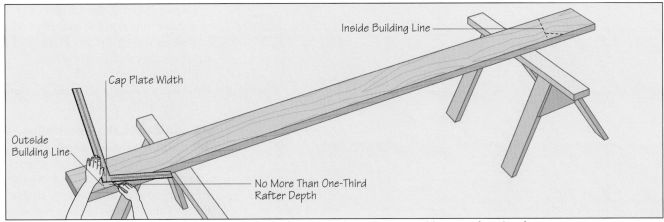

1 Use the framing square to mark the seat cut for the bird's mouths at the top and bottom of each rafter.

1 Mark the bird's mouths.

The seat cut, or the horizontal cut that allows the rafter to sit on the cap plate, should match the width of the plate. If you're framing the walls with 2×4s, the seat cut should be 3½ inches wide. Using the framing square, line up the blade with the building line and move the square up or down until the 3½-inch mark on the tongue intersects the underside edge of the rafter. Draw the 3½-inch-long seat-cut line. The plumb-cut line runs from where the seat-cut line intersects the building line (inside line for the top of the rafter and outside line for the bottom of the rafter) down to the rafter edge. The depth of the plumb cut should not exceed one-third the width of the rafter. Let's say you are framing with 2×8 rafters. The 2×8's actual width is 7¼ inches, and when it is tilted up at a 3-in-12 slope, it has an apparent width of about 8 inches. So the bird's-mouth depth of cut should be no more than about 2½ inches. Start the cuts with a circular saw, but finish them with a handsaw.

2 Position and fasten the rafters.
Position the shed rafters so they sit right above studs, not over the stud bays. The rafters should transfer the roof load to the studs in straight vertical lines. Toenail the rafters to the cap plates using 16d nails. Install outriggers and barge rafters for overhangs on each side of

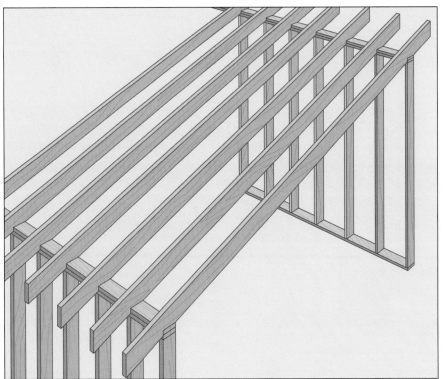

2 Put the rafters in place over the studs, and toenail them to the cap plates using 16d nails.

the roof (similar to gable-end overhangs) to match the overhang at the top and bottom. (See "Framing the Gable-End Overhang," page 133.)

Hip Roofs

Hip roofs are challenging to build. They require intermediate to advanced carpentry skills and the ability to do three-dimensional problem solving. Avoid hip roofs unless you are confident of your

skills. Ideally you'll have framed a gable roof and thoroughly understood those roof framing principles before attempting a hip roof.

Think of a hip roof as a common gable roof (the middle rafters) with two angled rafters on each end, running at 45-degree angles from the ridgeboard like angled sawhorse legs. The four rafters running at 45-degree angles are called hip rafters. Between these hip rafters and the cap plate run hip jack rafters of varying lengths.

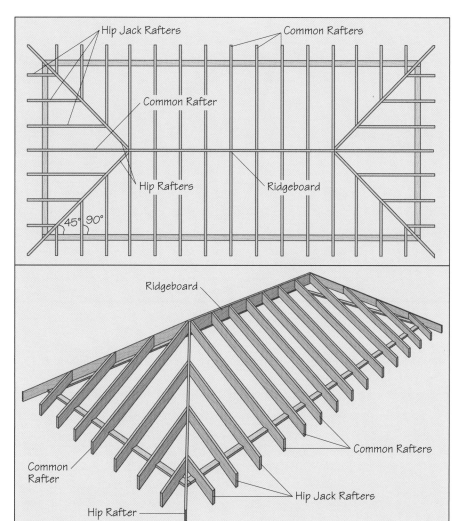

Hip Roofs. A hip roof is basically a gable roof with angled rafters on each end, making for complex angle cuts.

Beginning a Hip Roof

Difficulty level:

Tools and Materials

- Basic carpentry tools and nails
- Framing square
- Two-by ridgeboard and rafter stock

1 **Cut the ridgeboard and common rafters.** To obtain the ridgeboard length for a hip roof, take the length of the building, subtract the span (or two times the run), and add the thickness of the rafters. Cut the ridgeboard from appropriate two-by stock.

Determine the building's slope, and then cut the common rafters for a hip roof as you would cut them for

a common gable roof. There is no difference between a common rafter used on a hip roof and a common rafter used on a gable roof. The same principles of rise and run

apply, as do the principles for cutting the bird's mouths. (See "Gable-Roof Framing," pages 121–142.)

2 **Calculate the hip-rafter length.** Because the hip rafters run at a 45-degree angle, they will invariably be longer than the common rafters. When determining the rise and run of a common gable rafter in the previous chapter, you used a run figure of 12. For hip rafters, that run figure changes to 17. A hip rafter must run 17 inches to reach the same height that a common rafter reaches in 12 inches of run. Also, because the hip rafters run at a 45-degree angle, the cut at the ridge will actually be two side, or cheek, cuts so that each rafter can sit snugly between the perpendicular common rafters.

For this example, assume a 6-in-12 roof that rises 6 feet. The hip-rafter run is 17 feet. Notice in the drawing that the hip-rafter run is not half the building's span, but the distance from the building line at the corner to the center of the building's width at the ridgeboard.

Now use a framing square to find hip-rafter length. Note on the framing square that a unit length for a hip rafter on a 6-in-12 roof is 18. You'll find that number under the 6-inch mark on the second line of the table etched into the framing square, along the line marked "Length Hip or Valley Per Foot of Run." Multiply the roof run by

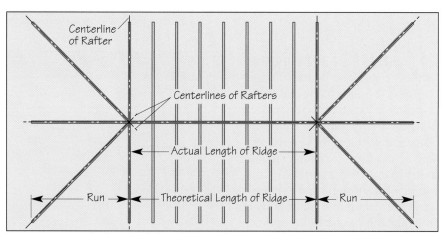

1 Determine the length of the ridgeboard; cut it; and install the common gable rafters.

the hip-rafter unit length: 12 × 18 = 216 inches, or 18 feet. The hip-rafter length for a run of 12 feet (at a 6-in-17 slope) is 18 feet.

3 **Shorten the hip rafter.** The hip-rafter length you just obtained is the theoretical rafter length, the distance from the building line to the center of the ridge along the roof's hip. Just as with common gable rafters, you must shorten the hip rafter to accommodate the thickness of the ridge. This procedure is complicated by the fact that the hip rafter fits between a common rafter parallel with the ridgeboard and the last true common rafter on the main part of the roof. So to get the actual hip-rafter length, you must deduct one-half the 45-degree thickness of the ridgeboard.

Draw a 45-degree line across the crown edge of the ridgeboard; then measure the length of this line and divide by two. Draw a square line across the crown edge at one end of the hip rafter. Measure back from the square line the amount at which you just arrived, and make a mark. Draw another square line through the mark, and find that line's center point. This is the line for the shortened hip rafter.

4 **Mark the ridge side cuts.** It's easy to mark for side, or cheek, cuts by using the framing square and rafter table. The last line on the rafter table reveals figures, by unit rise, for "Side Cut Hip or Valley."

For a roof with a 6-inch unit rise, the side cut figure is $11\frac{5}{16}$ inches. Place the framing square at the uphill end of the hip rafter on its crown edge, aligning 17 on the blade and $11\frac{5}{16}$ on the tongue to establish the proper side-cut angle. With the framing square in position, make a side-cut line across the crown edge of the rafter intersecting the center of the cut line for shortening the rafter. Turn the square over, align it again, and make the second side-cut line, forming a point with the other side-cut line.

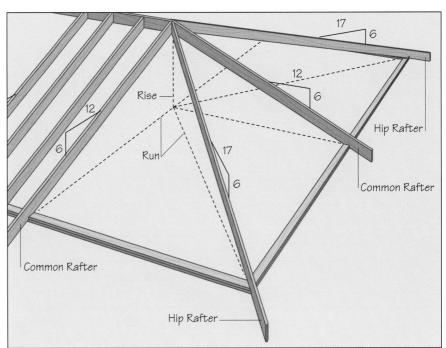

2 Determine the length of the hip rafters using a unit run of 17 inches instead of 12.

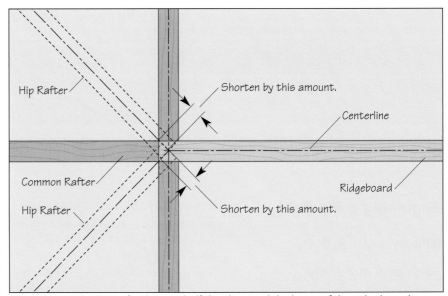

3 Shorten the hip rafter by one-half the diagonal thickness of the ridgeboard.

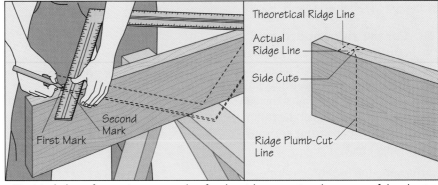

4 Mark the rafter on its crown edge for the side cuts using the center of the shortened mark as reference.

RAFTER TABLES ON A FRAMING SQUARE

Some people get a framing square and use it as a large square for standard carpentry. They are unaware of the wealth of information imprinted on its side. The rafter table found on a framing square contains much work-saving data essential to many framing calculations. Here's a description of the table line by line.

The first line in a rafter table gives unit lengths for common rafters. (See "Rafter Length Measurement," page 123.) Unit length is the common-rafter length required, in inches and decimals, at any given slope to gain a foot of run (a foot of horizontal distance). A rafter at a steep 10-in-12 slope has to be longer to cover a foot of run than a rafter at an 8-in-12 slope. The figures on the rafter table's first line break out those runs for you by the unit rise of your slope (as with all the figures on a rafter table). You look below the inch designation that corresponds to your unit rise to find the numbers you need. If you're framing an 8-in-12 roof, for example, look at the row of numbers below the framing square's 8-inch mark (that's the 8-inch mark on the square's blade, or wider portion). If you're framing a 12-in-12 roof, look under the number 12 on the blade of the square.

The second line of the rafter table gives the unit length, in inches and decimals, of hip or valley rafters per foot of run. This is the same principle as that described in the previous paragraph, but these unit-length figures are for hip or valley rafters instead of common rafters.

The third and fourth lines of the rafter table are the difference in jack-rafter lengths for either 16-inch (third line) or 24-inch (fourth line) on-center framing. When jack rafters run between the hip rafters and top plates of a building, they get smaller as they move away from the last common rafter and work into the corner of the building. The amount you decrease each jack in length is a predictable figure. That figure is dependent on slope and on-center spacing, however, so to determine how much to lop off a

jack rafter, check under the inch mark for your respective unit rise and look along the line marked for your on-center framing. You'll find the common length difference for jack rafters.

Slope also affects side cuts. When rafters meet, they don't always meet at 45 or 90 degrees. The angle varies and is affected by slope. To make a side cut, place a framing square along the crown edge of the rafter, with the 12 lined up on the blade and another figure lined up along the tongue, and mark the rafter along the blade. That second figure, the tongue figure, is the one that varies. For side cuts at the base of jack rafters, you'll find jack side cuts along the fifth line of the rafter table, under the inch mark that designates unit rise. For hip- or valley-rafter side cuts, move on to the sixth (last) line on the framing square.

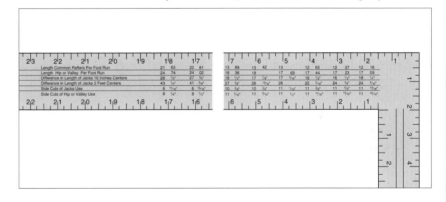

Length Common Rafters Per Foot Run	21 63	20 81	13 89	13 42	13
Length Hip or Valley Per Foot Run	24 74	24 02	18 36	18	17 69
Difference in Length of Jacks 16 Inches Centers	28 7/8	27 3/4	16 1/2	17 7/8	17 5/16
Difference in Length of Jacks 2 Feet Centers	43 1/4	41 5/8	27 3/4	26 19/32	26
Side Cuts of Jacks Use	6 11/32	6 15/32	10 3/4	10 3/4	11
Side Cuts of Hip or Valley Use	8 1/4	8 1/2	11 1/16	11 5/16	11

EASY SIDE CUTS

Here's an easy way to make ridge side cuts for a hip rafter. Set the framing square for the correct slope and mark along both sides of the tongue as shown. Adjust your circular saw to cut at a 45-degree angle by tilting the base plate of the saw. Check the cutting angle using an angle square. Make two 45-degree cuts with the circular saw, one from each side of the board, and you're done.

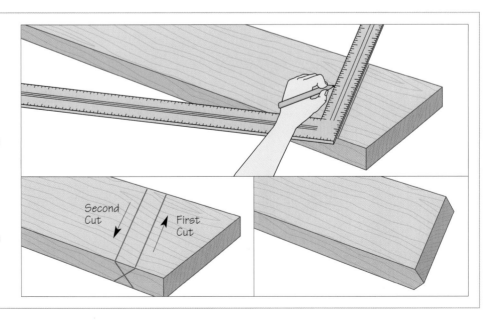

Second Cut · First Cut

Now turn the rafter on the flat. With the framing square set at 6 and 17, draw a plumb line from the back corner (downhill side) of one of the side-cut lines. Turn the rafter over and repeat the procedure. These are the ridge plumb-cut lines.

5 **Lay out the tail cuts.** Using the first square line you drew in Step 3, the theoretical ridge line, measure back the rafter length along the rafter's crown edge and make a square line. From the rafter-length line, draw a plumb building line with your framing square set at the proper rise and run. Using the building line as a reference, measure and mark a bird's-mouth seat cut just as you would on a common rafter. Next, determine the hip-rafter overhang. (See "Hip-Rafter Overhang," on page 151.) Read your framing square's rafter table to obtain the hip-rafter unit length for your roof's unit rise, and measure back for the desired overhang distance.

Square a line across the crown edge at the end of the rafter after calculating your overhang length; find the center point; and mark it. Draw side-cut lines, just as you did at the ridge, but this time the arrow these side-cut lines create will point downhill. At the uphill ends of the side-cut lines, draw a set of tail plumb-cut lines. The tail cut will accommodate fascia boards where they meet at the corner of the building.

6 **Cut the backing.** Before installing the hip rafters, cut an angled backing along the top edge with your circular saw. This is nothing more than a chamfer, or angled cut, that will allow the roof sheathing to rest flush against the top edge of the hip rafter. To determine the amount you must cut off, set the framing square so that the rise on the tongue aligns with the crown edge and 17 on the blade also aligns with the crown edge. Measure down the blade one-half the thickness of the rafter, and make a mark. Then draw a line along the length of the rafter corresponding to the mark.

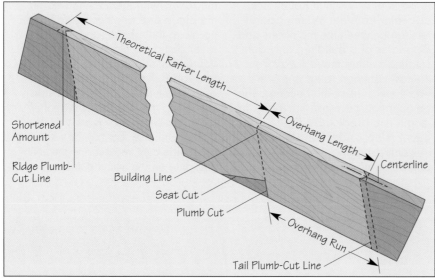

5 Measure the rafter length from the first ridge mark you made; mark the building line; then measure the overhang.

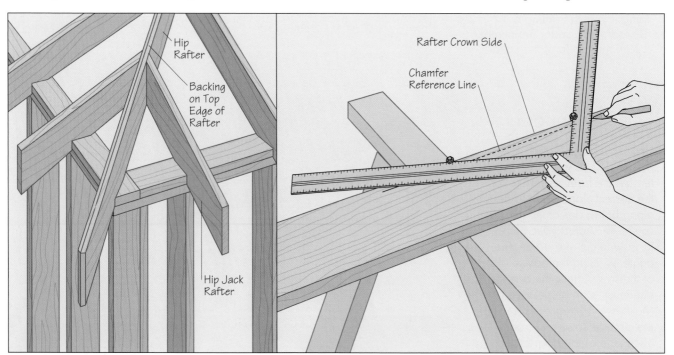

6 Chamfer the tops of the hip rafters before installing them by cutting down to the line you make with the square.

HIP-RAFTER OVERHANG

To mark for an overhang on hip rafters, you need to know that the run of all hip-rafter overhangs is 1.41 inches for every 1 inch of common-rafter overhang. That's because, being in the corner, the run of the hip-rafter overhang is the hypotenuse of a right triangle that has sides equal to the run of the common rafters and jack rafters. Theoretically speaking, think of a common-rafter overhang of 1 inch and use the Pythagorean theorem to determine the hip-rafter overhang (hypotenuse): $1^2 + 1^2 = 2$; the square root of 2 is 1.41.

Assume a common-rafter overhang of 12 inches and use the Pythagorean theorem to determine the hip-rafter overhang: $144 + 144 = 288$. The square root of 288 is 16.97 inches. Now if you multiply 12 x 1.41 (actually 1.4142135, the true square root of 2), you also get 16.97. Round off to 17 inches. That's the overhang the hip rafter must run to maintain a 12-inch common overhang. To determine the length the rafter must be to achieve the overhang of 17 inches (which also happens to be the unit run for a hip rafter), multiply the overhang by the unit length for hip rafters from the framing square's rafter table. Assuming a 6-inch rise, you'd multiply 1x18 = 18 inches. Measure down the rafter from the building line 18 inches to achieve the 17-inch overhang. The exactness of this measurement is crucial

because the fascia will bulge out or be indented if the hip rafter is too long or too short.

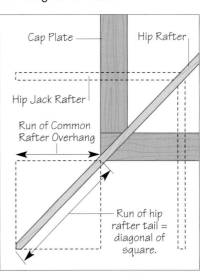

Installing Hip-Roof Jack Rafters

Hip-roof jack rafters run between the hip rafter and the top plates. Each jack rafter is a different length, but because the roof is symmetrical, you can cut two of them at a time, one for each side of the roof. Space the hip jack rafters using the same on-center spacing as you used for the common gable rafters.

As you move in from the end wall along the length of the building, the hip jack rafters gain in length until the one closest to the first common rafter is nearly as long as the common rafters. The difference in jack-rafter length is predictable, and is called the difference in length of jacks. After you determine the length of one hip rafter, you can determine the lengths of all the others by adding or subtracting this common length difference. The common length difference varies by slope, and you can find the common length differences on the rafter table imprinted on your framing square, listed along a line labeled "Difference in Length of Jacks" for either 16- or 24-inch-on-center framing.

Difficulty Level: 🔨🔨🔨

Tools and Materials

- Basic carpentry tools and nails
- Framing square
- Two-by rafter stock

1 Find the common difference in jack rafters. Use the framing-square rafter table to find the common difference in the

lengths of the jack rafters. For a roof slope of 6-in-12 (the common-rafter slope, not the hip-rafter slope), the figure is $17\frac{7}{8}$ inches for 16-inch-on-center framing and $26\frac{13}{16}$ inches for 24-inch framing. Keep those figures in mind.

2 Lay out the jack rafters. Just as with hip rafters, start by drawing a square line at the uphill end of the jack rafter. Measure one-

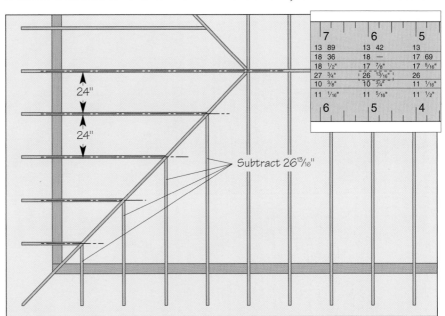

1 Hip jack rafters vary in length by a common difference. Line 4 on the table shows the difference in length of jack rafters spaced 24 in. on center.

half the 45-degree thickness of the hip rafter from the square line to shorten the rafter and draw a second square line. Find the center of the second square line. Using the framing square, measure and mark the side-cut line that corresponds to the unit rise of your roof. (See "Mark the Ridge Side Cuts," page 148.) There will be only one side cut for jack rafters, not two as in the hip rafters. With the framing square aligned for the slope of your roof, mark the ridge-cut line, starting from the end of the side-cut line.

Measure and mark the length of the first hip jack rafter from the square line you initially drew. This rafter will be shorter than the common rafters by the amount of the difference in jack rafter lengths ($17\frac{7}{8}$ or $26\frac{13}{16}$ in the example). At the lower end of the rafter, draw a building line and use it to mark the plumb and seat cuts for the bird's mouth. Add any overhang distance by measuring along the crown edge of the rafter using the unit length for your roof's unit rise. Mark a tail-cut line at the downhill end of the rafter. With all the rafters marked, cut them, preferably with a power miter saw or radial arm saw as these tools will provide the most accurate side cuts, although you can make these cuts using a circular saw.

3 **Install the jack rafters.** First, lay out the jack-rafter positions on the cap plates and hip rafters. Erect the jack rafters in pairs to prevent the hip rafters from being pushed out of line. Install the first pair about halfway between the wall plates and the ridge, making sure the hip rafter stays straight. Toenail the rafter to the cap plate with two 16d nails, one on each side; attach the top end to the hip rafter with two 12d nails.

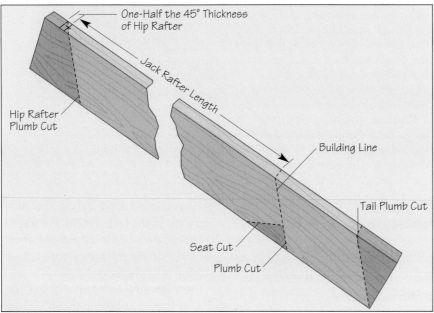

2 Measure and mark each rafter for length and various cuts.

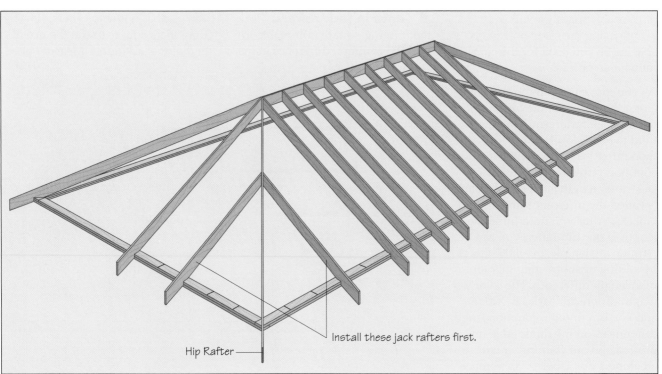

3 Install the jack rafters in pairs, starting midway up the hip rafter.

The Pros Know

REMOVING NAILS CLEANLY

A hammer will often mar lumber when you remove a nail. By using a block beneath the hammer, you can protect the surface of good lumber beneath it and gain extra leverage on the nail.

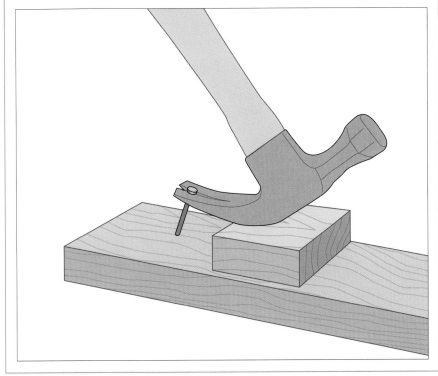

Gambrel Roofs

You probably have often seen gambrel roofs on barns and utility buildings. That is because the design allows for more usable headroom on the topmost floor. These roofs are also popular in house designs, and you'll see them on so-called Dutch Colonial-style houses both old and new. The design originally comes from the English countryside.

A gambrel roof is really a combination of two gable roofs of varying slopes. The part of the gambrel roof that rises directly off the top plates—the first gable—tends to have a severe slope, like 16 in 12 ($\frac{2}{3}$ pitch). The part of the gambrel roof that rises to the ridge—the second gable roof—has a less severe slope, say, 8 in 12 ($\frac{1}{3}$ pitch). Wherever the rafters meet from these varying pitches, you need a support such as a wall, purlin, or post. An exception to this rule may occur when you frame with gambrel trusses, in which case the truss engineer will alert you to any required support.

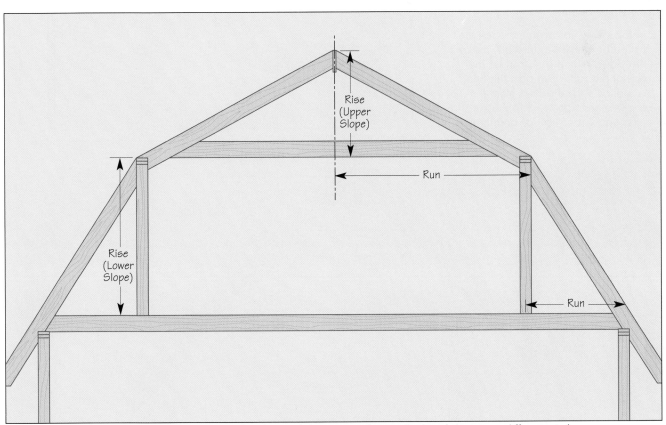

Gambrel Roofs. Believed to have originated in the English countryside, gambrel roofs have two different pitches.

For the example shown in this chapter, let's assume a 24-foot total span. That divides the gambrel roof into two different roofs with two different rises and runs. The total run for the lower part of the gambrel roof is 4 feet, found by measuring the distance from the cap plate of the building wall to the center of the cap plate of a mid-pitch supporting wall. The total rise is the distance the roof section rises from the floor to the top of the wall. The total run for the top part of the gambrel roof is 8 feet, found by measuring from the cap plate of the mid-span supporting wall to the center of the ridgeboard. The total upper-portion rise is the vertical distance from the support wall's cap plate to the center of the ridge.

EXPOSED RIDGE BEAMS FOR CATHEDRAL CEILINGS

Many cathedral-ceiling designs have an exposed ridge beam, a structural beam that supports roof loads. Note that a ridge beam must have support in the gable end of the structure that runs in an uninterrupted load line all the way down to the footings. A ridge beam made from an architectural-grade glue-laminated beam is common because you can sand the wood and coat it with polyurethane for an attractive finish. Traditional common-rafter framing has the rafters lying against the ridge, however, and with a structural ridge beam, the rafters should sit on top of the ridge. This means cutting bird's mouths not only where the rafter sits on the exterior-wall cap plate but also where the rafters sit on the ridge beam.

In this case, you won't shorten the rafter for the ridge. Instead, make the ridge plumb line, but let the rest of the rafter run past the line a foot or so. The rafters from the roof's other side will lap these rafters; you'll face-nail or bolt them together and trim them later. Measure back one-half the width of the ridge beam from the ridge plumb line for the seat cut. For a glue-laminated beam made from 2x4s, this figure is 1¾ inches; for one made from 2x6s, the figure is 2¾ inches. Make a plumb line, and cut out the bird's mouth.

Figure the rafter length in the usual way for gable rafters, and cut the lower bird's mouth. Note that the seat cut at the exterior walls' top plates must be the full width of the top plate, otherwise the drywall from the wall won't properly match the drywall on the ceiling.

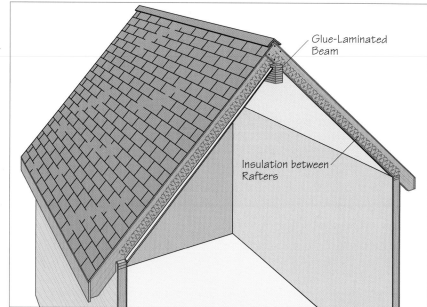

Glue-Laminated Beam

Insulation between Rafters

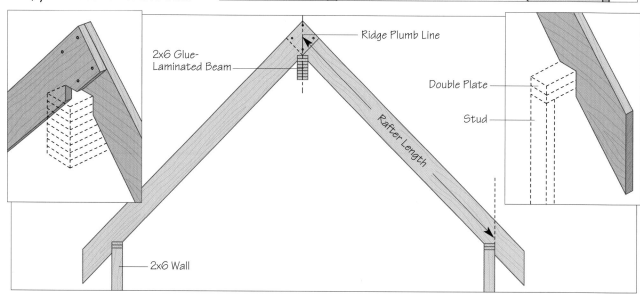

Ridge Plumb Line

2x6 Glue-Laminated Beam

Double Plate

Stud

Rafter Length

2x6 Wall

Laying Out a Gambrel Roof

Difficulty Level:

Tools and Materials

- Basic carpentry tools
- Framing square
- Two-by lumber stock

1 Lay out the upper rafters.
Obtain the slope and run of the upper roof section from the blueprints. Mark the ridge cut, and measure the pattern rafter as you would for any gable roof. (See "Rafter Length Measurement," pages 123–127.) At the plumb building line, subtract the width of the supporting-wall top plate (5½ inches for 2×6 walls; 3½ inches for 2×4 walls) and draw a second plumb line.

Using the building line as a reference point, mark a seat-cut line 90 degrees to it at the crown edge of the rafter. This seat cut is where the rafter will sit on the cap plate. The seat cut should be the width of the top plate, either 3½ or 5½ inches.

2 Lay out the lower rafters.
Obtain the slope and run of the lower roof section from the blueprints. Note that the tops of the lower rafters tuck under the double top plate.

At the top end of the rafter, mark a plumb line, setting your framing square to the correct slope. Measure down along the plumb cut the thickness of the two top plates, 3 inches for two-by lumber. Draw a seat-cut line 90 degrees to the plumb cut at this point; then cut out the resulting notch. At the other end of the rafter, mark the rafter length (obtained as for any common gable rafter) with a plumb building line. Using the building line as a reference, cut a bird's mouth at its base where the rafter will sit on the cap plate.

On the basis of the amount of overhang you desire, figure the rafter

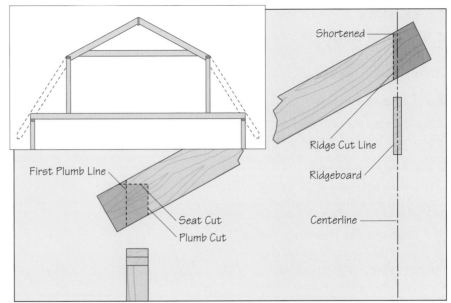

1 Lay out the upper rafters, and cut them to fit over the support wall.

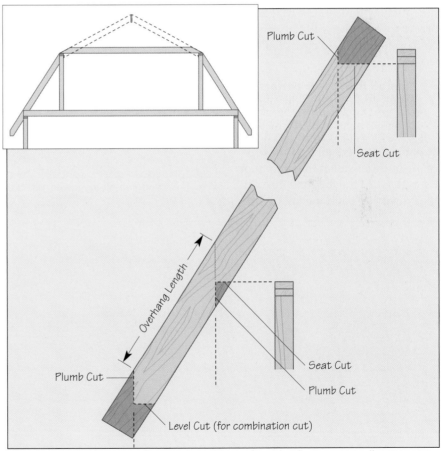

2 Lay out the bottom rafters, and cut them to fit under the support wall.

overhang length by stepping it off with a framing square, using the Pythagorean theorem, or using the framing square's rafter tables. (See Chapter 9, beginning on page 121.) Mark a plumb line at the

overhang length for the tail cut. If you want the rafters to end square, just make the square cut. If you want a combination cut, mark and cut along a line 90 degrees to the plumb cut near the end of the rafter.

Assembling a Gambrel Roof

Difficulty level: 🦇🦇🦇

Tools and Materials

- Basic carpentry tools and nails
- 2x4 partition wall in place
- 2x4 braces and cleats
- Two-by rafters and stock for collar ties (one for every third rafter).

1 **Prepare for framing.** Before assembling the gambrel roof rafters, put down the decking on your top floor in the area between where the two support walls will be. Erect 2×4 walls the entire length of the roof directly beneath where the rafters will meet. Use diagonal braces to keep the walls plumb. Nail off the braces to cleats nailed to your deck.

2 **Install the lower rafters.** With the support walls in place, erect and nail off all the base, or lower slope, rafters. Use 16d nails at both ends. Toenail into the top of the outside wall at the bottom of the rafters. At the top, nail through the crown edge and toenail up into the bottom of the partition wall's top plate.

3 **Install the upper rafters.** Once the lower rafters are in place, install the top, or upper slope, rafters, following the conventional gable-roof procedure.

(See "Ridgeboard & Rafter Installation," page 130.) Use 16d nails to secure the rafters to the support-wall cap plates and 8d nails at the ridge. Attach collar ties between every third rafter, face-nailing them to the rafters with four 16d nails on each end.

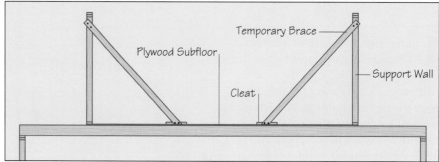

1 Lay a subfloor down the middle of the roof, and erect 2x4 support walls.

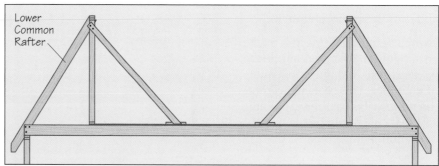

2 Erect and nail off the lower rafters using 16d nails.

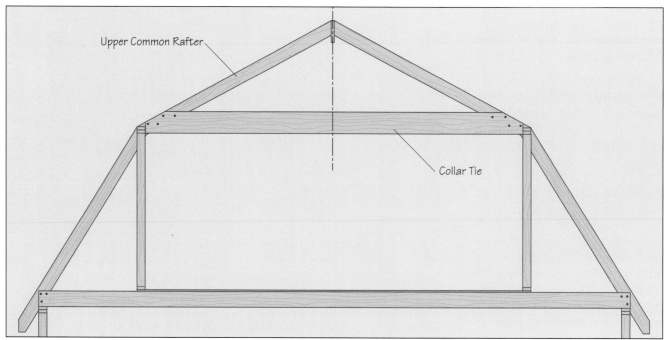

3 Erect the upper rafters with a collar tie every third rafter.

Framing Dormers

Because dormers serve both practical and aesthetic functions, adding them to your roof expands the design options available to you. On the practical side, a dormer allows you to install a window on a pitched roof, providing light and ventilation to what would otherwise be a closed-in space. The dormer construction adds useable living space and headroom to an area with a sloping ceiling. Aesthetically, dormers add architectural interest to the roof. Their presence helps identify specific styles of housing. The two main types of dormers are gable and shed dormers. Both types are easiest to incorporate into the design during the initial roof framing, although retrofitting a dormer is possible. Building any kind of dormer requires the use of the framing principles you've seen throughout this book. Gable dormers require some advanced rafter cuts for the valley rafters and valley jack rafters, similar to the cuts used in hip roofs. Shed dormers, with their flat roofs, are easier to build.

Gable Dormer

A gable dormer has a roof with two pitched planes that meet at a ridge, just as in any gable roof. The ceiling inside is usually flat, though sometimes it may be vaulted. The roof slope need not match that of the house, but designing a similar roofline may help the dormer fit in visually. The intersection of the dormer and house roof forms a valley to channel away water. Although a gable, or doghouse, dormer is good for creating natural light and ventilation, its proportions restrict its size, making it somewhat ineffective for increasing usable floor space.

Building a Gable Dormer

Difficulty level:

Tools and Materials

- Basic carpentry tools
- Two-by rafter lumber
- Two-by wall stud lumber
- Plywood sheathing

1 Establish the rough opening. Obtain the length of the rough opening you'll require in the roof from the blueprints. If you're adding the dormer on your own, you can calculate the length by determining the rough opening required for the window(s) you plan to install, and then adding wall space between them and to each side. In your planning, end the dormer at rafters on each side. These rafters will be the trimmer rafters. Double up the trimmer rafters. Note that because of ceiling-joist placement, the rafters get doubled on the right. Make sure the rafters are arrow straight.

2 Install the headers. Working with the depth of the dormer given in the plans, install double headers at the front and rear of the opening. Establish plumb lines on the trimmer rafters, and nail the headers in place with 16d nails. Cut and install short rafters above and

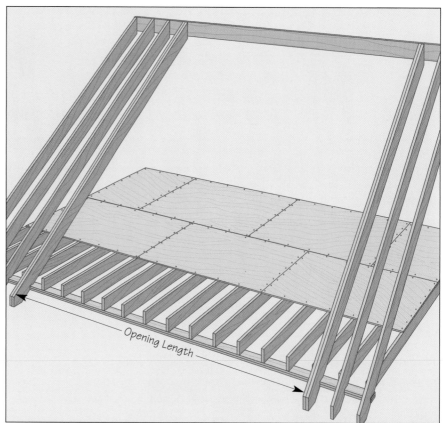

1 Determine the length of the rough opening, and install double rafters on each end.

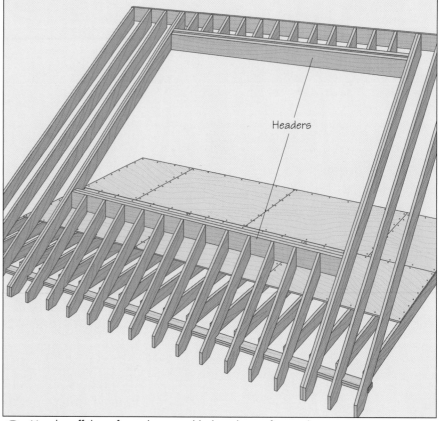

2 Header off the rafters above and below the roof's rough opening.

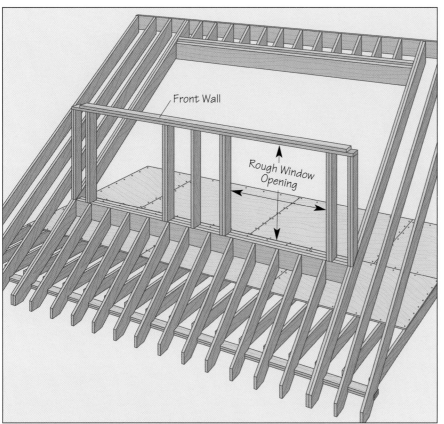

3 Build a stud wall on top of the lower header. Leave spaces on each end of the top plate so that the side walls can lock in.

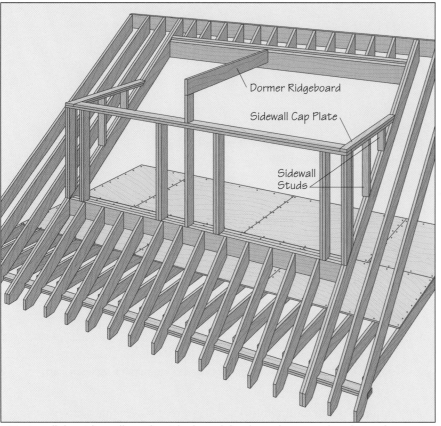

4 Install the side walls and a ridgeboard that butts the upper header and rests on a stud in front. Support the ridgeboard down to the header.

below the gable dormer, maintaining the rafter on-center spacing.

3 Frame the front wall. Use the rough-opening dimensions of your window to determine the height of the dormer's front wall. Frame the wall with two-by lumber, using double studs. Make sure the outside corner studs sit plumb, directly on top of the trimmer rafters, and cut them on an angle so that their ends bear fully on the trimmer rafters' crown edge. You can most easily acquire the angle by holding a stud plumb in place, drawing a line across the rafter's crown, and transferring that angle to the other studs after accounting for length. Make all the studs (including the side-wall studs, later) flush with the outside of the header and trimmer rafters, allowing any excess to protrude into the room, where you can deal with it when you finish the walls. Double the front wall's top plate, leaving spaces on both ends that will allow the cap plates on the adjacent walls to overlap it.

4 Install the side walls and ridge. To make the side walls, run top plates back from the dormer's front wall so they rest on the trimmer rafters. Cut the cap plates so they overlap the front wall's top plates where you left space on each end. Fill in the side walls with studs, matching the on-center framing of your front wall. These studs will get shorter as you work up the trimmer rafters.

With the walls standing in place, run a dormer ridgeboard from the upper header out above the front wall. If you want the ridge to overhang, be sure to account for this. With the ridgeboard in place, support it with a stud that runs from the center of the front wall's top plate to the underside of the board.

5 Attach the valley and common rafters. At the back end of the ridgeboard where it meets the header, run angled rafters from each side of this junction to the trimmer rafters. These two will be valley rafters. (See "Laying Out Valley Rafters," page 163.) Use standard common gable rise-and-run calculations to cut and install the dormer's common gable rafters above the front wall. (See "Rafter Length Measurement," page 123.)

6 Install the valley jack rafters. Valley jack rafters run between the ridge and the valley rafter and between the header and the valley rafter. The cut at the ridge and header is a plumb cut. At their bases, valley jack rafters have a side cut that corresponds with the roof's slope. (See "Lay out the jack rafters," page 151 for how to make side cuts.)

To lay out the rafters, determine the common difference in length from the rafter table on your framing square, just as you did for the hip-roof jack rafters. (See "Installing Hip-Roof Jack Rafters," page 151.) Make sure there's a common rafter at the base of the valley rafters, and use it as a basis for the length of the valley jack rafters. Begin measuring 16 (or 24) inches on center from the common rafter to position the valley jack rafters.

Square a line across the crown edge of each valley jack rafter near the uphill end. Shorten the rafter by one-half the thickness of the ridgeboard, and draw a second square line. Draw a ridge plumb-cut line from the second square line. Now from the first square line you drew, measure the length of the rafter and draw a square line across the rafter's crown edge. Shorten the rafter by one-half the 45-degree thickness of the valley rafter, and draw a second square line across it's crown edge. Mark the center of the line, and use this center mark to mark your side-cut lines. Draw a plumb-cut line on each side of the rafter from the side-cut line.

Make the side and ridge cuts with a circular saw, power miter saw, or radial-arm saw, and attach the rafters with 16d nails by nailing through the ridge and through the

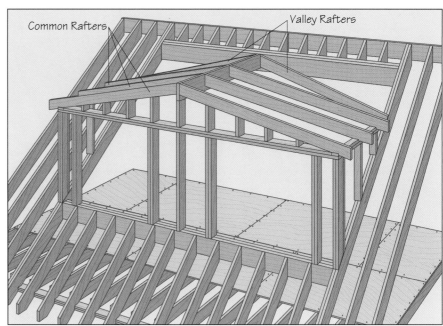

5 Install as many common rafters as the dormer design permits, plus valley rafters on both sides of the ridgeboard.

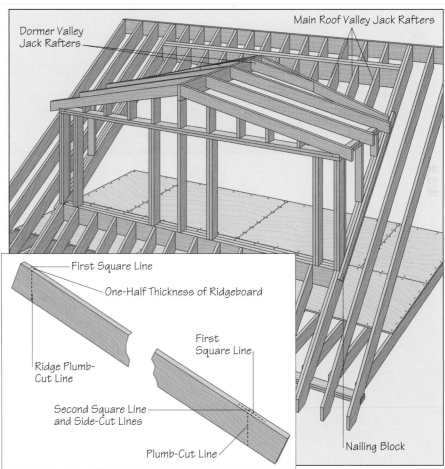

6 Valley jack rafters run between the dormer's ridge and the valley rafters.

valley rafters. Attach nailing blocks to the outside of the double rafters in the area of the dormer walls to accept roof sheathing. Once you've framed the dormer, sheathe it as you sheathe the roof and walls.

The Pros Know

STARTING HARD-TO-HOLD NAILS

Use needle-nose pliers to grip small, hard-to-hold nails or nails in a tight spot where it's difficult to fit your hand.

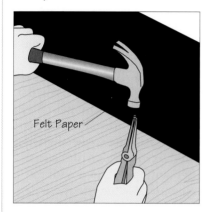

Felt Paper

Shed Dormer

A shed dormer differs from a gable dormer in a number of ways, but the principal difference is that rafters for a shed dormer run parallel with the main roof rafters, whereas the rafters in a gable dormer run perpendicular. For large shed dormers that have dormer rafters with a run as long as that of the main roof rafters, such as the one described below, there is no need to header-off the rafters above and below the rough opening in the roof; the shed dormer outright replaces the rafters in the area it occupies. For smaller shed dormers, however, you will header-off a rough opening in the main roof rafters and secure the dormer rafters to the header.

Building a Shed Dormer

Difficulty Level:

Tools and Materials

- Basic carpentry tools
- Two-by rafter lumber
- Two-by wall stud lumber
- Plywood sheathing

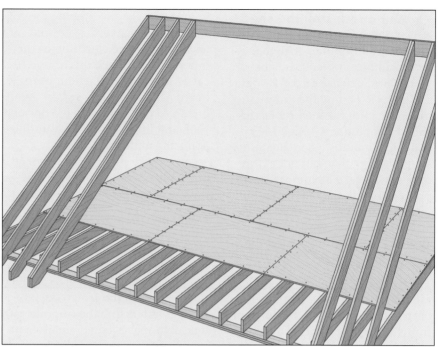

1 A shed dormer, like a gable dormer, begins with a rough opening. Double the trimmer rafters on each side.

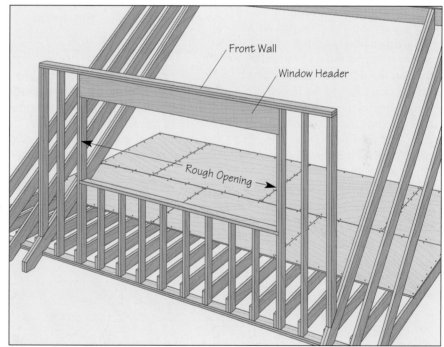

Front Wall

Window Header

Rough Opening

2 Build a simple stud wall on the double top plate of the building's wall for the front wall of the dormer.

1 Establish the rough opening. Just as with a gable dormer, doubled trimmer rafters establish the length of the dormer rough opening.

2 Erect the front stud wall. Build a stud wall on the front side of the dormer, right on the lower wall's cap plate. Follow the spacing of the studs below. Allow an adequate rough opening for your window(s). Use two-by studs, doubled at the wall's outside edges, and doubled where they define the window rough opening. Note that you need to cut the end studs to fit the slope of the roof.

3 **Cut and install the shed dormer rafters.** Determine the correct size rafter stock to use by consulting a rafter span table or your plans. Choose arrow-straight rafter stock. Follow the rafter-cutting principles for shed roofs. (See "Shed Roof Rafters," page 144.) Cut bird's mouths where the rafters sit on the top plate but not at the upper end; make a plumb cut at the proper slope so the rafters can butt the roof's main ridgeboard. To determine the slope, measure the rise and run of the dormer or get the figure from the plans.

The ridge-cut angle for the end rafters, which sit on top of the double trimmer rafters, will be different from the angle you cut for the other dormer rafters. The easiest way to determine this angle, which will be sharp, is to cut the end rafter to length and make a plumb cut and bird's mouth, just as you did with all the other dormer rafters. Next, temporarily rest the end rafter in place on the dormer's header, but run the rafter just to the inside of the trimmer rafters. Hold the end rafter in place, next to the trimmer rafter, and draw a cut line using the crown edge of the trimmer rafter as

your guide. Before drawing the cut line, though, make sure the end rafter is at the same elevation as the other rafters. Check this at two locations: first, install a temporary board across the other rafters about one-third of the way up the dormer roof, and lift the end rafter until it abuts the underside of this board; second, make sure the crown edge of the rafter's ridge end is flush with the top of the main ridgeboard.

Once you've drawn the cut line, remove and cut the end rafter; then set it in place directly over the trimmer rafters, flush with the outside. At the ridge end, predrill and nail down through the crown edge of the end rafters into the trimmer rafters; at the eaves end, toenail them into the wall plate using 16d nails.

Where the rest of the rafters butt the ridge, drive 16d nails through the face of the ridge into the rafter's end grain. Toenail the rafters at the top plate of the supporting wall using 16d nails.

4 **Frame the side walls.** Once the rafters are in place, the next step is to install notched two-by studs that run from the top of the trimmer rafters to the end rafters.

Because each stud must be a different length, you'll mark and cut each one separately.

The side-wall studs will have the same on-center framing as a typical two-by wall. Along the crown edge of the trimmer rafters, mark 16- or 24-inch on-center intervals, using level dimensions. Next, plumb-up a two-by stud on edge at each on-center mark, and hold it against the inside face of the trimmer rafter. For the bottom of the stud, draw a cut line using the crown edge of the trimmer rafters as a guide. For the top of the two-by, draw two lines: one aligned with the crown edge of the end rafter and one aligned with the bottom edge of the end rafter.

For the cut on the bottom of the stud, set your circular saw's sole plate to the angle marked using a sliding T-bevel, and cut across the entire width of the stud. For the top of the stud, cut across its entire width at the topmost mark only. For the lower mark, cut only to a depth of 1½ inches. Then rip down from the end of the board to cut a 1½-inch-wide notch that will rest against the inside face of the rafter.

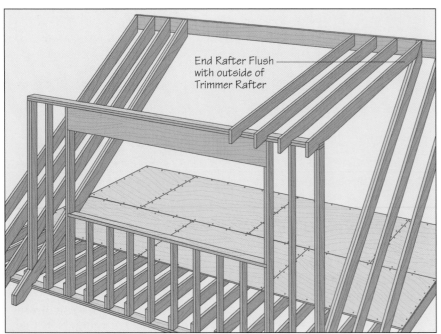

3 Cut and install the dormer rafters. Note that the end rafters require a special cut to sit on top of the roof rafters.

4 Plumb the side-wall studs, and mark three cut lines.

Cut the studs in pairs and use the second set on the other side of the dormer, but be sure to notch opposite edges. Work your way up the trimmer rafters, holding each stud in place as you go for each of the on-center marks. Attach 2×4 blocks to the trimmer rafters.

5 Install the collar ties. After all the studs and rafters are in place, install collar ties from the shed-dormer rafters across the width of the roof. Use whatever two-by stock you used for your shed-dormer rafters. Face-nail the collar ties in place with four 10d nails on each end. You'll find that you can't face-nail the collar ties to the inside face of your dormer's outside rafters because the studs block the collar tie from coming flush. Install a short two-by plate here, with standoff blocks, so you have a nailing surface.

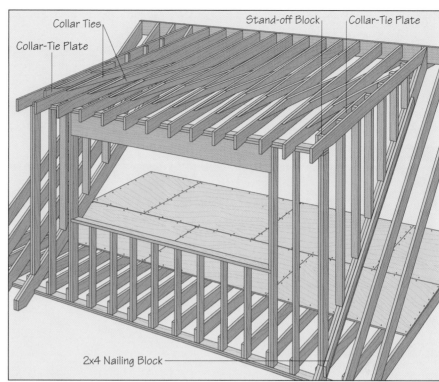

5 Face-nail collar ties using 10d nails. Use stand-off blocks and a two-by plate on the end rafters.

LAYING OUT VALLEY RAFTERS

Most gable-dormer designs require valley rafters. Cutting and installing valley rafters involves some challenging carpentry and calculation.

1 Measure and mark the rafter. Mark the top end of the valley rafter for side cuts just as you would mark a hip rafter. (See "Beginning a Hip Roof," page 147.) Remember the run is 17, not 12. Determine the rafter length using the "Length Hip or Valley" figure from the rafter table, just as you would for a hip rafter. When you shorten the length at the end of the rafter for a

gable dormer, take into account the thickness of the double common rafter. Shorten the valley rafter by one-half the 45-degree thickness of the outside rafter and the entire 45-degree thickness of the inside rafter.

2 Make the bottom side cut. Use the rafter-length mark as the center of a single side cut, so the rafter tail will sit flush against the trimmer rafter's face. Make the usual hip rafter's cut at the ridge. These will be compound angles, so use a compound miter saw if you have one.

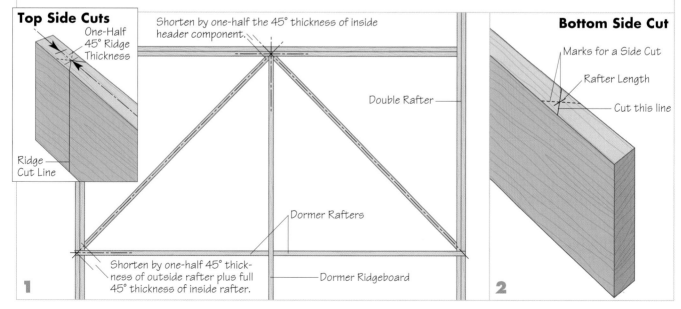

Section III

Framing Projects

12 Building Stairs   **166**

Design Ideas for Stairs   **190**

13 Basement Framing   **192**

Design Ideas for Basements   **204**

14 Installing a Bay Window   **206**

Design Ideas for Windows   **213**

Home Plans   **218**

12

Building Stairs

Stair construction appears challenging to all but the most experienced carpenters. But if you've mastered the other framing techniques presented in this book, you should be able to build stairs. This chapter presents several types of stairs, beginning with simple straight-run stairs. You'll learn to calculate the rise and run, to measure and cut materials, and to install the components. There is also information on installing L-shaped stairs and three-step winder stairs.

Straight-Run Basics

The closed-riser, notched-stringer staircase project in this chapter may be used as a main stairway or for connecting the basement with the first floor. This kind of staircase is also useful for porches, where closed risers block a view under the porch. For simpler, more basic utility stairs, leave out the risers.

Every situation is different. This chapter gives specific dimensions for building a specific staircase and assumes that you already have a framed stairwell opening. You should study the method used to help you make your own calculations. In most cases, these calculations will result in a few choices rather than a single solution. If given a choice, always opt for comfort and safety over meeting minimal standards.

Difficulty Level:

Tools and Materials

- Basic carpentry tools
- Router
- Power miter saw
- Plumb bob, level, framing square, and calculator
- Story pole
- 2x12s for stringers (length dependent on your stairs)
- ¾-inch plywood
- 1x12s for skirtboards
- 1x8 hardwood or softwood lumber for risers
- Standard hardwood stair treads
- Newel posts (if at least one side of the stairs is open)
- Balustrade (handrails and balusters)
- Angle brackets
- 4d, 8d, and 10d nails
- Adhesive
- Screws, lag screws, carriage bolts, and rail bolts

Calculating the Staircase Size

Rise and run, and the relationship between them, are critical features in staircase design. As in roof framing, rise refers to vertical distance and run to horizontal. The total rise is the total distance the stairs must climb vertically, while the total run is the total distance the stairs cover horizontally. Unit rise and unit run are layout terms that refer to the dimensions of each individual riser and tread. The rise and run on each step must be nearly identical. Stairs that vary in tread depth or riser height are dangerous. Codes require that the difference between the highest and lowest risers not exceed ⅜ inch. If you do your calculations in decimals with a calculator and round to the nearest ¹⁄₃₂ inch, you should be close enough. (See "Changing Fractions to Decimals," below.)

1 **Calculate the total rise.** You must calculate the total rise from finished floor surfaces. If you are installing stairs in a house where the finished flooring is not yet in place, find out the flooring thickness and factor it into the total rise.

To get an exact vertical measurement, run the measuring tape alongside a wall or plumb-bob

line. Measure the total rise at each corner of the stairwell. If the measurements differ, use the shortest dimension as the total rise and plan to shim under the stringers when you install them. In the stairs being

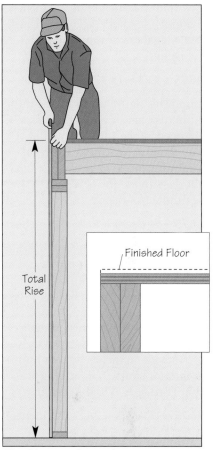

Finished Floor

Total Rise

1 Measure the total rise, ensuring that the measuring tape is plumb.

CHANGING FRACTIONS TO DECIMALS

¹⁄₃₂	0.0313	⅜	0.3750	²³⁄₃₂	0.7188
¹⁄₁₆	0.0625	¹³⁄₃₂	0.4063	¾	0.7500
³⁄₃₂	0.0938	⁷⁄₁₆	0.4375	²⁵⁄₃₂	0.7813
⅛	0.1250	¹⁵⁄₃₂	0.4688	¹³⁄₁₆	0.8125
⁵⁄₃₂	0.1563	½	0.5000	²⁷⁄₃₂	0.8438
³⁄₁₆	0.1875	¹⁷⁄₃₂	0.5313	⅞	0.8750
⁷⁄₃₂	0.2188	⁹⁄₁₆	0.5625	²⁹⁄₃₂	0.9063
¼	0.2500	¹⁹⁄₃₂	0.5938	²⁹⁄₃₂	0.9063
⁹⁄₃₂	0.2813	⅝	0.6250	¹⁵⁄₁₆	0.9375
⁵⁄₁₆	0.3125	²¹⁄₃₂	0.6563	³¹⁄₃₂	0.9688
¹¹⁄₃₂	0.3438	¹¹⁄₁₆	0.6875	1	1.000

used as an example in this chapter, the total rise is 106¾ inches.

2 **Calculate the unit rise.** The next step is to calculate the unit rise, which is the height of one step. Codes typically mandate that the maximum step height be 7¾ inches, so divide the total rise (106¾ inches) by the legal maximum unit rise (7¾ inches):

106.75 ÷ 7.75 = 13.77

Round this figure up to 14, the minimum number of risers the stairs will need, since 13 risers would push the unit rise above the legal maximum. Now, to determine the unit rise, divide the total rise by the number of risers:

106.75 ÷ 14 risers = 7.625 (7⅝ inches)

To meet most codes, this staircase would require a minimum of 14 risers, each measuring 7⅝ inches. Many people find a 7⅝-inch step to be too high, however. A more comfortable riser height for most people is 7 inches or even 6½ inches. (Consider 6 inches the minimum for interior stairs.) Try adding another riser or two to the formula:

106.75 ÷ 15 risers = 7.117 (7⅛ inches)

or

106.75 ÷ 16 risers = 6.672 (6¹¹⁄₁₆ inches)

Adding one or two risers makes for a more comfortable staircase. Before deciding on the number of risers, however, you need to calculate the unit run and total run; then determine whether you have adequate headroom and landing space.

3 **Calculate the unit run.** Unit run is the horizontal distance from the face of one riser to the face of the next riser. Codes sometimes refer to the unit run as the tread depth and require a minimum depth of 9 inches. Again, you don't have to build your stairs exactly to this dimension; in fact, 10 or 11 inches is a safer depth.

As a rule, deeper treads should have shorter risers. Carpenters have developed a variety of formulas for

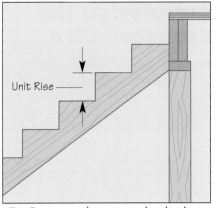

2 Determine the unit rise by dividing the total rise by the highest maximum unit rise code allows.

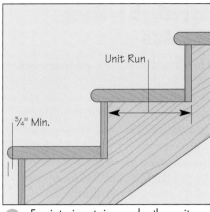

3 For interior stairs, make the unit run between 10 and 11 in., with at least a ¾-in. nosing.

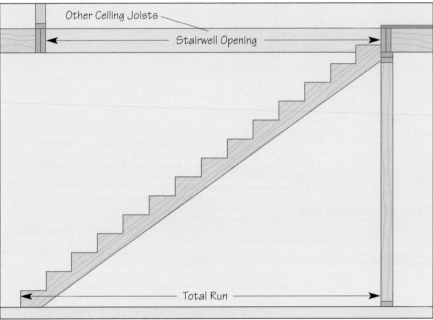

4 The total run is the distance covered by the stairs; it equals the unit run multiplied by the number of treads.

matching tread depth to riser height. Two simple ones are:

rise + run = 17 to 18 and

rise × run = 70 to 75

Using these riser/tread formulas and the target riser dimensions (7⅛ inches and 6¹¹⁄₁₆ inches), you can calculate the acceptable choices for unit run:

6¹¹⁄₁₆ riser + 11 tread = 17¹¹⁄₁₆

6¹¹⁄₁₆ riser × 11 tread = 73⁹⁄₁₆ or

7⅛ riser + 10 tread = 17⅛

7⅛ riser × 10 tread = 71¼

Because all the results fall within the formula targets, either choice

would make for an acceptable and comfortable stair.

4 **Calculate the total run.** Next, multiply the unit run by the total number of treads to reach the total run, which is the horizontal length of the entire stair. All stairs have one less tread than riser because the bottom landing, in effect, serves as one tread. So with 15 risers, the staircase has 14 treads, and 14 treads multiplied by the 10-inch unit run = 140 inches total run.

5 **Check landing clearance.** You may find that the calculated total run leaves insufficient room for a landing. Building codes may

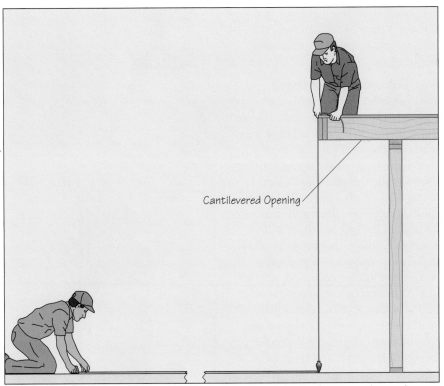

5 To make sure that the stairs won't run into any obstacles for a cantilevered opening, drop a plumb bob and measure the total run plus the landing.

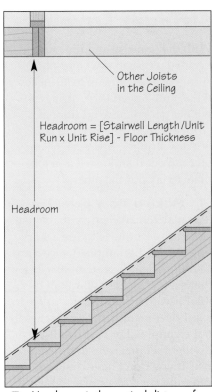

Other Joists in the Ceiling

Headroom = [Stairwell Length/Unit Run x Unit Rise] - Floor Thickness

Headroom

6 Headroom is the vertical distance from the nosing to any obstruction overhead.

require space at both ends of the stairs so that users have a place to enter or exit. Typically, the length of this space, or landing, equals the staircase width; if there will be a door at the top of the staircase that swings toward the stairs, the landing must be at least as long as the door is wide. If you have the space, remember that a deeper landing allows for moving larger items up and down the stairs.

The stairwell opening should have been positioned to allow enough room for a landing at the top of the stairs. Use the total run of your stairs to determine whether there's enough landing space at the bottom. Drop a plumb bob from the end of the opening where the top of the stairs will be; mark the floor; and measure out the distance of the total run plus the width of the staircase (for the minimum-size landing). If you run into something—a wall, for instance—before you've spanned the total run of the staircase plus the landing, the stairs may not be acceptable by code. Try reducing the unit run, the number of treads

(while increasing the unit rise), or both to make the stairs fit in the stairwell space. If you still don't have enough room, you'll have to build a different style of staircase.

6 Calculate the headroom.
Knowing the staircase layout also lets you know whether you can use the stairs and have sufficient headroom. The amount of clear space between the stairs and the stairwell header is called headroom, and it's measured vertically from an imaginary sloped plane connecting the nosings of the treads. On most stairs, the headroom is shortest just below the header to the stairwell, so check the size of your stairwell opening. Ideally, the total run should equal the length of the stairwell opening. If the opening is significantly shorter than the stairway's total run, you may not have sufficient headroom.

To find out exactly how much headroom your rise/run relationship yields, use this formula:

Headroom = [stairwell length ÷ unit run × unit rise] - floor thickness

In the example stairs, the stairwell is 133 inches long; the unit run is 10 inches; the unit rise is $7\frac{1}{8}$ inches, and the floor system thickness is $10\frac{3}{4}$ inches. When plugged into the formula, these figures produce 84 inches of headroom. Typical code requirements say that there must be a minimum of 80 inches (6 feet 8 inches) of headroom in all parts of the stairway. Again, that minimum figure is not necessarily ideal. A 6-foot 5-inch resident using such a staircase would still feel compelled to duck a bit. Seven feet of headroom is a more comfortable minimal target, and it provides more clearance for moving large objects up and down the stairs.

If you find that the headroom is too short, you can adjust the rise or run of the stairs or subtract a tread or two to gain a few inches of headroom. Lowering the unit run to $9\frac{1}{2}$ inches in the example staircase, for instance, yields 89 inches of headroom. If you still don't have enough headroom, consider enlarging the stairwell. (See "Rough Openings in Floor Joists," page 87.)

Stringer Layout

With the unit rise and unit run decided, you can start marking stringers. For stairs up to 40 inches wide, you'll need three stringers; wider stairs require additional stringers. You only need to lay out one stringer, however. Then you can cut it and use it as a template to lay out the others.

1 **Make a story pole.** The best way to make sure your dimensions are accurate is to use a story pole. Make this simple device from a straight board, preferably a 2×4, that's a few inches taller than the total rise. Mark off the story pole in exact riser increments (7⅛ inches in our example). For best results, use dividers set precisely to the unit rise. If you don't have dividers, carefully cut a piece of scrap wood exactly 7⅛ inches long to use as a spacer block, or simply use a measuring tape. Start from the bottom of the board and mark off the number of risers in the stairs. Set the story pole in the stairwell and check that the top mark aligns with the upper level finished floor. The story pole must be plumb to get an accu-

rate reading. If the top mark is not within ⅜ inch of the finished-floor height, you'll need to recalculate the unit rise.

2 **Calculate the stringer length.** To determine the length of the lumber needed to make the stringers, you need to know the total rise, the total run, and the Pythagorean theorem just as in determining rafter length. (See "Calculating the Length," page 125.) Using the example stair, the results produce a minimal stringer length of 14 feet 8 inches. Dimension lumber is sold in 2-foot increments, so 16-footers would be the shortest you'd want to buy. However, a safer length would be 18-footers, which ensures that you'll have enough room to lay out the stringers. The material should have straight grain and no defects.

3 **Lay out with a framing square.** Laying out stairs is similar to stepping off a rafter. (See "Stepping off the Length," page 127.) Set one stair button so the outside edge of the blade is at the 10-inch mark (for the tread) and the other button is on the outside edge of the tongue at the 7⅛-inch mark (for the riser).

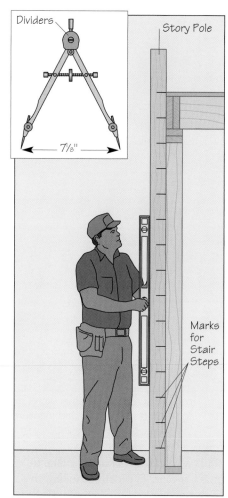

1 Before you lay out stringers, use a story pole to check that the top step will be even with the upper floor.

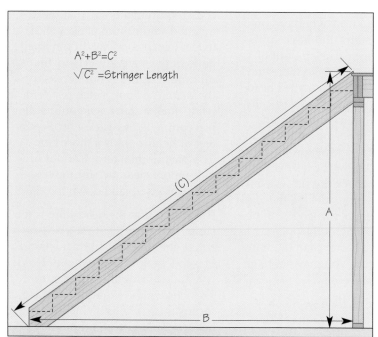

$$A^2+B^2=C^2$$
$$\sqrt{C^2}=\text{Stringer Length}$$

2 Plug your stairs' total rise and total run into the formula above to determine stringer length. (Example: $9^2(81) + 12^2(144) = 225$. The square root of 225 is 15, or a 15-ft stringer.

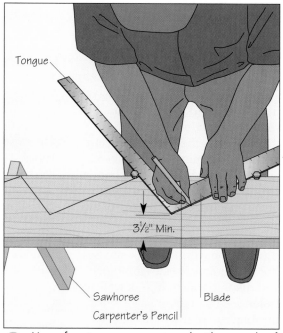

3 Use a framing square equipped with a couple of stair nuts to lay out the first stringer. Set the 2x12 across a pair of sawhorses.

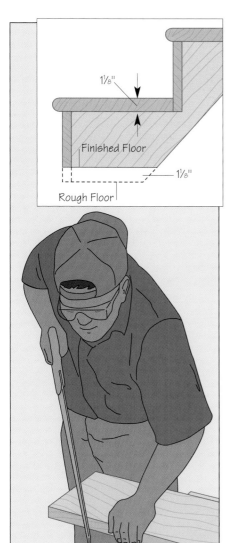

1⅛"

Finished Floor

1⅛"

Rough Floor

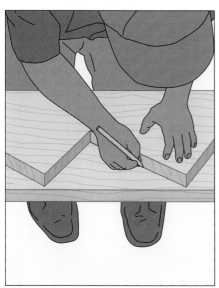

4 After the stringer has been laid out, trim one tread thickness from the bottom.

5 Use the first stringer as a template to lay out the other stringers.

Sight down the 2×12s, and lay out the stringers so that the crown side is up. With the stringer lying flat across a couple of sawhorses, place the square as shown so that its corner points away from the wood's crowned edge. Mark along the outside edges of the square, then slide it down the stringer so that it aligns exactly with the previous mark, and mark the next cutout. Number the cutouts as you go along.

4 **Drop the stringer.** On a finished floor, you need to shorten the bottom of the stringer by the thickness of one tread; otherwise, the bottom tread will be too high from the floor and the top tread will be too high for the floor above. Set a scrap piece of tread stock along the bottom cutoff line on the stringer and draw another line. Cut the stringer at this line.

5 **Cut the stringers.** With the master stringer laid out, cut it following the same technique as that used for cutting rafter bird's mouths. (See "Making the Bird's-Mouth, Ridge, and Tail Cuts," page 129.) You can then use the stringer to lay out the other stringers.

Set the stringer in the stairwell with the top of the stringer one riser plus one tread thickness below the finished floor surface. Place a 24-inch level on the tread cutouts to make sure they are at or close to level, and make sure there's enough landing space at the bottom of the stairs. Adjust the stringer up and down slightly until it rests flat against the floor and upper framing. If the bottom does not rest properly on the rough or finished floor, trim or shim accordingly, but verify the height of the first tread and check for level both the width and length of the tread.

Using the stringer you just cut as a template, lay it directly on top of another 2×12, and ensure that the edges are perfectly aligned. Be sure that any crown in the 2×12 will be along the cut edge. Mark and cut out the remaining stringers.

Staircase Installation

You install the stringers at the top one riser plus one tread thickness below the level of the finished floor. The outside stringers should be at least 1½ inches from the edge of the framed opening or wall framing. This gap allows plenty of room for drywall and a skirtboard.

1 **Install the hangerboard.** There are several ways to hang the stringers. For indoor stairs, usually the best choice is to nail the stringers to a hangerboard, a piece of ¾-inch plywood that you nail to the upper framing. Cut the hangerboard two risers wide (about 14 inches) and long enough to fit in the rough opening. Use 8d common nails to secure the hangerboard to the header.

2 **Lay out the hangerboard.** Measure down from the finished floor surface one unit rise (7⅛ inches in our example) plus the thickness of the tread (1⅛ inches), and make a mark on the hangerboard. Then use a 24-inch level to draw a level line at this mark across

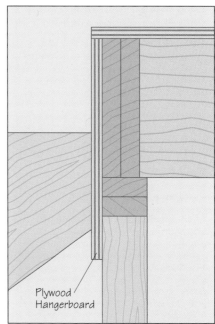

Plywood Hangerboard

1 Use 8d nails to fasten a ¾-in. plywood hangerboard to the stairwell header as a nailing surface for the stringers.

12 BUILDING STAIRS

the hangerboard. You'll install the stringers along this horizontal line.

3 **Install the stringers.** Attach each stringer along the layout line with a single 10d common nail, and check the fit. If there's not enough room for nailing through the back side of the hangerboard and into the stringers, use metal angle brackets to attach the stringers to the hangerboard. The stringers should lie flat against the hangerboard and bear fully on the floor. Place a level across the stringers at each step. If you find a stringer slightly out of alignment, try shimming the bottom. When the stringers are plumb and level, finish nailing.

TIGHT-FIT TREADS AND RISERS

Make a measuring jig for stair treads and risers, and you'll get tight-fitting parts without looking at a ruler. Cut three slots in a 1x4 as shown, and attach two ½-inch plywood end pieces with 1½-inch long machine screws, washers, and wing nuts. Adjust the panels when you come to each riser or tread width—even if it's out of square—and you'll have an exact template from which to cut your riser and tread pieces for a snug fit.

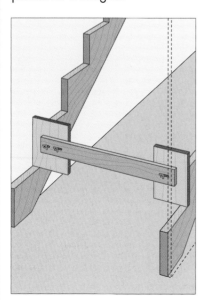

2 Measure down from the rough floor the combined distance of the finished floor surface, one unit rise, plus one tread thickness.

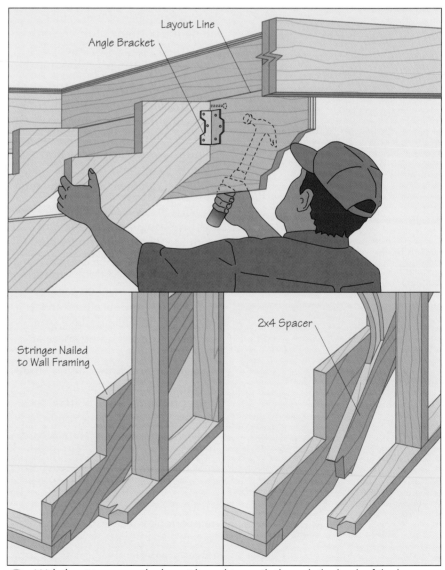

3 With the stringers on the layout line, drive nails through the back of the hangerboard into each stringer (top). Nail an outer stringer either to the wall framing (bottom left) or to a 2x4 spacer (bottom right).

If you have a wall on one or both sides, you can nail the stringers to the wall framing for a solid connection. If you plan to add drywall and a skirtboard or another surface material, however, this method would force you to notch the material to fit around the stairs. A better solution is to install the stringer away from the wall framing. Leave a space wide enough for the wall covering. A 2x4 makes a good spacer. First, set the stringer in place temporarily, resting against the wall, and then draw lines on the studs along the bottom of the stringer. Nail a 2×4 to the studs along this line, and then attach the stringer to it. This method creates a stronger connection and leaves a space for you to slip in drywall and a skirtboard. The treads and risers will cover the gap.

4 Anchor the bottom. Align the stringers so that they are square to the stairwell header, and space them at the bottom to match the spacing at the top. If you are adding a kickboard, cut a 2×4 to length, and then slip it into notches cut into the stringers and secure it to the floor. Alternatively, you can screw metal angle brackets to the floor and stringers.

5 Install the skirtboard. A skirtboard is a length of hardwood or softwood stock—typically 1×12—that's installed on the wall side of the stairs. Although a skirtboard isn't a necessity, it provides protection for the drywall and gives the stairs a finished look. Use a framing square to lay out cut lines at the bottom and top of the skirtboard, then nail the board to the stringer or the wall framing.

6 Cut and install treads and risers. Rip 1×8 lumber to $7\frac{1}{8}$ inches for the risers. Rip the bottom riser narrower than the others by the thickness of one tread. Crosscut and install the risers first. Then install the treads. Use 8d finishing nails or $2\frac{1}{4}$-inch drywall screws, driving three into each stringer. The treads on a closed-riser staircase must have a nosing between $\frac{3}{4}$ and $1\frac{1}{4}$ inches. You can buy hardwood treads with premilled nosings from lumberyards and home centers. For a more secure connection, spread construction adhesive along the mating surfaces, and then fasten the parts.

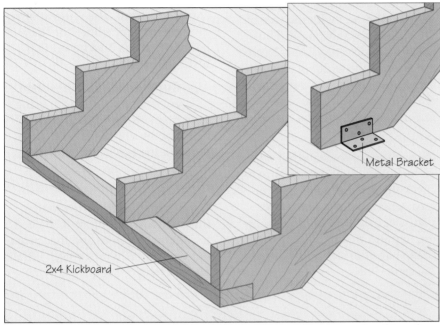

2x4 Kickboard

Metal Bracket

4 For a wood floor, cut in a kickboard; fasten it to the stringers; and nail it to the floor. Or you can use angle brackets (inset).

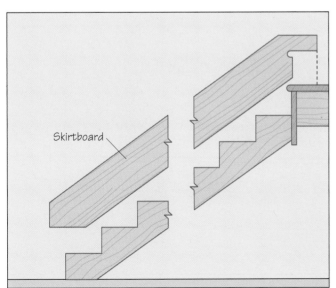

Skirtboard

5 Cut a 1x12 skirtboard, and install it between the stairs and a wall for a more finished look.

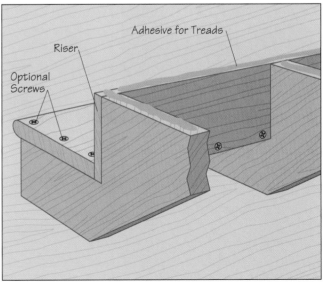

Adhesive for Treads

Riser

Optional Screws

6 Glue and screw the treads and 1x8 risers (ripped to width) to the stringers.

Balustrades

A balustrade, which is an assembly made up of a handrail and balusters, can be the most prominent and aesthetically significant feature of a stair. Balustrades also serve an important safety function, providing both a graspable handrail to steady the user and a blockade on an open staircase to prevent a fall over the side. There are two principal types of balustrades: post-to-post and over-the-post. The stairs in this chapter use a post-to-post railing, in which the handrail is cut to fit between newel posts and all of the sections of handrail are straight. Although many homeowners favor the flowing appearance of an over-the-post balustrade, fabricating one from scratch is difficult even for experienced stair builders. If your heart is set on an over-the-post balustrade, consider buying and installing a prefabricated system.

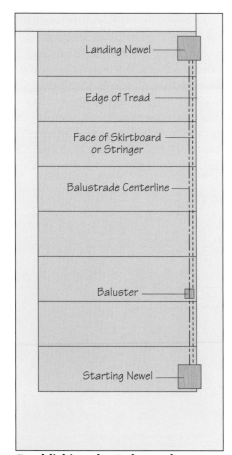

Establishing the Balustrade Centerline. The balustrade centerline locates the midpoint of the railing.

Establishing the Balustrade Centerline

If you want to build a balustrade system with balusters set in the treads, you first must establish the balustrade centerline. This is nothing more than a line along which you'll locate all of the components.

There are no hard and fast rules about where exactly to locate the balustrade centerline, but there are a few general rules of thumb. Begin with the location of the balusters on the treads. Balusters typically align on the side with the face of the stringer or skirtboard. Thus, the balustrade centerline is located exactly half the width of a baluster away from the face of the stringer or skirtboard. Mark the centerline in pencil on each tread.

Codes require at least 32 inches of clearance at the handrail on a 36-inch-wide stair, but be sure to check the requirements in your area. Check the clearance after you establish the centerline, keeping in mind that half the width of the handrail extends beyond the centerline.

Installing Newels

With the balustrade centerline determined, you can calculate where to locate the newels. The aim is to center each newel on the centerline. With the handrail centered over the balusters, this ensures that the handrail will fall in the center of the newel.

1 Lay out the newels. Use the centerline to determine where to notch the newel. Some newels require a notch on one face only; others must fit around the corner of a tread. The illustrations give general guidelines for calculating the notch on a newel that rests on the subfloor.

2 Cut the notches. You can cut a simple side notch using a circular saw and chisel. With the depth of the saw blade set to the depth of the notch, make a series of cuts. Then clean out the notch with a chisel.

Cut a corner notch with a router fitted with a straight bit. You need to rout on two sides and then clean out the corners with a chisel. If the bit isn't long enough to excavate

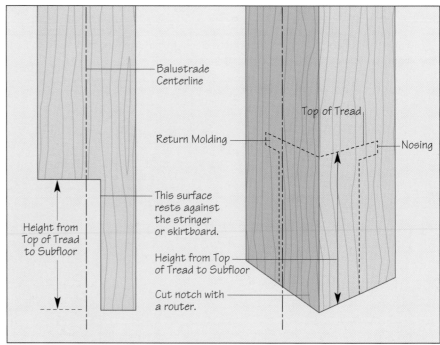

1 Use the balustrade centerline to determine the location of the newel and where to notch the newel so that it will fit over the tread. Cut the tread nosing notches using a router; you can use a chisel to make short work of the rest of the notch.

the entire depth of the notch, chisel out the excess wood, as shown. To guide the router in a straight line, use an edge guide if you've got one or clamp down some straight boards to guide the router.

3 **Attach the newel to a stringer.** Bolts make the strongest connection for attaching a newel firmly to a stringer. If you want to hide the bottom of the newel, notch it and install it on the inside of the stringer after installing the skirtboard and mortising the tread.

The more common approach is to notch the newel to fit around the corner of the bottom or top tread, which may have to be notched as well to accept the newel. In this case, the bottom of the newel will be visible. Drive carriage bolts or lag screws through the post on two sides. Make sure the newel post is plumb on two adjacent sides before tightening the fasteners. Countersink the holes, if you like, and then cover the bolt heads with wood plugs. Sometimes you can also just attach the top newel post to the upper floor wall.

Installing a Handrail

Handrails come in a variety of shapes and sizes. You can buy a manufactured handrail and cut it to length or make your own, but remember that the handrail serves one principal function: it gives you something to grasp when climbing or descending the stairs. If you can't grip the handrail, it can't do its job, which is why codes give specific instructions on the size and shape of

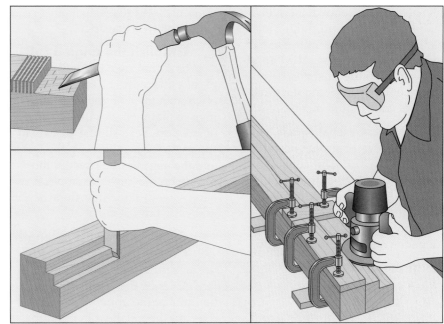

2 Use a circular saw and chisel to cut a side notch (top left). Use a router to cut a corner notch. Clamp straight boards to guide the router (right). Square the corners with a chisel (bottom left).

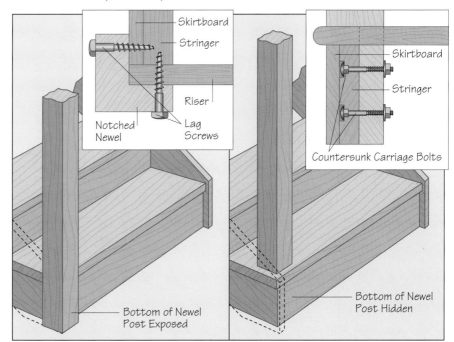

3 Notch the newel to fit over the outside of the stringer and tread (left) or over the inside of the stringer (right), and fasten it.

12

BUILDING STAIRS

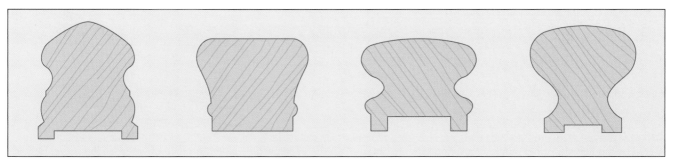

Installing a Handrail. Handrails come in a wide variety of styles and can be purchased with a flat or a dadoed (plowed) bottom.

the handrail. A round handrail with a diameter between 1¼ and 2 inches is the most effective style and dimension for grasping. Most building-supply outlets carry several styles of handrails manufactured to meet code requirements.

For a post-to-post balustrade, you fit the handrail between newel posts with a butt joint cut at the angle of the slope of the stairs. Attach the handrail to the newels with rail bolts. The height at which you should fasten the rail depends on local codes; usually,

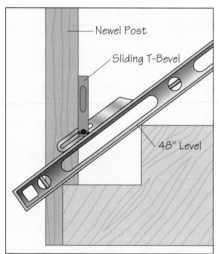

1 Find the angle of the stairs using a level and a sliding T-bevel.

you must set rails 30 to 38 inches above the tread nosing.

1 Establish the angled cut.
Find the angle to cut the ends of the handrail. Set a straight board or 48-inch level on the tread nosings so that it crosses the starting newel post. Set a sliding T-bevel to the angle formed between the level and the newel post. Transfer the setting on the bevel to a miter box, chop saw, or table saw, and then make the bottom cut.

2 Cut the handrails to length.
Lay the rail along the tread nosings flush with the starting newel. Scribe the length of the handrail at the upper newel, and then cut the rail. Bear in mind that this method will work only if both newel posts are exactly plumb; if they aren't, cut the handrail a little long, and trim it for a good fit.

3 Establish the handrail height. The height of the handrail, measured vertically from the nosing of the treads, is established by code. The minimum in most cases is 30 inches, and the maximum is 34 to 38 inches. Clamp a piece of wood on the newel post to hold the handrail at the appropriate height.

4 Fasten the handrail to the newels. There are several ways to attach the handrail to the newel post. The method you use may depend on the style of the handrail you choose. If you are using a handrail with a grooved, or plowed, bottom, you can drive two 2-inch wood screws through the underside of the handrail into the starting newel post at the base of the stairs. The baluster fillets will cover the holes.

Another method uses rail bolts. A rail bolt has machine-screw threads on one end and lag-screw threads on the other. With the handrail temporarily clamped in place, drill a pilot hole through the handrail 2 inches deep into the newel post for the bolt. Then drill a clearance hole through the handrail and a 1½-inch-deep countersink hole to fit the rail-bolt washer. Remove the handrail, and screw the lag-screw end of the rail bolt into the newel post. This will be easier if you spin a couple of nuts on the machine-thread end and use a wrench to grip the nuts and thread the bolt in. Remove the nuts; slip the handrail over the rail bolt; insert the washer and nut; and tighten the nut. You can cover the access hole with a wood plug.

2 Use the newels, rather than a measuring tape, to determine the length of the handrail.

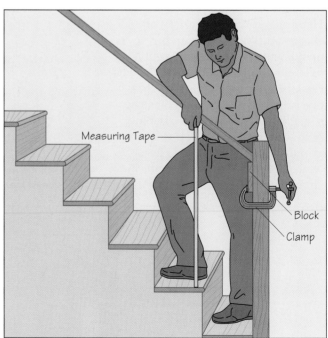

3 Temporarily clamp a piece of wood on the newel to hold the handrail at the right height.

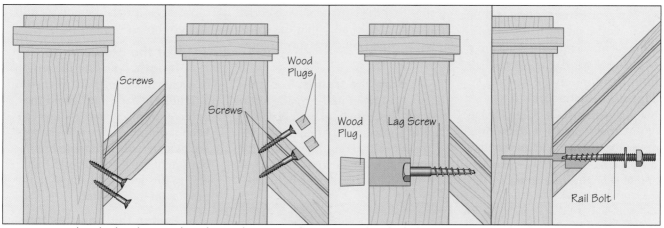

4 Fasten a handrail to the newels with wood screws or lag screws. Plug the holes, and sand them smooth. Or drill an access hole and pilot hole and install a rail bolt, slipping the handrail over the machine-thread end.

Or attach the top end of the handrail using lag screws through the bottom, or screws or a lag screw through the top. Plug the holes.

Installing Wall Rails

In an enclosed stairwell (walls on both sides of the stairs), you need only attach a rail to the wall. Building codes establish the height of the wall rail, usually the same as baluster handrails: between 30 and 38 inches. Also, you must maintain a space of at least 1½ inches between the rail and wall.

The easiest method for installing a wall rail is to attach a stock

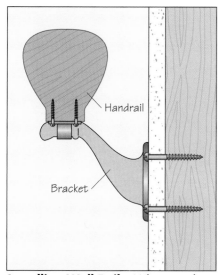

Installing Wall Rails. When attaching a handrail to a wall, screw the brackets to the wall, making sure you hit studs or blocking, and then screw the handrail to the brackets.

handrail to brackets that you've fastened to the wall. You must secure the brackets using screws long enough to penetrate at least halfway into the wall studs or blocking. With the brackets in place, cut the handrail to length and attach it to the brackets with screws.

Installing Balusters

Balusters, sometimes called spindles, aren't just pretty to look at; they also support the handrail and fill the gap between the handrail and treads. Building codes regulate the gap size permitted between balusters, normally 4 to 6 inches. This tight spacing not only prevents a child from falling through the balustrade, it also is intended to prevent a small child from slipping his head between balusters. (A 4-inch gap is much more effective in this regard.)

At one time, experienced stair builders attached balusters to treads with dovetail joints, but you rarely see such labor-intensive joinery in new construction. Today, manufactured balusters are available with 1-inch wood pins on the base that fit into holes bored in the treads. You drill the holes along the balustrade centerline. For balusters that you'll attach between treads and a handrail, note that you'll need two sizes. The baluster at the front of the tread is shorter than the back baluster. Also note that the ends of any

recess or chamfer on the baluster are an equal distance from the tread at the bottom but follow the slope of the handrail at the top.

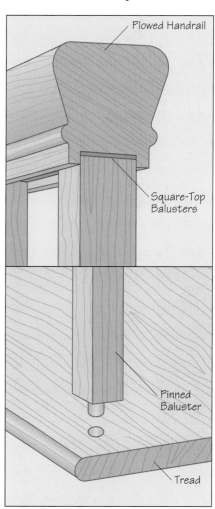

Installing Balusters. Square-top balusters usually require grooved handrails. Prefabricated balusters often have pins that fit into holes in the stair treads.

1 **Lay out the treads.** Having established the balustrade centerline, you've already done most of the work for laying out the baluster locations on the treads. On a typical balustrade, each tread holds two balusters. Align the face of the front baluster with the face of the riser beneath it, and center the back baluster between the risers. This layout procedure will en-

sure that the balusters have equal spacing. Make sure that the spacing between balusters meets your local code.

2 **Bore the treads.** You must drill holes in the treads for the premilled balusters with bottom pins. Draw straight diagonal lines in each baluster outline, and at the intersection of the lines, drill a hole 1 inch deep with a brad-point bit

of the appropriate diameter. Drill straight holes.

3 **Cut the balusters to length.** Measure the length of each baluster in place to ensure a tight fit at each joint. Hold the baluster in place, using a level to keep it plumb. Scribe a line across the baluster where it intersects the bottom of the handrail, and then add to this length the depth of the groove on the handrail.

4 **Fasten the baluster tops.** Toenail the tops of the balusters to the handrail through pilot holes. If the bottom of the handrail is flat, set the nails and fill the holes with putty.

On a grooved handrail, you fill the space between balusters with short pieces of wood called fillets. Handrail manufacturers make fillet stock to fit the groove in a plowed handrail, or you can make your own to match the wood on the handrail and balusters. Establish the angled end cuts of the fillets with a sliding T-bevel; cut them on a table saw or with a power miter saw; and fasten them between balusters with short finishing nails driven into the handrail.

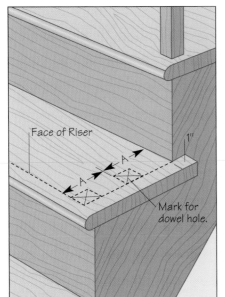

Face of Riser

_1"_

_A_   _A_

Mark for dowel hole.

1 The baluster at the front aligns with the riser beneath it; center the back baluster between the risers.

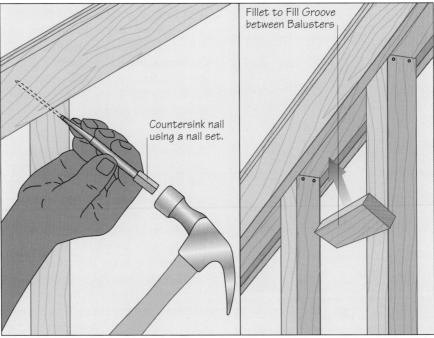

Countersink nail using a nail set.

Fillet to Fill Groove between Balusters

2 Bore holes in the treads at the intersection of the diagonal layout lines in the baluster outlines.

3 Plumb each baluster using a level, and mark the top for cutting.

4 Drill pilot holes for 4d finishing nails; toenail the balusters to the handrails; and then install fillets in the empty spaces.

About L-Shaped Stairs

Even if space isn't a factor, many people find L-shaped stairs to be more appealing than straight-run stairs. By turning the corner at 90 degrees, the L-shaped staircase breaks the direct visual line from top to bottom. If the landing can be equipped with a small window, the effect will be even more pleasing. Also, a landing installed midway between the upper and lower floors provides a convenient rest spot for those who have difficulty getting up and down stairs.

The L-shaped stairway with a landing is essentially nothing more than two straight-run stairs heading in perpendicular directions. In terms of calculating dimensions, treat the landing as just another tread.

The staircase in this chapter is a closed-riser model, with standard hardwood tread stock and matching hardwood risers. The landing can be covered with ¾-inch hardwood flooring installed over a ¾-inch plywood subfloor. Oak is the most popular hardwood for stairs, but other woods could be used as well. If you were building these stairs for utility purposes, such as building stairs leading to a basement, and you wanted to cut costs, you could use two-by lumber for the treads and leave out the risers. Be sure to adjust dimensions to your design variations.

Calculating Rise & Run

Treads and risers on an L-shaped stairway must meet the same minimal requirements as on straight-run stairs. Another point: it is essential that tread depth and riser height be identical on both the upper and lower staircase runs.

1   **Calculate the rise.** The total rise is the vertical distance be-

tween finished floors. In this case, the upper and lower floors will be finished with identical material (¾-inch hardwood flooring or ½-inch carpet). The total rise measures 105 inches. Divide the total rise by 7¾ inches (maximum riser height) to find the minimum number of risers the stairway will require. The result is 14 (rounded up from 13½).

Divide the total rise (105 inches) by 14 risers to find the unit rise (7½ inches). The stairway could be built with 15 7-inch risers ($15 \times 7 = 105$), but using 14 risers allows the landing to be located exactly halfway between the floors. As long as you're not constrained by a wall, it's easiest to build the landing halfway between floors because the stringers will then be identical for both flights of stairs, which will cut

down on the amount of measuring and cutting you will need to do later. If a wall limits the amount of space you have to build stairs, see "Limited Total Run," page 180.

2   **Calculate the landing height.** Divide the total number of risers in half ($14 \div 2 = 7$) because we have decided to place an equal number of treads on the upper and lower portion of the stairs. Then multiply the result by the riser height ($7 \times 7½ = 52½$). This establishes that the finished height of the landing should be 52½ inches. Because the landing will be covered with ¾-inch plywood and ¾-inch hardwood, subtract the combined thickness of these flooring materials from the landing height to find the framing height ($52½ - 1½ = 51$ inches).

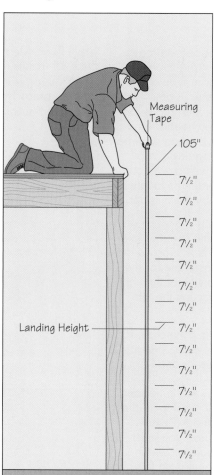

1 As with straight-run stairs, begin planning an L-shaped staircase by finding the total rise. Be sure that your measurement is from finished floor to finished floor.

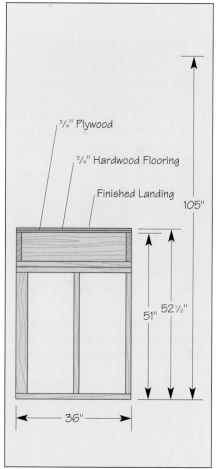

2 To determine the finished height of a landing located halfway between floors, divide the total number of risers in half and multiply the result by the unit rise.

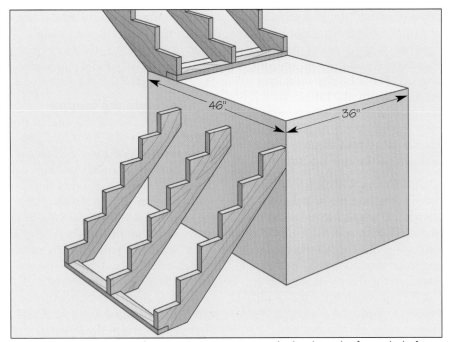

Determine the landing
size. When construction is complete, the finished landing on an L-shaped staircase should be square, with the sides equal to the width of the treads, which in this case is 36 inches. However, because the stringers for the upper section will rest on the landing, you need to frame the landing larger than its finished size. Build a rectangular platform during rough framing as shown left. The side of the frame to which the lower stringers will be attached should be built about 1 unit run longer than the other side, which will be framed to the length of the treads. In this case, the frame measures 36 inches by 46 inches because the unit run is 10 inches, as described in Step 4, opposite.

3 Because stringers to the upper stairway rest on the landing, the framed platform must be larger than the finished landing surface.

LIMITED TOTAL RUN

Sometimes, you need to install an L-shaped staircase because there isn't enough space for straight-run stairs. Maybe the stairs face a wall, or maybe a straight-run would extend into a hallway. In any event, the problem you face is that the total run is too short to put in straight-run stairs. So you need a landing for an L-shaped stairway, and the landing must be built in a particular spot, whether it's against a wall opposite the stairwell header or flush with a wall on one side of a hallway. Because the landing's location is fixed, its height will be determined by the number of steps needed to reach it.

First, figure out the total rise and the unit rise. For this example, 105 inches of total rise yields 7½ inches of unit rise. Then measure the total run available for the upper staircase. You must subtract the size of the landing from the total run, and then occupy the leftover space with treads.

If the total run for the upper staircase is 86 inches, for example, and the stairs are 36 inches wide, then the finished landing will be 36 inches square, and the space you have left over is 50 inches. If you will use a hangerboard to connect the stringers to the header, subtract ¾ inch from the total run. You need to fill the 50-inch space with treads. Having already determined that the unit rise will be 7½ inches, you must find a unit run that will fill the space and fall within the limitations set by the run-to-rise formulas. In this case, five 10-inch-deep treads work out perfectly. Because there's always one more riser than tread, you'll need six risers, each 7½ inches high, putting the finished landing surface 45 inches below the upper finished floor. Measure down from the upper finished floor 45 inches, and use a level and straightedge, line level, or water level to transfer this height to the landing area. Then build the landing as described in "Framing the Landing," opposite.

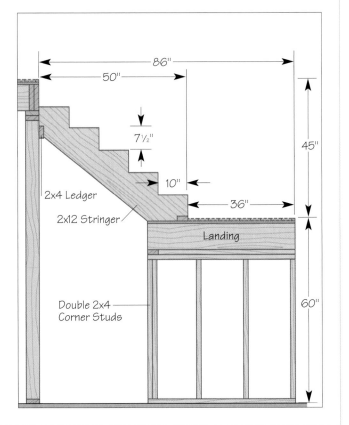

4 **Find the run.** To determine the unit run, use the run-to-rise formulas explained on page 168:

unit rise + unit run = 17 – 18

unit rise × unit run = 70 – 75

By applying the unit rise (7½ inches) to these formulas, you will find that 10 inches is a good unit run.

Next, find the total run for the upper stairs. Because there are seven risers, there will be six treads. Multiply the number of treads by the tread depth to find the total run (6 × 10 = 60 inches). The bottom riser will be located 60 inches from the hangerboard, measured horizontally. Use the same dimensions for the lower flight of stairs.

Framing the Landing

Typically, a landing on an L-shaped staircase is encased by walls on two sides. Joists for these sides can be nailed directly to the wall studs. The other two sides of the landing need to be framed using standard 2×4 framing techniques.

If the walls are covered with drywall, you need to locate the wall studs so that the joists can be nailed to them. If necessary, the entire landing can be set on three framed walls (if only one side abuts a wall) or four framed walls in case no side abuts a wall. If your landing is a different size from the example in this chapter, be sure that the studs and joists in the framing are located 16 inches on center.

1 **Attach joists to the wall.** Mark the height of the landing framing (51 inches) on one wall stud; then use a level to mark the rest of the studs. Nail a 46-inch-long 2×10 joist to the studs, even with the layout marks. Then nail a 33-inch-long joist at the same height on the adjacent wall.

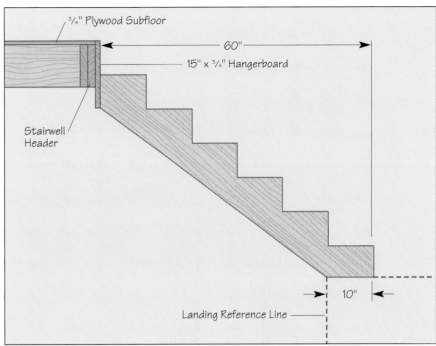

¾" Plywood Subfloor
15" x ¾" Hangerboard
Stairwell Header
60"
10"
Landing Reference Line

4 Use the run-to-rise formulas to determine acceptable tread and riser dimensions for upper and lower stairs. Then multiply the unit run by the number of treads to determine the total run and the landing location.

46"
51"
33"
Nail joist to wall at proper height.

1 With 12d common nails, attach 2x10 joists to the wall studs so that the finished floor will be at the proper height. Make sure the joists are perfectly level.

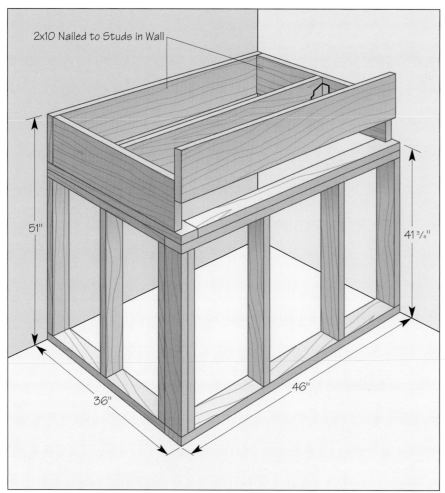

Label: 2x10 Nailed to Studs in Wall

Dimensions: 51", 41 ¾", 36", 46"

2 Build the walls for the landing with 2x4s spaced 16 in. on center. A double top plate ties the adjoining walls together, and 2x10 joists bear on the top plates.

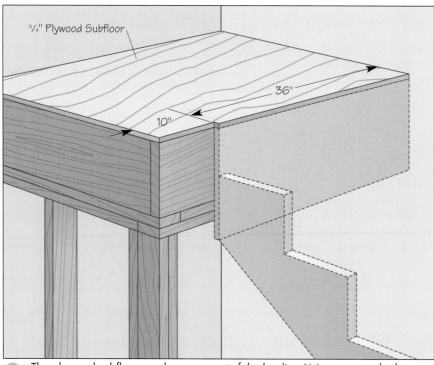

Label: ¾" Plywood Subfloor

Dimensions: 36", 10"

3 The plywood subfloor overhangs a part of the landing ¾ in. to cover the hangerboard. Glue and nail the subfloor to the joists.

Frame the landing walls.

2 The short walls that support the landing are framed like normal stud walls, with a bottom plate and a double top plate. Measure the distance from the floor to the bottom edge of the joists. If you used 2×10s at a 51-inch height, the distance should be 41¾ inches, but measure to be sure. This is the height of the landing wall.

Now subtract 4½ inches from this figure (the thickness of the three plates) to find the stud length (38¼ inches here). Cut eight 2×4s to this length. Attach studs to the bottom and top plates as shown, spaced no more than 16 inches apart.

Cut to length the two double top plates (42½ inches and 36 inches), then attach them to the top plates using 8d nails. The double top plate on the short wall should overlap the end of the wall 3½ inches; the double top plate on the long wall should stop 3½ inches from the end of the wall. Fit each wall under the end of the perimeter joist as shown, and secure the walls to the house framing and floor. Make sure the landing frame is square with the adjacent walls; then use 10d nails to fasten the landing walls together through the top plates and the corner joists.

Attach the other two perimeter joists along the tops of the landing walls. Toenail the joists to the top plate. Measure the distance between the joists (43 inches here). Cut and install the intermediate joist with joist hangers.

Install the landing sub-

3 **floor.** Cut a piece of ¾-inch plywood that is flush with the landing on three sides and overhangs the long side by ¾ inch. The overhang will cover the hangerboard. Notch the overhang so that it extends only as far as the outside stringer, as shown. Apply construction adhesive on the joist tops before using 8d common nails to fasten the subfloor to the joists.

Making the Stringers

You need to make a total of six stringers. If your landing is located exactly midway between the upper and lower floors (as in this example), and you will use the same flooring material for both floors and the landing, then all stringers will be identical. Lay out and cut one stringer, then use it as a template to lay out the others.

1 Choose the stringer stock. The stringers are made with 2×12 stock. To determine the minimum length for each one, use the Pythagorean theorem and the figures for total rise and total run on each section, as shown. Be sure to add one unit run to the total run in your calculations. Or you could convert the total rise and run to feet, and using the scale 1 foot equals 1 inch, mark these points on a framing square. Then measure the distance between these points to find the length of the stringers.

2 Lay out and cut the stringers. Use a framing square to lay out the stringers. Set a stair button on the outside edge of the blade to the unit run (10 inches) and another on the tongue to the unit rise (7½ inches).

With the stringer lying flat, place the square as shown, with the corner resting on the lumber. Mark along the outside edges of the framing square. Slide the square down the stringer so that it aligns exactly with the previous mark; then lay out the next cutout. Extend the top rise line to the bottom of the stringer. This will mark your plumb-cut line.

3 Drop the stringer. Usually, "dropping the stringer" means trimming the thickness of a tread from the bottom of the stringer. In this case, however, the tread stock is thicker than the hardwood flooring, which is not yet in place. So the bottoms of the stringers need to be shortened by the thickness of a tread minus the thickness of the finished flooring. The treads on this staircase will be ⅝-inch hardwood, which is 1⅛ inches thick, and the flooring will be ¾ inch thick. The difference between the two materials is ⅜ inch. Cut along a line ⅜ inch from the bottom of each of the stringers.

In some cases, the stringers must be dropped different amounts, such as when the bottom rests of a slab floor. In these cases, you will need to make two templates.

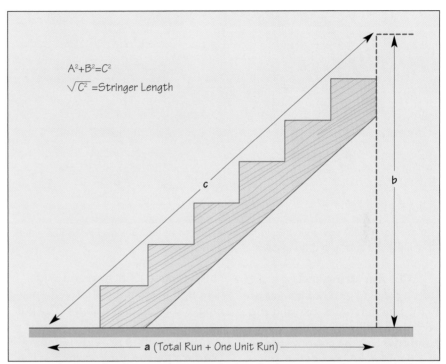

$$A^2+B^2=C^2$$
$$\sqrt{C^2} = \text{Stringer Length}$$

c

b

a (Total Run + One Unit Run)

1 Use the formula above to determine the length of stringer stock you need. Use only straight, solid boards for stringers.

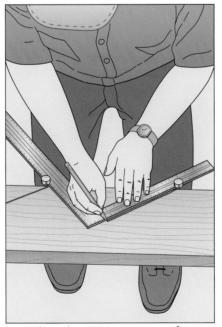

2 Place the 2x12s on a pair of sawhorses, and after attaching stair buttons to a framing square at the unit run and unit rise, lay out the stringer.

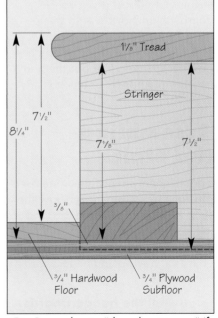

1⅛" Tread

Stringer

7½"

8¼"

7⅛"

7½"

⅜"

¾" Hardwood Floor

¾" Plywood Subfloor

3 Remember to "drop the stringer." If the flooring is not yet in place, calculate the difference in thickness between the treads and the flooring.

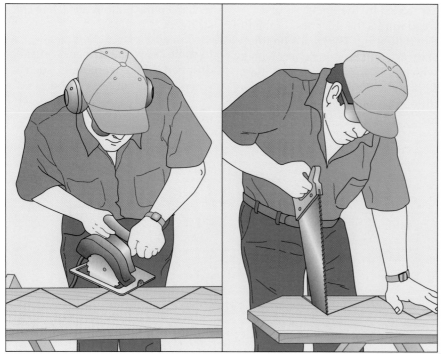

4 Use a circular saw to cut up to the intersections of the riser and tread lines; then finish the cuts with a handsaw.

5 Cut notches in the stringers for the 2x4 kickboard.

4 **Cut the stringer.** Use a circular saw to cut the stringer up to the junction of the rise and run layout lines. Finish cutting with a handsaw. Use the cut-out stringer as a template to lay out the others.

5 **Cut notches for the kickboards.** The bottom of the stringers will rest on 2×4 kickboards to anchor them to the lower floor and the landing. Use a piece of scrap 2×4 to lay out the notches on each stringer. Cut out the notches with a handsaw or electric saw.

Assembling the Stairs

The stringers are installed one riser plus one tread thickness below the finished flooring of both the landing and the upper floor. The stringers will be attached to hangerboards at the top and a kickboard at the bottom.

1 **Install the hangerboards.** A hangerboard is a piece of ¾-inch plywood that is nailed to the stairwell header and the landing. Cut both hangerboards two risers

high (about 15 inches) and wide enough to span the stairwell opening at the top of the stairs. The bottom hangerboard should be just wide enough to provide a nailing surface for the outer stringers. Use 8d common nails to nail the

hangerboards securely to the joists. Think about the finished ceiling now. If the hangerboard will interfere with the ceiling drywall, trim the hangerboard so that it will be flush with the bottom edges of the stringers.

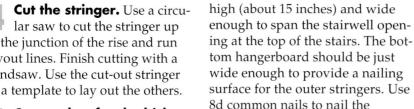

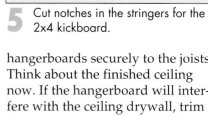

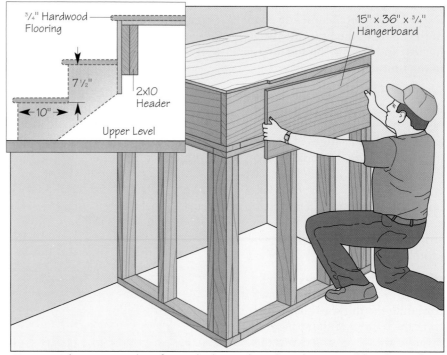

1 Use 8d common nails to fasten the hangerboards to the stairwell header and landing. If necessary, trim the top hangerboard to be flush with the bottom edge of the stringers.

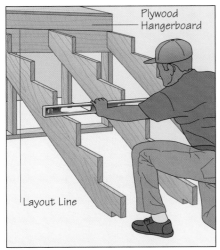

2 With a single nail, attach each stringer along the layout line. Check that the stringers are level and straight before you finish nailing.

2 Set the stringers. On each hangerboard, measure down from the finished floor surface one unit rise (7½ inches in our example) plus the thickness of the tread (1⅛ inches here), and mark a layout line on the hangerboard.

Attach each stringer along the layout line with a single nail; then check the fit. The stringers should lie flat against the hangerboard and be perfectly level with the floor. Place a level across the stringers at each step. If you find one stringer slightly out of alignment, shim the bottom level with the others.

3 Attach spacers to the walls. If you have a wall on one or both sides, you can nail the stringers directly to the wall framing. If you plan to add drywall and a skirtboard, however, leave a space wide enough for both between the wall and the stringer. Use a 2×4 spacer for this purpose. Position the stringer even with the layout line on the hangerboard. Check that the stringer butts tightly against both the hangerboard and the floor. Then mark the bottom edge of the stringer on the wall, and cut a 2×4 to fit along this line. Remove the stringer; spike the 2×4 spacer to the wall with 16d nails; then reset the stringer; and nail it to the 2×4 spacer with 16d nails.

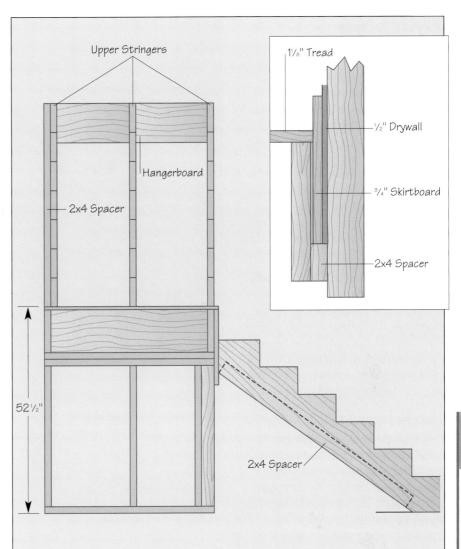

3 At a wall, attach a stringer to a 2x4 nailed to the wall. The gap created by the 2x4 provides space for a skirtboard and drywall.

4 Attach the stringers. If you have access to the back of the hangerboard, drive 12d nails through the back of the hangerboard into the stringers. If the framing on the landing prevents this, attach the stringers to the hangerboards with metal angle brackets. Attach the middle stringer so that it is centered between the outside stringers.

Make sure the stringers are square to the landing and the stairwell framing and that they're properly spaced at the bottom. To hold them in place, cut a 2×4 kickboard to length, slip it into the notches in the stringers, and then secure the kickboard to the floor and the stringers to the kickboard.

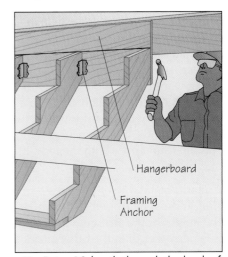

4 Drive 12d nails through the back of a hangerboard to fasten the stringers, or use metal framing anchors. Insert the kickboards into the notches at the bottoms of the stringers, and nail everything together.

12 BUILDING STAIRS

Finishing the Stairs

The stairs shown here have been designed to take 1⅛-inch hardwood treads, which are cut from standard tread stock available at lumberyards and building-supply outlets. Usually, the nosing on the tread stock is already rounded over, but you need to cut the boards to the right length and width before installing them. The risers and skirtboard could be made from the same type of wood, using ¾-inch boards.

1 Cut and install the treads and risers. To minimize squeaks, the treads should be attached to the stringers with screws and construction adhesive spread along all mating surfaces. Drill pilot holes before driving screws. Attach risers using 6d nails and construction adhesive. Use wood screws to fasten the bottoms of the risers to the back edges of the treads, too. If you are using hardwood treads and risers, countersink the screws, and cover them with wood plugs that match the tread stock. On the risers, use a nail set to drive the heads of the nails below the surface, then plug the holes with matching putty. Sand or plane the surfaces flush.

The treads must be at least 36 inches wide. If you are using hardwood tread stock and you want the treads to overhang the side a bit, you might want to shape the tread ends to match the rounded nosing. Use a router fitted with a roundover bit to shape the ends, as shown. You will need to round over both the top and bottom.

Cut and install the bottom riser first. It must be ripped to match the height of the stringer. Note that it is narrower than the other risers by the thickness of a tread. Then cut and install the second riser before installing the first tread. Install the third riser, followed by the second tread, and continue up the stairway.

The easiest way to get a perfect fit against a skirtboard is to position the riser or tread tightly against the skirtboard, and then use a compass to scribe the exact shape of the skirtboard on the end of the tread. If you need to install a skirtboard on an open side, use a framing square to lay out cut lines at the bottom and top, and then nail the skirtboard to the stringer.

The treads on a closed-riser staircase must have a nosing between ¾ inch and 1¼ inch.

2 Attach the angle blocks. Another way to prevent squeaky stairs is to install angle blocks. Cut the triangular blocks out of scrap two-by lumber, and attach them with adhesive and nails to the underside of the stairs where the tread meets the riser. Attach two or three to each step.

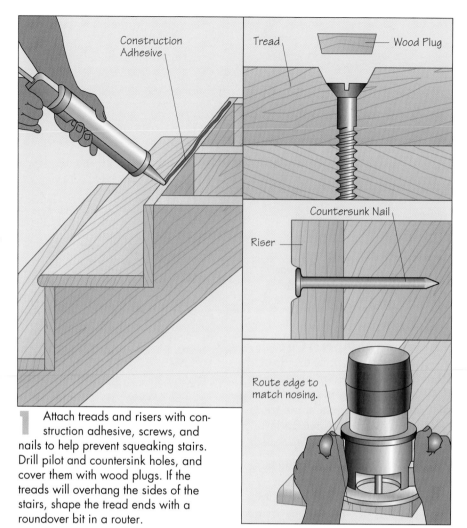

1 Attach treads and risers with construction adhesive, screws, and nails to help prevent squeaking stairs. Drill pilot and countersink holes, and cover them with wood plugs. If the treads will overhang the sides of the stairs, shape the tread ends with a roundover bit in a router.

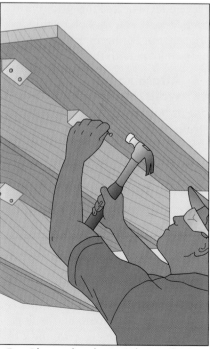

2 Glue and nail triangular angle blocks under the treads and risers to keep them from squeaking.

Winder Pros & Cons

Winders are not as safe as straight-run stairs or stairs with a landing. Use a winder only if you have no other choice. For one thing, the irregularly shaped treads present a hazard. An important component of stairway safety is ensuring that the movement from step to step is routine and repetitive. By their nature, winders require users to adjust their routine as they move around the corner. Also, users who try to climb the stairs using the narrow section of the winder may find insufficient support for their feet. Finally, while a landing is likely to break a fall down the stairs, winder stairs would not.

Restrictions. Winders are often closely regulated by codes. In some areas you may not be allowed to build a winder as the main stairway in a house. Many codes won't allow winders in which the treads come to a point. Instead, treads are required to be at least 10 inches deep along the "line of travel," usually defined as the line running 12 inches from the narrow edge of the treads.

Some codes additionally stipulate that the minimum width of treads be no less than 6 inches at any point. A continuous handrail is required along the side with the narrower treads. Be sure to check your local code carefully.

Saving Space. A winder introduces a shortcut in the line of travel, similar to cutting across a corner lot rather than following the sidewalk. The reduced impact on the floor plan is most apparent when the winder treads come to a point, as shown in the drawing. When space is too limited even for a winder, you may have to consider spiral stairs.

Building a Basic Winder

As with all stairs, you need to find the total rise, then calculate a comfortable unit rise and unit run. To illustrate better the differences between stairs with winders and stairs with a landing, the instructions below will assume the same total rise (105 inches) and number of risers (14) as the L-shaped stairs

described on pages 179 to 186. Be sure to read those pages carefully before attempting to build a winder.

You need to frame a landing and build two sets of stringers. The differences here are that one set of stringers is reduced by two treads, whose place will be taken by the two winder steps you will install on top of the landing. Also, the upper stringers won't rest on the landing. Instead, they are hung with joist hangers off the side of the top winder step. This allows you to build a smaller frame.

1 Build the landing. Two sides of the 36-inch by 36-inch landing rest on short framed walls. The joists for the other two sides are attached directly to the house framing. If your landing is freestanding (that is, not adjacent to walls), you can frame short walls to the other two sides to support the other two sides. In the example stairs, the landing serves as the fifth tread from the bottom, and the total height of the landing is 37½ inches (using a unit rise of 7½ inches). Use construction adhesive and 8d common nails to install the landing subfloor.

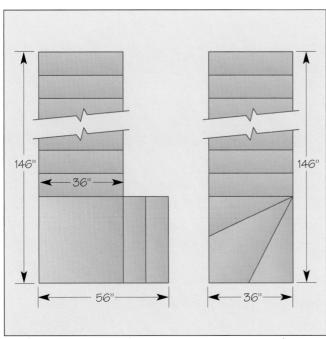

Saving Space. A winder staircase is more compact than L-shaped stairs because the landing is replaced by three pie-shaped treads, called winders.

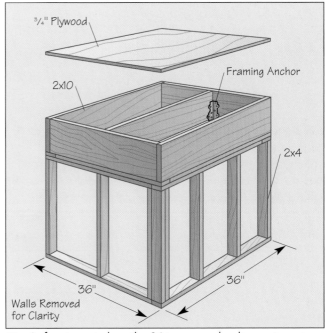

1 In framing winders, the 36-in.-square landing rests on two framed walls for support. The other two sides are attached to the house framing.

2 Lay out the winders. Use a 36 × 36-inch piece of ¾-inch plywood to lay out the winders. Lay out three treads so that the tread width along the line of travel (usually 12 inches from the narrow end of the treads) is equal on each tread. An easy way to ensure this is to draw a diagonal line on the land-ing, as shown. Measure in from each corner 18¾ inches, and mark these spots on the diagonal line. Then draw a line from the inside corner of the plywood through each of the two marks. This divides the plywood into three pie-shaped wedges. Each wedge serves as a layout for one tread.

Note that this 18¾-inch dimension is good only on a 36 × 36-inch land-ing. For other sizes, you can experi-ment with the layout until the tread width along the line of travel is equal from step to step.

3 Cut the treads. Cut out one of the treads. This piece will be the top tread, and the remaining two-thirds piece will be the middle tread. The landing itself will serve as the bottom tread.

4 Build the winders. You need to build frames for the top two steps of the three-step winder. The unit rise on this exam-ple staircase is 7½ inches. From this dimension, subtract the thickness of the plywood treads (¾ inch). The result, 6¾ inches, is the height of each frame. Rip several 2×8s to 6¾ inches, then cut and assemble the frames using 10d nails.

5 Assemble the winder. Keeping the sides flush, toe-nail the larger of the two frames to the landing using 8d ring-shank nails for extra holding power. Then nail the larger plywood tread to the frame. Finally, fasten the small-er riser frame and tread.

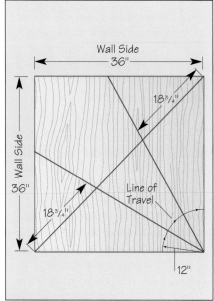

2 Draw a diagonal line and measure 18¾ in. from each corner. Then draw lines from an adjacent corner through the 18¾-in. marks just made.

3 Cut as shown above. The smaller piece will be the top tread; the larger piece will be the middle tread; and the landing will be the bottom tread.

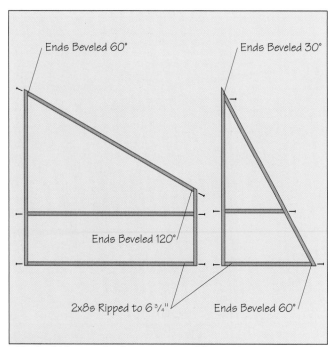

4 Build frames for the top and middle winders using two-by lumber and 10d nails. The height of each frame plus tread equals the unit rise.

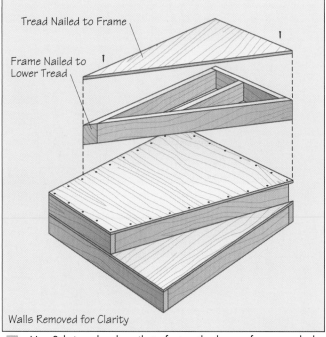

5 Use 8d ring-shank nails to fasten the larger frame and ply-wood tread to the landing, and the smaller winder to the larger one.

Adding Nosings

With the winder stairs built and the stringers cut and attached, you can now cut and install the remaining treads and risers, using ¾-inch plywood. If the stairs are going to be carpeted, you may not have to include a nosing on the treads. This is often determined by the local building code, so check the code for building requirements.

If you need to add a nosing for carpeted stairs, cut the treads accordingly. Because you can't use a router on the plywood winder treads, you can add nosings to the winder treads by installing half-round molding, which is available in a variety of sizes. Cut the molding to the width of the tread; apply construction adhesive or glue to the mating surfaces of the molding and the winder; and then drive 4d or 6d finishing nails through the molding and into the winder.

If the winder treads are going to be covered with hardwood, you don't need to worry about the nosing at this rough stage. Instead, the finish treads—with one edge bullnosedfor the nosing—can be cut to allow for the proper overhang.

6 Use joist hangers or framing anchors to attach the stringers to the upper winder and hangerboards for the tops of the stringers.

6 Install the stringers. The stringers are cut and installed much like those in the previous chapter. The one difference is that the stringers for the upper staircase section do not rest on the platform. Rather, they are hung from the back side of the upper riser with joist hangers. Do not "drop the stringer" in this case. Instead, clip off a flat edge on the stringer bottoms so that they can rest in the joist hangers. If the end stringers are flush with the edge of the platform, you won't be able to install joist hangers properly. Instead, use framing anchors.

You will need to "drop the stringer" on the lower stringers. Both sets of stringers can be attached at the top with hangerboards.

12 BUILDING STAIRS

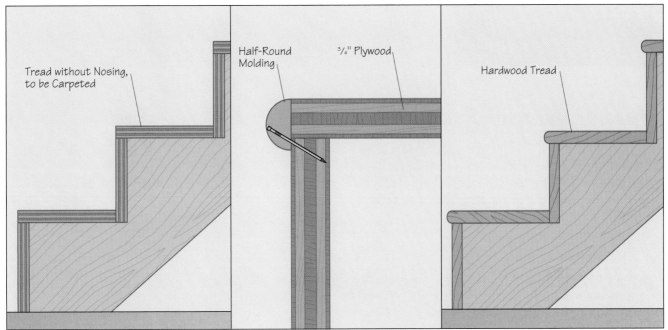

Adding Nosings. Before carpeting the stairs, use half-round molding attached with 4d or 6d finishing nails and construction adhesive to create nosings. Hardwood can be installed so that it overhangs the risers.

design ideas for stairs

Left Stairs with landings save valuable floor space, and they provide an elegant touch to the design of the entire room.

Above Balustrades can be as simple or as intricate as you wish. This unusual design is a focal point for this room.

Right A simple staircase has a few distinctive touches to make it more appealing, such as the matching treads and railing and the unusual treatment for the newel post.

Above A winder staircase makes an elegant addition to this room. Windows along a stair or on a landing usually flood both floors with light.

Above right Distinctive newel posts and balusters are available from home centers, lumber yards, and custom woodworking shops.

Right Treat a stair as the architectural detail it is. Here a distinctive Arts and Crafts-style stair ties the designs of the two floors together.

13

Basement Framing

Using steel studs to convert an unfinished basement to useable living space is a practical solution for families with space problems. While you could use wood to accomplish the same goal, steel does have advantages over wood. Every component of a steel framing system is the same as the other components, there is no shrinking or warping. Steel is resistant to rot, and it is fireproof. Assuming the basement is dry and does not have leakage problems, divide the project into five tasks: furring or building stud walls that face on masonry walls, building stud partition walls that divide interior space, installing a ceiling, installing a floor, and concealing pipes, ducts, beams, and columns. Here's how to finish a basement using steel framing.

Estimating Materials

If you have scaled plans for your basement project, you can use them to estimate materials. If you don't have plans, the easiest course is to measure the basement area and then figure your materials. The basic materials for simple wall framing include channel-shaped steel studs, U-shaped steel track (for the top and bottom plates) in which you place the studs, and low-profile self-tapping screws with Phillips heads for attaching the studs to the tracks. (Some pros use clinching tools for this.) If you were framing 24 inches on center and the basement was 24 feet long, 16 feet wide, and 8 feet high, for example, you'd need 13 studs for each long wall, 9 studs for each short wall, and 160 feet of track for the top and bottom plates. Multiply total wall length by height and add 15 percent, and you'd get the required square footage of vapor barrier (sheet plastic you apply to keep moisture that may seep through the masonry away from the new wall).

Basement Walls

There are two strategies for framing walls that face onto masonry walls: attaching wood or steel furring directly to the masonry or building stud walls independent of the masonry walls. The kind of walls you build depends on two things: the condition of the masonry and the amount of insulation you require. If the masonry walls are flat and in good shape and you can get by with ¾-inch rigid foam insulation panel with an insulating value of about R-5, you can use furring on masonry. If the basement walls are irregular (like stone) or you require more insulation, build stud walls. You'll also use stud walls as partition walls, though you'll build them slightly differently. The projects that follow entail building steel-stud walls.

Building Stud Perimeter Walls

Difficulty Level: 🦅🦅

Tools and Materials

- Basic carpentry tools
- Polyethylene vapor barrier
- Construction adhesive
- Steel framing (studs, track, and ceiling channel)
- Metal snips
- Powder-actuated fastener
- Drill and/or screw gun
- ½-inch #8 low-profile self-tapping screws

---

1 **Attach a vapor barrier to the masonry.** Check the basement walls for moisture problems, and correct them before proceeding. Cover the masonry with a 6-mil polyethylene vapor barrier. Mil is a thickness rating in which 1 mil is equal to ¹⁄₁₀₀₀ inch. Glue the vapor barrier to the concrete using mastic paste or construction adhesive. Overlap the plastic 6 inches along the seams.

Unfortunately, adhesives don't have great reliability over time. To ensure that the plastic vapor barrier stays in place, use furring strips, positioned vertically, over the plastic at each seam, at each end of the wall, and every 8 feet in between.

Fasten the strips using at least four fasteners per section. For 1×2 material use 1¾-inch masonry nails, 1¾-inch concrete screws (first predrilling holes using a masonry bit loaded in your hammer drill), or 1½-inch nails driven by a powder-actuated fastener (PAF). A PAF is a special gun that shoots pin-like fasteners into concrete using a .22- or .25-caliber blank cartridge called a powder load. Use PAF nails only in concrete or concrete block, not cinder block. After you drive the

1 Attach a 6-mil vapor barrier to the masonry wall using mastic or construction adhesive and furring strips.

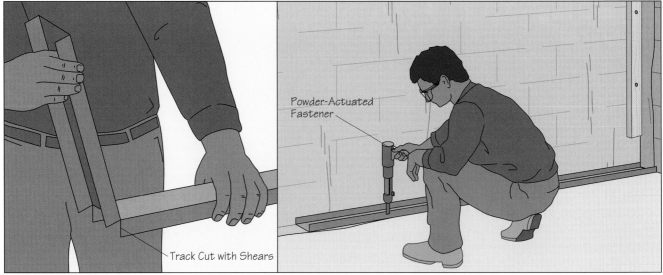

Powder-Actuated Fastener

Track Cut with Shears

2 Cut the bottom track to length, and attach it to the concrete floor using 1-in. fasteners. An easy way to attach the track is to use a powder-actuated fastener.

first PAF nail, check the nailhead to make sure it's seated well in the built-in washer. If the head is protruding, use a stronger powder load, each of which is color-coded for power. One charge doesn't suit all walls because concrete density and strength vary. If you don't own a PAF or can't borrow one, you may be able to rent a unit locally.

2 Lay the bottom track. At both ends of each basement wall, measure 1 to 6 inches from the wall (depending on how much space you want between the masonry and the new stud wall), and make a mark on the floor. You'll need at least a 1-inch space for air circulation and to account for any irregularities in the masonry wall. Now make a second mark 3½ inches into the room from each of the first marks and snap a chalk line. (Steel studs come in sizes from 1½ to 5½ inches wide. We're using 3½-inch studs.) The chalk line will act as a guide for the inside edge of the bottom track. Lay the track, and fasten it using 1-inch concrete screws or a PAF with 1-inch nails. If you need to cut the track, use metal snips to cut the two flanges; then bend back the track and cut the web. Mark the track for studs 16 or 24 inches on center.

3 Attach the top track. Use a plumb bob to locate the top

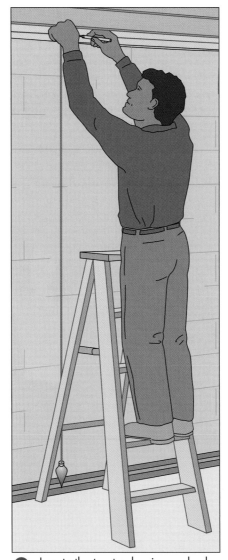

3 Locate the top track using a plumb bob, and attach it to the ceiling joists with 1¼-in. drywall screws.

AVOIDING STEEL-STUD STRIPING

Often, vertical stripes appear after a while on steel-stud walls. This occurs because steel studs easily transfer heat, making surfaces in contact with the studs cooler than the rest of the room. Dust in the air may stick to the cooler surfaces, causing striping. To prevent this, install rigid-foam insulation under the drywall. Also, use plywood or 1x2 spacers to bridge the thermal-break air space (as mentioned in Step 2) and maintain stiffness in the steel studs, which may not be sturdy when covered with drywall on only one side.

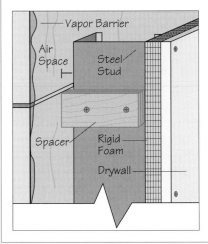

Vapor Barrier

Air Space

Steel Stud

Spacer

Rigid Foam

Drywall

4 Attach the wall studs 16 or 24 in. on center using ½-in self-tapping screws. Insulate the walls and apply a vapor barrier.

track directly over the bottom track. Attach the track to the underside of the ceiling joists with 1¼-inch drywall screws. If the track runs parallel with the joists, install 1×4 or 1×6 blocking in the joist bays to provide an attachment surface for the track.

4 **Install the studs.** Install metal studs between the top and bottom tracks 16 or 24 inches on center, just as with conventional wall framing. (See "Wall Framing," page 94.) Attach the studs with ½-inch self-tapping screws. These screws have a shallow head that doesn't interfere with installation of drywall. Insulate the wall with fiberglass batts by tucking one side of the batt inside the open flange of a stud and pressing the other side into the wall cavity. Friction should hold the batts in place until you install drywall. Apply a 6-mil polyethylene vapor barrier across the studs before you attach the drywall. It might seem like overkill to put a vapor barrier on both the masonry wall and the

warm side of the stud wall, but it's not. The vapor barrier on the masonry wall will stop excess moisture from migrating into the room from

outside. The vapor barrier on the stud wall prevents warm, moist air in the heated living area from migrating through the wall and condensing on the insulation when it meets the cold air in the unheated area of the basement.

Building Partition Walls

Difficulty Level: 🦇🦇

Tools and Materials

- Basic carpentry tools
- Steel framing (studs, track, and ceiling channel)
- Metal snips
- Powder-actuated fastener
- Drill and/or screw gun
- ½-inch #8 low-profile self-tapping screws

1 **Install the top track.** Cut the top and bottom tracks to the length of the wall you plan to build, and mark the top one for the position of the studs at 16 or 24 inches on center. Determine where you want the wall, and attach the top track using one screw at each end. After you've double-checked the

1 Attach the top track to joists or to blocking nailed between the joists if it runs parallel.

track position, you'll drive a screw at each intersecting joist or into blocking between two joists. Be sure you can see the stud layout.

2 Measure with the 3-4-5 triangle. Before you fasten the track in place, use the 3-4-5 triangle method (or a proportional version) to be sure the track is perpendicular: measure along the intersecting wall (presumably one of the basement walls) 3 (or 6) feet from one side of the partition wall (point A) and make a mark (point B). Now from point A, measure 4 (or 8) feet along the partition wall to point C. If the partition wall is at a right angle to the intersecting wall, the diagonal between point C and point B will be 5 (or 10) feet; if it's not, move the partition wall track until the diagonal measures correctly.

3 Locate the bottom track. Hang a plumb bob from the top track in several locations, and make marks transferring its position to the floor. Align the bottom track with the layout marks you just made. When the bottom track is directly below the top, attach it to the floor. (See "Lay the Bottom Track," page 194.) Mark the track for studs as you did the top track.

4 Install the studs. Measure between the tracks at each stud location, and cut studs to fit using metal snips. The studs will be close to the same length unless the floor or the joists are greatly out of level. Put a stud in position; align it with the layout marks on the top track; and fasten it using a ½-inch self-tapping screw. Plumb each stud, and fasten it to the bottom track. To frame for a door opening, follow conventional rough-opening layout procedures. (See "Marking Plates for Door Rough Openings," page 101.) Assemble two studs back to back as a king stud with a section of track as a jamb. (See the drawings on page 197.) Cut a section of track as shown in the drawings for the header. Once you've framed the wall, apply drywall with screws.

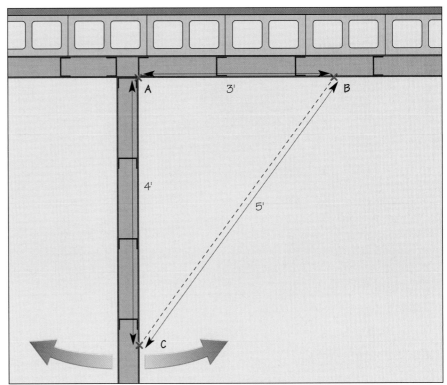

2 Use the 3-4-5 triangulation method to be sure that the partition wall is square to the outside walls. For better accuracy, use 6-8-10 ft.

3 Transfer the position of the partition wall's top track to the floor using a plumb bob. Use the marks as guidelines for the bottom track.

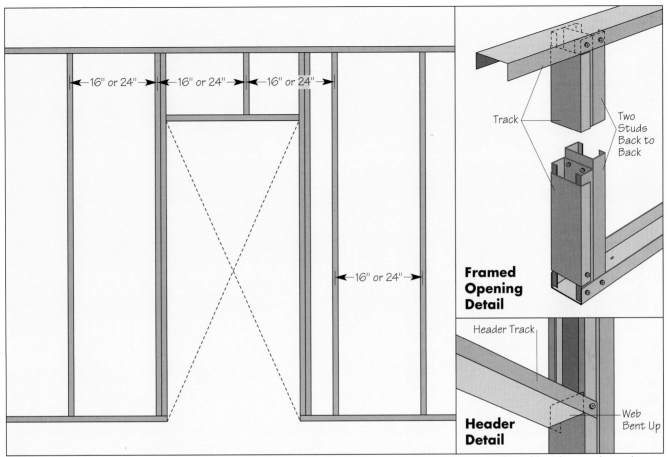

Track

Two Studs Back to Back

Framed Opening Detail

Header Track

Header Detail

Web Bent Up

 Install the studs 16 or 24 in. on center, and frame window and door openings with jamb studs and headers made as shown.

If you're installing a ceiling, cover the ceiling with drywall before covering the walls.

Basement Ceilings

You have several options when it comes to installing a ceiling in the basement. You can hang a suspended ceiling that uses a grid to hold acoustical tiles. This option is a good idea if you must have access to utilities like electrical or plumbing and you can afford to lose a few inches of headroom. According to most building codes, there must be at least 90 inches of headroom (84 inches in kitchens, hallways, and bathrooms) in a finished basement. If headroom is tight, you can install drywall and paint it or glue acoustical tile to it. Don't attach drywall directly to the underside of the ceiling joists, however;

use wood or metal furring attached perpendicular to the joists and shimmed. For furring you can use wood 1×3s or resilient steel channel (ceiling channel tracks), as in the procedure that follows.

Installing a Drywall Ceiling

Difficulty Level: 🐟🐟

Tools and Materials:

- Basic carpentry tools
- String
- Shims
- Furring
- 8d nails
- Drywall
- Tape and joint compound
- Drywall screws
- A drywall jack or T-brace

1 **Check the joists.** In some homes the ceiling joists may be inconsistent; that is, they are at different elevations. This can cause an unevenness in the ceiling finish. Before you install the ceiling channel tracks, pull a string across the underside of the joists to check for high spots, which you'll have to shave, or low spots, which you'll have to shim.

2 **Install the furring.** Set the ceiling channel track in place, and attach it to the underside of the ceiling joists 16 or 24 inches on center by driving 1½-inch drywall nails or 1¼-inch drywall screws into the flanges on each side at each joist. As you install the channel, use a level to double-check for consistency from row to row. Shim where necessary.

3 **Apply the drywall.** When you've leveled, shimmed, and installed the furring, apply drywall

1 Pull a string across the joists and nail it off to check for high and low spots.

2 Attach metal resilient channel across the joists, checking for level and shimming as necessary.

2x4 T-Brace

3 Install drywall on the ceiling, attaching it to the metal channel and holding it in place with a T-brace.

The Pros Know

LIFTING PANEL MATERIALS

Use a lever and block to position panel materials. Control the lever with your foot. When the panel is properly positioned, secure it with a couple of nails or screws. Then remove the lever and finish fastening the panel.

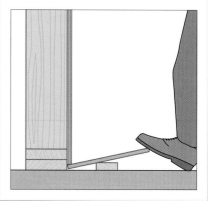

as you would to any ceiling. You'll be working over your head, so you may want a helper, and you may want to construct a T-brace to help you hold the drywall in place. A T-brace is a T-shaped two-by device that is just a bit longer than the distance from the strapping to the floor. Wedge it beneath a piece of drywall on one end, so you can have your hands free to screw or nail at the other end. In place of a T-brace, you could use a drywall jack, which you might be able to rent locally. Drywall jacks are more versatile than T-braces, allowing you to work alone if necessary, and are usually inexpensive to rent.

Basement Floors

Untreated wood will eventually rot when moisture comes into contact with it, so whatever design you use to install a wood floor on a concrete floor must keep moisture from entering. All good concrete-under-wood-floor projects begin with a 6-mil polyethylene vapor barrier.

You might think you can attach wood floors directly to concrete if you use the right adhesive. However, even so-called waterproof adhesives will eventually fail, and besides, you need a vapor barrier, remember? One solution is a floor design that will create an insulated platform slightly above the concrete floor, which you've already covered with a vapor barrier. To this platform you might attach wood flooring, resilient flooring, or carpeting. You can also build the stud walls on top of this subfloor. If headroom is tight, a better option might be a newer development in floors: floating laminate flooring, page 201.

Installing an Insulated Subfloor

Most likely there's no insulation beneath your basement slab. One exception might be an unfinished daylight basement, where at least one wall is exposed to the grade. An uninsulated slab is uncomfortably cold in the winter, so contact the builder, if possible, to determine whether insulation exists.

An insulated subfloor installed over a concrete slab isolates the finished floor from the slab, resulting in a warmer floor and helping to prevent moisture from damaging the flooring. The insulated subfloor consists of water-resistant plywood that's nailed to sleepers, usually pressure-treated 2×4s laid flat. Rigid insulation fits between the sleepers. You can use either square-edge or tongue-and-groove-edge plywood; tongue-and-groove plywood eliminates the need for blocking placed beneath unsupported plywood edges. Remember that according to most building codes, you must have at least 90 inches of headroom in most of the basement's living area (84 inches in kitchens, hallways, and bathrooms), measured from the *finished floor*.

Build the platform before installing walls, and attach the bottom tracks to the subfloor.

Difficulty Level:

Tools and Materials

- Basic carpentry tools
- Polyethylene vapor barrier
- Construction adhesive
- Caulking gun
- Pressure-treated 2x4s
- PAF or 2¼-inch masonry nails
- Extruded polystyrene foam panels
- ¾-inch plywood
- 6d common nails

1 **Put down a vapor barrier.** After sweeping the floor slab, cover it with sheets of 6-mil polyethylene plastic. Overlap each seam by at least 6 inches. Lift up the edges of the polyethylene, and use a caulking gun to put down dabs of construction adhesive to hold it in place.

2 **Install the perimeter sleepers.** Use 2¼-inch nails fired from a PAF or 2¼-inch-long masonry nails to fasten pressure-treated 2×4 sleepers around the perimeter of the room. Because sleepers expand and contract with changes in temperature and moisture, leave a ½-inch gap between the edge of a sleeper and the wall. If the lumber is dry and straight, a nail or two installed every several feet will suffice. Shim the sleepers where needed. Mark these perimeter sleepers for additional sleepers 24 inches on center. This spacing is acceptable for ¾-inch plywood.

3 **Install interior sleepers.** Align the interior sleepers square to the marks on the perimeter sleepers. Sight the floor with a straight 2×4 on edge and a level to determine where to shim the sleepers because of unevenness in the concrete. Use one fastener at the end of each sleeper and one about every

1 Sweep the slab and lay 6-mil plastic sheeting as a vapor barrier, overlapping the seams by 6 in.

2 Fasten pressure-treated 2x4 sleepers around the perimeter of the room on top of the vapor barrier.

48 inches. Position the sleepers end to end, but leave a ½-inch gap between the ends for expansion.

4 **Insert the foam panels.** Medium-density extruded polystyrene foam is best for concrete floor slabs. Use a thickness that matches the thickness of the sleepers, about 1½ inches. Cut the pieces to fit between the sleepers and insert them.

5 **Attach the subfloor.** Use ¾-inch plywood subflooring, either square or tongue-and-groove edge. Cut the plywood to run perpendicular to, rather than parallel with, the sleepers. Lay the panels with staggered joints, and fasten them using 6d galvanized nails. Install a wood floor or carpeting right on the subfloor, or nail down an underlayment on top of the subfloor for a resilient floor.

Laminate & Engineered Flooring

As its name suggests, prefinished flooring comes with a factory-applied, finished topcoat. There are two basic varieties. There installation methods are similar, but you should check with the manufacturer concerning your requirements.

Laminate flooring is generally made of high-strength hardboard that is sealed, top and bottom. The top surface is decorative, high-pressure melamine laminate resembling wood or natural stone. Laminate flooring can be installed over any substrate.

The other kind is manufactured by cross-laminating layers of wood veneer and is called Engineered flooring. The top layer is usually a hardwood veneer that is finished with a number of coats of UV-cured urethane. The ½-inch-thick flooring comes in strips 2 to 4 inches wide or planks more than 4 inches wide. The planks often contain a number of narrow strips and resemble strip flooring when installed.

Because it's made from layers of wood plies or sealed hardboard, these products are more stable than solid wood, and you can install them where ordinary wood flooring might have problems, say below grade and directly over concrete. This stability also allows you to install the flooring as a floating floor system over a ⅛-inch-thick layer of high-density foam underlayment. You glue the tongue-and-groove joints, using no nails in the installation. Some systems are glueless. You simply click the tongue-and-groove sections together.

3 Space the pressure-treated sleepers 24 in. on center, and fasten them using a powder-actuated fastener with 2¼-in nails.

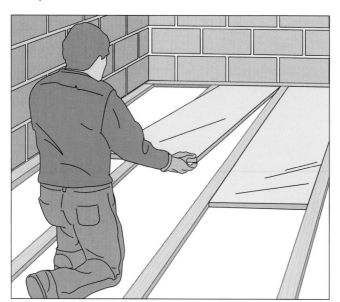

4 Cut 1½-in.-thick extruded-foam panels to fit between the sleepers, and lay them in place.

5 Attach ¾-in. plywood panels perpendicular to the sleepers, staggering the joints.

Installing a Floating Floor

Difficulty Level:

Tools and Materials

- Polyethylene vapor barrier
- Foam underlayment and tape
- Laminate flooring and glue
- Measuring tape, pencil, and hammer
- Handsaw, circular saw, utility knife

1 Prepare the floor. Lay a vapor barrier of polyethylene sheeting that is at least 6 mil thick. Overlap the vapor-barrier joints by at least 6 inches, and tape them with duct tape. Roll out the foam underlayment, and cut it to fit the room. Butt the joints, and seal them with duct tape.

2 Lay the planks. Leave a ½-inch expansion gap around the perimeter of the room. Start the installation on one of the long walls of the room, with the panel's groove facing the wall.

3 Join the planks. Try to work in room-length runs. Join the planks by running a bead of white glue or carpenter's glue in the bottom edge of the groove as you install each succeeding section.

4 Finish the job. Tap the sections together tightly with a hammer on a hammering block. Flooring from some manufacturers comes with a plastic hammering block; if yours doesn't, use a scrap piece of flooring. Mark, cut, and install planks in irregular areas just as you would a normal wood floor.

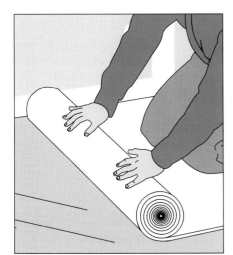

1 Lay a polyethylene vapor barrier; then roll out the foam underlayment and trim it to fit the room. Tape all joints.

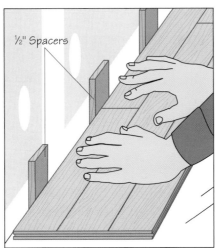

½" Spacers

2 Leave an expansion gap of ½ in., and lay the planking with the grooved edge facing the wall.

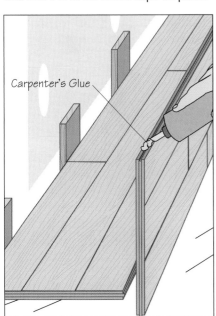

Carpenter's Glue

3 Squeeze carpenter's glue into the bottom of each groove, and then join the panels, tongue to groove.

4 Tap the joints tight with a hammer and a scrap of flooring or plastic hammering block.

Beams, Ducts, Pipes & Columns

Basements often contain beams, ducts, pipes, and columns, all of which you should cover when converting the space into a living area. Don't ever remove beams and columns. They were originally installed for required structural support, and removing them may cause serious structural damage. The best thing to do with such permanent obstructions is to box them in with framing and drywall or one-by pine.

Framing and covering pipes, thin (4-inch) columns, and small ducts (6 × 6 inches, for example) with drywall may be more trouble than it's worth, so simply use one-by pine to box them in. There is no need to miter the pine boards, since you can nail them where their edges butt, but you may want to do so for a neater appearance.

Concealing Beams and Ducts

The task of concealing a wood beam or post isn't difficult. You might nail plywood paneling or drywall to a wood beam or post and treat the edges just as you would walls finished with the same materials. Or simply sand the beam or post smooth; round over or chamfer the edges with a router; and paint it.

A steel beam, on the other hand, isn't easy to conceal because it's difficult to fasten material to it. To get around this problem, you can secure paneling or drywall to wood framework that's nailed to the underside of the ceiling joists. First build two wood "ladders" made of 2×2s. Place the ladders against the beam, toenail them to the joists, and attach crosspieces between the ladders using 2½-inch screws. Attach drywall on all three sides, also using screws. Before finishing the walls,

cover the drywall corner joints with corner bead—a metal strip made at a 90-degree angle, which you nail to outside drywall corners to protect them—or with molding.

A large, rectangular, sheet-metal duct, called a trunk, often leads from a furnace to the farthest points of a house. You'll often find trunks along attic floors and basement ceilings. Smaller ducts branch off the trunk and distribute warm air to each room served. The ducts in a central air-conditioning system may have a similar layout. If the ducts obstruct headroom, it may be possible to move them, but this

definitely is a job for a heating-and-cooling contractor. In most cases, it's easier and less expensive to leave the ducts in place. With an informal decor, you can just paint the ductwork to match the ceiling color. It may also be possible to enclose them within the confines of a suspended ceiling. If not, you can box the ducts within a wood framework similar to that for a beam and cover the frame with drywall or paneling.

Concealing Soil Pipes

The soil pipe, the main drainpipe of the plumbing system, conducts water and waste away from the house. Typically, it's the largest pipe in the house and may be plastic or cast iron. If possible, enclose the pipe within a box or soffit as shown in the drawing below. Predrill through the joists and bottom 2×4 for the 2½-inch screws, and attach the drywall using screws. It's a good idea to wrap the pipe in insulation before you box it in, especially if it's plastic. The insulation reduces the sound of rushing water. Be sure to take measurements in several places along the length of the pipe before making the box because the pipe slopes at least ¼ inch per foot for proper drainage. If you'll cover the pipe's clean-out plug by the concealment process, provide access to the plug.

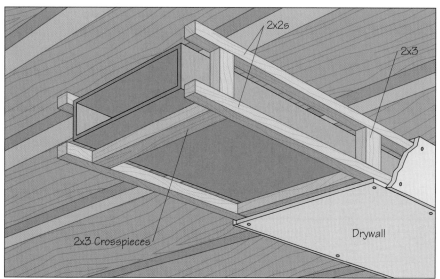

Concealing Beams and Ducts. Build a framework of 2x2 "ladders;" attach it to the joists; and cover it with drywall.

2×2s

2×3

2x3 Crosspieces

Drywall

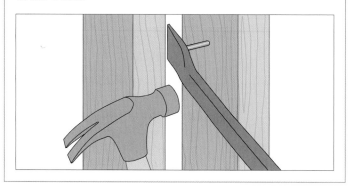

The Pros Know TIGHT-QUARTERS NAILING

To drive nails where you can't reach them, lay the flat end of a wrecking bar on the nailhead, then whack the bar with a hammer as close as possible to the nail. You'll be able to drive the nail flush with the surface of the wood.

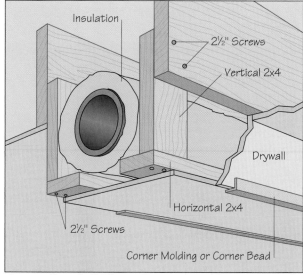

Insulation

2½" Screws

Vertical 2x4

Drywall

Horizontal 2x4

2½" Screws

Corner Molding or Corner Bead

Concealing Soil Pipes. Frame around large pipes with 2x4s as shown, and attach drywall.

13

Boxing around a Post

A good way to conceal a lally column, a smaller duct, or a pipe is to create a wood box to surround it. This method consumes less space than a frame and drywall. Use one-by stock to build the box; pine or a hardwood such as oak is appropriate. You can paint or stain pine, and while you can stain hardwood, you can also leave it natural and coat it with a clear varnish or sealer.

Difficulty Level:

Tools and Materials

- Basic carpentry tools
- Framing square
- One-by lumber
- Table saw (or circular saw)
- Wood glue and clamp
- 6d finishing nails
- Wood putty
- Sandpaper

1 **Lay out the box.** Use a framing square to lay out the inside perimeter of the box. You can then draw the outside perimeter ¾ inch outside the first line, providing the exact outside dimensions of the box.

2 **Cut the sides.** Measure the distance between the floor and ceiling; then subtract ¼ inch from the measurement to provide a fitting allowance. Cut four pieces of stock to length. Use a table saw or circular saw to miter each edge at a 45-degree angle if desired. Test-fit the assembly around the post.

3 **Assemble and install the box.** Spread a thin film of wood glue on the edges, and use 6d finishing nails to nail three sides of the box together. Then slip the three sides over the post, and clamp and nail the fourth side into place. Toenail the box to the floor and to the beam above. If you can't toenail the bottom, apply a bead or two of construction adhesive under the box to hold it in place.

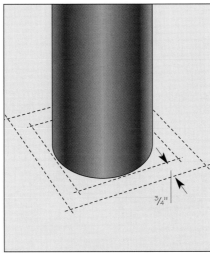

1 Use a framing square to draw a full-scale layout of the one-by wood box on the floor.

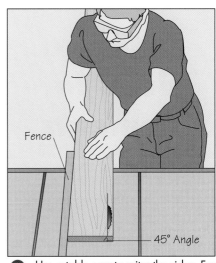

2 Use a table saw to miter the sides. For safety, use a blade guard (not shown), and tilt the blade away from the fence.

Fence

45° Angle

Miter Joints on All Edges

Finishing Nails

3 Glue and nail three sides together; slip the assembly over the post; and nail on the fourth side. Toenail the box to the floor and to the beam.

4 **Finish the box.** Use sandpaper or a rasp to round over the edges of the box. Rounding the edges minimizes impact damage, both to

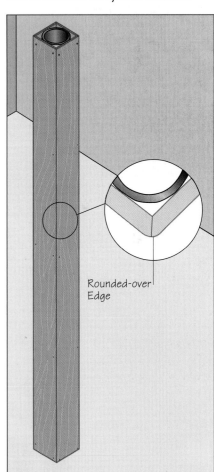

Rounded-over Edge

4 Fill the nailholes with wood putty, and then use sandpaper to smooth them and to round over the corners. You can stain or paint the box later.

the box and to those who may bump into it accidentally. Use wood putty to fill all nailholes, and then sand them smooth. Paint or stain the box.

design ideas for basements

Above Get in shape by converting part of a basement to a home workout center.

Left If creating a family room, add a wet bar and cabinets for extra convenience.

Opposite Built-in display cabinets add an elegant touch to this television room.

Left An unused basement may be the only space large enough for a home theater system.

Right A dry basement that receives some natural light is a great spot for an extra bedroom.

14
Installing a Bay Window

O ne way to gain a little extra space, or at least the illusion of space, is by adding bay windows to your home's design. As shown at right, a bay window projects out from the plane of the wall, giving you extra floor and shelf space inside. The large amount of glass helps open up the interior, providing the illusion of more space. Most aspects of a bay window are simple to frame, except the short roof rafters. These rafters are tricky to lay out and involve cutting compound angles. But the work is not so difficult that it can't be handled with the right tools, some care, and the use of a calculator.

Bay Windows

A bay window—also called an oriel—can add a surprising amount of light and space to a room, not to mention a panoramic view of the outdoors. You can buy prefabricated bay windows in 30-degree, 45-degree, and 90-degree (box) bays. You can also create your own bay by building angled walls and framing for double-hung or casement windows combined with fixed units.

This chapter describes installing a prefabricated 45-degree bay window. Although you can bump out the entire wall when you install a bay window and gain extra floor space, we show installing the unit in a conventional window rough opening, which results in a large windowsill area that provides shelf space. (See "Floor-Support Alternatives," page 210, for information on creating a bump-out.) When you install a bay window in this manner, you can support the unit using decorative brackets for structural support or—as we do—using diagonal lumber braces covered with a plywood skirt that's sided to match the house. Some window manufacturers employ a cable support system in their bay-window units, which requires no additional support from below. Carefully read the instructions that come with your window to determine the support required.

Framing for a Bay Window (Oriel)

Difficulty Level: 🦇🦇

Tools and Materials

- Basic carpentry tools
- Bay window
- Two-by framing lumber
- One-by trim lumber
- ½-inch CDX plywood

1 Build the rough opening and upper and lower support frames. The rough opening

for the bay window will be a hole in the side of the building like that used for a standard window. Read the literature enclosed with the unit to determine the dimensions for the opening. (See "Walls & Partitions," starting on page 93, for how to frame a window rough opening.)

With the rough opening formed and the wall sheathed, you'll attach two frames—one above and one below—that protrude horizontally from the side of the house. The frames will support the bay window from below and support the bay window's roof above. Build two 2×4 "footprints" of the bay-window shape, sheathed on one side with ½-inch CDX plywood, to act as the support frames. Instructions that come with the window

will give you dimensions or even a full-size pattern to use. Most bay windows have a large face and two smaller sections, one on each side. The side windows meet the face window at a 135-degree angle in a 45-degree bay unit. (See the drawing.) Assemble the frames using 12d nails.

2 Install the lower support frame. Attach one of the 2×4 support frames to the house at the bottom of the rough opening. After leveling, nail through the back 2×4 into the house studs using 16d nails.

In some cases you'll attach the frame so that its plywood top is flush with the sill plate of the rough opening. In other cases you'll attach the frame below the sill plate to allow for

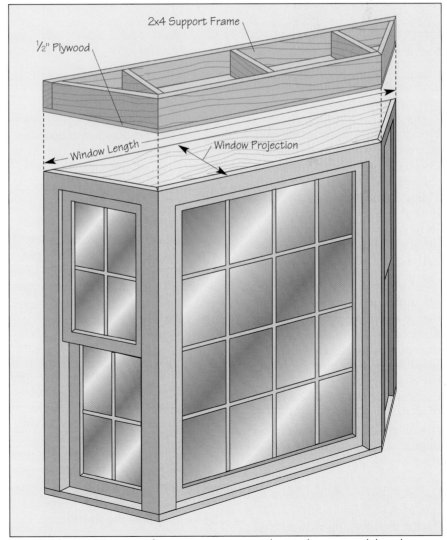

2x4 Support Frame

½" Plywood

Window Length

Window Projection

1 Build two 2x4 support frames, one to support the window unit and the other as a base for the roof. Match the shape of the bay window, and use 12d nails.

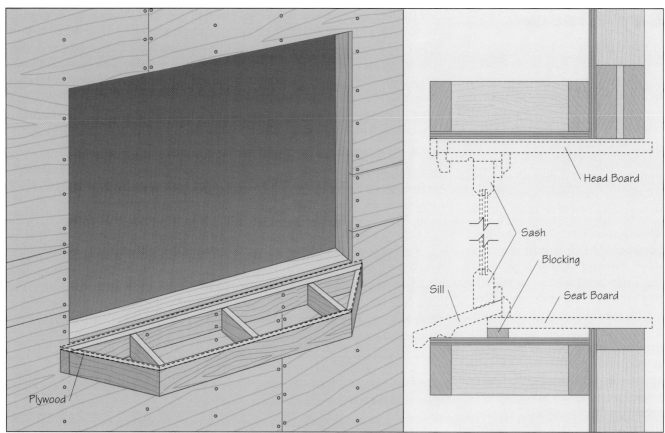

Plywood

Head Board

Sash

Blocking

Sill

Seat Board

2 Attach the lower support frame to the house framing using two 16d nails in each stud. You may have to account for blocking (right). See the manufacturer's literature before you install the frame.

blocking. This is because the angled sill on many bay-window units doesn't allow the window to sit flush on the support frame. By providing blocking, you allow the window to sit above the decking, with its base level, the window frame plumb, and the angle of the sill maintained in its proper position.

The literature provided by the manufacturer will provide the height of the required blocking. Look for a drawing similar to the one above (right). Some bay windows require blocking above the head board as well as below the seat board. The cross-sectional view of the window will show the placement of any blocking (top or bottom) and its dimensions. Install the blocking along the full length of each side of the plywood decking and along each end, creating a box on which the window will sit. Fasten the blocking with 8d nails, and then install rigid or fiberglass-batt insulation between the blocks

so that the window's seat board will enclose a layer of insulation between it and the support frame.

3 **Install bracing.** To support the 2×4 frame, install a 2×6 ledger board that spans two-thirds the width of the bay window, centered below the unit. As for elevation, the braces supporting the bay window will sit at 45-degree angles, and their position will dictate the elevation of the ledger board. (See the drawing.)

Attach the ledger to wall studs using at least two 3-inch-long, ½-inch-diameter lag screws. Drill pilot holes for the lag screws into the studs, and drill clearance and countersink holes in the ledger. If you are installing the window on a house that has already been sided, remove the siding where the ledger board contacts the house. The ledger should sit flush against the sheathing.

Run braces at a 45-degree angle from the underside of the 2×4 sup-

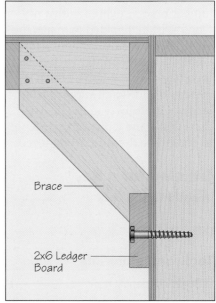

Brace

2x6 Ledger Board

3 Lag-screw the ledger board to wall studs at a height that will support braces attached at 45-degree angles. Notch the braces over the ledger.

port frame to the ledger board, as shown in the drawing. Notch the braces over the ledger as shown, and attach them to the 2×4 frame

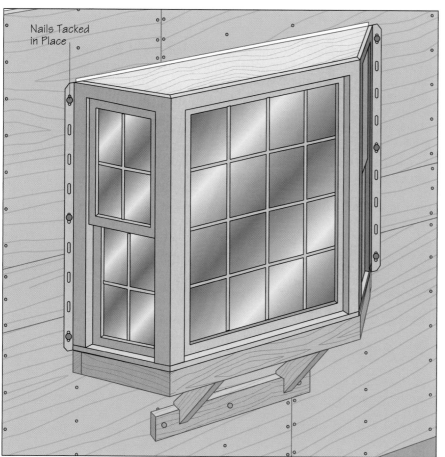

Nails Tacked in Place

"joists" using three 10d nails or 2½-inch deck screws. You'll probably want to hide these braces from view later by building a plywood skirt around the base of the bay window. The skirt will also cover any insulation you choose to add to the underside of the 2×4 support frame.

4 Place the window. With at least one other person helping you, position the window on top of the 2×4 support frame. Tack the window to the house with a few 10d nails through the window's brickmold or nailing flange. Do not drive the nails home.

5 Install the top support frame. Set the top 2×4 support frame in place on top of the bay window. After you've positioned the frame squarely, nail it to the house framing (through the back 2×4 into the opening header) using 16d nails. Remove the tacked nails, and level and plumb the window. Use cedar shims to hold the window in place. Nail through the window flange or brickmold into the window-opening framing.

4 Once you've initially positioned the bay window with the assistance of a helper, tack it in place with 10d nails.

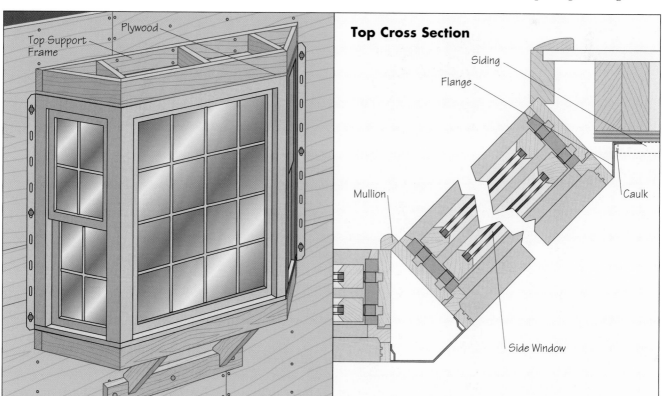

Top Support Frame

Plywood

Top Cross Section

Siding

Flange

Mullion

Caulk

Side Window

5 Install the top support frame by nailing it to the house studs; then remove the tacked nails; plumb and level the window; and nail it in position. Siding will butt the window frame (right).

FLOOR-SUPPORT ALTERNATIVES

If you want to gain square footage by bumping out a wall to hold a bay window, you'll need to provide support for a floor—unless your project is new construction and you've accounted for the bump-out in the original foundation footprint.

You have at least three choices if you're adding floor support: a cantilevered floor, a post-supported floor, or a slab-on-grade floor.

For a cantilevered floor, you have to cut out a section of the rim joist and add sister joists to the floor joists that run from the foundation wall to another support, such as a beam. (See "Cantilevered Joists," page 88.)

A post-supported floor requires that you set footings below the frost line and pour at least two concrete piers to support a header to which you'll attach the floor joists. Attach the other end of the joists to the house's rim joist using hangers.

If you have a slab-on-grade foundation, you can pour an add-on slab to support the new bay-window bump out. You'll need to attach the new slab to the existing one, though. Attachment entails drilling holes in the existing concrete to accept rebar rods, which will in turn extend into the new slab and tie it to the house foundation.

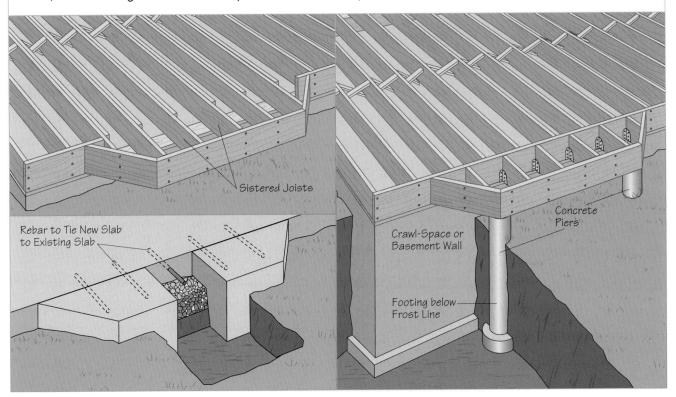

Sistered Joists

Rebar to Tie New Slab to Existing Slab

Crawl-Space or Basement Wall

Concrete Piers

Footing below Frost Line

Building the Bay-Window Roof

With the bay window in place, it's time to build the roof. To save yourself the rafter calculations (which are challenging), you can install a prefabricated roof, often clad with copper, offered by window makers.

If you decide to build your own bay-window roof, match the main house's roof slope for the best appearance. To better envision the bay-window roof, think of it as one-half of a modified hip roof.

There are three kinds of rafters and one "ridge" in a bay window roof.

The ridge is only as long as the front face of the center window. Two plumb-cut rafters will sit perpendicular to the ends of the ridge. These rafters are the bay window "commons." You'll bevel the crown edge and the plumb-cut end of the rafters as though they were hip rafters because this is where the plywood sheathing and the fascia boards will meet from different angles.

The second kind of rafter is the "wall rafter." The wall rafters run from each end of the ridge to the top support frame at the same slope as the bay-window commons. These

rafters have an angle cut across the crown edge that matches the roof slope so that the plywood roof sheathing can sit flush against the wall rafters where it meets the house siding.

The third kind of rafter is the "side rafter," and it runs, just like a hip rafter, from the junction of the wall rafter and the common rafter. You might want to cut these rafters (after you've installed the others) by trial and error until they fit to avoid difficult calculations.

All three rafters have bird's-mouth cuts where they meet the "top plate" (the 2×4 top support frame).

Installing the Bay-Window Roof Framing

Difficulty level:

Tools and Materials

- Basic carpentry tools
- 2x6 lumber, 12d nails
- ½-inch CDX plywood

1 Measure and cut the common rafters. Once you've decided on the slope, determine the rise using calculations explained earlier in this book for common gable roofs. (See "Figuring Total Rise," page 122.) Once you know the rise and run of the roof, calculate the length of the common rafters. (See "Calculating the Length," page 125.) With the rafter length in hand, mark and cut the rafters. The "building line" will be the outside edge of the top support frame. (See "Marking the Rafter Length," page 128, and "Making the Bird's-Mouth, Ridge & Tail Cuts," page 129.) Bevel one side of the crown edge and the plumb-cut rafter tail to accommodate the two roof planes, which meet at each common rafter. (See the drawing.)

2 Measure and cut the wall rafters. Mark and cut the wall rafters as you would commons, after determining their rise and run with a measuring tape. Along the crown edge of the wall rafters, rip an angle that corresponds to the slope of the bay's roof. For an 8-in-12 roof, that angle is just over 33 degrees. At the tail, cut a 45-degree angle.

3 Measure and cut the side rafters. The side rafters are also cut like commons. Though they will have the same rise as the two common rafters you first cut, they will have a shorter run. But at the ridge, the side rafters are cut like hip rafters, with two side cuts corre-

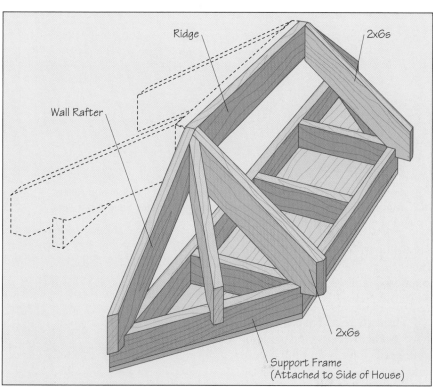

Building the Bay-Window Roof. A bay-window roof is essentially one-half of a hip roof with the corners clipped. The common rafter, side rafter, and wall rafter are all cut and beveled differently.

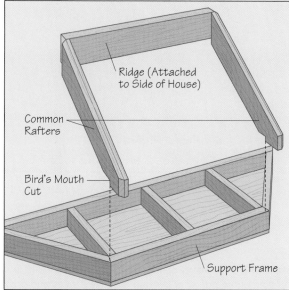

1 Determine the rise and run; then cut the common rafters and ridge and attach them to the side of the house. Bevel the rafters' outside edge and outside end.

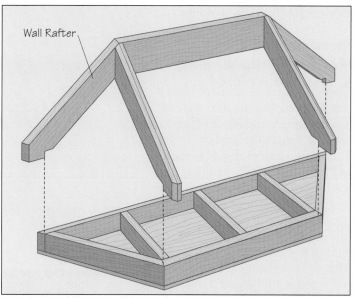

2 Cut and then install the wall rafters as you did the commons. For each rafter, bevel the top edge to fit the slope and the plumb-cut edge at 45 degrees to match the window's angle.

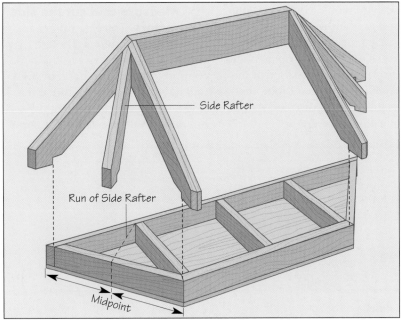

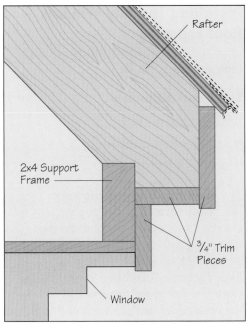

3 Install the side rafters between the wall rafters and the common rafters. Make side cuts at the top of the rafters as though they were hip rafters. You don't have to bevel the upper edge.

4 Trim the bay-window roof with one-by material to form the fascia/soffit and to cover the joint between the window and support frame.

sponding to the slope of the roof. (See "Mark the Ridge Side Cuts," page 148.) There is no need to bevel the crown edge.

4 Install roof fascia and soffit. Because the common rafter tails have been plumb-cut and beveled, it's easy to trim out the connection between the window and the upper 2×4 support frame with one-by pine to form a fascia and small soffit. (See the drawing for one way to do the job.)

Trimming Out the Bottom of the Window

Build a 2×4 frame similar to that in the drawing to echo the shape of the support frames. Build the frame deep enough to at least cover the braces and ledger. Small blocks with a beveled edge installed on each side of the front vertical members provide nailing surfaces for the side pieces of plywood. Sheathe the skirt frame with plywood and siding to match the house. If you choose not to build a skirt, install a plywood soffit beneath the lower template, trimmed out with one-by pine. Paint the braces and ledger to match the color of the house.

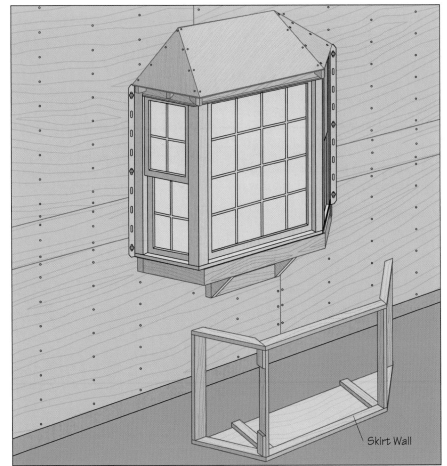

Trimming Out the Bottom of the Window. Build a 2x4 frame and sheathe it with plywood to enclose the bottom of the bay window and hide the braces and any insulation. The frame is built to the same outside dimensions as the lower support frame. Beveled blocking provides nailing for plywood at the outside corners. This treatment looks best with a foundation.

design ideas for windows

Above A cushioned window seat provides additional seating in this breakfast nook.

Above right The angles created by a bay window create a peaceful sitting area.

Right This style bay window combines fixed glass and operable casements.

design ideas for windows

Left Mid-height curtains provide a sense of enclosure and privacy to people sitting on this sofa.

Opposite Similar to bay windows, bow windows also provide light and a distinctive design.

Above A floor-to-ceiling bay is unusual, but it affords great views and helps the room seem light and airy.

Right A bay window with a built-in window seat is the perfect spot to get away from it all. This design gives you the opportunity to try creative window treatments.

PLANS to Help You Build Your
Dream Home

How Many Plans Should You Order?

Standard 8-Set Package. We've found that our 8-set package is the best value for someone who is ready to start building. A number of people will require their own set of blueprints. This package provides plans for you, your builder, the subcontractors, mortgage lender, and the building department.

Minimum 4-Set Package. If you are in the bidding process, you may want to order only four sets for the bidding round and reorder additional sets as needed.

1-Set Study Package. The 1-set package allows you to review your home plan by providing a study print. It is illegal to build a house from a study print and a violation of copyright law to reproduce a blueprint without permission.

Buying Additional Sets

If you require additional copies of blueprints for your home construction, you can order additional sets within 60 days of the original order date at a cost of $45.00 for each additional set.

Reproducible Masters

If you plan to make minor changes to one of our home plans, you can purchase reproducible masters. Printed on vellum paper, an erasable paper that you can reproduce in a copying machine, reproducible masters allow an architect, designer, or builder to alter our plans to give you a customized home design. You can make copies of reproducible masters.

Mirror-Reverse Sets

Plans can be printed in mirror-reverse—we can "flip" plans to create a mirror image of the design. This is useful when the house would fit your site or personal preferences if all the rooms were on the opposite side than shown. As the image is reversed, the lettering and dimensions will also be reversed, meaning they will read backwards. Therefore, when ordering mirror-reverse drawings, you must order at least one set of right-reading plans. A $50.00 fee per order will be charged for mirror-reverse.

EZ Quote: Home Cost Estimator

EZ Quote is our response to one of the most frequently asked questions we hear from customers: "How much will the house cost me to build?" EZ Quote: Home Cost Estimator provides a calculated building cost to construct your new home, based on labor rates and material costs in your zip code area. This summary provides the total construction costs before you purchase the plans. The cost is $29.95 for the first EZ Quote and $14.95 for each additional one. Available only in the U.S. and Canada.

CompleteCost Estimator

CompleteCost Estimator is a valuable tool for use in planning and constructing your new home. It combines the detail of a materials list with line-by-line cost estimating. The result is a complete, detailed estimate—similar to a bid—that will act as a checklist for all the items you will need to select or coordinate during the building process. CompleteCost Estimator is only available for certain plans and may only be ordered with the purchase of a set of home plans. The cost is $125.

Materials List

The Materials List provides you an invaluable resource in estimating the cost of your home. Each Materials List outlines the quantity, dimensions, and type of materials needed to build your home (with the exception of mechanical systems). A Materials List may only be ordered with the purchase of a set of home plans.

Terms & Copyright

These home plans are protected under the terms of United States Copyright Law and may not be copied or reproduced in any way, by any means, unless you have purchased reproducible masters, which clearly indicate your right to copy or reproduce. We authorize the use of your chosen home plan as an aid in the construction of one single-family home only. You may not use this home plan to build a second or multiple dwellings without purchasing another blueprint or blueprints, or paying additional home plan fees.

Architectural Seals

Because of differences in building codes, some cities and states now require an architect or engineer licensed in that state to review and "seal" a blueprint, or officially approve it, prior to construction. Delaware, Nevada, New Jersey, and New York require that all plans for houses built in those states be redrawn by an architect licensed in the state in which the home will be built. We strongly advise you to consult with your local building official for information regarding architectural seals.

Order Toll Free by Phone
1-800-523-6789
By Fax: 201-760-2431

Regular office hours are
8:30AM–7:00PM ET, Mon–Fri

Orders received 3PM ET, will be processed and shipped within two business days.

Order Online
www.ultimateplans.com

Mail Your Order
Creative Homeowner
Attn: Home Plans
24 Park Way
Upper Saddle River, NJ 07458

Canadian Customers
Order Toll Free 1-800-393-1883

Mail Your Order (Canada)
Creative Homeowner Canada
Attn: Home Plans
113-437 Martin St., Ste. 215
Penticton, BC V2A 5L1

Before You Order

Our Exchange Policy

Blueprints are nonrefundable. However, should you find that the plan you have purchased does not fit your needs, you may exchange that plan for another plan in our collection within 60 days from the date of your original order. The entire content of your original order must be returned before an exchange will be processed. You will be charged a processing fee of 20% of the amount of the original plan set, the cost difference between the new plan set and the original plan set (if applicable), and shipping costs for the new plans. Contact our customer service department for more information. Please note: reproducible masters may only be exchanged if the package is unopened.

Building Codes and Requirements

At the time of creation, our plans meet the building code requirements published by the Building Officials and Code Administrators International, the Southern Building Code Congress International, the International Conference of Building Officials, or the Council of American Building Officials. Because building codes vary from area to area, some drawing modifications and/or the assistance of a professional designer or architect may be necessary to comply with your local codes or to accommodate specific building site conditions. We strongly advise you to consult with your local building official for information regarding codes governing your area.

Blueprint Price Schedule

Price Code	1 Set	4 Sets	8 Sets	Reproducible Masters	CAD	Materials List
A	$290	$330	$380	$510	$950.00	$60
B	$360	$410	$460	$580	$1,100.00	$60
C	$420	$460	$510	$610	$1,200.00	$60
D	$470	$510	$560	$660	$1,300.00	$70
E	$520	$560	$610	$700	$1,400.00	$70
F	$570	$610	$670	$750	$1,500.00	$70
G	$620	$670	$720	$850	$1,600.00	$70
H	$700	$740	$800	$900	$1,700.00	$70
I	$810	$850	$900	$940	$1,800.00	$80

Note: Prices subject to change

Shipping & Handling

	1-4 Sets	5-7 Sets	8+ Sets or Reproducibles
US Regular (7–10 business days)	$15	$20	$25
US Priority (3–5 business days)	$25	$30	$35
US Express (1–2 business days)	$40	$45	$50
Canada Regular (8–12 business days)	$35	$40	$45
Canada Express (1–2 business days)	$60	$70	$80
Worldwide Express (2–5 business days)	$80	$80	$80

Note: All delivery times are from date the blueprint package is shipped (typically within 1–2 days of placing the order).

Order Form

Please send me the following:

Plan Number: _____

Price Code: _____

Indicate Foundation Type: (see plan page for availability)
☐ Slab ☐ Crawl space ☐ Basement ☐ Walk-out basement

Basic Blueprint Package — Cost
☐ Reproducible Masters — $_____
☐ 8-Set Plan Package — $_____
☐ 4-Set Plan Package — $_____
☐ 1-Set Study Package — $_____

☐ Additional plan sets:
__ sets at $45.00 per set — $_____
☐ Print in mirror-reverse: $50.00 per order — $_____
__ sets printed in mirror-reverse

Important Extras
☐ Materials List — $_____
☐ CompleteCost Materials Report at $125.00 — $_____
☐ Zip Code of Home/Building Site_____
☐ EZ Quote for Plan #_____ at $29.95 — $_____
☐ Additional EZ Quotes for Plan #s_____
at $14.95 each — $_____

Shipping (see chart above) — $_____
SUBTOTAL — $_____
Sales Tax (NJ residents only add 6%) — $_____

TOTAL — $_____

Order Toll Free: 1-800-523-6789 By Fax: 201-760-2431
Creative Homeowner
24 Park Way
Upper Saddle River, NJ 07458

Name _____
(Please print or type)

Street _____
(Please do not use a P.O. Box)

City _____ State _____

Country _____ Zip _____

Daytime telephone (____)_____

Fax (____)_____
(Required for reproducible orders)

E-Mail _____

Payment ☐ Check/money order *Make checks payable to Creative Homeowner*

☐ VISA ☐ MasterCard ☐ American Express Cards ☐ Discover

Credit card number _____

Expiration date (mm/yy) _____

Signature _____

Please check the appropriate box:
☐ Licensed builder/contractor ☐ Homeowner ☐ Renter

SOURCE CODE **CA602**

Plan #131027

Dimensions: 62'4" W x 53'6" D
Levels: 2
Square Footage: 2,567
Main Level Sq. Ft.: 2,017
Upper Level Sq. Ft.: 550
Bedrooms: 4
Bathrooms: 3
Foundation: Crawl space, slab, or basement
Materials List Available: Yes
Price Category: F

Images provided by designer/architect.

The features of this home are so good that you may have trouble imagining all of them at once.

Features:

- Great Room: Imagine a stepped ceiling, corner fireplace, built-in media center, and wall of windows with a glass door to the backyard—in one room.

- Dining Room: A stepped ceiling and server with a sink add to the elegance of this formal room.

- Breakfast Room: Eat at the bar this room shares with the island kitchen, and admire the 12-ft. cathedral ceiling and bayed group of 8- and 9-ft. windows. Or go through the sliding glass door to the covered side porch.

- Master Suite: The bedroom has a tray ceiling and cozy sitting area, and a whirlpool tub, shower, and walk-in closet are in the skylighted bath.

- Optional Study: The private bath near bedroom 2 makes it ideal for a study or home office.

- Bonus Room: Enjoy the extra 300 sq. ft.

Main Level Floor Plan

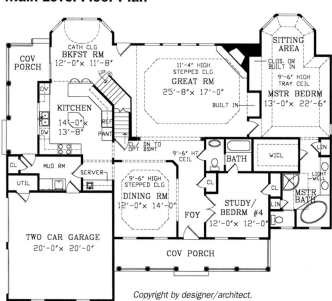

Copyright by designer/architect.

Upper Level Floor Plan

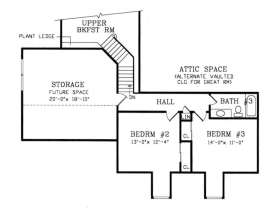

Plan #131003

Dimensions: 60' W x 39'10" D
Levels: 1
Square Footage: 1,466
Bedrooms: 3
Bathrooms: 2
Foundation: Basement, crawl space, or slab
Materials List Available: Yes
Price Category: B

Images provided by designer/architect.

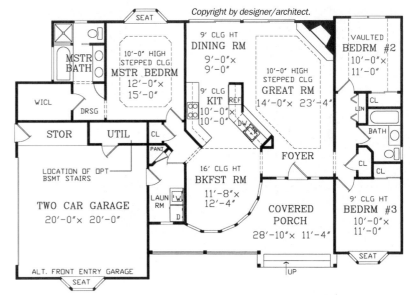

Copyright by designer/architect.

Victorian styling adds elegance to this compact and easy-to-maintain ranch design.

Features:

- Ceiling Height: 8 ft.

- Foyer: Bridging between the front door and the great room, this foyer is a surprise feature.

- Great Room: A 10-ft. ceiling adds to the spacious feeling of this room, while the corner fireplace gives it an intimate feeling. Sliding glass doors at the rear of the room open to the backyard.

- Dining Room: This formal room adjoins the great room, allowing guests and family to flow between the rooms.

- Breakfast Room: Turrets add a Victorian feeling to this room that's just off the kitchen and overlooks the front porch.

- Master Suite: Privacy is assured in this suite, which is separated from the main part of the house. A compartmented bath and large walk-in closet add convenience to its beauty.

Breakfast Room

MASTER SUITE
16'-0" X 13'-5"

PLANT LEDGE

BREAKFAST
12'-9"
X 13'-3"

GLASS SHOWER

PORCH

MASTER BATH

BEDROOM-2
11'-1"
X 10'-0"

BOOKS

EATING BAR

UP

HALL

CL.

GREAT ROOM
17'-8" X 16'-5"

D.W.

REF.

STOR.

CL.

F/P

KIT.

1/2 BATH

UTIL.

CAB.

F W D

CL.

R

STOR.

BATH-2

CL.

CTS.

DINING
12'-0"
X 11'-0"

59'-8"

LIN.

BEDROOM-3
11'-1"
X 10'-0"

CL.

BEDROOM-4
11'-0"
X 12'-6"

FOYER

DOUBLE GARAGE
20'-0" X 20'-0"

PORCH

STORAGE

65'-0"

Plan #241002

Dimensions: 65' W x 59'8" D

Levels: 1

Square Footage: 2,154

Bedrooms: 4

Bathrooms: 2½

Foundation: Slab, crawl space, or basement

Materials List Available: No

Price Category: D

Main Level Floor Plan

MASTER BEDROOM
14'-0" x 15'-6"
9' CH

LIVING / DINING
25'-6" x 13'-0"
11' to 14' CH

PORCH
13'-6" x 8'-8"

KITCHEN
19'-0" x 15'-0"
9' CH

MASTER BATH
9' CH

PWDR.

LIBRARY
HALL
15'-3"
x 14'-8"
9' CH

UP

FAMILY ROOM
14'-4" x 15'-0"
9' CH

2 STORY ENTRY
13'-7" x 10'-6"
21'-2" CH

MASTER CLO
12'-0" x 11'-0"
8' CH

PORCH
8'-6" x 9'-0"

GARDEN

GARDEN

BRKFST
9'-8" x 9'-8"

DN

OV

UTIL
12'-4" x 9'-2"

60'-8"

DBL GARAGE
21'-4" x 22'-4"
9' CH

Copyright by designer/architect.

DBL GARAGE
21'-4" x 22'-4"
9' CH

82'-0"

Upper Level Floor Plan

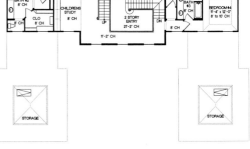

BEDROOM #2
12'-0" x 13'-6"
8' CH

UNFIN. STORAGE
22'-8" x 14'-2"
14'-6" CH

BEDROOM #3
12'-10" x 12'-0"
8' CH

SHWR

BATH #2
8' CH

CLO
8' CH

CLO

CHILDRENS STUDY
8' CH

UP

2 STORY ENTRY
21'-2" CH

DN

BATH
#3
8' CH

CLO

BEDROOM #4
11'-4" x 12'-0"
8' to 10' CH

11'-2" CH

UNFIN. LOFT
13'-7" x 10'-6"
7' CH

STORAGE

STORAGE

WIDOW'S WALK

Plan #121049

Dimensions: 82' W x 60'8" D

Levels: 2

Square Footage: 3,335

Main Level Sq. Ft.: 2,054

Upper Level Sq. Ft.: 1,281

Bedrooms: 4

Bathrooms: 3½

Foundation: Slab

Materials List Available: Yes

Price Category: G

CAD FILE AVAILABLE

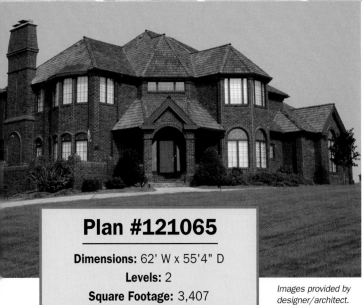

Main Level Floor Plan

Plan #121065

Dimensions: 62' W x 55'4" D

Levels: 2

Square Footage: 3,407

Main Level Sq. Ft.: 1,719

Upper Level Sq. Ft.: 1,688

Bedrooms: 4

Bathrooms: 2½

Foundation: Basement

Materials List Available: Yes

Price Category: G

Images provided by designer/architect.

Upper Level Floor Plan

Copyright by designer/architect.

HOME PLANS

Plan #101005

Dimensions: 63' W x 57'2" D

Levels: 1

Square Footage: 1,992

Bedrooms: 3

Bathrooms: 2½

Foundation: Slab, crawl space, or basement

Materials List Available: Yes

Price Category: D

Images provided by designer/architect.

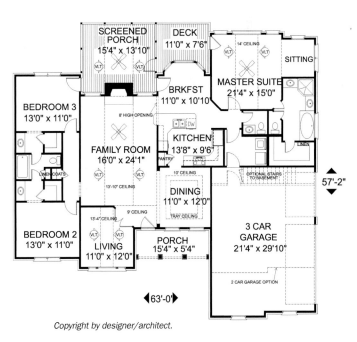

Copyright by designer/architect.

Plan #111004

Dimensions: 76' W x 85' D

Levels: 1

Square Footage: 2,968

Bedrooms: 4

Full Bathrooms: 3½

Foundation: Slab

Materials List Available: No

Price Category: F

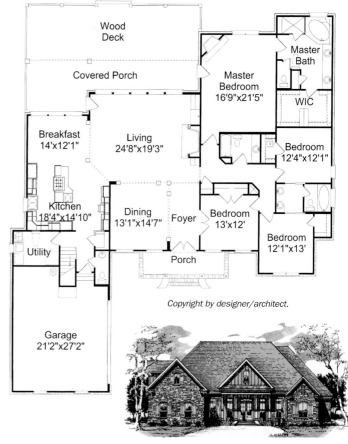

Images provided by designer/architect.

Copyright by designer/architect.

Plan #101011

Dimensions: 71'2" W x 58'1" D

Levels: 1

Square Footage: 2,184

Bedrooms: 3

Bathrooms: 3

Foundation: Slab, crawl space, walk-out or basement

Materials List Available: Yes

Price Category: D

Images provided by designer/architect.

CAD FILE
CAD
AVAILABLE

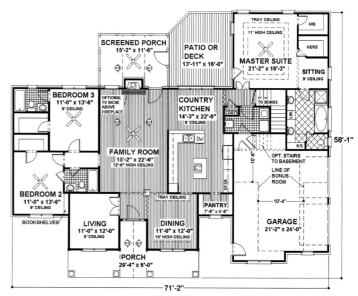

Copyright by designer/architect.

order direct: 1-800-523-6789

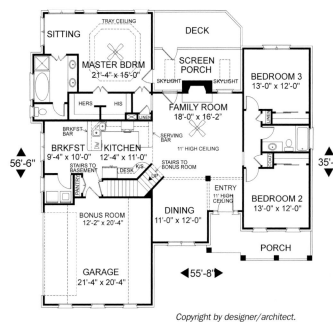

Images provided by designer/architect.

Copyright by designer/architect.

Plan #101004

Dimensions: 55'8" W x 56'6" D

Levels: 1

Square Footage: 1,787

Bedrooms: 3

Bathrooms: 2

Foundation: Slab, crawl space, or basement

Materials List Available: Yes

Price Category: C

Images provided by designer/architect.

Copyright by designer/architect.

Plan #151002

Dimensions: 67' W x 66' D

Levels: 1

Square Footage: 2,444

Bedrooms: 3

Bathrooms: 2½

Foundation: Basement, crawl space, or slab

CompleteCost List Available: Yes

Price Category: E

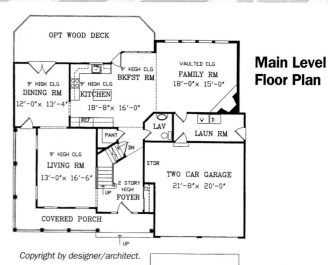

Main Level Floor Plan

OPT WOOD DECK

DINING RM
12'-0"x 13'-4"
9' HIGH CLG

KITCHEN
18'-8"x 16'-0"
9' HIGH CLG

BKFST RM
9' HIGH CLG

FAMILY RM
18'-0"x 15'-0"
VAULTED CLG

REF

LAV

LAUN RM

W D

PANT

LIVING RM
13'-0"x 16'-6"
9' HIGH CLG

DN

STOR

TWO CAR GARAGE
21'-8"x 20'-0"

UP

2 STORY HIGH FOYER

COVERED PORCH

UP

Copyright by designer/architect.

Plan #131030

Dimensions: 51' W x 41'10" D

Levels: 2

Square Footage: 2,470

Main Level Sq. Ft.: 1,290

Upper Level Sq. Ft.: 1,180

Bedrooms: 4

Bathrooms: 2½

Foundation: Crawl space, slab, basement, or walk-out basement

Materials List Available: Yes

Price Category: F

Images provided by designer/architect.

Entry

Upper Level Floor Plan

SKYLITE

MSTR BATH

WICL

LIN

WICL

WICL

BEDRM #2
12'-0"x 11'-0"

UPPER FAMILY RM

RAIL

LIN

BATH #2

CL

CL

MSTR BEDRM
13'-0"x 19'-0"
VAULTED CLG

BALC

DN

UPPER FOYER

BEDRM #4
10'-0"x 12'-0"

BEDRM #3
11'-4"x 12'-0"

Plan #151050

Dimensions: 69'2" W x 74'10" D

Levels: 1

Square Footage: 2,096

Bedrooms: 3

Bathrooms: 2½

Foundation: Crawl space, slab, or basement

Complete Cost List Available: Yes

Price Category: D

Images provided by designer/architect.

CAD FILE AVAILABLE

69'-2"

WORK SHOP / GARAGE
23'-0" X 20'-0"

Copyright by designer/architect.

COVERED GRILLING PORCH
30'-6" X 12'-6"

GAS DROP

STRG.

BRKFAST RM.
12'-4" X 9'-6"

GARAGE
23'-0" X 22'-4"

74'-10"

WHP TUB

M.BATH
15'-2" X 18'-0"

LIN

GREAT RM.
17'-0" X 22'-8"
9' BOXED CEILING

OPT ISLAND

REF

DW

LAU.

W

D

BEDROOM 3
11'-8" X 14'-8"

BOOK SHELVES

GALLERY

KITCHEN
12'-4" X 12'-0"

OVEN

PAN

BOOK SHELVES

MASTER SUITE
15'-2" X 16'-0"
9' BOXED CEILING

FOYER
9' CEILING

COVERED PORCH
17'-0" X 5'-0"
9' CEILING

DINING RM.
12'-4" X 12'-0"
9' BOXED CEILING

BEDROOM 2
13'-4" X 10'-8"

order direct: 1-800-523-6789

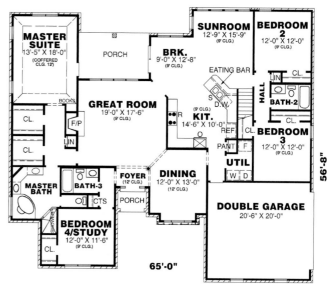

Plan #241008

Dimensions: 65' W x 56'8" D

Levels: 1

Square Footage: 2,526

Bedrooms: 4

Bathrooms: 3

Foundation: Slab, crawl space, or basement

Materials List Available: No

Price Category: E

Images provided by designer/architect.

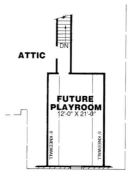

Copyright by designer/architect.

Plan #161016

Dimensions: 59'4" W x 58'8" D

Levels: 2

Square Footage: 2,101

Main Level Sq. Ft.: 1,626

Upper Level Sq. Ft.: 475

Bedrooms: 3

Bathrooms: 2½

Foundation: Basement

Materials List Available: Yes

Price Category: D

Images provided by designer/architect.

Main Level Floor Plan

Copyright by designer/architect.

CAD FILE AVAILABLE

Rear Elevation

Upper Level Floor Plan

www.ultimateplans.com

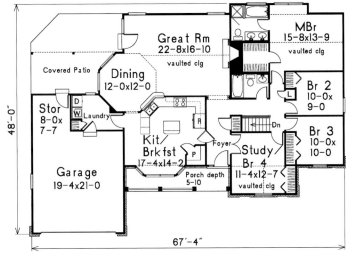

Images provided by designer/architect.

Plan #321003

Dimensions: 67'4" W x 48' D

Levels: 1

Square Footage: 1,791

Bedrooms: 4

Bathrooms: 2

Foundation: Basement

Materials List Available: Yes

Price Category: C

Copyright by designer/architect.

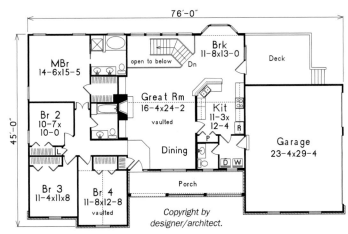

Plan #321006

Dimensions: 76' W x 45' D

Levels: 1, optional lower

Square Footage: 1,977

Optional Basement Level Sq. Ft.: 1,416

Bedrooms: 4

Bathrooms: 2½

Foundation: Basement

Materials List Available: Yes

Price Category: D

Images provided by designer/architect.

Copyright by designer/architect.

Optional Basement Level Floor Plan

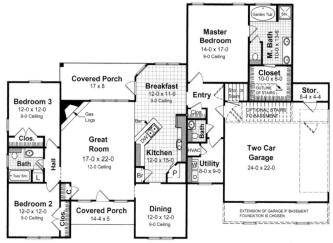

Copyright by designer/architect.

Images provided by
designer/architect.

Kitchen/Great Room

Plan #351001

Dimensions: 72'8" W x 51' D

Levels: 1

Square Footage: 1,855

Bedrooms: 3

Bathrooms: 2½

Foundation: Basement, crawl space, or slab

Materials List Available: Yes

Price Category: D

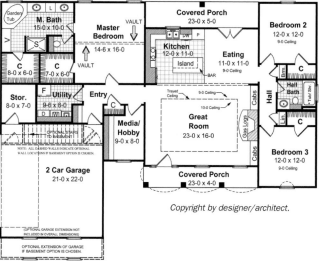

Images provided by
designer/architect.

Copyright by designer/architect.

Plan #351002

Dimensions: 64' W x 45'10" D

Levels: 1

Square Footage: 1,751

Bedrooms: 3

Bathrooms: 2

Foundation: Basement, crawl space, or slab

Materials List Available: Yes

Price Category: C

Resource Guide

The following list of manufacturers and associations is meant to be a general guide to additional industry and product-related sources. It is not intended as a listing of products and manufacturers represented by the photographs in this book.

APA – The Engineered Wood Association
7011 South 19th
Tacoma, WA 98466
253-565-6600
www.apawood.org
APA is a nonprofit trade association that works to promote the growth of the engineered wood industry. The company's Web site has information about engineered wood products, including technical reports and comprehensive market studies.

International Code Council
5203 Leesburg Pike, Suite 600
Falls Church, VA 22041
703-931-4533
www.iccsafe.org
The International Code Council provides the construction codes and standards that are used on job sites throughout the country. By combining the efforts of various regional code organizations, ICC has created a universal set of requirements for construction in the United States.

NAHB – National Association of Home Builders
1201 15th St., NW
Washington, DC 20005
800-368-5242
www.nahb.org
Trade association that helps promote the policies that make housing a national priority. Find more information at the organization's Web site.

AWCI – The Association of the Wall and Ceiling Industries International
803 West Broad St., Suite 600
Falls Church, VA 22046
703-534-8300
www.awci.org
AWCI provides services and undertakes activities that enhance the ability of contractors to operate successful businesses.

Senco Products, Inc.
8485 Broadwell Rd.
Cincinnati, OH 45244
800-543-4596
www.senco.com
Manufacturer of air-powered fastening tools. Visit the company's Web site to view its line of pneumatic tools, or to locate a dealer.

Southern Forest Products Association
P.O. Box 641700
Kenner, LA 70064
504-443-4464
www.sfpa.org
SFPA works to develop and expand market opportunities for Southern Pine forest products. Visit the Web site for industry statistics, or to sign up for their weekly newsletter.

Timber Framers Guild
P.O. Box 60
Becket, MA 01223
888-453-0879
www.tfguild.org
The organization is dedicated to establishing training programs for timber framers, disseminating information about timber framing, and generally promoting the craft.

Trim-Tex
3700 W. Pratt Ave.
Lincolnwood, IL 60712-2508
800-874-2333
www.trim-tex.com
Manufactures and distributes vinyl drywall beads and drywall finishing accessories. Visit the company's Web site for a catalog and gallery.

Werner Co.
93 Werner Rd.
Greenville, PA 16125-9499
724-588-8600
www.wernerladder.com
Supplies aluminum, wood, and fiberglass ladders, step stools, and ladder accessories, such as planks and platforms. See the company's Web site for a photo gallery of their products in action.

Wolmanized Wood
Arch Wood Protection, Inc.
1955 Lake Park Dr., Suite 100
Smyrna, GA 30080
866-789-4567
www.wolmanizedwood.com
Manufactures various forms of treated lumber for diverse projects. Read more about their offerings at their Web site.

Glossary

Actual dimension (lumber) The exact cross-sectional measurements of a piece of lumber after it has been cut, surfaced, and dried.

Actual length (rafters) Length of a rafter after half the thickness of the ridgeboard has been subtracted.

Air-dried lumber Wood seasoned by exposure to the air without use of artificial heat.

Allowable span Distance allowed between two contact points for load-supporting lumber such as rafters, girders, beams, and joists.

Anchor bolt Bolt set in concrete or held in place by friction or epoxy that is used to fasten lumber, columns, girders, brackets, or hangers to concrete or masonry walls.

Angle iron Structural steel bent at 90 degrees and used for fastening a range of framing connections.

Asphalt shingle Shingles made of felt that has been soaked in asphalt; asphalt shingle tabs are coated with granular minerals.

Attic The space between the rafters and the ceiling joists.

Backfill Soil or gravel used to fill in between a finished foundation and the ground excavated around it.

Backing (hip rafter) Bevel cut along the crown edge of a hip rafter that allows plywood from opposing roofs to meet at a clean angle flush with the rafter.

Barge rafters The last outside rafters of a structure. They are usually nailed to outriggers and form the gable-end overhangs. Sometimes called flying rafters.

Batt insulation A mineral fiber material, delivered in rolls and typically paper- or foil-faced, that is installed in stud bays to provide insulation.

Batten Narrow one-by or two-by wood strips that typically cover vertical joints between siding boards in board-and-batten siding.

Batter board A level board attached to stakes and used to position string in foundation and footing outlines. Notches in batter boards determine the position of foundation guideline strings.

Bay window A window, typically three sided, that projects from a wall, creating a recessed area in the structure's interior. Also called an oriel.

Beam A steel or wood member installed horizontally to support some aspect of a structure's load.

Beam hanger A metal pocket- or shelf-like hanger that supports a beam where it butts into another member.

Bevel An angled surface not at 90 degrees, typically cut into the edge of a piece of lumber. Also a tool for making such an angle.

Bird's mouth The notch cut near the tail end of a rafter where it fits on a cap plate or horizontal framing member.

Blocking 1) Horizontal blocks inserted between studs every 10 vertical feet to defeat the spread of fire. 2) Lumber added between studs, joists, rafters, or other members to provide a nailing surface for sheathing or other material.

Board-and-batten siding A siding style that uses long siding boards installed vertically, right next to one another, with the gaps between them covered by one-by or two-by battens.

Board foot Unit of volume for a piece of wood 12 inches square and 1 inch thick.

Bottom plate The horizontal plate at the base of a wall.

Bridging Wood blocks installed in an X-shape between floor joists to stabilize and position the joists.

Built-up beam or girder A beam or girder made of smaller component parts—for example, nailing together three 2×12s for a "built-up" beam.

Butt joint The junction where the ends of two pieces of lumber or other members meet in a square-cut joint.

Cantilever Joists projecting from a wall to create a porch or balcony floor without supports.

Carriage bolt A bolt with a slotless round head and a square shoulder below the head that embeds itself into the wood as the nut is tightened.

Caulk Tube-delivered plastic-and-silicon substance that cures quickly and is used to seal gaps in wood to prevent air or water leakage.

Cedar shingles Tapered 16- to 18-inch-long pieces of western cedar used for shims, siding, or roofing.

Check (in lumber) A defect in lumber caused by a separation lengthwise between the wood's growth rings.

Chords In triangular trusses, the wood members that form the two sides of the roof and the triangle's base.

Cleat A small board fastened to a surface to provide support for another board, or any board nailed onto another board to strengthen or support it.

Clinching The practice of driving an overlong nail through two boards and bending the protruding end over.

Code The rules set down by various regional code bodies that specify minimum building practices.

Collar tie A horizontal board installed rafter to rafter for extra stiffness.

Column A wood or metal vertical support member.

Common length in jack rafters The amount that jack rafters increase or decrease in length as they run between two angled rafters or an angled rafter and a top plate.

Common rafter Rafter in a gable-type roof that runs from the ridge to the double top plates.

Composite board Panel material similar to plywood but made up of reconstituted wood particles at its core and sometimes softwood veneer on its faces.

Core The middle veneer layer in plywood or the center section of material in a composite panel.

Corner boards One-by or two-by boards nailed vertically to the corners of a building that serve as a stopping point for siding and as an architectural feature.

Cornice Also called roof overhang, the part of the roof that overhangs the wall.

Cricket A small gable-like structure installed on a roof to divert water, usually from a chimney.

Cripple studs Short studs that stand vertically between a header and top plate or between a bottom plate and the underside of a rough sill.

Crosscuts Cuts made width-wise, or across the grain of lumber.

Crown The natural bow along the edge of a joist, rafter, stair stringer, or other member. It should almost always be placed facing up.

Cup A distortion in wood across the grain caused by warpage.

Dead load The weight of the building components, including lumber, roofing, windows, doors, and flooring.

Deflection The bending of wood due to live and dead loads.

Diagonal bracing 1) Braces running from corner to corner used to stiffen walls and prevent racking. 2) Braces nailed off to cleats or stakes to support a standing wall.

Door sill The same as a threshold. A piece of lumber beveled along each edge and nailed to a floor to cover a floor joint or to mark a door passageway.

Dormer A shed- or doghouse-like structure that projects from a roof and can add space to an attic.

Double top plate The double tier of two-by lumber running horizontally on top of and nailed to wall studs.

Drip edge A metal piece bent to fit over the edge of roof sheathing, designed to shun rain.

Drywall Gypsum sandwiched between treated paper. Used as an interior covering material. Also called gypsum board or wallboard.

Eaves The part of a roof that projects beyond its supporting walls to create an overhang.

Elevation The same as height. When referred to in transit use, the height above or below a transit instrument.

End grain The end of a crosscut piece of wood.

Expansion bolt A bolt used to anchor lumber to masonry walls. The jacket of an expansion bolt expands to grip the side walls of a pilot hole due to wedge pressure at its base or the wedge force of a bolt screwed into it.

Facade The exterior front of a building.

Face-nailing Nailing perpendicularly through the surface of lumber.

Factory edge The edge finish put on wood and panels at the mill.

Fascia One-by or two-by trim piece nailed onto the end grain or tail end of a rafter to form part of a cornice.

Fiberglass Spun glass fibers used in insulation and roof shingles.

Finishing nail A smooth nail with a tiny round head, normally set below the surface of finished wood with a countersink tool, or nail set.

Fire blocking Horizontal blocking installed between studs to defeat the upward progress of fire.

Flakeboard The same as particleboard.

Flashing Thin aluminum or copper strips or coil stock used to bridge any space between roof and framing, shingles and framing, or windows/doors and any part of the structure. Also, the metal strips used to protect corners and valleys in roof construction.

Floor plans Drawings that give a plan view (bird's-eye view) of the layout of each floor of a building.

Footing The base, usually poured concrete, on which a foundation wall is built. With a pressure-treated wood foundation, a gravel or soil footing may be used.

Framing anchor Metal straps, pockets, or supports used to reinforce or strengthen joints between wood framing members.

Frieze board Trim board nailed horizontally on a building wall directly beneath rafters to provide a nailing surface for soffits and cornice trim.

Frost line The maximum depth to which soil freezes in the winter. Frost lines change regionally.

Furring strips Narrow one-by or two-by wood strips used be create space— for example, between ceilings and ceiling joists or between insulated walls and masonry walls.

Gable roof A triangular-shaped roof.

Gable end The triangular section at the ends of gable roofs.

Gambrel roof A roof design common on barns and utility buildings that combines two gable roofs of differing slopes. Sometimes mistakenly called Dutch Colonial-style roof.

Gauge A measurement of wire thickness. The higher the gauge, the thinner the wire.

Girder A horizontal wood or steel member used to support some aspect of a framed structure. Also called a beam.

Girder pocket The let-in and seat created in a foundation wall in which a girder sits.

Glue-laminated lumber Stacked dimension lumber glued together to create a beam.

Grade 1) The identification class of lumber quality. 2) Ground level. The slope of the ground on a building site.

Ground-fault circuit interrupter (GFCI) A device that detects a ground fault or electrical line leakage and immediately shuts down power.

Gusset plates Metal or plywood plates used to hold the chords and webs of a truss together.

Gypsum board See "Drywall."

Hardwood Wood that comes from deciduous trees.

Header The built-up horizontal framing member that runs above rough openings to assume the loads that would have otherwise been carried by the studs that have been removed or omitted below to create the opening.

Heartwood The part of the wood between the pith and the sapwood.

Heel (rafter) When a rafter is in position at pitch, the end grain of a rafter closest to the rafter's underside.

Hip jack rafter A rafter that runs from a top plate to a hip rafter.

Hip rafter A rafter that runs at a 45 degree angle from the end of a ridge to a corner of a building.

Hip roof A roof that has a central ridge and that slopes in all four directions.

I-beam A beam, typically steel, with a vertical middle section and flat webs on the top and bottom.

Incline (roof) Same as pitch.

Jack rafters Short rafters that run between a rafter and a top plate or between two rafters.

Jack stud See "Trimmer stud."

Jamb The finished frame of a doorway.

Joist Framing lumber placed on edge horizontally, to which subfloors or ceilings are attached.

Joist hanger Bracket used to strengthen the connection between a joist and a piece of lumber into which it butts.

Kerf A shallow slot cut into a piece of lumber usually measured by the width of the saw blade.

Keyway A flat-bottomed notch or indentation created at the top of a footing to allow foundation walls to interlock.

Kiln-dried lumber Wood dried in a kiln, or a large oven, rather than by natural air currents.

Lag screw A large screw with a pointed tip and a hex head.

Lally column A steel pipe usually filled with concrete and used as a support column beneath girders and beams.

Ledger A horizontal board attached to a beam or other member and used as a shelf-like support for lumber that butts against the beam.

Level A hand tool for checking that any piece is perfectly horizontal or vertical. Also a term meaning horizontal.

Live load All the loads in a building not part of the structure—furniture, people, snow, wind.

Masonry wall A wall made of concrete, cinderblock, or brick.

Mastic A thick, pasty adhesive.

Miter box A hardwood open-topped square box with precut cut lines to guide angled or square saw cuts.

Moisture content (in wood) The amount of water contained in wood, expressed as a percentage of the dry weight of wood.

Mudsill Same as sill plate.

O.C. An abbreviation for "on center."

Oriented-strand board (OSB) Panel material made of wood strands purposely aligned for strength and bonded by phenolic resin.

Overhang The part of the tail end of a rafter that projects beyond the building line. Often it's enclosed by a soffit.

Particleboard Panel material made from wood chips and flakes held together by resin.

Partition wall A nonload-bearing wall built to divide up interior space.

Penny Abbreviation: d. Unit of measurement for nail length, such as a 10d nail, which is 3 inches long.

Pier (concrete) A round or square concrete base used to support columns, posts, girders, or joists.

Pilot hole A hole drilled before a screw is inserted to defeat splitting.

Pitch (roof) Loosely, the slope or angle of a roof; technically, the rise of a roof over its span.

Plates Horizontal two-by lumber at the top and bottom of a wall, or any horizontal lumber at the base of a wall.

Platform framing The framing method that builds walls, one story at a time, on top of platforms that are built on joists.

Plumb Vertically straight. A line 90 degrees to a level line.

Plywood A wood panel composed of cross-laminated veneer layers.

Prehung door A door that's already set in a jamb, with hinges (and sometimes a lockset) preinstalled, ready to be installed in a rough opening.

Pressure treatment A factory process of using pressure to force preservatives into wood.

Pump jack A working platform system that is raised and lowered along vertical 4×4s using a pumping action.

Quartersawn lumber Lumber milled from quartered logs, typically very stable, close-grained wood.

Rafter table The table of rafter lengths and cut angles found etched in the side of a framing square.

Rebar Short for "reinforcement bar." Metal bars laid in a grid used to reinforce concrete.

Resilient flooring Flooring that has memory and returns to its original shape after it is indented, usually made of vinyl and available in large sheets or smaller tiles.

R (resistance, in insulation) The measure of a substance's resistance to heat flow. An R-value is a number assigned to thermal insulation. The higher the number, the better the insulation.

Ridge The highest point of a roof.

Ridgeboard The horizontal board that defines the roof's highest point, or ridge.

Ridge cut The cut at the uphill end of a rafter, along the ridge plumb line, that allows the rafter's end grain to sit flush against the ridgeboard.

Rim joists Joists that define the outside edges of a platform. Joists that run perpendicular to floor joists and are end-nailed to joist end grains are known as header joists. Also called band joists.

Rip To cut wood in the same direction as the grain.

Rise In a roof, the vertical distance between the supporting wall's cap plate and the point where a line, drawn through the outside edge of the cap plate and parallel to the roof's slope, intersects the centerline of the ridgeboard.

Rough sill The horizontal framing member that defines the underside of a window's rough opening.

Run In a roof with a ridge, the horizontal distance between the edge of an outside wall's cap plate and the centerline of the ridgeboard.

Sapwood The living wood near the outside of a tree trunk that carries sap.

Scab A short piece of wood nailed on the face of two boards where they join to help position or strengthen them.

Scaffold A temporary working platform and the structure that supports it.

Scarf joint Where the end grain of two pieces of lumber meet in the same plane at a 45-degree angle.

Seat cut (rafter) The horizontal cut in a bird's mouth that fits on a top panel or horizontal framing member.

Shakes Same as cedar shingles, but rougher in texture because they are split rather than sawn.

Shear wall A wall, typically covered with carefully nailed plywood, that is designed to resist lateral force.

Sheathing Panel material, typically plywood, applied to the outside of a structure on which siding is installed.

Shed roof A roof that slopes in one direction only.

Shim A thin wedge of plastic or wood (typically cedar) used as blocking to level or plumb doors, windows, and framing lumber.

Siding Finish material applied to the outside of a building, either on top of the sheathing or directly nailed into studs and blocks.

Sill (window) The piece of wood at the bottom of a window frame, typically angled to shun water.

Sill anchor Threaded metal anchors set in concrete to which mudsills are attached with washers and nuts.

Sill plate The horizontal two-by lumber attached directly to the masonry foundation on which stand the building's walls. Same as sole plate and mudsill.

Slab-on-grade Monolithic concrete foundation that serves as both the building's first floor and the structure's perimeter footings.

Sliding T-bevel An adjustable pivoting straightedge that can be set at a number of different angles. Also sometimes called a bevel square.

Slope The rise of a roof over its run, expressed as the number of inches of rise per unit of run (usually 12 inches). For example: 6 in 12 means a roof rises 6 inches for every 12 inches of run.

Soffit The board that runs the length of a wall, spanning between the wall and the fascia on the underside of the rafters

Sole plate Same as sill plate.

Span Distance between supports, such as the outside walls of a building or a structural wall and a beam.

Staging Same as scaffold.

Staple Hand or pneumatically driven U-shaped metal fastener used to hold shingles, roofing, and finished wood in place.

Story pole A piece of lumber (usually a 2×4) marked off in required dimensions to determine stair-height layouts and other elevations.

Stud Vertically standing two-by lumber that extends from the bottom plate to the top plate of a stud wall.

Subfloor Structurally rated plywood or oriented-strand-board decking installed on sleepers or joists.

Tail (rafter) The base, or downhill end, of a rafter.

Tail cut The plumb or square cut at the tail end of the rafter.

Theoretical rafter length The rafter length before it is shortened to accommodate ridgeboard thickness.

Timber Lumber pieces, larger than a nominal 4×4, typically used as columns or beams.

Toe-nailing Driving a nail at an angle into the face of a board so it penetrates another board beneath or above it.

Tongue and groove (T&G) Boards that have a groove on one edge and a tongue on the other so that other similar boards can fit into one another along their edges.

Top plate The horizontal two-by board nailed to the top of wall studs.

Total rise The ridge height of a roof measured from the top plate of the structure's wall.

Total run One half the building span.

Transit A telescope mounted on a swiveling plate that can view a perfectly level line 360 degrees once it has itself been leveled.

Trim One-by lumber used as siding corner boards or as finish materials around windows and doors, under eaves, or around cornices.

Trimmer joist A second joist added to reinforce a floor joist that defines a rough opening in floors.

Trimmer rafter A second rafter added to reinforce a rafter that defines a rough opening in roofs.

Trimmer stud Stud that runs from the bottom plate to the underside of a header. Also called jack stud.

Underlayment Highly stable, often water-resistant veneer-type panel material (a kind of plywood) installed on top of a subfloor but beneath resilient flooring or other finish floor material.

Unit rise Number of inches a common rafter will rise vertically for every 12 inches of run.

Unit run Unit of the total run, based on 12 inches for common rafters and 17 inches for hip rafters.

Valley jack rafter A rafter that extends from a valley rafter to a ridge.

Valley rafter A rafter that extends from a ridge to an intersecting corner of a building or to another rafter.

Veneer A thin piece or section of wood, typically a layer of plywood.

Waferboard Panel material made from wood wafers bonded with an exterior-grade resin.

Waler Horizontal lumber pieces used to span or stiffen walls.

Wallboard See "Drywall."

Warp Uneven shrinkage in wood causing bending or twisting.

Web (truss) The truss's inner members that tie together the chords.

Index

A

Abbreviations on blueprints, 34
Air-dried lumber, 15
Aluminum ladders, 47
Anchor bolts, 56–58, 78
   extended, 110
   self-drilling, 58
Anti-kickback saw blades, 43, 67
Appearance grades, 20
Architectural-grade beams, 20
Ascender-type rope grab, 52
Asphalt shingles, 140
Awning windows, 113

B

Balloon framing, 94
Balusters, 191
   installing, 177–78
Balustrades, 174–78, 190
   establishing centerline, 174
Basement floors, 199–201
Basement framing, 192–205
   ceilings, 197–98
   estimating materials, 193
   walls, 193–97
Basement-wall foundation, 74–75
Bay window, 206–15
   building roof, 210
   floor-support alternatives, 210
   framing for, 207–9
   installing roof framing, 211–12
   trimming out bottom of window, 212
Beams, 28–29
   architectural-grade, 20
   bearing, 29
   cantilevered, 31
   concealing, 201–2
   exposed ridge, 154
   I-, 76–77, 80–81
   industrial-grade, 20
   nonbearing, 29
   premium-grade, 20
   steel I-, 77–78
   wood I-, 21–22
Bearing beams, 29
Bearing walls, misaligned, 25–26

Bird's mouth cut, 124, 146
Blocking, 84
   installing, 85
Blueprints, 31–32, 32–34, 217–27
   abbreviations on, 34
   dimensions on, 33
   door sections on, 36
   elevation on, 34
   floor plans, 34
   lines on, 32–33
   ordering, 217–27
   utility symbols on, 33
   wall symbols on, 33–34
   window sections on, 36
Bolts, 59
   anchor, 56–58
   carriage, 59
   epoxy, 58
   extended anchor, 110
   friction-held, 57–58
   latch, 117
   rail, 176
   self-drilling anchor, 58
Boxing around post, 203
Brickmold, installing windows with, 114–15
Bridging, 84
   installing, 84–85
Building codes, 103, 228
Building loads, 24–26
   defining, 24
   deflection, 24
   paths, 24–26
Building plans, 31–36
Bump-out, 207, 210

C

Cantilevered joists, 88–89
Cantilevers, 31
Cap plate, 109
Carriage bolts, 59
Casement windows, 113
Casing nails, 115
Cathedral ceilings, exposed ridge
   beams for, 154
Cat's paw, 42

Ceilings
   basement, 197–98
   drywall, 197–98
   exposed ridge beams for cathedral, 154
Chipboard, 18
Chromated copper arsenate (CCA), 16
Circular saws, 42–43, 65
   avoiding kickback, 67
   choosing blade, 65
   cutting lumber and plywood, 65–67
   making square cuts, 65
   safe use of, 64–65
Clinching, 64
   tools for, 193
Collar ties, 28
Columns, 26
   installing, 78–80
   post attachment and, 80
Combination blades, 65
Combination square, 40
Composite board, 18
Concrete slab, 73
Connectors, 20
   choosing right, 82
   hurricane ties and, 54–56
   missing, 136
Cordless drills, 44
Corners
   marking plates for inside, 97–98
   marking plates for outside, 98–99
   nailing, 99
   stud configuration for, 97
Crawl-space foundation, 73
Cripple studs, 95, 100–101
Crosscut blades, 65
Crosscuts, 65–67
Cut lines, drawing, 62

D

Deadbolt, 117
Dead load, 24
Deck screws, 59
Deflection, 24
Digital level, 39–40
Dimension lumber, 13

Dimensions on blueprints, 33
Door frame, 118
Doors
    on blueprints, 36
    flush, 117
    installing prehung, 117
    marking rough openings for, 101
    panel, 117
    prehung exterior, 117
Dormers, 157–63
    building shed, 161–63
    gable, 157, 158–61
    shed, 157, 161–63
Double-hung windows, 112–13
Drills, 44
    cordless, 44
Drip edge, 140
Drywall ceiling, installing, 197–98
Drywall jacks, 198
Drywall screws, 113
Ducts, concealing, 201–2
Ductwork, accommodating, in flooring,
    86
Dust mask, 38

E

Elevation on blueprints, 34
End-nailing, 63
Engineered flooring, 200
Engineered lumber, 20–22
    glue-laminated, 20–21
    laminated-veneer, 21
    parallel-strand, 21
    steel studs, 22
    wood I-beams, 21–22
Engineering basics, 23–36
    beams, rafters, and collar ties,
        27–31
    building loads, 24–26
    building plans, 31–36
Epoxy bolts, 58
Expansion shields, 58
Exposed ridge beams for cathedral
    ceilings, 154
Exposure, 19
Extended anchor bolts, 110
Extension ladders, 46

F

Face-nailing, 63
Fall-arrest systems, 50–52
Fiberglass ladders, 47

Fiberglass shingles, 140
Finger-jointing, 20
Finishing of stairs, 186
Fire blocking, 103
Fixed windows, 112
Flakeboard, 18
Flashing, installing, 139
Floating floor, installing, 201
Floor(s)
    avoiding spongy, 91
    basement, 199–201
    installing floating, 201
Floor framing, 72–92
    lally-column installation, 78
    steel I-beams, 77–78
    structural support, 73–76
    wood girders, 77
Flooring. See also Subflooring
    accommodating ductwork, plumbing,
        or wiring in, 86
    engineered, 200
    laminate, 200
Floor joists, 27, 81–89
    installing, 82–83
    preparing girders and I-beams for,
        80–81
    rough openings in, 87
    span ratings, 26
Floor plans on blueprints, 34
Floor-support alternatives, 207
Flush door, 117
Fold-up ladders, 46
45-degree angles, drawing, 124
Foundations
    basement-wall, 74–75
    crawl-space, 73
    pier, 76
    slab-on-grade, 210
    wood, 76
Framing dormers, 157–63
Framing hammer, 41
Framing hardware, 53–60
    anchor bolts, 56–58
    bolts, 59
    connectors and hurricane ties, 54–56
    nails, 54
    screws, 59–60
    staples, 60
Framing materials, 12–22
Framing members, drilling and
    notching, 28
Framing square, 40, 170–71

rafter tables on, 149
Framing tools, 37–44
    hand tools, 41–42
    levels, 39–40
    marking tools, 41
    measuring tools, 38–39
    power tools, 42–44
    safety equipment and, 38
    squares, 40
Freeze-thaw cycles, 73
Friction-held bolts, 57–58
Frost heaving, 73
Full-body harnesses, 50, 52

G

Gable dormers, 157, 158–61
    building, 158–61
Gable-roof framing, 121–42
    calculating rafter length, 123–30
    installing flashing, 139
    installing ridgeboards and rafters,
        130–34
    pitch and slope, 122–23
    roof loads, 122
    roof sheathing, 138, 140–42
    skylights, 137
    trusses, 134–36
Gable roofs, 143
Gambrel roofs, 143, 153–56
    assembling, 156
    laying out, 155
Girders, 28
    preparing, for floor joists, 80–81
Glue-laminated lumber, 20–21
    appearance grades, 20
    connectors, 20
    residential grade, 20
Grade stamps, 15–16
Grading
    air-dried lumber, 15
    grade stamps, 15–16
    kiln-dried lumber, 15
    moisture content, 15
    native green lumber, 15
    pressure-treated lumber, 16
    structural grade, 15
Guard rails, 50

H

Hammer
    framing, 41
    handling your, 68

Handrail, installing, 175–77
Handsaw, 42
Hand tools, 41–42
Hardboard, 92
Hardwood, 13
Headers, 29–31
    installing joists, 83, 87
    span table for, 30
Head jamb, 118
Hearing protection, 38
Heartwood, 13–14
Hip-rafter overhang, 151
Hip roofs, 143, 146–52
    beginning, 147–48, 150
    installing jack rafters, 151–52
Hold-down anchor, 110
Homemade ladders, 47–48
Howe truss, 134
Hurricane ties, connectors and, 54–56

I

I-beams, 76–77
    preparing, for floor joists, 80–81
    steel, 77–78
    wood, 21–22
Industrial-grade beams, 20

J

Jack studs, 95
J-bolts, 57, 78
Joist hangers, sizing correctly, 54
Joists
    cantilevered, 88–89
    floor, 27, 81–89
    tapering, 83
Juvenile wood, 17

K

Kickback, 67
Kiln-dried lumber, 15
King studs, 95, 102

L

Ladder jacks, 48
Ladder leveler, 48
Ladders, 46–50
    accessories, 47–48
    aluminum, 47
    extension, 46
    fiberglass, 47
    fold-up, 46
    homemade, 47–48

ratings of, 47
safe use, 47
step, 46
wooden, 47
Ladder stand-off, 47–48
Lag screws, 59
Lally-column installation, 78
Laminated-veneer lumber, 21
Laminate flooring, 200
Latch bolt, 117
Lean-to-roofs, 143
Levels, 39–40
    digital, 39–40
    spirit, 39
    torpedo, 40
    water, 40
Lines on blueprints, 32–34
Live load, 24
Load-bearing cantilevers, 89
Load-bearing LB structural studs, 22
Load paths, 24–26
Locksets, 117–20
    installing, 119–20
Long tape, 39
L-shaped stairs, 179
Lumber. *See also* Wood
    air-dried, 15
    common problems, 16–18
    dimension, 13
    engineered, 20–22
    fighting crooked, 69
    glue-laminated, 20–21
    juvenile wood, 17
    kiln-dried, 15
    laminated-veneer, 21
    nail popping and, 17
    native green, 15
    parallel-strand, 21
    plainsawn, 14
    pressure-treated, 16
    quartersawn, 14
    shrinkage in, 16–17
    sizing, 27
    strength of, 15
    troubleshooting problems, 68–69
    veneer-core, 18
    weather protection, 17–18
Lumber-core plywood, 18

M

Marking plates
    for inside corners, 97–98

for outside corners, 98–99
Marking tools, 41
Masonry, attaching vapor barrier to, 193–94
Measuring
    accuracy in, 62–63
    tools for, 38–39, 62
Measuring tape, 38–39, 62
Milled dimensions, 14
Milling methods, 14
    plainsawn lumber, 14
    quartersawn lumber, 14
Mill number, 19
Misaligned bearing walls, 25–26
Misplaced struts, 25
Moisture content, 15
    in grading lumber, 14–15

N

Nailing
    basics of, 63–64
    end, 63
    face, 63
    tight-quarters, 202
    tips for, 142
Nail pouch, 42
Nails, 54
    blunting points of, 54
    casing, 115
    choosing right, 54
    as pilot bits, 115
    popping of, 17
    removing cleanly, 153
    removing finishing, 118
    sizing, 54
    starting, 67
    starting hard-to-hold, 161
Nail wax, drilling for, 114
National evaluation report (NER), 19
Native green lumber, 15
Needle-nose pliers, 161
Newels, 191
    installing, 174–75
NLB drywall studs, 22
Nonbearing beams, 29
Nosings, adding, 189

O

Oriented-strand board (OSB), 18, 90, 92, 138
Overhang
    calculating, 127

creating, 125
framing gable-end, 133–34

P

Panel doors, 117
Panel grade, 19
Panel materials, lifting, 198
Panel products, rating
  exposure, 19
  mill number, 19
  panel grade, 19
  span rating, 19
  thickness, 19
  veneer grades, 19
Parallel-strand lumber, 21
Particleboard, 18, 92
Partition walls, building, 195–97
Performance-rated panel standard
    (PRP), 19
Phillips bit, 59–60
Pier foundations, 76
Pilot bits, using nails as, 115
Plainsawn boards, 16
Plainsawn lumber, 14
Platform framing, 12, 94
  floor system in, 72
Platform jacks, 48–50
  ladder jacks, 48
  pump jacks, 49–50
  roof jacks, 49
Pliers, needle-nose, 161
Plumb cut, marking, 129
Plumb-cut rafters, 210
Plumbing, accommodating, 113
  in flooring, 86
Plumb lines, marking, 62–63
Plumb walls, 107
Plywood, 18–19, 92
  cutting guide for, 66–67
  lumber-core, 18
Pneumatic nailers, 44
Point load, 24
Post attachment, columns and, 80
Posts
  boxing around, 203
  cutting square, 79
  installing, 78–80
Powder-actuated fastener (PAF), 193–94
Power miter box, 102
Power miter saw, 43
Power tools, 42–44
Prehung exterior doors, 117

Premium-grade beams, 20
Pressure-treated lumber, 16
Pump jacks, 49–50
Pythagorean theorem, 151

Q

Quartersawn lumber, 14
Quick-set framing, 97

R

Rafters, 27–28
  calculating length of, 123–30
  installing, 130–34
  marking length of, 128
  span ratings of, 27
Rafter tables, 125
  on framing square, 149
Rafter tails, marking, 128–29
Rail bolts, 176
Rails, installing wall, 177
Reciprocating saw, 43
Residential grade, 20
Respiratory protection, 38
Ridgeboards, installing, 130–34
Ridgeboard thickness, subtracting, 128
Ridge cut, 124
Rip blades, 65
Risers, tight-fit, 172
Roofing felt, laying, 140
Roof jacks, 49
Roof loads, 122
Roof pitch and slope, 122–23
Roof sheathing, 138, 140–42
Rough carpentry, 61
Rough openings, 100–101
  in floor joists, 87
  framing, 87–88
  marking plates for door, 101
  marking plates for window, 100–101

S

Safety
  with circular saw, 64–65
  ladders and, 47
Safety equipment, 38
Safety glasses, 38
Sapwood, 13–14
Saturated organic base, 140
Saw guides, 65
Saws, 42–43
  circular, 42–43
  hand, 42

making cuts, 130
power miter, 43
reciprocating, 43
using safely, 43–44
Scaffolds, 50
  assembling, 50
Screws, 59–60
Screw's gauge, 59
Seat cut, marking, 129–30
Seismic anchors, 55–56, 110
Seismic bracing, 109–10
Self-drilling anchor bolts, 58
Shear load, 24
Sheathing, 110–12
  installing, 111–12
Sheathing staples, 60
Shed dormers, 157, 161–63
  building, 161–63
Shed rafters, marking, 144–45
Shed roofs, 143
  framing, 144–46
  installing rafters, 145–46
Shingles
  asphalt, 140
  fiberglass, 140
  installing, 140
Shrinkage, 16–17
Side cuts, 149
Side rafter, 210
Sill plates, 56, 75, 118
  attaching, to foundation, 74–75
Single-hung window, 113
Skylights, 137
  framing for, 137
Slab-on-grade, 73
Slab-on-grade foundation, 210
Sliding T-bevel, 40
Sliding windows, 113–14
Softwoods, 13, 17
Soil pipes, concealing, 202
Soundproofing, 120
Southern Pine Inspection Bureau, 14
Span rating, 19
Speed square, 40, 44
Spirit level, 39
Spongy floors, avoiding, 91
Spread load, 24
Springy floors, avoiding, 91
Squares, 40, 44
Stairs, 167–91
  adding nosings, 189
  assembling, 184–85

balustrades, 174–78
calculating rise and run, 179–81
calculating staircase size, 167–69
design ideas for, 190–91
finishing, 186
framing landing, 181–82
installing handrail, 175–77
installing newels, 174–75
installing wall rails, 177
L-shaped stairs, 179
making stringers, 183–84
staircase installation, 171–73
straight-run, 167
stringer layout, 170–71
Staples, 60
Stationary windows, 112
Steel I-beams, 77–78
Steel studs, 22, 192
Steel-stud striping, 194
Stepladders, 46
Stepping off the length, 127–28
Stops, 118
Strap-type connectors, 110
Strike plate, 118
Stringers, making, 183–84
Structural grade, 15
Struts, misplaced, 25
Stud perimeter walls, building, 193–95
Studs
configuration of, for corners, 97
cripple, 95, 100–101
jack, 95
king, 95, 102
load-bearing LB structural, 22
marking for, 99
sizing, 28
steel, 197
trimmer, 95, 102
wall, 95
Subflooring, 90–91
installing, 90
installing insulated, 199–200
Sway braces, installing, 132–33

T

Tacking, 64
Tail cut, 124
Tail joists, installing, 88
T-brace, 198
Thickness, 19
3-4-5 triangle, measuring with, 196
Threshold, 118

Tight-quarters nailing, 202
Toenailing, 63, 133
Tool belt, 42
Torpedo level, 40
Treads, tight-fit, 172
Trimmer joists, installing, 87
Trimmers, 87
Trimmer studs, 95, 102
Trusses, 134–36
erecting, 135–36

U

Underlayment, 90, 92
installing, 92
nailing schedule, 92
types of, 92
Utility knife, 41
Utility symbols on blueprints, 33

V

Valley rafters, laying out, 163
Vapor barrier, 199
attaching to masonry, 193–94
Veneer-core lumber, 18
Veneer grades, 19

W

Waferboard, 18, 90
Wall(s)
basement, 193–97
bearing stud perimeter, 193–95
misaligned bearing, 25–26
partition, 195–97
plumb, 107
Wall assembly, 102–10
cutting and installing studs and
headers, 102–3
erecting walls, 105–6
final plumbing and alignment of
walls, 107–9
framing connectors, 109–10
squaring and bracing walls, 103–5
Wall framing, 94–99
laying out plates, 95–97
marking plates for inside corners,
97–98
marking plates for outside corners,
98–99
nailing corners, 99
stud configuration for corners, 97
2x4s vs. 2x6s, 94–95
Wall rafter, 210

Wall studs, 95
Wall symbols on blueprints, 33–34
Water level, 40
Weather protection, 17–18
Weatherstripping, 118
Wedges, easy-cutting, 116
Western Wood Products Association, 14
Winders, 187
building basic, 187–89
Winder staircase, 191
Windows, 112–16
awning, 113
bay, 206–15
casement, 113
double-hung, 112–13
fixed, 112
installing, with brickmold, 114–15
installing flanged, 116
sections of, on blueprints, 36
single-hung, 113
sliding, 113–14
stationary, 112
Wiring, accommodating, 113
in flooring, 86
Wood. *See also* Lumber
grading, 14–16
milled dimensions, 14
milling methods, 14
working with, 13–14
Wood casings, 118
Wooden ladders, 47
Wood foundations, 76
Wood girders, 77
Wood I-beams, 21–22
Wood-post installation, 79
Wood rule, 39
Wood screws, 59
Work gloves, 38
W-type truss, 134

Photo Credits

T: Top; R: Right; B: Bottom; L: Left; C: Center

p. 1: David Geer
p. 2: Southern Forest Products Association
pp. 6–7: (top row) David Geer; David Geer; David Geer; (R) Western Wood Products Association; (bottom row) www.creatas.com; David Geer; Western Wood Products Association; David Geer; David Geer; David Geer
p. 11: Kim Jin Hong Photo Studio
p. 12: Bonnie Sue
p. 23: David Geer
p. 37: APA–The Engineered Wood Association
p. 45: David Geer
p. 53: John Parsekian/CH
p. 61: Weyerhaeuser
p. 71: Brand X Pictures
p. 72: APA–The Engineered Wood Association
p. 93: Southern Forest Products Association
p. 121: David Geer
p. 143: Southern Forest Products Association
p. 157: David Geer
p. 165: www.indexstock.com
p. 166: David Geer
p. 190: (T) Mark Lohman; (C) Bill Rothschild; (L) www.davidduncanlivingston.com
p. 191: (TL) www.davidduncanlivingston.com; (TR) Bill Rothschild; (BR) www.davidduncanlivingston.com
p. 192: Steel Framing Alliance
p. 204: (T) Phillip H. Ennis, design: Siskin Vails, Inc.; (BR) Phillip H.Ennis; (BL) Phillip H. Ennis, design: KJS Interiors; (LC) Phillip H. Ennis, design: Anne Cooper Interiors
p. 205: Kraftmaid Cabinetry
p. 206: Andersen Windows
p. 213: (T) Jessie Walker; (C) www.davidduncanlivingston.com; (B) Andersen Windows
p. 214: (T) Mark Lohman; (B) Jessie Walker, design: Shea Lubeke; (L) Jessie Walker
p. 215: Andersen Windows
p. 228: (T) David Geer; (B) Bill Rothschild; (L) American Plywood Association
p. 229: (T) Southern Forest Pine Association
back cover: (T) Brand X Pictures; (BL), (BC) Trus Joist MacMillan; (BR) David Geer

Metric Equivalents

Length

1 inch	25.4 mm
1 foot	0.3048 m
1 yard	0.9144 m
1 mile	1.61 km

Area

1 square inch	645 mm^2
1 square foot	0.0929 m^2
1 square yard	0.8361 m^2
1 acre	4046.86 m^2
1 square mile	2.59 km^2

Volume

1 cubic inch	16.3870 cm^3
1 cubic foot	0.03 m^3
1 cubic yard	0.77 m^3

Common Lumber Equivalents

Sizes: Metric cross sections are so close to their U.S. sizes, as noted below, that for most purposes they may be considered equivalents.

Dimensional lumber	1 × 2	19 × 38 mm
	1 × 4	19 × 89 mm
	2 × 2	38 × 38 mm
	2 × 4	38 × 89 mm
	2 × 6	38 × 140 mm
	2 × 8	38 × 184 mm
	2 × 10	38 × 235 mm
	2 × 12	38 × 286 mm
Sheet sizes	4 × 8 ft.	1200 × 2400 mm
	4 × 10 ft.	1200 × 3000 mm
Sheet thicknesses	¼ in.	6 mm
	⅜ in.	9 mm
	½ in.	12 mm
	¾ in.	19 mm
Stud/joist spacing	16 in. o.c.	400 mm o.c.
	24 in. o.c.	600 mm o.c.

Capacity

1 fluid ounce	29.57 mL
1 pint	473.18 mL
1 quart	1.14 L
1 gallon	3.79 L

Weight

1 ounce	28.35g
1 pound	0.45kg

Temperature

Fahrenheit = Celsius × 1.8 + 32
Celsius = Fahrenheit – 32 × 5⁄9

Nail Size & Length

Penny Size	Nail Length
2d	1"
3d	1¼"
4d	1½"
5d	1¾"
6d	2"
7d	2¼"
8d	2½"
9d	2¾"
10d	3"
12d	3¼"
16d	3½"

Have a home improvement, decorating, or gardening project? Look for these and other fine
Creative Homeowner books wherever books are sold.

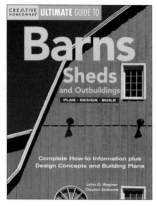

How to build and finish a utility building. Over 850 photos and illustrations. 240 pp.; 8$^{1}/_{2}$"×10$^{7}/_{8}$"
BOOK #: 277812

How to improve your home by adding a deck. Over 750 photos and illos. 288 pp.; 8$^{1}/_{2}$"×10$^{7}/_{8}$"
BOOK #: 277168

600 best-selling designs from leading architects. Over 500 color photos. 528 pp.; 8$^{1}/_{2}$"×11"
BOOK #: 277039

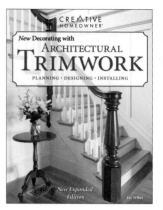

Transform a room with trimwork. Over 550 photos and illustrations. 240 pp.; 8$^{1}/_{2}$"×10$^{7}/_{8}$"
BOOK #: 277500

How to work with concrete, brick, and stone. Over 800 photos and illustrations. 272 pp.; 8$^{1}/_{2}$"×10$^{7}/_{8}$"
BOOK #: 277110

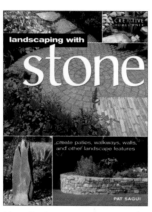

Ideas for incorporating stone into the landscape. Over 400 color photos and illos. 224 pp.; 8$^{1}/_{2}$"×10$^{7}/_{8}$"
BOOK #: 274172

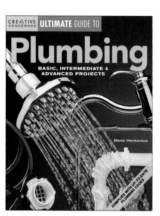

Take the guesswork out of plumbing repair. More than 750 photos and illustrations. 272 pp.; 8$^{1}/_{2}$"×10$^{7}/_{8}$"
BOOK #: 278210

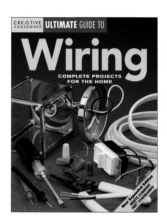

Best-selling house-wiring manual. Over 925 color photos and illustrations. 288 pp.; 8$^{1}/_{2}$"×10$^{7}/_{8}$"
BOOK #: 278237

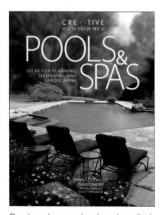

Pool and spa selection, installation, landscaping. Over 300 photos and illos. 224 pp.; 8$^{1}/_{2}$"×10$^{7}/_{8}$"
BOOK #: 277853

How to work with space, color, pattern, texture. Over 440 photos. 288 pp.; 9"×10"
BOOK #: 279672

Impressive guide to garden design and plant selection. More than 950 photos and illos. 384 pp.; 9"×10"
BOOK #: 274610

Lavishly illustrated with portraits of over 100 flowering plants; more than 500 photos. 208 pp.; 9"×10"
BOOK #: 274032

For more information and to place an order, go to **www.creativehomeowner.com**